Managerial Communication

Sixth Edition

sixth
edition

Managerial
Communication
Strategies and Applications

Geraldine E. Hynes
Sam Houston State University

SAGE

Los Angeles | London | New Delhi
Singapore | Washington DC | Boston

Los Angeles | London | New Delhi
Singapore | Washington DC | Boston

FOR INFORMATION:

SAGE Publications, Inc.
2455 Teller Road
Thousand Oaks, California 91320
E-mail: order@sagepub.com

SAGE Publications Ltd.
1 Oliver's Yard
55 City Road
London EC1Y 1SP
United Kingdom

SAGE Publications India Pvt. Ltd.
B 1/I 1 Mohan Cooperative Industrial Area
Mathura Road, New Delhi 110 044
India

SAGE Publications Asia-Pacific Pte. Ltd.
3 Church Street
#10-04 Samsung Hub
Singapore 049483

Printed in the United States of America

Library of Congress Cataloging-in-Publication Data

Hynes, Geraldine E.

Managerial communication : strategies and applications / Geraldine Hynes.—Sixth edition.

pages cm
Includes index.

ISBN 978-1-4833-5855-0 (hardcover: alk. paper)

1. Communication in management. 2. Business communication. I. Title.

HD30.3.H95 2016
658.4'5—dc23   *2014045581*

This book is printed on acid-free paper.

Acquisitions Editor: Maggie Stanley
Associate Editor: Abbie Rickard
Digital Content Editor: Katie Guarino
Editorial Assistant: Nicole Mangona
Production Editor: Jane Haenel
Copy Editor: Patrice Sutton
Typesetter: C&M Digitals (P) Ltd.
Proofreader: Sarah J. Duffy
Indexer: Terri Corry
Cover Designer: Anupama Krishnan
Marketing Manager: Liz Thornton

15 16 17 18 19 10 9 8 7 6 5 4 3 2 1

Brief Contents

Detailed Contents

5 Making Presentations 116

13 Managerial Negotiation

14 Conducting Interviews

Preface to the Sixth Edition

The roots of this textbook extend back to 1984, when John Wiley and Sons published *Managerial Communication: A Strategic Approach,* by Larry Smeltzer and John Waltman. Their practical, results-oriented examination of managerial communication was ground-breaking at the time. In the Preface they stated the book's objective: "to develop managers who communicate in a creative manner by understanding and strategically applying appropriate concepts." That objective is still valid.

A second edition added Don Leonard as third author in 1991. I adopted the 1994 edition, authored by Larry Smeltzer and Don Leonard, by then titled *Managerial Communication: Strategies and Applications*. I had been looking for a graduate-level text that presented a balanced approach to workplace communication and that was written for managers and executives.

These strengths drew me to that early edition:

- A strategic approach

- A solid research base

- Comprehensive coverage of contemporary issues

- An even-handed examination of oral and written communication channels

- A focus on managerial rather than entry-level competencies

I came onboard as third author with Smeltzer and Leonard for the 2002 edition and obtained sole authorship starting with the 2008 edition. As I revise yet again, my goal is to ensure that the qualities that made the original book unique and successful are still present in this sixth edition. Truth is truth. It does not change with the times. Therefore, my task is to bring timeless communication principles into the contemporary workplace. To meet the needs of today's busy manager/student, I updated the chapters, describing current business practices, summarizing relevant research, and providing guidelines for strategic managerial communication.

The reality is that an effective contemporary manager must possess a wide range of skills. While being accountable to an executive team and a customer base, a manager must be able to motivate subordinates and cross functional work groups with diverse back-grounds, interpret complicated rules, foster process improvement, and meet sometimes-unclear organizational expectations. Furthermore, today's manager often must use new technology to accomplish these tasks. Since these advanced abilities do not necessarily come from prior work experience, communication education is a vital component in managerial development.

Working on the sixth edition of this textbook has been both enjoyable and challenging. It has forced me to evaluate the content of the managerial communication course I teach in our MBA program at Sam Houston State University, to sort out what is important and what is no longer important for my students to know and be able to do. I hope that the results of these efforts satisfy other students' professional communication needs as well. After all, we know for sure that effective communication leads to managerial and organizational success. The value of the course is not controversial; the key is to keep the course content fresh.

What's New in This Edition

Many adopters of the fifth edition of *Managerial Communication: Strategies and Applications* indicated that major strengths are its balanced approach to managerial writing and oral communication, the end-of-chapter cases and exercises that offer opportunities for practice and application of the principles, and the comprehensive instructor supplements. So I retained these strengths in the sixth edition. On the other hand, this edition shakes things up a bit. After hearing adopters' suggestions, I made changes to the content of the chapters as well as to their sequence; the new features are described below.

BOOKWIDE CHANGES

My rationale for restructuring the book's topics is that instructors said that they form student teams early in their course and that they work on oral communication skills first. Therefore, it made sense to move forward the chapters on team communication strategies and on presentations; these chapters now constitute Part II. Since instructors said that writing is another topic they typically address early, Part III now covers writing skills; Part IV addresses strategies for understanding messages, and Part V examines interpersonal communication strategies.

A second major improvement to the sixth edition is that new cases focusing on technology appear at the end of every chapter. Instructors said that brief cases with discussion questions are an important resource because they provide opportunities for students to apply the chapter material to realistic scenarios. Furthermore, cases centering on emerging technologies are the most useful. So I added new cases with a focus on technology to the best cases and end-of-chapter exercises from earlier editions. They reflect important trends such as globalization and workplace diversity as well as the technology trend, and they are appropriate for both individual and group assignments.

Another new addition will improve students' critical thinking skills. Called Stop and Think, this feature appears several times in every chapter and consists of questions that encourage readers to analyze the principles in the chapter, apply them to their own experiences, and promote synthesis. Although the Stop and Think inserts act as strategic pauses to solidify students' understanding, they also can be used for class discussions or debates.

A fourth change to the content of this edition is expanded coverage of ethics. I introduced ethics in the first chapter and added coverage in subsequent chapters. This integrated approach seems more appropriate than a separate chapter on ethics, since ethical considerations are important in every managerial communication situation.

The final general change worth noting here is the addition of more visual aids. Sample documents in textboxes, tables, figures, charts, and checklists are found in each chapter. Summary tables may be especially helpful for visual learners; they also help break up large blocks of text.

CHAPTER-SPECIFIC CHANGES

Chapter-specific improvements in the sixth edition include the following:

- Chapter 1 ("Communication in Contemporary Organizations") has an expanded consideration of ethics and an expanded discussion of leadership orientations and managerial goals. I updated all the statistics and replaced obsolete descriptions and references.

- Chapter 2 ("The Managerial Communication Process") includes a clearer discussion of the strategic communication model, four Stop and Think inserts, five new summary tables, a new case focusing on technology, and refreshed, updated citations.

- Chapter 3 ("Communicating with Technology") is updated to include dos and don'ts for texting, blogging, and instant messaging. Emphasis is on the principles and best practices that apply to both emerging technologies and better-established technologies, such as e-mail and videoconferencing. A new section on surveillance warns students to expect that their employers will monitor their technology use.

- Chapter 4 ("Managing Meetings and Teams") is the chapter that reviewers ranked as the most important one in the text. It includes a considerably expanded, up-to-date discussion of electronic meetings, a section on team projects, and strategies for managing virtual teams.

- Chapter 5 ("Making Presentations") has a new section on team presentations, a new section on impromptu speaking and informal briefings, and an expanded discussion of ethical persuasion.

- Chapter 6 ("Contemporary Managerial Writing") introduces the plain language movement and provides examples of conversational style in business and government documents. I updated the references, added an end-of-chapter case, and inserted four Stop and Think pauses.

- Chapter 7 ("Writing Routine Messages") offers guidelines for formatting and designing e-mail, letters, and memos. The chapter presents two basic organizational patterns and explains when each is appropriate. The discussion of negative messages includes the impact of apologies. I added more examples and expanded the discussion of positive, negative, and persuasive messages.

- Chapter 8 ("Writing Management Reports and Proposals") takes an in-depth look at special business reports, including proposals and analytical reports. I included a description of PowerPoint decks as reports, additional examples of memo and letter reports, and more information about graphics. The parts of a formal business report are now more clearly labeled, explained, and exemplified.

- Chapter 9 ("Managerial Listening") has a new section on networking skills and an expanded section on specific techniques for interactive listening. I inserted five Stop and Think pauses, a new case focused on technology, and a nifty group exercise at the end of the chapter. You will also see several new examples, updated references, and more.

- Chapter 10 ("Nonverbal Communication") now includes an interesting section about recent research on nonverbal behavior in the workplace that uses electronic sensors. The discussion is expanded considerably, several citations are new or updated, and it has a new end-of-chapter case. I inserted five Stop and Think pauses and added three new tables, too.

- Chapter 11 ("Intercultural Managerial Communication") explores cultural differences in the meanings of colors, paralanguage, and time, with cases and examples of the concepts drawn from today's global marketplace. It emphasizes the relational meanings that multicultural workers see in their communication. The chapter includes a stronger focus on multinational corporations and on global business, such as translation software. I also updated the statistics, added a new end-of-chapter case on technology, and included a new class exercise for small groups.

- Chapter 12 ("Conflict Management") has new material on the benefits of conflict, the importance of shared perception, and the impact of power on conflict.

- Chapter 13 ("Managerial Negotiation") includes a major new section that describes how networking can increase influence at work.

- Chapter 14 ("Conducting Interviews") presents guidelines for networking as an employment search tool. It also has a new section explaining legal issues for performance reviews.

Acknowledgments

Most importantly, I wish to acknowledge John Waltman, Larry Smeltzer, and Don Leonard, who pioneered this textbook. They explicated the centrality of communication for managerial success, which I now know is an enormous undertaking. I deeply respect their wisdom and vision.

Many people helped make this edition a reality. Britany Vinsant, my graduate research assistant and right hand, performed her tasks with diligence, accuracy, and good cheer. I also wish to warmly thank contributing authors Robert Stretcher, Matt O'Rourke, Stephen Hunt, and Anna Turri. Maggie Stanley, my SAGE acquisitions editor, smoothed the way with her perspicacity and dependability. Katie Guarino, Jane Haenel, and Patrice Sutton also deserve recognition as key members of my SAGE team. A special thanks goes to Dave Fosnough, former Irwin/McGraw-Hill field sales supervisor, who started me down this path in 1993, and to Patricia Quinlin, former SAGE business editor, who turned me in the right direction. I am where I am today because they believed in me.

Several reviewers offered valuable insights and suggestions that shaped this edition. They are Jerry Jordan, University of Cincinnati; Sharyn Gardner, California State University, Sacramento; Jessica Rack, University of Cincinnati; Dionne Davis, University of Louisiana at Lafayette; Marguerite Joyce, Texas A&M University-Prairie View; Bob Gregory, Bellevue University; Chris Daly, Eastern Michigan University; Marcel M. Robles, Eastern Kentucky University; and Nancy Schullery, Western Michigan University.

I am forever grateful to my family—Jim, Maureen and Erasmus, Kellie and Bob, and my incandescent grandchildren, Ben, Aaron, Trixie, Samuel, and Clara—for their unreserved love and support.

Finally, I salute my students because they are dedicated to improving their managerial communication skills and strategies, and because they believe that I can help them do it. This book is for you.

—Geraldine E. Hynes

About the Author

Geraldine E. Hynes, PhD, is a professor in the College of Business Administration, Sam Houston State University, Huntsville, Texas, USA, where she has taught business and managerial communication at the undergraduate and graduate levels since 2001. She is also a communication consultant, executive coach, and contract trainer for business, government, and not-for-profit organizations. Her award-winning research has been published in scholarly journals and books in several countries and languages. She provides leadership to her discipline through the Association for Business Communication and was elected ABC president in 2010.

To Jim, who has been my center for more than forty-five years.

Managing in Contemporary Organizations

CHAPTER 1

Communication in Contemporary Organizations

Extremists think "communication" means agreeing with them.

—Leo Rosten, US (Polish-born) author and political scientist

In the second decade of this century, management communication is both challenging and exciting. It is challenging because organizations are becoming much more complex, and many new forces confront the manager. Greater competitive pressures, shorter product life cycles, increased demands for quality and service, more regulatory constraints, greater concerns for cost containment, heightened awareness of environmental concerns, and renewed emphasis on human rights are just some of the pressures increasing the complexity of the manager's job. But these pressures also make managerial communication exciting. The contemporary manager has a greater opportunity than ever to make a significant difference in the success of the organization and increase the quality of work life for fellow employees. But that requires effective managerial communication skills, which are becoming more complex, making them more difficult to master.

The workplace is much more diverse and complex than it was just a few decades ago, and it requires more sophisticated management communication skills. At the start of the 20th century, heavy manufacturing was the industrial base of Western countries. Products changed little from year to year, and the workforce consisted mainly of white males. But today, products and entire management systems change rapidly, and employees must adapt just as quickly. In addition, work teams are extremely diverse. At Intel, one of the world's largest and highest valued semiconductor chip makers, it is not uncommon to have a design engineer from Singapore working with a purchasing manager from Ireland and an accountant from California. This means the project manager must have the sophisticated skills required to communicate to a diverse work group in a rapidly changing environment.

Technology helps with this communication challenge, but it also adds new requirements. Advances in telecommunications have increased our communication capabilities, but we must learn how to best use these capabilities. In addition, the improved communication systems mean we have greater abilities to interact with multiple cultures, which require that we become better cross-cultural communicators. Furthermore, as technical products and services become more complex, we must be able to communicate about more complicated concepts than in the past.

Effective communication has been shown to be a leading indicator of financial performance. Towers Watson, a global company that provides human capital and management consulting services, conducted research on 651 organizations from a broad range of industries and regions over a ten-year period. They found that those companies that communicate effectively are 3.5 times more likely to significantly outperform their industry peers than those companies that do not communicate effectively. Other key findings include these approaches:

- Managers at the best companies are three times more likely to communicate clearly to their employees the behaviors that are expected of them, instead of being focused on cost.

- Managers at the best companies pay careful attention to their employees in their change planning; they communicate reasons for changes, provide training, and support the employees, instead of using a top-down approach. Extensive managerial communication improves the likelihood of successful change.

- Managers at the best companies are more than twice as likely to use new social media technologies to facilitate collaboration on work projects. Furthermore, they typically see better employee productivity and financial performance.[1]

Communication and its role in the life of an organization will continue to evolve. As a result, we must think about how communication will occur in the future. One way to understand what this will mean for managerial communication behavior is to look at the different stages through which managerial communication has already passed. As you read the following pages and note how managerial communication has changed over time, it is interesting and valuable to speculate how it will change during your career. Knowledge of the past will help us prepare for the future.

A BRIEF HISTORY OF MANAGERIAL COMMUNICATION

Managers communicated with subordinates in markedly different ways in the past than they do today. To best understand these changes, it is helpful to review the eras of management as listed in Table 1–1. After an overview of each era, the management communication strategies and techniques appropriate for that era are discussed.

Table 1–1   Historical Perspective of Managerial Communication

Era	Characteristics	Communication
Ancient and medieval	Initial efforts to organize commerce	Written records
Scientific management	Clearly defined job duties, time specifications for completing the task, and adherence to rules	One-way communication, heavy reliance on written job instructions and rules
Administrative management	Emphasis on authority and discipline	Similar to scientific management: one-way communication
Human relations	Relationship among managers and workers is important	Listening and two-way communication
Behavioral	Complexity of organizational behavior and communication recognized	Difficult to apply theories
Empowerment	Distribution of power to everyone in the organization	Two-way communication; participation of employees
Contingency	Interdependence of jobs, organizations, and people	Communication strategy must be applied to the situation

Management Communication in Ancient Times

The earliest known example of managerial communication may be the record keeping procedure developed by Sumerian priests around 5000 BCE. Business transactions were recorded north of the Persian Gulf as early as 3200 BCE. It is interesting to note that these records reflect cross-cultural business transactions. The Egyptians recognized the importance of putting requests in writing—a written code of conduct can be found circa 1750 BCE with the Code of Hammurabi. The ancient Romans were the first managers, using commercial languages to negotiate with suppliers, network with customers, and exchange business gifts between 1000 BCE and 1 CE. The first committee may have been organized around 325 BCE as Alexander the Great organized staff groups.

STOP AND THINK

1. Do you suppose managers complained about meetings in ancient times as much as they do now?

2. Other than technology use, what has changed in the way business is conducted?

Venice, Italy, was a major center for merchants and economic exchange during medieval times. Merchants built warehouses and used an inventory system that required periodic reports for the city governing body.[2] These brief examples indicate that since the beginning of commerce, some type of managerial communication has been practiced.

The Industrial Revolution and Scientific Management

Although managerial communication occurred in ancient times, the systematic evolution of managers as communicators began with the Industrial Revolution. The philosophy most generally associated with the early Industrial Revolution is *scientific management*. This philosophy and set of methods and techniques stressed the scientific study and organization of work. During this era, it was believed that the greatest levels of efficiency could be obtained with extremely precise job instructions and that subordinates should not second-guess the instructions. Thus, managerial authority was not to be questioned.

The background to the scientific management philosophy helps us understand its relationship to communication. Frederick Taylor created scientific management. He was a supervisor at the Philadelphia Midvale Steel Company in the late 1800s when he became interested in ways to improve lathe work. Taylor studied the work of individual lathe workers to discover exactly how they performed their jobs; he identified each aspect of each job and measured anything and everything that could be measured. He believed it was possible to develop a science that could indicate the most efficient and effective manner for performing a task; then, this technique could be written in elaborate job designs and communicated to employees through extensive training. Taylor treated individual employees as another element in the scientific formula.[3]

Several disciples of the scientific management theory espoused by Taylor developed these concepts further. Frank Gilbreth developed the study of motion to the highest level of perfection. To ensure precision, he invented the microchrometer, a clock with a sweeping second hand that could record time in 1/200 of a minute. Gilbreth's most famous accomplishment was a bricklaying study. After carefully analyzing the procedures followed by bricklayers, he reduced the number of motions from an average of 18 to 4.5 per brick on exterior brick and from 18 to 2 on interior brick.

A second disciple was Harrington Emerson, who developed twelve principles of efficiency for the railroads. One of his most repeated principles was discipline, which included adherence to rules and strict obedience. In other words, he believed management's role was to establish a set of elaborate rules and ensure that employees followed them.[4]

Scientific management attempted to systematize the work environment by reducing individual variance. This made the job easier for both the managers and the workers because unique situations were eliminated. No deviations from the norm were allowed. The manager was simply required to communicate the job specifications and the related work rules.

Scientific management is most often associated with the manufacturing efficiencies of the Model T Ford. These efficiencies allowed every working person of the day to drive a car. But we also see heavy reliance on the scientific method today in such businesses as McDonald's. The founder, Ray Kroc, used scientific management techniques to bring quality, service, cleanliness, and value to the fast-food industry. Every employee has a precise job description, each task is to be completed in a specified period, and there is strict adherence to rules. These procedures allow employees to be trained in a short time and reduce the number of unique conditions to which managers must adapt. Only limited strategic managerial communication is required.[5] Rules and job tasks are clearly explained, and employees are expected to follow them. No negotiations or deviations are expected.

The Administrative Approach

While scientific management was receiving extensive attention, a second branch of early management thought was developing, called *administrative theory.* Although this approach to management emerged during the same era as scientific management, its focus was quite different. While scientific management was concerned mainly with the individual workers and efficiency at the operational level, administrative theory focused on broader issues facing all managers.

A key figure in developing this theory was Henri Fayol, who developed fourteen principles of management.[6] Table 1–2 presents six of these principles of managerial communication. Note that two-way communication between the manager and subordinate is limited; the manager's authority is emphasized. The manager's role is to give orders and maintain discipline; little attention is placed on listening skills. Extensive use of groups and participative decision making are not integral to administrative theory. This approach is similar to the military model of the time, in which officers were extremely autocratic—subordinates were not encouraged to provide feedback to them, and the officers seldom listened. It is also comparable to the political system used in totalitarian governments.

The sixth principle, scalar chain, has special importance in our discussion of managerial communication. Fayol recognized the traditional organization hierarchy as important in establishing the chain of command. However, he also saw inefficiencies in the system when employees at the same level needed to communicate. Figure 1–1 shows how employee B would communicate with employee J according to prevailing thought at the time. The employee would have to send the message up the organization's chain of command to the top; then, the message would come down through another chain of

Table 1–2   Six of Fayol's Principles

1. Division of work. Efficiency requires that the total task be broken into small component parts assigned to workers who specialize in these limited tasks.
2. Authority. Managers have the formal authority to give orders. However, to be effective leaders, they must also possess personal authority deriving from their skill, experience, and character.
3. Discipline. Workers should willfully obey the rules and leaders of the organization.
4. Unity of command. Each subordinate should receive orders from only one supervisor.
5. Subordination of individual interest to general interest. The company's interest always takes precedence over the individual's interests.
6. Scalar chain. An unbroken line of authority runs from the top manager of an enterprise to the lowest levels of the organization. For giving orders and reports, this line should normally be observed.

Source: Fayol, 1949.

Figure 1–1   Following the Hierarchy

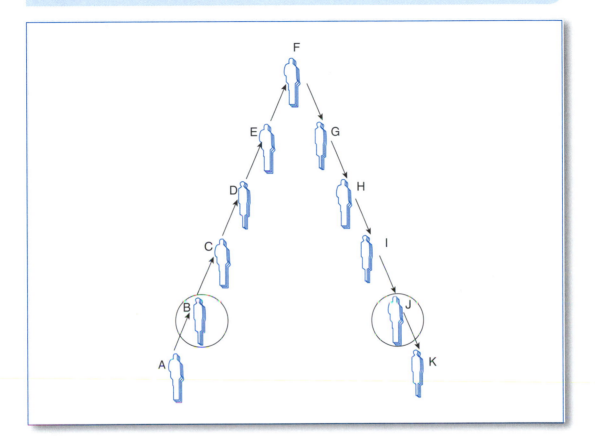

command. The implications for inefficiency and ineffectiveness are clear to contemporary managers.

To bypass these problems, Fayol developed what is now famously known as the gangplank theory. According to this theory, employee B would be allowed to communicate directly with employee J if each had permission from their immediate supervisors to do so and they kept the supervisors apprised of the communication. Figure 1–2 diagrams informal networks and horizontal communication. Gangplank theory was the first formal recognition of horizontal communication and acknowledged the importance of informal communication networks, which are now taken for granted in most contemporary organizations. But a strict chain of command is still used in some organizations. Throughout this book, we will discuss how organizations differ and how these differences must be considered when communicating.

Figure 1–2 Gangplank Theory

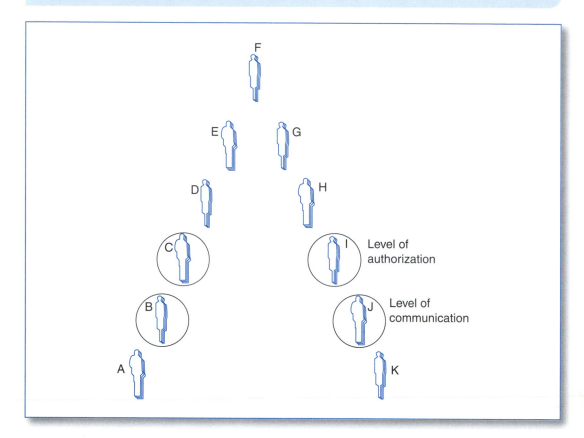

The Human Relations Approach

During the early 1900s, the nature of management and the manager's job became the focus of attention. Little was being said about how the manager related to employees. But this began to change in the 1920s and 1930s as the relationships between organizational members began to receive attention.

Dale Carnegie

Dale Carnegie was one of the first writers to link communication skill with managerial effectiveness. He wrote extensively about the social and psychological aspects of "winning friends and influencing people."[7]

Carnegie argued that gaining compliance from other people depends on interpersonal dynamics of attraction and influence. He offered his own prescriptions for influencing others by listening, showing an interest in their concerns, and gaining their confidence. Although his primary audience was not managers, his message to them was clear. Obtaining employee commitment to the organization does not depend solely on economic motivators or the authority of a manager's position. Commitment is gained through interpersonal communication skills. This was a radical change to those who previously believed a manager could "buy" commitment.

Before Dale Carnegie's death in 1955, nearly 5 million people had purchased his book, and thousands of managers had flocked to Dale Carnegie seminars.[8] His legacy continues today through the Dale Carnegie Training institute, which has expanded into sales, leadership, and presentations training for business professionals in 80 countries and in 25 languages.

Hawthorne Studies

About the same time that Dale Carnegie was presenting his seminars, a group of Harvard professors, led by Elton Mayo, was conducting a series of studies that became known as the Hawthorne studies.[9] The studies were conducted at Western Electric Company's Hawthorne plant in Illinois, where management followed the scientific management principles in the production of telephones. Little personal communication occurred between managers and employees; job specifications and work rules were spelled out; and the manager's job was to enforce them through authority and discipline.

Originally, a group of industrial engineers designed the Hawthorne studies to show the effect on productivity of increasing the light in work areas. The engineers set out to find the optimum conditions by experimenting with the lighting, but the results of the study defied explanation. Productivity increased regardless of what the researchers did to the lighting. When light was increased, productivity went up. When light was held constant, productivity still went up. Even when the level of light was decreased, productivity continued to increase until workers could no longer see what they were doing.

The results of these illumination studies were disturbing to engineers schooled in scientific management principles. To further study why their principles failed, researchers isolated and observed a small group of workers. These studies included changes in compensation, rest periods, work schedules, and work methods. In general, productivity increased during the studies regardless of changes in the work conditions. The researchers finally concluded the *relationship* between the researchers and the workers accounted for the results. The researchers had shown a great personal interest in the workers as they consulted with and kept them informed about changes. The relationship established between the researchers and the employees was quite different from that of the managers and employees in other parts of the plant.

Because the results differed from what was expected, the industrial engineers continued to study working conditions. During the next phase, the researchers interviewed thousands of employees to discover their attitudes toward working conditions, managers, and work in general. This was probably the first time extensive interviewing was conducted in the workplace. Traditionally, scientific management advocates simply observed workers as the researchers sought the most efficient way to organize a job. Now the Hawthorne researchers were asking employees about their feelings. Questioning or interviewing became part of the work environment.

The interviews indicated that people who work under similar conditions experience these conditions in different ways and assign different meanings to their experiences. The research concluded that employees' attitudes depend on the social organization of the group and their positions in these groups. One of the primary researchers, Elton Mayo, recommended that managers be friendly in their relationships with workers, listen to workers' concerns, and give workers a sense of participation in decisions so they could meet their social needs.[10] In many respects, both Mayo and Carnegie were similar in their advice, and both were in stark contrast to the scientific management philosophy.

Or were they? Did this human relations approach really differ from the scientific management approach? Some would argue that both Mayo and Carnegie were promoting highly manipulative, managerial communication strategies intended only to gain compliance from workers and to promote acceptance of managerial authority. The heart of the human relations approach is that attention to social needs and participation improve morale. In turn, this morale leads to greater compliance with managerial authority. In the human relations approach, managerial communication is seen as a tool for controlling organizational processes.

Although the general orientation of management during that era may have been manipulative, the human relations approach pointed out the importance of interpersonal communication. Because of the human relations approach, managing groups, listening, and interviewing are now all considered integral to managerial communication. In addition, the administrative approach highlighted the importance of organizational structures. Without the administrative and human relations orientations, the only focus of managerial communication would be keeping records, giving orders, and maintaining discipline.

But managerial communication goes beyond these functions. Each era approaches communication differently but helps us better understand communication within contemporary organizations and the type of communication that may be appropriate in the future. For instance, the gangplank concept is not totally accepted today in some organizations. Will it be accepted in 2020? What will be the acceptable rule for communicating with other employees?

The Behavioral Approach

The perspectives on managerial communication changed during the 1950s. Managers' behavior, including communication, received extensive attention. Economics, anthropology, psychology, and sociology were all applied to understanding communication on the job. The general orientation was to view organizational members as full human beings, not just as tools used to complete a job. Peter Drucker was among the first management gurus to assert that workers should be treated as assets, not as liabilities. He originated the view of the corporation as a human community built on trust and respect for the worker and not just a profit-making machine.[11]

Many management theories emerged during this era, such as McGregor's theory X and theory Y, Maslow's hierarchy of needs, Likert's four systems of management, Blake and Mouton's managerial grid, and Herzberg's motivational model. These theories, explained in most comprehensive management textbooks, have valuable information about what is required for effective managerial communication. Unfortunately, the theoretical explanations of managerial behavior became extremely complex, too complex for most managers to understand and apply. Many training programs were developed to help managers apply these theories, but often little benefit resulted.

While theories were being developed about behavior at work, much also was being done in the area of communication theory. For instance, J. L. Austen developed the speech act theory, which maintains that certain communication conventions must be used to be effective, and David Berlo developed a model emphasizing two-way communication.[12] Also, attention was given to social influences on communication, but unfortunately, the social context of managers was given little or no attention.[13]

In addition, the nature of organizational structure received extensive attention. Organizations of the 1950s and 1960s were recognized as being different from the social organizations of the early 1900s. Karl Weick developed a theory of organizing that helped us understand the nature of organizations and how communication operates within them. Weick and others made it clear that organizations are not stable, static entities; rather, they are continually evolving. In addition, both internal and external communication networks are continually evolving, and they must be considered by managers when communicating. For instance, the importance of rumors and informal communication began to receive attention. Also, the types of information managers need were changing from day to day. Earlier, Fayol recognized the importance of communication networks and organizational structure when he presented the gangplank concept. Now, entire organizations and their structure were receiving renewed attention.[14]

The nature of managerial and employee behavior, the study of communication, and an analysis of the nature of organizations all had important implications for managers as communicators. However, as mentioned earlier, these studies resulted in a complex body of knowledge that was difficult for managers to use. Out of this behavioral approach, the era of employee empowerment emerged.

Empowerment

The 1990s may be termed the era of empowerment. Empowerment is power sharing, the delegation of power or authority to subordinates in the organization.[15] In the traditional organization, all the power to make decisions was vested in top management, but since the emergence of the behavioral approach, we have seen a major shift away from the centralization of power. Empowerment encourages employees to participate fully in the organization. We now began to see power being given to others in the organization, so they could act more freely to accomplish their jobs.

As companies experienced more intense global competition and rapidly developing technology, many top managers believed giving up centralized control would promote faster product development, flexibility, and quality. In a study, 74 percent of the chief executive officers surveyed reported they were more participatory, more consensus oriented, and relied more on communication than on command. They found less value in being dictatorial, autocratic, or imperial.[16]

The chief executive officer's letter to the General Electric stockholders in the 1990 annual report provides an example of the empowerment philosophy. In this letter, the CEO asserted that managers must learn to delegate, facilitate, listen, and trust. He talked about the sharing of ideas to develop one vision for the huge corporation.

Sharing a vision means sharing information. In the traditional organization, the top managers are frequently the only ones that know the financial condition of the company, but in organizations that attempt to empower employees, information is shared with everyone. For instance, at Springfield Remanufacturing Center Corp. in Springfield, Missouri, workers on the line know—and are taught to understand—almost everything the president knows about costs and revenues, departmental productivity, and strategic priorities.[17]

The empowerment movement can be seen in union–management relations; union members have become more involved in management decisions as management provides more information to them. In fact, information sharing is often part of contract negotiations.[18] Both management and union members can be found on work quality and productivity improvement teams.

You may not be surprised that attempts at empowerment faced many challenges. Caterpillar Inc., the heavy-equipment manufacturer, made employment involvement a near religion in the late 1980s; however, when the industry met financial troubles, the employee involvement program became the victim of a bitter battle between the company and the United Auto Workers. An adversarial relationship between union and management returned; accordingly, one-way communication was more frequent than would be expected in an environment of empowerment.

Although efforts today to empower employees may run into problems, a number of strategies for empowering employees can be attempted. Such strategies as autonomous work groups, self-leadership, work-out groups, and quality circles should increase employee empowerment. But as mentioned in the discussion of the behavioral approach, some of the theories and programs for empowerment can become so complicated they are difficult to apply and are not suitable for every contemporary organization. As a result, the contingency approach has emerged as a management philosophy that makes sense in the early 21st century.[19]

The Contingency Approach to Management Communication

Managers who are effective see the interdependence of the various aspects of jobs, organizations, and communication. The basic idea of the contingency approach is that there is no one best way. The appropriate communication strategy varies from one situation to another. The most effective and efficient strategy depends on a number of factors. Accordingly, a communication method highly effective at one time and place may be ineffective in another situation. The contingency approach recognizes the importance of matching different situations with varying communication strategies. The scientific approach may be more appropriate in one situation, while extensive efforts to empower employees may be better in another setting.

For example, during a crisis, a manager may yell at subordinates and tell them exactly what to do because two-way communication might waste time. But during more tranquil times, discussion between the manager and subordinates may be appropriate. Time allows discussion. Each communication strategy—the direct autocratic approach and the participative approach—is appropriate in different situations.

The contingency approach has grown in popularity recently because of the complexity of organizations. Especially in multinational and multicultural organizations, managers must understand that there is no one best way of communicating; effective communication is contingent on the situation. That is not to say, however, that contemporary organizations are managed chaotically. On the contrary, accountability and oversight systems have been emphasized since the meltdown of multinationals such as Enron, Adelphia, and WorldCom in the early 2000s. The Sarbanes-Oxley Act of 2002 (especially Section 404) stresses the need for business control and auditing processes. The point is that, as corporate governance becomes more transparent, information flows more freely and that effective managers adapt to the complexities of each situation when communicating.

In summary, good ideas can be drawn from the scientific, administrative, human relations, behavioral, and empowerment approaches to communication. Creative analysis is required to ensure that communication strategies adapt to the varying contingencies.

STOP AND THINK

1. What are some of the complexities in today's business environment that make the contingency model so appropriate?

2. How can today's managers identify the contributing factors in their particular situation?

FACTORS AFFECTING COMMUNICATION CONTINGENCIES

The nature of communication and a model of managerial communication are presented in Chapter 2. This discussion presents three contingencies that should be considered when developing a strategy for managerial communication. It is impossible to review all contingencies because every manager faces many unique situations. However, it is possible to review the major current events that may influence a manager's environment. The following sections review major social and business influences that affect managerial communication contingencies, particularly diversity, competition and product quality, and ethics.

Diversity

Today, everyone works with more diverse populations than just a few decades ago. Beginning in the 1960s, the United States embraced tolerance and diversity as a strategic mission. However, minimizing cultural bias in the workplace continues to be a challenge for managers. This challenge, which is discussed throughout this text, means managers must not only be able to communicate with a greater variety of audiences but also must help their employees see diversity as a corporate asset rather than a liability. The contemporary manager should be particularly aware of four types of diversity that are becoming more predominant: gender, culture, age, and education.

Gender Diversity

During the past three decades, much has been written about how men and women communicate differently. Attention has also been given to how women and men communicate with each other. Many questions have been asked: Are men more assertive than women? Do women show more social support and sympathy to colleagues? Do men and women provide different types of feedback? Do leadership styles of men and women differ? Do women convey a different nonverbal message with the same gesture? Do men use space differently with other men than with women? Do men and women use different persuasive strategies?

In many cases, the answers to these and similar questions are not clear; furthermore, there is evidence that the answers evolve as general social changes occur. Sexual harassment is an example of a factor that affects communication between the genders at work. When some people think of sexual harassment, they think of touching or making physical advances. However, to others, sexual harassment can be an overheard ribald joke, extensive eye gaze, or even unexpected and unwelcome proximity. (Chapter 10 outlines the most common consequences of misinterpreted nonverbal behaviors.) Another possible example of sexual harassment in the workplace is a supervisor's sudden change in work schedules that makes it difficult for a worker to arrange child care or transportation to work.[20] The point here is that the definition of workplace harassment is evolving and broadening to reflect such perceptions.

Because of the evolving nature of communication and workplace relationships between the genders, definitive answers on gender differences in communication are difficult. But strong arguments for differences have been presented. In her best-selling book, Deborah Tanner makes a case for supporting the differences in communication styles of men and women. In doing so, she also presents interesting reasons men and women have difficulty communicating with each other. These reasons include both inherited traits and learned behavior.[21]

The differences in communication between genders are important because of the increasing gender diversity of the workforce. Both men and women will have difficulty succeeding if they cannot successfully communicate with each other. During the Industrial Revolution when scientific management practices prevailed, women had certain types of jobs, and men had other types. Women had either mostly routine, low-level manufacturing or clerical jobs; if they wanted to be a professional, their choices were teaching and nursing. Meanwhile, men had a greater variety of jobs such as management and engineering. Overall, men worked mostly with men, and women worked with other women or children.

But women have greater opportunities today and have access to most professions. Women represented 40 percent of the US workforce in 1976, and that number grew to more than 47 percent by 2010.[22] The US Bureau of Labor Statistics projects that the participation rate of women will increase by another 5.4 percent by the year 2022, which would make women the majority of the workforce.[23] Women are also moving into management. In 1983, only about a third of managers were women, but by 2012, according to the US Census Bureau, women filled 51.5 percent of management, professional, and related occupations.[24] Furthermore, the number of women serving as corporate officers in the top ten Fortune 500 companies doubled in less than twenty years—from 8.7 percent in 1995 to 17 percent in 2014.[25]

As mentioned earlier, a strong argument can be made that men and women communicate differently, causing men and women to experience miscommunication with each other at work. Furthermore, women in management are typically more risk averse than men, take a longer-term perspective, and are more relationship oriented. Such gender differences should be considered complementary rather than problematic since research shows that diversity in work teams leads to better outcomes. (See Chapter 4 for a thorough examination of team communication.) Effective managers must be sensitive to gender differences and make special efforts to adjust their communication.

Cultural Diversity

Managers must be able to communicate with people from other cultures as well as people of different genders. The increasing diversity of the US workforce is a reflection of the increasingly diverse population. This demographic phenomenon brings a range of interests, languages, and cultures that impacts the way business is conducted. No longer can we assume that the typical business professional is a non-Hispanic white. In 2012, the percentage of the population classified as non-Hispanic white by the US Census Bureau was 63.03 percent, and it is expected to decrease to 60.9 percent by 2017. If current rates of national population change continue as they have for the past twenty years, by 2035 non-Hispanic whites will be outnumbered by minorities. In fact, the states of Hawaii, California, New Mexico, and Texas already have minority non-Hispanic white populations.[26]

Furthermore, official population estimates indicate that the Hispanic community is the United States' largest ethnic community, with a population of 52.8 million in 2012 (16.9 percent of the population), reaching a projected 18.4 percent of the population by 2017.[27] The African American population was estimated at 39.5 million (12.6 percent of the population) in 2012 and is expected to decline to 12.47 percent by 2017. The Asian American population was estimated at 15.2 million (4.9 percent of the US total) in 2012 and is expected to increase to 5.2 percent by 2017.[28]

It is critical for businesses to know the demographic makeup of geographical regions so they can effectively localize products, services, and marketing. Hispanics have increased greatly in many southwestern US cities, while the African American population is the majority in some areas in the southeastern United States. Native Americans are the predominant minority in parts of New Mexico and Arizona. In Honolulu and San Francisco, Asians are the largest minority. California and Hawaii are also the states with the highest diversity index, which is a measure of the likelihood that two persons, chosen at random from the same area, belong to different racial or ethnic groups. These demographic statistics are relevant to managers because different cultures possess different work values and communication styles. Managers must learn to communicate with other managers and employees of all cultural backgrounds. In less than twenty years, there will be no majority race in the United States, at which point using the term *minority* will no longer make sense.

Managers must be able to work with diverse cultures both within their own organizations and from other organizations. Communication with employees and managers from other cultures will increase as transportation and telecommunications improve. For example, executives such as purchasing managers must be familiar with cross-cultural communication due to the increase of international business. International purchasing alliances too frequently fail because of poor communication.[29] This may be termed *intercultural business communication,* which is discussed in detail in Chapter 11.

In an effort to capture the growing multicultural market, US businesses are offering different products and services, and they are using new advertising and promotional appeals. According to the Selig Center's annual *Multicultural Economy* report, minority consumers had $2.6 trillion in disposable income in 2012. This is a significant and influential force in the US economy. The Hispanic market alone is larger than the entire economies of all but 13 countries in the world, and it is expected to increase as more Hispanics enter the workforce.

STOP AND THINK

1. Recall a recent TV commercial or advertisement of one of your favorite products. How does the persuasive message appeal to multicultural audiences?

2. How could it be improved?

Age Diversity

A third kind of diversity that managers must recognize is age diversity. Americans are living longer, and the average employee is getting older. By 2022, 38 percent of the US population will be over age fifty-five. For the first time in history, four generations are working together. According to the US Bureau of Labor Statistics, on average, more than 16 percent of employed Americans last year were between ages fifty-five and sixty-four. Roughly 5 percent were at least sixty-five years old. Added together, about one-fifth of employed workers were at least fifty-five years old.[30]

The worker who is thirty years old in 2015 has lived in a much different world from that of the worker who is sixty. The thirty-year-old, born in 1985, did not experience the national turmoil of the Vietnam War, grew up in an era of relative affluence, and is an avid techie. Multicultural social networks are important. The sixty-year-old remembers the Vietnam War and was affected by the global economic collapse of 2008. Economic and national securities are major concerns.

These differences in age and experiences may result in even greater communication difficulties than are normally caused by cultural differences. For instance, consider a woman of Korean descent and one of Hispanic descent who are both thirty years old, born and raised in a suburb of Dallas, educated at the University of Texas, and working in Dallas. These two women may have more in common and find it easier to communicate with each other than with the sixty-year-old Hispanic or Southeast Asian immigrant women they supervise.

Communication across these age differences can be a major challenge in the workplace, a challenge that companies can ill afford. Every generation is different, and generation gaps are natural, but generational tensions seem especially strong between managers and leaders in their thirties and early forties (called Generation X) and workers in their twenties (called Millennials). According to Harvard Business School researchers, Gen Xers started working when the economy was slow, and their career paths were rocky. Feeling vulnerable, they made personal and family sacrifices to achieve success. Today, their young employees are less willing to sacrifice their time with their families. They expect to be evaluated for productivity, not hours at their desk, especially when tech tools make their geographic location irrelevant. Their loyalties lie with their social network rather than their job, and they do not fear change.[31] Clearly, when values clash between bosses and their subordinates, effective communication across the generational divide becomes even more important. Managers must consider this contingency because of its implications for employee retention, harmony, and workplace efficiency.

Education Diversity

The fourth kind of diversity that managers should recognize as a contingency is educational level, because the workforce's education is changing dramatically. According to the US Census Bureau, 88 percent of US residents twenty-five and older are at least high school graduates. The bureau reported record high educational levels for nearly every racial and ethnic group and the nation overall. Furthermore, approximately 32 percent of the civilian labor force has a college degree.[32] Greater education levels mean employees will readily question managers and will want a say in any decision that affects them. In the scientific management era of Frederick Taylor, a manager could simply tell an educated employee what to do; however, today managers must listen to the employee and seek assistance with problem solving.

In summary, gender, culture, age, and educational diversity are major factors affecting a manager's communication contingencies. Given the increasingly diverse workforce, today's managers need to develop competencies that will enable effective communication internally with bosses, subordinates, and coworkers and externally with customers, suppliers, vendors, regulatory agencies, and the public. About half of the Fortune 500 companies employ diversity officers.[33] These officers have a variety of responsibilities; but at such companies as Colgate-Palmolive and General Electric, they provide individual assistance and conduct specialized training programs for managers in an attempt to help them see that workplace diversity is a benefit rather than a challenge.

Competition and the Drive for Quality

As explained in the previous section, diversity is an important managerial communication contingency. A second is quality, which is a competitive advantage for business. In the late 1960s, the French journalist Jean-Jacques Servan-Schreiber received considerable notoriety for his book *The American Challenge*.[34] In this book, he warned Europeans that American industry was well ahead of the industrialized world and the United States was widening its lead. But in 1992, such books as *Quality or Else: The Revolution in World Business* emphasized that quality must be improved if the United States is to remain competitive.[35] A pioneer of the drive for quality, W. Edwards Deming, pointed out that in order to continuously improve quality, systems must be in place for gathering feedback from the employees and customers. Contemporary managers now accept the idea that business is a globally competitive game and quality is the key to victory. *Competitive advantage* and *quality* are common words in business today. But what do the terms mean?

Competition may be considered as the effort of two or more parties acting independently to secure the business of a third party by offering the most attractive terms. A competitive environment means the organization must produce a product or service in a more efficient and effective manner than its competitors. Also, the service or product must possess greater value at the same or lower price. Little room exists for errors; defective parts must be minimal, few or no reworked parts can be allowed, few product repairs can be tolerated, and delivery cycles must be short. Continuous efforts are required to find new ways to improve the product or service while reducing costs.

Some of the characteristics an organization needs to gain competitive advantage in today's markets include the ability to do the following:

- Access resources

- Add value

- Develop a good skills base among the workforce

- Attract investment

- Develop nonprice characteristics that appeal to other markets

- Be price competitive

- Be efficient

- Use technology

- Be innovative

As you look over this list of factors, note how many directly rely on management's communication competencies. Yes, most of them. Today's managers must be able to gather information and ideas, share data, and promote and persuade to ensure continuous process improvement. Managers must be efficient and effective communicators in a fast-paced, highly competitive environment. Limited time exists to relax and contemplate communication strategies.

Let us look at an example. Toyota is the number one automaker in America (by production). As of January 2014, it was the fourteenth-largest company in the world (by revenue). Toyota relies on manufacturing systems, statistical process control, and other proven methods under a continuous improvement strategy to produce high-quality products that consumers demand. All the elements, including management's communication with dealers, suppliers, and employees, contribute to Toyota's reputation for quality.[36]

To enhance their competitiveness, many organizations use cross functional work teams in which employees learn a variety of tasks and work together. It is almost the direct opposite of the scientific management approach. When cross functional work teams are used, managers must understand and coordinate a variety of activities. They must be able to communicate from a variety of perspectives.

In some cases, entire organizational cultures must be changed from one in which quality is of little importance to a culture that says, "Quality is Job One," Ford Motor Company's motto since the 1980s. The slogan succinctly represents the corporate cultural changes that many companies are attempting. This means managers must be able to communicate a real interest in quality, and they must be willing to listen to employees about quality improvements. In 2003, as Ford celebrated its 100th anniversary, Chairman and Chief Executive Officer Bill Ford said, "Our success always has been driven by our products and our people. . . . We're going to apply fresh thinking and innovative technology to everything we do, from our basic business processes to the products that define who we are as a company." This dedication to quality appears to be paying off. In 2013, Ford gained more market share in the United States than any other automaker.[37]

Here is a simple example of how the organization's quality culture works. A Ford automobile assembly worker believed he had a better way to mount the door mirror. After several discussions with the departmental managers, a better procedure was implemented.[38] If managers are not willing to listen about quality improvements, they will not be successful in implementing the necessary corporate culture.

Ethics

A third major contingency that managers should consider when communicating is business ethics. The dangers of unethical behavior have been exemplified in recent years by major scandals in both the political and corporate worlds. Ethics charges filed against the most visible executive officer in the United States—President Bill Clinton—brought about his impeachment in 1998. A decade later, Rod Blagojevich became the first Illinois governor in history to be impeached after being accused of abuse of power, amid charges that he tried to sell the US Senate seat once held by President Barack Obama.

In the early 21st century, executives at Adelphia, Arthur Andersen, Enron, WorldCom, Martha Stewart Omnimedia, HealthSouth, and other corporations were charged with major ethics violations—accounting fraud, stock manipulation, obstructing justice, lying, and so on. In many cases the accused executives were convicted, and in some cases, their companies were even destroyed. Such events have triggered renewed concern for ethical standards in business.

Ethical dilemmas and temptations face managers at all levels, not just the political leaders and corporate executives who receive the attention of journalists. The top ethical issues in business today include corporate accounting practices, the use of social media among employees, workplace relationships (harassment), and pay equity.[39] Consider the following examples of ethical issues in managerial communication.

- The supervisor of a travel agency was aware his agents could receive large bonuses for booking 100 or more clients each month with an auto rental firm, although clients typically wanted the rental agency selected on the basis of lowest cost. The agents worked on a commission basis. Should the supervisor "warn" his subordinates, or should they be trusted to use their best judgment?

- The executive in charge of a parts distribution facility told employees to tell phone customers that inventory was in stock even if it was not. Replenishing the items took only one to two days; no one was hurt by the delay. Is it ethical for the company to omit this information?

- The project manager for a consulting assignment wondered whether some facts should be left out of a report because the marketing executives paying for the report would look bad if the facts were included. What is the project manager's ethical responsibility?

- A North American manufacturer operating abroad was asked to make cash payments (a bribe) to governmental officials and was told it was consistent with local customs, despite being illegal in North America. Should the manufacturer make such payments?

STOP AND THINK

Examine the code of conduct for a company, profession, or industry you are interested in.

1. Who wrote the code of conduct?

2. What are the consequences of honoring it?

3. What are the consequences of violating it (if any)?

4. What do you consider the most important reason that codes of conduct exist?

Answers to these questions are not easy, and in today's atmosphere of cynicism and mistrust, little room for error exists. Chapter 2 discusses the concept of communication climate and points out that trust is essential to developing a positive communication climate. Unfortunately, managers have difficulty developing trust when so many blatant examples of mistrust surface and individual managers face conflicting ethical demands.

No concrete set of ethical rules exists. There is no law to follow. Many behaviors have not been codified, and managers must be sensitive to emerging norms and values. Sensitivity to the nuances of ethical communication is the only way to maintain employee trust.

Because no universal laws exist, what one person or group considers ethical may be unethical to another. The question of taking bribes is a good example; they are quite ethical in one country but unethical and even illegal in another. Organizations are assisting managers with the many ethical quandaries they face when communicating by providing guidelines, seminars, and workshops. In 2005, companies spent an estimated $6.1 billion on ethics training. This effort is partly in response to the Sarbanes-Oxley Act of 2002, which makes corporate executives responsible for the unethical behavior of their employees—unless they can show that they provided ethical training for them.[40]

Another strategy many companies use to improve communication ethics is to develop a formal code of ethics. The code clarifies company expectations of employee conduct and makes clear that the company expects its personnel to recognize the ethical dimensions of corporate behavior and communication. A code of conduct may be broad or specific and most address managerial communication. For instance, the following is taken from International Paper's code of conduct, which is published on the company's website.

This Code of Conduct is designed to communicate our core values of commitment, ownership, respect, and excellence, and the standards that govern our business. It also provides guidelines for navigating successfully through ethical challenges. In our competitive global environment, we sometimes encounter situations that test our judgment and integrity. When that happens, this Code will help us respond in such a manner as to uphold the IP Way and comply with the spirit and letter of the law.[41]

Another possibility is an ethics committee or an ethics ombudsperson. With this approach, either one executive or a panel of executives is appointed to oversee the organization's ethics and serve as a consultant to other managers. This provides an opportunity for a manager to go to one person or a group of people to seek advice when confronted with an ethical issue. The importance of such a position is demonstrated by Xerox, where the ombudsperson reports directly to the CEO.

THE TRANSITION

This introductory chapter presents a historical overview of managerial communication, concluding that the contingency approach is the most appropriate, and it reviews three factors that affect contingencies. But organizational management and the corresponding communication are in constant transition. Managers do not communicate today as they did fifteen to twenty years ago, and communication styles and strategies will continue to change. Our challenge is to understand management communication and begin to prepare for these changes.

In 1982, John Naisbitt wrote a widely read book titled *Megatrends*.[42] In this book, he presented ten major predictions. Four of them are particularly pertinent to management communication. First, he stated we would be moving from an industrial society to an informational society. This movement has occurred with the tremendous influence of computer technology and global telecommunications.

The other three trends are highly related: moving from centralized to decentralized decision making, participatory governance replacing representation, and networking becoming more important than traditional hierarchies. Each of these trends implies that both written and managerial communication will become more frequent and intense. Evidence of these trends is increased communication training for managers, more emphasis on work groups, and decision making through governance teams that include all stakeholders. Examples of such governance teams range from the board of directors level to the project level, and they are particularly common in information technology (IT) management.

During the past few years, these trends seem to have grown in importance. Eight years after the original book, Naisbitt and Aburdene wrote a follow-up to the original *Megatrends,* titled *Megatrends 2000*.[43] In this later book, the authors again listed many of the same trends that appeared in the first book. In addition, intercultural communication was emphasized. Naisbitt's predictions that managerial communication would grow in intensity and importance and would take on an increased international and intercultural significance have all come true.

The Project Management Institute, Inc., headquartered in Pennsylvania, has provided solid evidence for the claim that managerial communication is a critical core competency for business success. In 2013, PMI published an in-depth report, *Pulse of the Profession: The High Cost of Low Performance: The Essential Role of Communications*. The report was the result of research conducted among over 1,000 project managers, executives, and business owners involved in large capital projects (at least US$250,000) worldwide. PMI's study revealed that US$135 million is at risk for every US$1 billion spent on a project, and a startling 56 percent is at risk due to ineffective communication with stakeholders. Undoubtedly, effective communication is the most crucial success factor in a complex and competitive business climate. The report concludes, "organizations cannot afford to overlook this key element of project success and long-term profitability."[44]

This book discusses the strategies and applications that are required for effective managerial communication. But as mentioned previously, not every contingency can be discussed. Managers must remain creative and strategic as they communicate in many unique and challenging situations.

SUMMARY

Management communication has gone through a number of changes since ancient and medieval times. Seven separate eras are presented in this chapter: ancient and medieval, scientific management, administrative management, human relations, behavioral, empowerment, and contingency. In each of these models, increasingly more attention has been given to managerial communication.

To better understand managerial situations, several contemporary dynamics affecting communication are presented. Different types of diversity are reviewed: gender, culture, age, and education. The work population will probably become more diverse in the majority of these attributes.

The drive for competitive advantage through improved product and service quality also affects managerial communication. As a result, everything will occur in shorter time cycles, and less room for error will exist as a result of quality demands.

Ethics is another contemporary dynamic that must be considered. Although management ethics can create difficult communication decisions, organizations provide assistance with training programs and codes of ethics. In addition to these dynamics affecting contemporary communication, trends imply that communication will become more frequent, intense, and intercultural as it grows in importance.

Cases for Small-Group Discussion

CASE 1–1

Ethics and Technology

Chris smiled as he received the analysis packet from his supervisor. He had been working from home for GEH Mortgage Company, analyzing mortgage applications, for the past three years. This particular application involved not just a home mortgage but also an entire farmstead, a home and business. Whenever he received an assignment he did not know how to analyze, he would call on his friend Joel, whom he had known since high school, to help him accomplish such tasks. He compensated Joel, usually with a case of beer, when they got together on the weekends. Chris knew he could trust Joel to do a good job on the analysis, because Joel had double majored in finance and accounting at a regional university. Chris would then tailor the analysis according to the way the firm expected reports to be submitted. He quickly e-mailed the application packet to Joel.

Chris was perceived as one of the most dependable analysts in the division because of his past work, much of which had been farmed out to Joel. He had received accolades and raises as a result and was enjoying his successful career with the firm.

QUESTIONS

1. The method used by Chris is obviously successful, and the company is satisfied with the results. Is it just good business, or is there an ethical dilemma present?

2. Should Chris confess to his supervisor or just continue the successful deception?

3. What are the privacy issues, since the information used in these analyses is proprietary and sensitive?

4. Does this activity fit the notion of plagiarism?

5. Do electronic communication and the telecommuting arrangement make Chris's actions more likely?

CASE 1–2

A 120-Year Difference

A historian has said this about Gen. George A. Custer: "Generals who led men were rare; generals who won battles were rarer. It is no wonder that he was idolized from President Lincoln down. All the world loves a winner." On June 26, 1876, Custer's 261 soldiers were killed at the Battle of the Little Bighorn. Another historian asks, "Was Custer a hero or a fool?"

On February 27, 1991, the allied coalition forces of Operation Desert Storm led by Gen. H. Norman Schwarzkopf overcame the armies of Iraq's Saddam Hussein in a victory that quickly became known to the world as "The 100-Hour War." Shortly before the war, Schwarzkopf is quoted as saying, "I told my family that during the first month of any military campaign, the guy in charge is a hero, and it's downhill after that."

We don't normally think of military leaders as managers, but they are responsible for the actions of numerous subordinates in critical times. They must be effective communicators to carry out this mission. Generals Custer and Schwarzkopf help demonstrate the differences in managerial communication that have occurred during the past 120 years.

General Custer led his 261 men on horseback in southeastern Montana. Compare this to General Schwarzkopf as you think about him stepping quickly toward the podium in a fourth-floor ballroom at the Hyatt Regency Hotel in Riyadh to address two hundred reporters from around the world. No doubt these two managers had different communication support systems, but they also had different respon-sibilities. General Custer was managing an operation of 261 horse soldiers. General Schwarzkopf was coordinating a half-million-strong international military force including the US Air Force, Navy, and Army as well as the first Tank Division of the United Kingdom and corps from Egypt, Saudi Arabia, and France.

What a difference! But in some ways, their training was quite similar. Both were educated at West Point, went through army war colleges at Fort Leavenworth, were stationed at Fort Riley, and had front-line battle experience. Both had experienced defeat and victory.

QUESTIONS

1. Compare the management communication systems of these two managers. How are the basics similar? What was the role of technology?

2. Which of the two generals had the easier job? Consider this question carefully because Custer had a much smaller group of men, but Schwarzkopf had sophisticated technology and organizational structure.

3. Which of the two managers required more advanced training in management communication? Why?

4. How would you compare these two generals to business managers during the same era?

CASE 1–3

Like Grandfather, Like Granddaughter?

Clarence opened a farm supply store in Montana during the early 1900s. His neighbors in the county were also his customers. Every person who walked into his store felt comfortable. In fact, they would often sit, sip a cup of coffee or shell some peanuts, and solve the world's problems before loading up their purchases. Clarence prided himself on knowing what his customers needed to be successful farm-ers, and he freely gave them advice about which brand of flea dip would work best on their cattle and which tonic would help a colicky horse. By the time he retired and his son Seth took over, the company had expanded to three stores in three towns and had fourteen full-time employees.

As a youth, Seth had attended the state college and earned a degree in agricultural business. He eagerly applied what he had learned to the family business. He was convinced that technology was the key to success, not personal relationships. Over the years, he struggled to convert all his father's old, handwritten records to electronic files. Eventually, he installed a completely computerized information system that tracked inventory, personnel, and accounts. He sometimes boasted about being an entrepre-neur, but Clarence snorted at that term. "Just do what's right for your customers and you'll be doing what's right for yourself," he would retort.

When Seth retired, his daughter Kathy took over the company that now has twenty-three stores with 228 employees in three states and one wholly owned subsidiary of eighteen gas stations. Kathy's vision involves offering a broader range of products than farm supplies. She wants to sell the image of the fam-ily farm. Her stores stock western clothing; boots, hats, and jewelry; home furnishings; and even CDs featuring country and western music.

Kathy finds herself traveling extensively from the corporate office to the various stores. Finding time to manage everything is a problem, but she has a staff of twelve professionals in the corporate office to assist her. A computer network, e-mail, and fax machines help tremendously.

QUESTIONS

1. How have communication requirements differed for Clarence in the early 1900s and Kathy in the early 2000s?

2. How do you think the management behaviors differed for Clarence and Kathy?

3. In what ways do you think Clarence and Kathy were alike as company presidents?

Student Study Site

Visit the Student Study Site at **study.sagepub.com/hynes6e** for web quizzes, video links, web resources, and cases studies.

Notes

1. Towers Watson, Inc., "Change and Communication ROI: The 10th Anniversary Report," (2013–2014), accessed May 10, 2014, www.towerswatson.com.
2. C. George, *The History of Management Thought* (Englewood Cliffs, NJ: Prentice Hall, 1972), chaps. 1 and 2.
3. Edwin A. Locke, "The Ideas of Frederick E. Taylor," *Academy of Management Journal,* January 1982, pp. 41–44.
4. William F. Muks, "Worker Participation in the Progressive Era: An Assessment by Harrington Emerson," *Academy of Management Review,* January 1982, p. 101.
5. "McRisky," *BusinessWeek*, October 21, 1991, pp. 114–117.
6. Henri Fayol, *General and Industrial Management* (London: Sir Isaac Pitman and Sons, 1949), pp. 3–13.
7. M. Richetto, "Organizational Communication Theory and Research: An Overview," in *Communication Yearbook* 1, ed. B. D. Rubin (New Brunswick, NJ: Transaction Books, 1977).
8. Dale Carnegie, *How to Win Friends and Influence People* (New York: Simon & Schuster, 1936).
9. F. L. Roethlisberger and W. Dickson, *Management and the Workers* (New York: Wiley & Sons, 1939).
10. E. Mayo, *The Human Problems of an Industrial Civilization* (Boston: Harvard Business School, 1947).
11. John A. Byrne, "The Man Who Invented Management: Why Peter Drucker's Ideas Still Matter," *BusinessWeek,* November 28, 2005, pp. 97–106.
12. J. L. Austen, *How to Do Things with Words* (Oxford: Oxford University Press, 1962); and David K. Berlo, "Human Communication: The Basic Proposition," in *Essay on Communication* (East Lansing, MI: Department of Communication, 1971).
13. Larry R. Smeltzer and Gail F. Thomas, "Managers as Writers: Research in Context," *Journal of Business and Technical Communication* 8, no. 2 (April 1994): p. 186.
14. K. Weick, *The Social Psychology of Organizing,* 2nd ed. (Reading, MA: Addison-Wesley, 1979).
15. Edwin P. Hollander and Lynn R. Offermann, "Power and Leadership in Organization," *American Psychologist* 45 (February 1990): pp. 179–189.
16. Thomas A. Stewart, "New Ways to Exercise Power," *Fortune,* November 6, 1989, pp. 52–64.

17. John Case, "The Open-Book Managers," *Inc.,* September 1990, pp. 104–105.
18. Stephenie Overman, "The Union Pitch Has Changed," *HR Magazine,* December 1991, pp. 44–46.
19. Robert L. Rose and Alex Kotlowitz, "Strife Between UAW and Caterpillar Blights Promising Labor Idea," *The Wall Street Journal,* November 23, 1992, p. 1.
20. Fatima Goss Graves, Liz Watson, Katherine Gallagher Robbins, Lauren Khouri, and Lauren Frohlich, "Seventeen Million Reasons Low-Wage Workers Need Strong Protections from Harassment" (National Women's Law Center Report, April 1, 2014), http://www.nwlc.org/sites/default/files/pdfs/final_nwlc_vancereport2014.pdf.
21. Deborah Tanner, *You Just Don't Understand* (New York: Ballantine Books, 1990).
22. U.S. Census Bureau, *Statistical Abstract of the United States: 2012*. Labor Force, Employment, and Earnings, Table 616, p. 393.
23. Mitra Toossi, "Labor Force Projections to 2022," *Monthly Labor Review,* December 2013, www.bls.gov/EMP.
24. U.S. Census Bureau, *Statistical Abstract of the United States: 2012*. Labor Force, Employment, and Earnings, Table 616, p. 393.
25. Sallie Krawcheck, "Diversify Corporate America," *Time,* March 24, 2014, pp. 36–37.
26. Esri, "Minority Population Growth: The New Boom. An Analysis of America's Changing Demographics" (2012), www.esri.com/data.
27. Ibid.
28. Ibid.
29. Michiel R. Leenders, Harold E. Fearon, and Wilbur B. England, *Purchasing and Materials Management,* 10th ed. (Burr Ridge, IL: Richard D. Irwin, 1993), p. 480.
30. Philip Moeller, "Challenges of an Aging American Workforce," *U.S. News & World Report,* June 19, 2013, http://money.usnews.com/money/blogs/the-best-life/2013/06/19/challenges-of-an-aging-american-workforce.
31. Tammy Erickson, "Ten Reasons Gen Xers Are Unhappy at Work," *Harvard Business Online*, May 15, 2008, accessed August 20, 2008, http://www.businessweek.com.
32. U.S. Census Bureau, *Educational Attainment in the United States, 2013*, https://www.census.gov/hhes/socdemo/education/data/cps/2013/tables.html.
33. Julie Amparano Lopez, "Firms Elevate Heads of Diversity Programs," *The Wall Street Journal,* August 8, 1992, p. B1.
34. Jean-Jacques Servan-Schreiber, *The American Challenge* (New York: Atheneum, 1968).
35. Lloyd Dolyns and Clare Crawford-Mason, *Quality or Else: The Revolution in World Business* (New York: Houghton Mifflin, 1992).
36. Mary Connelly, "Toyota's Ad Constants: Stress Quality, Seek a Feel-Good Connection," *Automotive News*, October 29, 2007.
37. Daniel Miller, "One Way that General Motors Trails Cross-Town Rival Ford Motor Company," *The Motley Fool*, March 20, 2014, http://www.fool.com/investing/general/2014/03/20/one-factor-where-general-motors-trails-cross-town.aspx.
38. *Netpiper Auto News,* July 6, 2003, accessed January 16, 2006, www.autoemirates.com/netpiper/news/details.asp?NID = 997.
39. Jonathan Lister, "Top Ethical Issues Facing the Business Community," *Houston Chronicle,* May 14, 2014, http://smallbusiness.chron.com/top-ethical-issues-facing-general-business-community-25417.html.
40. William Raspberry, "Straighten the Crooked and White-Collared? Good Luck," *Houston Chronicle,* November 21, 2005, p. B7.
41. http://www.internationalpaper.com/documents/EN/Ethics/IPCodeofConduct.pdf.
42. John Naisbitt, *Megatrends* (New York: Warner Books, 1982).
43. John Naisbitt and Patricia Aburdene, *Megatrends 2000* (New York: William Morrow, 1990).
44. Project Management Institute, Inc., *Pulse of the Profession™ In-Depth Report: The High Cost of Low Performance: The Essential Role of Communications*, May 2013, p. 2, accessed August 5, 2014, http://www.pmi.org/Knowledge-Center/Pulse/Pulse-Communications.aspx.

The Managerial Communication Process

Today, communication itself is the problem. We have become the world's first overcommunicated society. Each year we send more and receive less.

—Al Ries, Chairman, Trout & Ries Advertising, Inc.

Whether working for a hospital, manufacturer, or service firm, more than 75 percent of a manager's time is spent communicating. Considering the amount of information for which a manager has responsibility, this is not surprising. General managers face two fundamental challenges: figuring out what to do as they sort through enormous amounts of information and getting things done through a diverse group of people.[1] Effective communication is the key to planning, leading, organizing, and controlling the resources of the organization to master these challenges.

Communication—the essential process that managers use to plan, lead, organize, and control—is not easy. To understand a manager's message you must be able to perceive and interpret it. The process becomes more complex when communicating to a group of people because of the variety of perceptions and interpretations possible.

At the most general level, the communication process consists of an exchange of messages that are comprised of a set of symbols, such as words or gestures. Understanding the messages depends on a common meaning or frame of reference for those symbols. When sending a message, a manager may have the meaning of the symbols clearly in mind, but if someone receiving the message attributes a different meaning, the message is misunderstood. The process is made even more complicated because the symbols' meanings not only differ between people but also change as the experiences of the people involved change.

In this chapter, we examine those aspects of developing and exchanging symbols that relate to managerial communication, and we analyze the human factors that aid or hinder understanding. Further, we present a model of the strategic approach to communication that managers should follow when developing messages. Finally, we discuss three critical errors that managers must avoid when seeking effective communication.

LEVELS OF MANAGERIAL COMMUNICATION

Managerial communication may occur at five different levels:

1. Intrapersonal
2. Interpersonal
3. Group
4. Organizational
5. Intercultural[2]

One level is not more important than another. Communication may occur at any or all of these levels simultaneously.

Intrapersonal communication focuses on internal behavior, such as observing, listening, and reading. Most of these activities involve the seeking of information; consequently, this communication level is extremely important for managerial decision making and problem solving because effective decisions require accurate information.

The second category is the interpersonal level of communication. At this level, two or more people exchange thoughts. They may be sharing information, providing feedback, or simply maintaining a social relationship.

Group communication is a third level. The most common form of group communication is the meeting, which may be either formal or informal. Chapter 4 discusses the various functions of formal meetings.

Fourth, the organizational level of communication operates within the networks that link members of a company or other organization. Organizational communication is also concerned with how a group of tasks is linked to complete a job.

Fifth, the intercultural level of communication concerns interactions among people of different cultures. As discussed in the next section of this chapter, intercultural communication is occurring more frequently due to improved telecommunications and transportation.[3] Because of its importance, Chapter 11 is dedicated to intercultural communication.

Communication is a behavior we engage in throughout life and often take for granted. You may reach a managerial position yet never deliberately analyze your communication because it has become such common behavior. However, a lack of strategic decision making can cause communication problems for you as a manager. Just as a complex fiscal transaction triggers many different accounting decisions, a communication situation should trigger strategic communication decision making. The accountant does not intuitively enter a transaction as a debit or credit. She makes a series of analytical decisions to ensure that every transaction is correct. Unfortunately, the same accountant may communicate in a critical situation in a style that seems correct without making a similar strategic analysis.

A STRATEGIC APPROACH

The following discussion analyzes separate elements of a strategic approach to communication. However, these variables do not actually occur separately, nor can they be analyzed separately in the managerial context. They are highly interdependent and affect each other concurrently. For instance, the power of the person sending the message, the intended receiver, the message's purpose, and the organizations involved are all interrelated. Each strategic component is reciprocally interdependent. Although the following discussion considers each of the components separately, remember that each variable affects the others.

The strategic approach could be compared to an onion. The strategy is at the very core of the onion, but one must peel away several layers to get to the core. The outer layer of the onion, which we will examine first, can be compared to the context in which the communication event occurs.

The First Layer

The first layer consists of communication context. Context includes a consideration of the organization's climate and culture, both of which are discussed in the following subsections.

Communication Climate

Past communication, such as whether employees and managers have been trusting and open or closed and defensive, has a cumulative effect.[4] A trusting, open climate makes it much easier to communicate in an organization. And there seems to be a positive correlation between communication openness and trust. Major events in an organization's life cycle can affect the communication climate. For example, often when a company is restructuring or a merger is planned, managers reduce the amount of information flowing through the formal channels. The result of this information "vacuum" is employee anxiety and distrust. In such a climate, employees turn to each other, relying on the rumor mill to learn about impending changes and layoffs. Not surprisingly, productivity drops off.

On the other hand, success breeds success. Effective communicating results in trust and openness, which generally improve job performance.[5] In turn, future effective communication will get easier because of the trust and openness that has developed. A positive climate is fragile, however. After only one or two critical errors, a positive environment can quickly change to one of distrust and closed communication, making future communication more difficult. This is why the skills and principles discussed in the following chapters are so critical—managers must avoid communication errors that may result in a negative climate.

Cultural Context

The second factor in the outermost layer of our model is culture. All communication occurs within a culture. Culture is the social glue that binds members of nations and organizations together through shared values, symbols, and social ideals. Culture generally remains below the threshold of conscious awareness because it involves taken-for-granted assumptions about how one should perceive, think, and feel. But it is ubiquitous.

STOP AND THINK

1. How strong is the grapevine at your workplace compared to the formal communication channels?

2. How accurate are the rumors compared to the formal messages?

3. How complete are the rumors compared to the formal messages?

4. From which source would you prefer to get the information you need to do your job?

5. What can managers do to strengthen or weaken the grapevine?

To a large extent, national culture determines how we communicate. Obviously, language differs among cultures, but managers need to be aware of many more subtle conventions. For example, a US manager may perceive his British associates as reserved but his Italian connections as outgoing. Autocratic management is acceptable in India in businesses, while a more participative approach is expected in the United States. Chapter 11 discusses more thoroughly how national culture affects business communication.

Organizational culture also affects how managers communicate. If you think about companies with strong cultures, such as Southwest Airlines, Zappos, Google, Stonyfield Farms, or Whole Foods, you will realize that building an organizational culture takes hard work. The leaders are great communicators and motivators who clearly and consistently explain the organization's vision, mission, and values. Research shows that there is a link between culture and organizational success—performance-oriented cultures possess statistically better financial growth.[6] Additional benefits of a strong culture are high employee involvement and commitment, work team cohesiveness, clear focus on goals throughout the organization, and well-developed internal communication systems.

To diagnose the health of your company's culture, look around you during your next meeting or while eating lunch. Listen to the interactions. Watch how the leaders make decisions and disseminate them. For example, in some organizations, e-mail is used for every request, suggestion, and information exchange, whereas in another organization face-to-face conversation is the norm.

But an organization's culture affects more than preferences for a particular communication channel. The culture, as reflected in an organization's physical space, can encourage or discourage information flow. Office design can consist of closed doors; long, empty hallways; surveillance cameras; and sparse furniture. How many casual conversations are likely to take place among employees who work in such a culture? By contrast, office design can consist of a large, open space free of walls, with lots of seating, music, food, live plants, a waterfall, and employees' work spaces all visible to one another. In such an environment, the organization's cultural values regarding open communication are clear.

STOP AND THINK

1. How does your employer's culture affect you on a daily basis?

2. Does it inspire you or get in your way?

3. What drives your culture?

4. Who are the opinion leaders that reinforce your organization's values?

Figure 2–1   The First Layer of the Strategic Model

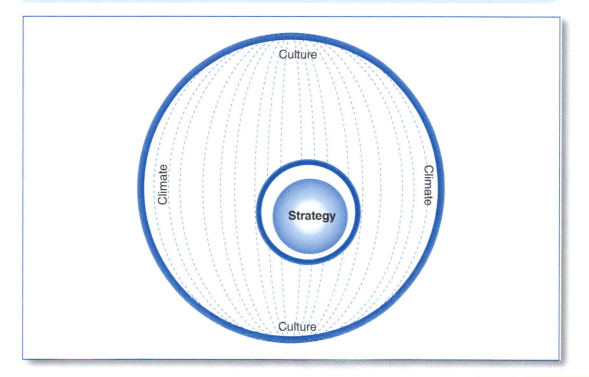

A cultural analysis does not provide definitive answers, but it gives an understanding of generally accepted values. In organizations, these values are manifested in communication practices. For instance, if independence is valued, a persuasive approach rather than a demanding approach may be required. If formality is valued, a formal hard copy memo rather than a telephone call may be necessary. If extensive technical details are part of the organizational culture, all reports may require technical elaboration. If collaboration is valued, then information flows smoothly and freely among all networked stakeholders.

Because culture and climate provide generally accepted patterns of communication, they are depicted as the outer layer of our analysis. Or, to use our analogy, they constitute the outer layer of the onion, as depicted in Figure 2–1. This layer must be analyzed first as managers develop the communication strategy.

The Second Layer

In addition to reviewing the climate and cultural aspects of the communication context, managers should consider the sender, receiver, and the purpose of the communication.

Figure 2–2 shows these three variables as the second layer of the strategic model of communication. Note that the relationship of the three variables is circular rather than linear. Each affects the other concurrently; one does not necessarily come before the other. To simplify our discussions, the manager will be considered as the encoder.

Sender (Encoder)

The manager encodes a message's meaning depending on his or her personality and experiences. Managers must analyze their own frames of reference and communication preferences to determine how they will affect the outcome of the communication.[7] Thus, self-awareness is critical for effective communication.

For instance, what strategy is best when persuading a work group to accept a new procedure? A manager may have realized he is most comfortable talking with just one person rather than a group, has trouble with grammar but can usually find the right words, is a patient listener, and holds a company position that makes it difficult to place demands on others. Consequently, the manager decides it would be best to meet with employees individually in a face-to-face setting to persuade them to accept the new procedure. The manager thus has strategically analyzed his own frame of reference and his role in the communication situation.

Figure 2–2   The Second Layer of the Strategic Model

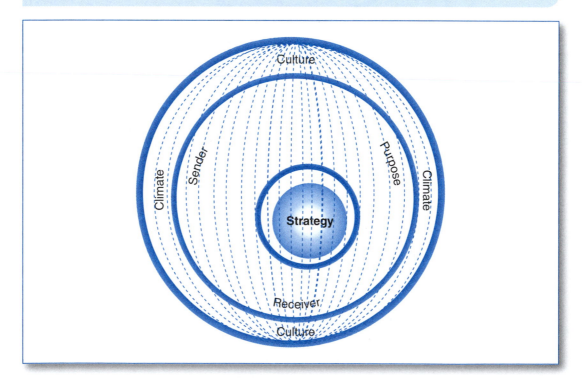

Receiver (Decoder)

Now we can add the second element to this layer: the receiver, or decoder. Managers must continually adapt communication to different receivers to be effective.

Several characteristics of the receiver require analysis: personal relationship of the receiver to the sender, status, interest in the message, feelings toward the message, knowledge about the subject of the message, and the communication skills of the receiver. Together, these characteristics may cause distortions to the intended message. They are sometimes referred to as "internal noise." A review of these items indicates the types of strategic communication decisions a manager must make relative to the receiver.

Relationship. Participants in a friendly relationship tolerate error and initial misunderstanding more than do those in a neutral or hostile relationship.[8] Friendly participants need less time and concentration when communicating than is required in a hostile relationship. For instance, suppose a manager discussing a report with a colleague finds a certain table difficult to read. A friendly colleague will be more tolerant and more willing to ask for clarification than will a hostile one who might criticize the report rather than seek clarification or provide constructive criticism.

Status Difference. Status differences between senders and receivers deserve attention. Status may require that certain customs or traditions be integrated into the communication. For example, the manager may need to refer to certain people as sir, Mr., Ms., doctor, or chief in some organizations to avoid offending the receiver. Also, the manager may need to stand when addressing a person of higher status, but it may be appropriate to sit down with a person of equal or lower status. People of different status levels may easily interpret words and gestures differently.[9] Suppose a manager says, "Can I meet with you for a few minutes?" This simple statement may be a request or a demand, depending on the receiver's status. Obviously, verbal emphasis needs to be adapted to different audiences.

Receiver's Interest. A third type of "noise" is caused by the interest level of the receiver. Thus, a manager may have to make another strategic consideration.[10] If the receiver has low interest, some persuasive elements may be appropriate to get the person's attention even when the ultimate goal of the message is to inform. The audience's interest level may affect the objective of the communication. The manager must adapt the nature of the message to fit the interests of the receiver rather than just the manager's personal interest.

Receiver's Emotional State. The receiver's emotional state at the time of communication may affect how the message is received. A receiver upset about something requires a different communication strategy than that used with a relaxed person. When a receiver is upset, the sender needs to deal first with the person's feelings and attempt to relax the individual, so the receiver is more receptive to the main message. In addition, strategic analysis of the possible emotional reaction to a message makes it possible to be on guard without getting caught up in the emotion.

Receiver's Knowledge. Remember that technical words and examples are appropriate in a message only if everyone involved in the communication transaction understands the terminology; unfortunately, technical concepts may add confusion if receivers do not understand them. Would it be appropriate to ask, "Have you checked the FAR on the VOR at LAX?" How many technical terms may one use with this particular reader or listener? Will certain concepts need explaining? Incorrectly assuming the receiver has considerable knowledge may result in a communication breakdown. But assuming too low a level of knowledge may waste time and insult the receiver. A receiver's level of knowledge can be gauged quickly by asking questions and getting feedback. The answer given to an open-ended question on a specific topic is often the best indication of a receiver's level of knowledge.

Receiver's Communication Skills. The receiver, as well as the sender, must be a competent communicator.[11] Can the receiver communicate clearly? Does the receiver get nervous in communication situations? If the receiver cannot express concepts clearly or becomes nervous when communicating, a manager needs to exercise patience and assist or even relax the person as much as possible.

In summary, a manager should consider six characteristics of the receiver before communicating, as summarized in Table 2–1: personal relationship, status, interest in the message, feelings, knowledge, and communication skills. Knowing one's audience is a critical strategy. Next, the manager needs to analyze the purpose of the message for effective communication in critical situations.

Table 2–1   Checklist for Analyzing the Receiver

What is the personal relationship of the receiver to the sender?
What is the receiver's relative status?
How interested in the message is the receiver?
What are the receiver's feelings toward the message?
How much does the receiver know about the topic of the message?
What are the communication skills of the receiver?

Purpose of the Message

Unless managers analyze their goals, the resulting communication may waste time and effort. Before reviewing the purpose of a communication, managers should first determine whether it is best to verbalize a message at all.

A manager has four major reasons for choosing to communicate. First, the mere act of communicating with a fellow worker may be enjoyable. Communication does not always have to mean business, although one should not confuse working with socializing. At work, some socializing by managers can boost employee morale.

Second, managers communicate to present information and, third, to gain information. Ironically, not all managers distinguish between gaining and presenting information. Many managers tend to do all the talking when they are trying to gain information. While it seems to be human nature to tell others everything one knows, managers must resist this tendency if they wish to gain information.

Fourth, managers communicate to persuade.[12] Managers with persuasion as a goal must develop an appropriate persuasive strategy. Would a rational-logical approach be best, or should it be an emotional appeal? This question of goals can become complicated because goals may be combined. For instance, a goal may be to inform a subordinate of a new procedure while also persuading her to accept the procedure. In these situations, managers need to identify goals clearly and develop appropriate strategies; otherwise, they may achieve neither goal.

The communication goal or purpose often defines the strategy appropriate for a given situation; consequently, effective managers are keenly aware of their communication goals. Subsequent chapters explain how this strategy relates to the audience and the goal and present several examples. For instance, in our discussion of memos and letters in Chapter 7, we explain when a deductive, or *direct*, approach should be used, and when an inductive, or *indirect*, approach should be used.

The Third Layer

To review, we have seen that when a manager is determining a communication strategy, he should begin by considering the context. Next, the manager should consider the purpose, sender, and receiver of the message. We now come to the third layer of the strategic model, which includes four more elements the manager should consider:

- The specific content of the message
- The message's channel
- The physical environment in which it occurs
- The time the communication occurs

Figure 2–3 presents the complete strategic managerial communication model. These four elements appear as the layer closest to the core strategy because they depend on the sender, receiver, and purpose of the message, as well as on the culture and climate. For purposes of discussion, we review each component separately. But again, remember that in reality, a manager needs to consider all interrelationships when developing a communication strategy. Neglecting any one component when analyzing a critical situation may result in a communication failure.

Figure 2–3   The Complete Model

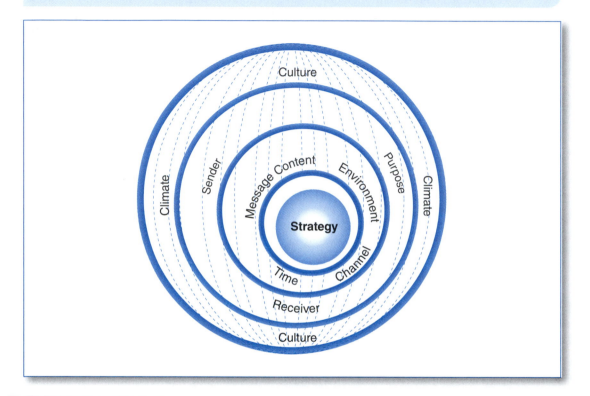

Message Content

We can simplify our discussion by classifying the content of a message according to four factors.

First, will the receiver perceive the message as *positive, negative,* or *neutral?* When the message is positive, the best strategy is to present the good news immediately; however, with a negative message, it is usually best to present neutral information before the negative news.[13] To determine whether the message is positive or negative, consider the receiver's perspective. What may seem positive to a manager may be negative to the receiver.

For example, the manager of an accounting firm was ecstatic as she announced a new contract with a growing firm. But staff members were unhappy with the news because they already felt overworked.

Second, does the message deal with *fact* or *opinion?* A fact may be established with concrete information, but opinion is largely based on assumption. The manager should critically analyze the objective basis of his message because he may feel so sure about his opinion, he will present it as fact. When the manager presents opinions as facts, the receivers may be deceived.

Third, to what extent is the message *important* to the receiver? If the message is important to the manager, but not to the receiver, the manager has to emphasize attention-getting techniques. He would structure such a message according to the needs of the receiver rather than those of the sender. A manager needs to determine how to make the content of the message important to the receiver and then integrate that importance into the information. For instance, an announcement that a staff meeting is to be held at 2 p.m. may not capture an employee's interest; however, if the notice states one of the items on the agenda is a new incentive program, employees are more apt to pay attention.

Fourth, to what extent is the message *controversial?* A controversial message calls for neutral words that can reduce the emotional response. In these situations, phrases such as "Surely you realize," "Everyone else believes," "Can't you see," or "You have to understand" can make the receiver defensive and create conflict.

Effective managerial communication requires analysis of the content factors summarized in Table 2–2. An effective communicator will consider these factors simultaneously with the sender, receiver, and purpose, because they all affect one another when developing a communication strategy.

Table 2–2   Checklist for Determining Message Content
Will the receiver consider the message to be negative or positive?
Will the message deal with facts or opinions?
How important will the message be to the receiver?
How controversial will the message be?

Channel of the Message

With the advent of sophisticated telecommunications and instant delivery, the question of how the message is to be sent becomes increasingly complicated. Habits further complicate channel selection. Managers find ways of communicating that are comfortable for them and continue to use the same methods, even when they are inappropriate. One accounting manager was known for communicating by Post-it notes. While these small adhesive papers are handy for commenting on documents, this manager used them to communicate with his subordinates all the time. He would silently approach an employee in her cubicle, attach the Post-it note to her monitor, and walk out again. How do you think the employee reacted?

Which channel is appropriate for which message? Written communication (memos, letters, reports) provides the opportunity for permanent records and may be precise and clear; however, it usually does not provide the opportunity for immediate feedback. E-mail is thought of as less formal and is often hastily written, but it has the advantages of immediacy, speed, and permanence. Oral communication is often more persuasive than a written message. Texting and phoning can be quick, but they generally provide no permanent record of the conversation. Also, while phone calls allow oral feedback, the participants cannot observe nonverbal behaviors. Since so many factors are involved, it is difficult to declare one channel invariably preferable to another.

The question becomes one of minimizing costs while maximizing communication effectiveness. Consider just these basic options: (1) oral, (2) written, (3) oral and written, and (4) visual. Now subdivide these further into formal and informal approaches. Table 2–3 presents some of these options. But let us complicate the options even further by adding technologically mediated communications, such as video teleconferences, electronic mail, and fax. It quickly becomes apparent that the correct channel choice is not simple. This is why Chapter 3 presents an extensive discussion of communication channels mediated by some form of technology.

Should the message be presented to one individual at a time or to a group? While individual communication allows the manager to adapt the message to each person, group communication is quicker and cheaper. The manager needs to decide if individual adaptation is necessary or if the time saved with group communication is more important. The chapter on meetings will detail this later.

Table 2–3 Channels of Communication

	Informal	Formal
Oral	Personal conversations Interviews and counseling Telecommunication Employee plant tours (orientation)	Staff meetings Public address system Conferences Directives and instructions Briefings
Written	Bulletin boards Daily news digests E-mail Blogs	Policy manuals Management newsletters Intranets Reports Company website
Both oral and written	Face-to-face contact between superior and subordinate where written information is exchanged	Company meetings where reports and data are presented
Visual	Sound-action exhibits Closed-circuit TV Satellite downlinks	Videos PowerPoint slide decks Chart talks

The question of individual versus group is a key to persuasive communication. In some situations, it may be easy to persuade a group of people; however, in other situations, one-to-one communication may be more effective. The manager must strategically analyze all the factors to determine which would be best in a given situation.

Not surprisingly, cost affects all questions regarding channel selection. A letter requires time for drafting and typing. A group meeting requires many individuals to commit their time, and that pooled time can be expensive. These costs need to be balanced with the fact that groups allow for input and feedback from different employees. A telephone call may be quick, but long-distance rates can add up. A formal report may be extremely time consuming to put together, but others may refer to it again later, whereas an oral report is temporary. Thus, managers balance cost and time factors when selecting the appropriate channel for their communication.

Physical Environment

The environment in which communication occurs has a clear effect. Just as receiver characteristics may cause internal noise, so elements of the physical environment may cause "external noise." The result is message distortion. Ask four questions when you analyze the environmental factors in strategic communication:

1. Is it a public or private situation?

2. Does it involve a formal or informal setting?

3. What is the physical distance between the sender and the receiver?

4. Is it a familiar or unfamiliar environment?

The answers to each of these questions can significantly affect the communication strategy.

Privacy. A congratulatory comment may be best in a public forum, while a sensitive question is best asked in a private setting. Some choices between public and private settings are obvious. For instance, neither the manager nor the subordinate would want their annual performance appraisal interview to be conducted in the company cafeteria. But choosing the correct environment for other situations is more difficult. For instance, should a team's performance problem be discussed with each person individually, or should the discussion be held with all members of the team in a public forum? In the past, managers were advised to "praise in public, punish in private." But this simplistic approach to employee feedback can backfire. Singling out subordinates for special attention can result in other employees ostracizing them as the "boss's pet." The outer layer of the strategic model reminds us to consider culture and climate when deciding whether privacy is important as a communication strategy.

Formality. The formality of the setting affects the wording of the message as well as the opportunity for feedback. Thus, while official titles may be appropriate when presenting a formal oral report, they may restrict communication in an informal group discussion. Also, feedback is often more difficult to obtain in a formal setting because questions may seem inappropriate or the questioner may be shy. Finally, people are generally more reserved in their nonverbal behavior in a formal setting, which makes their feedback more difficult to read.

Physical Distance. A third variable to consider is the physical distance between the sender and receiver. In oral communication, physical distance mutes the variations in the voice's tone and loudness and in the participants' gestures and posture. Thus, it is less effective to use these strategies for emphasis when distance is great. Proximity, on the other hand, makes messages compelling. In written communication, distance also affects feedback and time. The quality of feedback for a report mailed from Lima, Ohio, to Lima, Peru, may be less timely (and, consequently, less useful) than it is for a report exchanged in one building. A manager can expect less comprehensive feedback as distances increase. Distance also makes persuasion more difficult because opposing arguments cannot be answered immediately. A manager may have to decide if it is better to wait until a face-to-face opportunity is available or if the persuasive efforts should occur over a greater distance for the sake of timeliness.

Familiarity. The final factor to consider when discussing environment is its familiarity. This concept needs to be analyzed from the perspective of the manager as well as the receiver. A familiar environment allows the participants to be relaxed, which is important when controversies or feelings are involved. When communicating in an unfamiliar environment, a manager should anticipate the distractions that may occur. Distractions that we might be accustomed to in our own environment can be unnerving when we encounter them in unfamiliar surroundings. Something as seemingly simple as heavy traffic outside an office window can be a distraction when we are not used to it.

Table 2–4 summarizes the factors that managers must strategically analyze when considering the physical environment of a communication event.

Table 2–4   Checklist for Analyzing the Physical Environment

Is the environment public or private?
Is the environment formal or informal?
What is the physical distance between the sender and the receiver?
Is the environment familiar or unfamiliar?

Time

Time affects all elements of management, and it has a ubiquitous effect on communication. Clearly, the adage that "time is money" is appropriate here. Managers need to consider the amount of time spent in preparing to communicate and the amount of time spent in the process. Consider the time of both managers and receivers to obtain cost and communication efficiency. Thus, while a meeting may at first seem advisable because it allows for questions and feedback, it may not be efficient because of the time required to assemble people. Consequently, an e-mail or text message may be more efficient in certain situations. This effort is the type of strategic time decision a manager must make.

Remember also that time is power and time is status. People with busy schedules are perceived as more important than those whom you can approach at any time. Also, while the subordinate must make an appointment to see the manager, the manager, who has higher status, can drop in on the employee without notice. Status is also communicated by the amount of time a person is kept waiting.

The actual timing of the communication is another important consideration. Communication behavior appropriate at one time may be inappropriate or even detrimental at a different time. It is not appropriate to try to get the attention of someone immediately before an important meeting. Also, it is highly unlikely that a report will receive much attention if it arrives late on a Friday afternoon. As another example, consider the timing of an announcement made at a large urban hospital consisting of several buildings. For several years, landscaping improvements were being installed to improve water runoff. The grounds were beautiful on completion. But as the project was completed, layoffs of hospital staff were announced. It appeared the landscaping was done at the expense of jobs. Understandably, many employees were bitter about the allocation of funds.

FEEDBACK AND MEASURES OF EFFECTIVENESS

Integral to a strategic management communication approach are feedback and measures of effectiveness. These variables are not included in the strategic model (Figure 2–3) because they are so pervasive. They are inherent in each variable and cannot be separated. Feedback is important in two ways. First, it should be continually obtained to determine how changing events may affect the overall strategy. For instance, a manager determines that an e-mail about a new procedure was not as clear as he thought because many questions were being asked. Based on this feedback, he quickly calls a meeting to clarify the procedure. In this case, the channel is changed to improve the communication strategy.

Second, feedback may be obtained to determine if the strategy was effective even though it may be too late to change it. Unfortunately, many managers may avoid this feedback because they believe nothing can be done about it. For example, an advertising agency submits a proposal for an ad campaign. When the contract is given to another agency, the tendency is not to evaluate the effectiveness of the written proposal. After all, nothing can be done about it now. But this is the opportunity to thoroughly evaluate all aspects of the proposal, including such items as an analysis of the receiver, writing style, and timing. Lessons thus learned should be applied to the next proposal. Postmortems, while unpleasant and often avoided, are valuable tools for organizational improvement.

Obtaining feedback and measuring effectiveness may be extremely difficult. In one case, a regional insurance manager is disappointed in sales. She writes a number of letters, makes

STOP AND THINK

Consider a time when you failed to reach your goal, whether in sports or on a work project.

1. How welcome was the feedback you received?

2. What did you do differently the next time you faced a similar challenge?

phone calls, and personally meets with her independent sales agents to motivate them, yet sales continue to slide. She contracts a management consultant to determine how she can improve her motivational strategies. However, it cannot be determined if poor sales were the result of communication with the sales agents or the insurance products themselves. Managerial communication is so interrelated with other factors that it is often difficult to determine effectiveness.

CRITICAL ERRORS IN COMMUNICATION

Despite consideration of all the foregoing elements, managers make communication errors. The communication process depends on the personalities of those involved and the environment in which they operate. This process creates a dynamic interaction, and as the strategic communication model shows, this interaction is not perfect.

Even when people believe they are communicating what is real, they are communicating only what is reality in their own minds. No perfect correspondence exists between what is real in the world and the reality perceived by the mind because of the mental filters. This imperfect correspondence is manifested in a person's attempt to communicate real events of the world. These critical but common errors arise from problems in our mental filters: the assumption-observation error, the failure to discriminate error, and the allness error.[14]

The Assumption-Observation Error

An assumption occurs when people accept something as valid without requiring proof. Every day we must act on assumptions. For example, we assume the food in the cafeteria is not toxic (despite our persistent jokes to the contrary), the ceiling in the office will not fall, and numbers being used in a report are valid. Assumptions are essential and desirable in analyzing materials, solving problems, and planning.

When we drop a letter in the mailbox, we assume it will reach its destination in a reasonable time. But is this assumption completely accurate or safe? Evidence suggests the letter may be lost, delayed, or even destroyed. Nevertheless, we take a calculated risk, and the act seems to be relatively safe. But if the same envelope contains something valuable, we insure the envelope's contents.

At what point is insurance necessary? That is, when is an assumption safe, and when is it a risk? Strategic communication continually addresses this question. Strategic communicators must avoid assumptions that may be incorrect and unreliable and that result in miscommunication. Consider the following example.

The manager of the quality control department noticed that Andre, a new chemist, was extremely conscientious. Andre remained after work at least a half hour every night to check all the figures. The manager was so impressed with Andre's commitment that she wrote a special commendation letter for his personal file. Later, the manager discovered Andre was really having a lot of difficulty with the tests and was remaining late to correct the many errors he normally made.

To avoid the assumption-observation error, a manager should ask, "What are the facts?" We must determine the extent of risk that a statement is true for a specific situation. Once done, the resultant communication should be stated as either a fact or an assumption. For instance, "I see we got a shipment of copper [fact]." On the other hand, expressions such as "In my opinion," "It looks to me as if," and "I am assuming" can help us to differentiate between fact and assumption. Just as these phrases can help managers to clarify in their own minds when they are using assumptions, they also give the receiver a clearer understanding of the message.

The Failure to Discriminate

The failure to discriminate is the failure to perceive and communicate significant differences among individuals or changes in situations. This failure to make clear distinctions or to differentiate can lead to the neglect of differences and the overemphasis of similarities. One of the consequences of the failure to discriminate is what William Haney calls "hardening of the categories." A leading researcher in the field of interpersonal communication and organizational behavior, Haney observed:

> Most of us have a penchant for categorizing—for classifying. Show someone something he has never seen before and one of his first questions is likely to be: "What kind is it?" We meet a new person and we are uneasy until we can pigeonhole: What is she? How is she classified? Is she a salesperson, plumber, farmer, teacher, painter? Is she Protestant, Catholic, Jew, atheist? Democrat, Republican, independent? Lower, middle, upper "class"?[15]

This hardening of categories can result in stereotypes because people may apply their set image of the group to any individual in the group; consequently, inappropriate labels may be applied. One common example concerns managers who are interviewing job applicants. An applicant may have attended a school whose graduates the interviewer categorizes as undesirable. Therefore, the interviewer does not fully listen to the applicant. The hardening of categories can also cause a person to communicate in terms of general categories rather than specifics and thus lose valuable information. For example, "Joyce is a union member" omits the fact that she is the most qualified inspector in the department.

The potential danger is that those who put everything into a category are usually not aware they are doing it. This blindness makes failure to discriminate an extremely difficult tendency to overcome. However, Haney provides two valuable suggestions.[16] The first is to internalize the premise of uniqueness—that is, to develop a sensitivity to all the differences in the world. No two things, whether snowflakes or siblings, have ever been found to be exactly the same. A second technique is to index evaluations. This means each person, thing, or situation should be indexed according to some unique characteristic. This can soon lead to the conclusion that everything and everyone is unique and, in turn, provides sensitivity to differences.

Polarization is a special form of discrimination involving "either-or" thinking. Some situations are true dichotomies that can be stated in terms of either-or: an employee is either absent or present; a person is either male or female. However, we cannot accurately describe many situations in either-or terms: a product is neither good nor bad; a person works neither fast nor slow. Polarization occurs when a person deals with a situation involving gradations and middle ground in strict either-or terms. Thus, someone may state he will either succeed or fail in a job and may truly believe that no middle ground or success exists. Conversely, if a person is told the only options are either success or failure, the person may begin to believe that in-between possibilities do not exist. When managers are wary of either-or statements, they can more accurately distinguish the degree of differences between two items and more accurately perceive the world.

Frozen evaluation is another failure to discriminate. It occurs when people disregard possible changes in persons, places, or things. Because everything in the world changes, evaluations cannot remain static. However, while it is easy to say that change is a major aspect of business, it is often difficult to adapt to that continuous change. Frozen evaluation can result in an inaccurate perception of the world, and management errors may result.

The key to avoiding frozen evaluations is to remember that all things change. The manager who continually asks when and what has changed avoids assuming that events are static, thus preventing this common and critical communication error. A simple question a manager may ask is "What labels have I applied to this situation?"

Allness and the Process of Abstraction

A third critical error that a manager must conscientiously avoid is allness. People commit this error when they structure communications as if what they are stating is all there is to know about a subject. The astute person knows that reality is too complex for anyone to know all there is to know about something. However, the error is still made. Haney states that allness is the result of two false beliefs: (1) It is possible to know and say everything about something, and (2) what I am saying (or writing or thinking) includes all that is important about the subject.[17] Normal communication patterns contribute to the problem of allness because people abstract as they speak. Abstracting is the process of focusing on some details and omitting others. When communicating, we need to select some details and omit others. The very process of abstracting, however, can conceal that we have selectively omitted certain data. As a result, the listener, and in some instances the speaker, has no warning that certain information is being left out. Sometimes the more that is omitted, the harder it is to recognize that one has left out anything.

A conspicuous example of the allness error is the following: A high school sophomore was chatting with a man who (unknown to the student) was a distinguished scientist devoting his lifetime to studying botany. The smug sophomore commented, "Oh, botany? I finished studying all about that stuff last semester." As Bertrand Russell stated, "One's certainty varies inversely with one's knowledge."

Almost everything we do involves some level of abstraction, so the solution to the allness error is not simply to omit abstraction. Rather, it is important to be aware of the level of abstraction occurring. Once the person is aware of the level of abstraction, the message can be phrased accordingly: "as far as I know," "according to the information I have," or "this is what I consider to be the critical information." To help overcome the allness error when listening, ask "What has been omitted?" or simply "What else?" Also, if it is possible to put the phrase *et cetera* at the end of a sentence, ask what that would include.

Table 2–5 summarizes the questions to ask in order to avoid committing three critical errors when communicating.

Table 2–5   How to Avoid Critical Errors

Critical Error	Question to Ask
Assumption-Observation	What are the facts?
Failure to Discriminate	What labels have I applied to this situation?
Allness	What else is going on?

The foregoing critical errors—assumption-observation, failure to discriminate, and allness—were discussed largely from the perspective of the intrapersonal and interpersonal levels of communication. However, management communication seldom operates at just the intra- or interpersonal level. The process may become more complex as more people become involved. In a meeting, the three communication errors discussed exist, and specialized problems inherent in groups must also be considered. When a manager of one department communicates with a group in another department, organization-level dynamics become involved. In both of these cases, the basic errors presented in this chapter can occur, and specialized types of potential errors must be considered also. More is said about group and organizational levels of communication in Chapter 4, which is dedicated to meetings and group dynamics, while Chapter 11 addresses intercultural communication.

SUMMARY

Managerial communication occurs at five levels: intrapersonal, interpersonal, group, organizational, and intercultural. Each of these levels is considered in this text.

This chapter also presents a model for strategic managerial communication that may help managers reduce errors in critical situations. While it is not possible to present concrete rules that will serve in every instance, we explored factors the manager should review before communicating.

These factors are presented as three layers of a strategic model. The first layer includes climate and culture. The communication strategy must be consistent with the context of national and organizational cultures. The second layer involves the sender, receiver, and purpose of the message. The third layer includes the message, channel, environment, and time of communication. The appropriate strategic implementation of these factors—the model's core—depends highly on these three layers of variables.

Considering these elements during the developmental phase, however, is insufficient to ensure communication success. Managers must also seek feedback and measures of effectiveness to ensure continuous improvement of their interaction skills.

Finally, this chapter examined critical errors in the communication process. The most common are (1) the assumption-observation error, (2) the failure to discriminate, and (3) the allness error. The assumption-observation error results when a manager communicates something as real when no observable evidence is present. The failure to discriminate is the failure to perceive and communicate changes in events or significant differences between things. The error of allness occurs when a person structures communication as if it states all there is to know about a subject. Managers need to consider all these factors and human foibles when communicating.

Cases for Small-Group Discussion

CASE 2–1

The Shroud of Technology

Ben knocked on the door of Nancy Kerr, his supervising director.

"Come in," Nancy said, and Ben entered. He was frustrated, and his demeanor reflected it.

"I need to talk to you about Stacey Burton, who works in the office beside mine," Ben said. "Ever since we rearranged the office suite about a month ago, Stacey has been coming by and standing in the door of my office, just to flirt and to chat. It interrupts my work, and I'm uncomfortable with the overt attention, especially flirtatious attention," Ben continued. "I'm also getting deluged with non-work-related e-mails from Stacey."

"Have you asked Stacey to stop?" asked Nancy.

"Well, not really. The interaction could easily be taken as office banter, if you just heard the words. It is the way Stacey gestures and speaks and looks at me that makes it flirting," Ben said. "I'm really not comfortable with initiating a confrontation with Stacey and thought maybe you would be willing to say something instead."

"I'll be happy to—probably today," Nancy replied. "I'll send an e-mail now. Thanks for bringing this to my attention."

Nancy sent an e-mail to Stacey to come to her office briefly at 2:00 p.m.

At 1:55, Nancy heard a knock and said, "Come in."

A smartly dressed young man came in and sat down. "Can I help you?" Nancy asked.

"Well, you said you wanted to talk to me. What can I do for you?" he asked.

"I wanted to talk to you?" asked Nancy.

"Yes," the young man replied. "I'm Stacey Burton."

QUESTIONS

1. What assumption-observation error might be made in this scenario?

2. To what extent did the use of technology for these message exchanges contribute to the miscommunication between Nancy and Stacey?

3. What gender stereotypes discussed in Chapter 1 apply to this case?

4. How would you, in Nancy's shoes, handle the awkward moment and the ensuing discussion?

CASE 2–2

Developing a Brochure

Mitch Finley, a twenty-nine-year-old with a degree in finance, began working as a loan officer at a bank two years ago. Later, he began consulting for other businesses in financial planning. His career goal has been to start his own business.

Recently, Finley opened The Suite Thing, a development company using one of his original business ideas—the construction of two large hotel-like buildings containing suites (living room, bedroom, kitchen) rather than single rooms.

The hotels are located in two cities that are important regional centers for the oil industry. Instead of renting the suites, he is selling them to large oil companies to meet entertainment and tax planning needs.

Finley had been using a brochure his architects put together, but he was not pleased with its presentation. He had collected other company brochures that he liked and decided to call an advertising firm to design a new brochure and logo for his company.

In the initial meeting, Finley told the advertising representative he needed a new company logo and a brochure folder that would hold his leaflets. Most important, the logo and kit had to be completed as soon as possible, because time was money to him.

The advertising representative (very new on the job) acknowledged that his company could do logo and brochure layouts. The representative then asked Finley a few general questions about his two projects—what they involved, where they were located, and their surroundings. The agency rep said he would return within one week with his ideas.

Two-and-one-half weeks later, Finley called the advertising agency and wanted to know if it had developed the materials. The representative came by later that afternoon with his idea. The agency's approach centered on a hard-sell theme of "Beat the Hotel Game with the Suite Thing." Finley, frustrated by the response delay and the inconsistency between the advertising agency's offering and his own image of the project, said, "No, that's not at all what I want." The advertising representative, taken aback, sat in silence for a time before responding in a frustrated voice, "Well, what do you see your project as being?" and reminded him of the time constraints Finley had given. Finley said he did not see hotels as his competitors, and he wanted a brochure and logo that used soft sell to introduce his idea to top-level executives as an investment.

The next day the advertising representative returned with a more conservative, soft-sell piece. Finley said, "That's *kind of* what I want, but not really."

Finley cannot understand why he did not get what he wanted the first time because "that's their business and they should know how to do it."

QUESTIONS

1. What are some possible causes of Finley's communication problem? Of the advertising representative's?

2. Identify how assumptions caused communication problems in this case.

3. What actions would you recommend to the advertising representative to ensure this does not happen again?

4. Do you believe there is a communication deadlock? If so, what should the participants do to resolve it?

CASE 2–3

Why Is Jones Changing?

The Finance Investment Company is located in Houston, Texas. The company is only two years old, but it has made the headlines in regional magazines as "the company to watch." It is staffed with three investment analysts and four secretaries. The firm occupies a fairly small space, with the secretaries in the front office and the analysts' offices adjacent to the front office.

Mr. Jones, a top-notch analyst, is very unfriendly. He runs the company with an iron fist. Jones is the first one at work and the last one to leave. Promptness is his motto.

The women working in the office think the middle-aged Jones is attractive. One secretary commented to another, "I wonder what it's like to be married to him. He's so good looking, but he's such a geek. He couldn't be that much fun to be married to." Jones never talked to them; it seemed as if business was the only thing on his mind.

Recently, Jones began coming in late, taking long lunch hours, and leaving earlier. One of the secretaries commented, "Wow, what a change in Mr. Jones. I wonder what's going on?" Another secretary replied, "You're right; I've noticed a change in him also. He started all this about the time that new woman began working here."

The secretaries did not like the new woman in the office. She was tall, blonde, and beautiful. She talked little, could hardly type, and knew little about computers. The other secretaries wrote her off as a "dumb blonde." One secretary commented to another, "Old Jonesey is not only coming in from lunch late, but lately he's been in the best moods. He even talked to me today!" Another said, "I noticed that, and I also saw his secretary coming in the door right after he did. And a woman calls about 6 p.m. every afternoon for Mr. Jones, but he has been leaving the office at 4:30 and cannot take the call." The other secretary said, "Well, I can put two and two together. Can't you?"

QUESTIONS

Evaluate each of the following statements as true (T), false (F), or questionable (?). Do not reread the story before evaluating the statements, and do not change any of your answers.

1. Financial Investment Company is located in Houston, Texas.
2. Financial Investment Company is the fastest-growing company in Houston.
3. The building has four offices.
4. Jones is unfriendly.
5. Jones is very prompt.
6. Jones owns the company.
7. Jones has an iron fist.
8. Jones is about forty-five years old.
9. Jones is married.
10. Jones hired a new secretary.
11. The new secretary is a gorgeous blonde.
12. The new woman types well.
13. Jones returns to the office in a good mood.
14. The secretaries in the office think that Jones is having an affair with the gorgeous blonde.
15. Jones is having lunch with his secretary.
16. Jones is not going home after work.
17. A woman calls Jones every day at 6 p.m.
18. Jones's wife is probably looking for him.
19. Jones is going through his midlife crisis.

What critical communication error is demonstrated with this exercise? Explain.

CASE 2–4

Resigning from the TV Station

Jane Rye is a student of advertising at the local state university and will graduate at the end of the next term. She has a part-time job in the sales department at a local television station. When hired, Rye thought she was very lucky to have a job there, not only for the money but also for the work experience.

Pat Trent, the sales manager who hired her, was Rye's immediate supervisor. Rye was doing a very good job and received considerable support from Trent. In fact, the sales manager had nothing but praise for Rye's work when reporting to top management. Trent often told her subordinate that her work was exceptional and Trent would like to hire her on a permanent basis after graduation to head a new media research department for the station. The job seemed to promise a challenging and rewarding career.

While Rye was flattered by the offer, she was not interested in the position because she found her present job unsatisfying. However, she never told Trent her feelings about the job or the possible appointment. Because Trent had trained Rye and had promoted her to everyone, Rye had become very loyal and grateful to her sales manager. Thus, Rye thought she would betray Trent if she were to refuse the job. After six weeks, however, Rye decided to quit and work part-time at the university, but she did not know how to approach her boss.

Rye, feeling unable to say anything unpleasant to Trent, let time pass until the day she was ready to quit to start her new job. When Rye got to work that day, the sales manager was scheduled to leave town later that morning. Rye was forced to go into Trent's office while two other people were there discussing another matter. Trent asked Rye what she wanted, and Rye replied, "I am resigning." The sales manager was taken completely by surprise, asked Rye why she was resigning, and wondered what was to be done with the project Rye was handling. Rye apologized for such short notice. Rye explained that she was taking a part-time job at the school starting tomorrow. Trent, very disappointed in her subordinate, said, "If you had told me sooner, I could have phased out the project to someone else—now I'm in a bind."

QUESTIONS

1. How should Rye have handled her resignation?

2. Where, when, and how do you think Rye should have resigned? Do you think Trent would have understood under different circumstances?

3. How did Trent foster Rye's reluctance to communicate?

4. What are some possible long-term repercussions of the way Rye handled her resignation?

Student Study Site

Visit the Student Study Site at **study.sagepub.com/hynes6e** for web quizzes, video links, web resources, and cases studies.

Notes

1. John P. Kotter, "What Effective General Managers Really Do," *Harvard Business Review* 77, no. 2 (1999): pp. 145–158. For a list of key managerial skills, see the American Management Association's "2001 Managerial Skills and Competencies Survey" results, available online at http://www.amanet.org/research/archive_2001_1999.htm.

2. Lee Thayer, *Communication and Communication Systems* (Burr Ridge, IL: Richard D. Irwin, 1968).

3. Harry C. Triandis and Rosita D. Albert, "Cross-Cultural Perspectives," in *Handbook of Organizational Communication,* eds. F. Jablin, L. Putnam, K. Roberts, and L. Porter (Newbury Park, CA: Sage, 1987), pp. 264–295.

4. M. S. Poole, "Communication and Organizational Climate: Review, Critique, and a New Perspective," in *Organizational Communication Traditional Themes and New Directions,* eds. R. D. McPhee and P. K. Tompkins (Beverly Hills, CA: Sage, 1985), pp. 79–108.

5. Raymond L. Falcione, Lyle Sussman, and Richard P. Herden, "Communications Climate in Organizations," in *Handbook of Organizational Communication,* eds. F. Jablin, L. Putnam, K. Roberts, and L. Porter (Newbury Park, CA: Sage, 1987), pp. 195–227.

6. Shawn Parr, "Culture Eats Strategy for Lunch," *Fast Company*, January 24, 2012, www.fastcompany.com/1810674/culture-eats-strategy-for-lunch.

7. John Petit, Jr. and Bobby C. Vaught, "Self-Actualization and Interpersonal Capability in Organizations," *Journal of Business Communication* 21, no. 3 (1984): pp. 33–40.

8. Joseph N. Cappella, "Interpersonal Communication: Definitions and Fundamental Questions," in *Handbook of Communication Science,* eds. C. R. Berger and S. H. Chaffee (Newbury Park, CA: Sage, 1987), pp. 184–238.

9. C. L. Hale and J. G. Delia, "Cognitive Complexity and Social Perspective-Taking," *Communication Monographs* 43 (1976): pp. 195–203.

10. Kitty O. Locker, "Theoretical Justifications for Using Reader Benefits," *Journal of Business Communication* 19, no. 3 (1982): pp. 51–66.

11. Gary F. Soldow, "A Study of the Linguistic Dimensions of Information Processing as a Function of Cognitive Complexity," *Journal of Business Communication* 19, no. 1 (1982): pp. 55–70.

12. Mohan R. Limaye, "The Syntax of Persuasion: Two Business Letters of Request," *Journal of Business Communication* 20, no. 2 (1983): pp. 17–30.

13. Mohan R. Limaye, "Buffers in Bad New Messages and Recipient Perceptions," *Management Communication Quarterly* 2, no. 1 (1988): pp. 90–101.

14. Much of this discussion is drawn from William V. Haney, *Communication and Interpersonal Relations: Text and Cases,* 6th ed. (Burr Ridge, IL: Richard D. Irwin, 1992).

15. Ibid., pp. 359–381.

16. Ibid., p. 368.

17. Ibid., pp. 320–357.

Communicating with Technology

In the last decade, we have gone from a connected world to a hyperconnected world. In the hyperconnected world . . . managers and entrepreneurs everywhere now have greater access than ever to the better and best people, robots and software everywhere.

—Tom Friedman, author, *New York Times* columnist, and three-time Pulitzer Prize winner

If you spend as much time as most managers do creating and responding to e-mail, texting your staff, blogging, participating in webinars and virtual meetings, and compulsively checking your smartphone at stoplights, you may well assume that developments in technology will determine the future of business communication. Where does a discussion of technologically mediated communication begin? Technology is changing so quickly that it sometimes seems impossible to get a focus on the topic. Forty years ago, a communication theorist stated, "Communication is essentially a social affair . . . but life in the modern world is coming to depend, more and more, upon 'technical' means of communication, telephone and telegraph, radio and printing."[1] That observation was prescient.

Think about all the technology that has developed in the past fifty years. Only a couple of generations ago, the communication revolution meant the long-distance telephone. Thirty-five years ago, the discussion of telecommunication included the definition of *floppy disk* and what was meant by a personal computer. Thirty years ago, many textbooks like the one you are reading would have dedicated much space to an explanation of the difference between hardware and software, the purpose of a modem, and how word processing could soon replace the electric typewriter. Fifteen years ago, managers did not routinely look at a candidate's Facebook page as a step in the hiring process. Ten years ago, businesses were unaware of the power of Twitter for reaching out to their market. And just five years ago, no one had a tool like the Wall Street Scanner, an app for a handheld device that synthesizes the stock markets, social networks, headlines, and corporate sites, to instantly report on economic trends and the forecast for the next day.

Today, electronic communication channels are an integral part of our work lives. The whole rationale for reliance on technology is increased efficiency and productivity, and recent research does provide some evidence to support this assumption. But technology is not merely a beneficial tool, it's a force that must be constantly reassessed. Technological innovation is not always good merely because it is innovative. It's a thin line to walk, and it requires some creative thinking to stay balanced between technological aptitude and overkill.[2]

Given the speed with which business communication technology changes, it is unrealistic to assume that this chapter will accurately reflect what is going on both when I wrote it and when you read it. So instead of describing "current" practices, the chapter focuses on *best practices*, time-honored principles for using technology in the workplace. Reading it will help you develop a framework for making strategic decisions in the use of whatever technologically mediated communication tools are available at that time.

STOP AND THINK

1. How often are you interrupted by incoming e-mail, instant messaging, or text messages at work?

2. How does that impact your productivity?

3. Given that 28 percent of a typical office worker's time is spent being interrupted, to what extent does technology help versus hinder efficiency?

A FRAMEWORK FOR USING TECHNOLOGICALLY MEDIATED COMMUNICATION

The decision to use a telephone, e-mail, text message, or teleconference can be complicated because of the many variables involved. To understand these variables, refer to Chapter 2 and the discussion on strategy. With technologically mediated communication, a technological channel transmits the communication. Thus, the main difference is in the channel. However, as the strategic communication model in Chapter 2 indicates, every other variable is also affected by the technology. Four concepts help us understand the use of technologically mediated communication: *bandwidth, perceived personal closeness, feedback*, and the *symbolic interactionist perspective*.[3]

Bandwidth

Communication occurs along five sensory channels: visual, auditory, tactile, gustatory, and olfactory.[4] Bandwidth is the information transmission capacity of the available sensory channels. Face-to-face communication between two people within an arm's length of each other has a wide bandwidth because it can use all five channels. When a manager first meets a job applicant, the two people usually shake hands. They are concurrently sharing visual, auditory, tactile, and olfactory cues, so this communication has a wide bandwidth.

Mediated communication generally omits one or more of the channels. For instance, a videoconference omits tactile and olfactory channels or cues, while the telephone omits tactile, olfactory, and visual cues.

How many messages sent via different channels can the mind comprehend at one time? This theoretical question has plagued communication researchers for centuries, but it remains a relevant question when considering technologically mediated communication. To help understand this question, imagine a Y. Assume that each communication message or bit is a ball that approaches our brain—the base of the Y—along an arm of the Y. The arms of the Y are different communication channels. What happens if both balls approach the intersection of the Y concurrently, but there is room for only one ball? Information jamming will occur. In terms of information theory, selective attention results, so the receiver pays attention to only one of the information bits while ignoring the others. In other words, the mind decides which ball can proceed to the base of the Y. This process is diagrammed in Figure 3–1.

The goal is to have as much information as possible processed in the central nervous system without jamming. How many cues from different sources can be processed simultaneously?[5] This leads to the concept of between channel redundancy (BCR). BCR results in multichannel communication when information is shared among auditory, olfactory, tactile, gustatory, or visual channels.

Consider meeting a job applicant. When auditory and visual channels transmit identical information, BCR is complete. This would occur when the person dresses neatly and

Figure 3–1 Information Processing

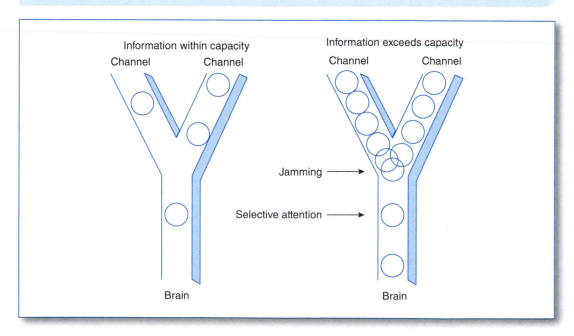

speaks in an articulate, precise manner. Both of these cues are complementary because they signal that the person is a professional. BCR is mixed or incomplete when different channels transmit conflicting or incongruous information. BCR is zero when each channel transmits completely different or contradictory information. Other things being equal, information transfer is theoretically most effective when BCR is complete. Interference is highest when BCR is zero.

Information theory has not been able to totally determine what information humans process or how they process it. However, several conclusions can be stated. First, we can process only a limited amount of information. Second, certain types of information over-power other types of information.[6] Both of these conclusions have powerful implications for strategic managerial communication. Managers must determine how much information can be valuable in various situations. Only valuable information—cues—should be provided so a person's information-processing capabilities are not overpowered with useless cues.

The choice between video networking, videoconferencing, and audio conferencing indicates why this is important for technologically mediated communication. Management may be tempted to use video networking because it provides real-time interactive video, audio, and data sharing via the Internet. Videoconferencing provides visual cues in addition to audio cues. But the cost of setting up online collaboration tools and videoconferences is much higher, and it may not be justifiable. Sharing data and files in real time during a meeting may not be important. Even visual cues may be of little value or even distract from the critical audio message that can be provided with a simple, audio-only teleconference.

On the other hand, managers typically should not choose communication channels with narrow bandwidths for emotional messages. Text messaging an employee that she has been terminated or e-mailing an expression of sympathy for the loss of a loved one are "tech-etiquette" blunders that are becoming all too common. And the broadest bandwidth channel, face-to-face, may be crucial for effectively communicating with key clients, especially in certain cultural contexts, as discussed in Chapter 11.

If circumstances require the use of a narrow bandwidth channel to transmit a sensitive message, managers should do their best to offset the consequences. A recent example was provided by a major corporation that used e-mail to notify four hundred employees of layoffs. While initial reactions to that channel choice for termination notices may be critical, a closer look shows that the company chose e-mail because it was efficient and practical for the mass announcement. In addition, company officials had held a series of meetings (a broad bandwidth channel) during which they explained the method they would use. Employees also could use the company intranet site to find answers to their questions.[7] Thus, managers should consider using multiple channels of varying bandwidth for important, emotional messages.

In addition to the concept of bandwidth, the theory of *electronic propinquity*, or perceived personal closeness, provides a framework for understanding technologically mediated communication.

Perceived Personal Closeness

Participants in the communication process can feel either attached or removed from each other. Two people in the same room may feel miles apart, whereas those on different continents may feel close to each other. Many factors such as the history of the two people as communication partners can affect this feeling of closeness. Of particular concern here is how media affect the feeling of closeness, or propinquity.

Much research indicates electronic media affect the extent to which people feel close to each other. For instance, some people are much more apprehensive about leaving voice-mail messages than others and feel uncomfortable even when making a simple call.[8] When this apprehension exists, telephone conversations will not help a person feel psychologi-cally close to another. Indeed, the psychological distance could be increased because of the accompanying apprehension. Some suggest it is the inability of the communicator to read nonverbal communication that causes this apprehension.[9] Others, however, may prefer and enjoy some form of technology over face-to-face communication. Some people actu-ally warm up to the technology. An example is young people's reliance on their smart-phones for friendly interactions. When a person feels warm to the technology, psychological distance may be decreased.

Telecommunications may actually increase a person's sense of closeness. One study found that participants in certain situations enjoyed group meetings more when mediated by technology than when everyone was physically present.[10] Another example of prefer-ence for technology as an interpersonal communication tool is the use of text messaging. Instant messaging (IM) has become the long-distance communication medium of choice for young adults. More similar to an electronic conversation than e-mail, IM is used by nearly three-quarters of teens online, and most use it every time they log on.[11] More rele-vant to this discussion is the fact that about a third of today's 200 million IM users world-wide are doing it at work.[12] Text messaging is also popular among business professionals. Smartphones allow remote e-mail access and web browsing. Some managers prefer texting coworkers rather than e-mailing or leaving voicemail messages because they ensure quick, brief responses especially when they are in the field rather than in their offices.

Interestingly, voicemail is becoming obsolete as an interpersonal communication tool. While a human voice may seem to convey personal closeness more successfully than text, the number of steps required for dialing in and checking voicemail messages, recording the phone numbers, redialing, and leaving a return message may be more trouble than it is worth. Research shows that employees take longer to reply to voice messages than other types of technology—more than 30 percent of voice messages are not retrieved after three days. By contrast, 91 percent of people under 30 respond to text messages within an hour, according to a 2008 study. But substituting text for talk is not just a generational phenomenon. Even adults over 30 are twice as likely to respond within minutes to a text as to a voicemail message.[13]

In summary, the impact of electronic media on feelings of personal closeness has not yet been adequately determined. But there is some evidence for an inverse relationship between technology use and closeness. Preliminary research on this question indicates that overuse of technology does indeed affect interpersonal relationships. For example, a research team led by Brian Wansink at Cornell University found that children and adults who avoid or are denied eye contact are more likely to suffer from feelings of isolation and to exhibit antisocial traits and other psychological problems. The researchers hypothesize that people who spend more time looking at their mobile devices than at one another suf-fer impaired emotional intelligence and social facility.[14]

Managers need to determine the extent to which perceived personal closeness is important in different situations. Also, to what extent do various types of technology affect this closeness between the sender and receiver? If this question is not addressed, inappropriately used technology designed to enhance managerial communication may be destructive rather than constructive.

In addition to bandwidth and electronic propinquity, we should consider a third factor, *feedback*, when discussing technologically mediated communication.

Feedback

Feedback binds the sender and receiver together so they truly communicate with each other. Feedback is always present if it is sought. To understand fully the implications of this statement in relationship to mediated communication, it is important to consider both bandwidth and perceived personal closeness.

Mediated communication may reduce channels for obtaining feedback. When using the telephone, we do not see the facial expression of our communication partner. Thus, feedback is reduced. Also, when managers are not totally comfortable with a particular medium, they may ignore potential feedback cues. Consider a conference call involving five people at five locations. Such a call requires a different set of skills than a normal conversation, and the manager may not be totally comfortable with the situation. Not only are different skills required to monitor feedback, but the manager's anxiety may also reduce attention to feedback.

Time is related to feedback. The feedback cycle can be dramatically shortened with technology. For example, an Arco purchasing manager sent a rather long contract via fax to a vendor. The manager used fax because the contract was long and complex—too long to send via e-mail. Immediately after sending the contract, the sender went to another person's office for a meeting. On returning, the manager checked the voicemail system and found that the receiver of the contract called to indicate it had arrived and was being reviewed. About two hours later, the purchasing manager received an e-mail indicating how the vendor wanted the second paragraph changed. This was all done in a matter of a few hours even though the transaction occurred in two cities a thousand miles apart. Also, no busy telephone lines interrupted the process and no administrative assistants were required to draft letters.

Videoconferencing affects feedback in several ways. First, although visual feedback is present, it is reduced. Also, it is not possible to make eye-to-eye contact. However, the time required to arrange for the communication is greatly diminished. The major advantage, and the ultimate reason that many companies use videoconferencing, is that travel time for meetings is reduced.[15] A meeting with participants miles apart can be arranged without accounting for travel time, an important consideration for geographically dispersed members of an organization.

At the same time, the reduced time for feedback can cause problems. Although, according to information theory discussed earlier, we have limited capabilities to process information, managers may be pressured to decipher information and respond quickly just because the technology allows it. Imagine a manager who receives about two hundred e-mails and text messages daily. These media represent speed and responsiveness. But constant interruptions such as e-mail alerts may result in stress and overload. Recent research examining the effects of interruption overload and continuous partial attention is alarming. Higher cognitive functions, starting with decision making, can be impaired. Fragmentation of attention also appears to impede creativity.[16] Multitasking, rather than a step toward efficiency, apparently prevents us from focusing on anything in a significant way.[17] Managers need to be aware that continuous availability for feedback may have damaging consequences on their thought processes.

The impression that a manager must respond quickly brings us to our discussion of the fourth concept that helps us understand technologically mediated communication, *symbolic interactionism*.

A Symbolic Interactionist Perspective

Symbolic interactionism is a concept that can be used to explain sociological and psychological phenomena. In the imagery of symbolic interactionism, we view society as a dynamic web of communication. Thus, society and every organization in which managers function is an interaction. An interaction is symbolic because, through their interactions, people assign meaning to things and events. Over time, many symbols evolve within the organization and take on an agreed-upon meaning.[18]

<table>
<tr><td>

STOP AND THINK

1. Pretend that a close coworker has just suffered the loss of a family member. You wish to express your condolences. Which channel will you use: a paper sympathy card sent by snail mail, an e-mail, a phone call, or a post on the coworker's Facebook page? Why?

2. Which channel do you think the coworker will appreciate the most? Why?

3. What is the symbolic value of each channel?

</td><td>

The media that managers choose to use for communication may be based partially on symbolic reasons. Some argue that managerial communication behavior represents ritualistic responses to the need to appear competent, intelligent, legitimate, and rational.[19] For example, a face-to-face medium may symbolize concern or caring. Conversely, the manager who congratulates a subordinate on twenty-five years of service with an e-mail message may unintentionally communicate a lack of personal concern. A handwritten note or a special card would symbolize more personal warmth to some people.

</td></tr>
</table>

A comprehensive study of managers and their communication media indicates that channel choice was highly symbolic.[20] Managers interviewed in this study said they choose the face-to-face channel to signal a desire for teamwork, to build trust or goodwill, or to convey informality. Both face-to-face and telephone communication symbolized urgency, showed personal concern, and signaled deference to the receiver who preferred that medium. By contrast, written media were thought to show authority, make a strong impression, and be legitimate and official. Written media were also used to get attention and to comply with protocol.

The results of this study indicate that managers should not simply rely on the channel they feel most comfortable with when communicating; they should consider its symbolism.

Here is a true story that demonstrates this principle. There once was an accounting department manager who relied solely on sticky notes for communicating within his department, to the extent that he would silently tack the note onto a subordinate's computer monitor, even while the subordinate was sitting right in front of it. How do you think the employee felt about the manager and his message?

In summary, managers should consider four factors when deciding on the most effective and efficient use of mediated communication: bandwidth, perceived closeness, feedback, and symbolism. The choice of technology has become rather complicated, and it is difficult to generalize from one situation to another. But certain general conclusions can be stated.

MATCHING TECHNOLOGY AND THE MESSAGE

The discussion so far has emphasized how the channel may vary when communication is mediated by technology. Now consider matching the message and the technology. Not all technology is appropriate for all types of messages. To facilitate this discussion, messages are categorized along these continuums: sensitivity, negativity, complexity, and persuasiveness (as illustrated in Figure 3–2).[21] The challenge is to consider the message and how it fits into the various categories; then, match it with the appropriate technology.

Figure 3–2   Message Types

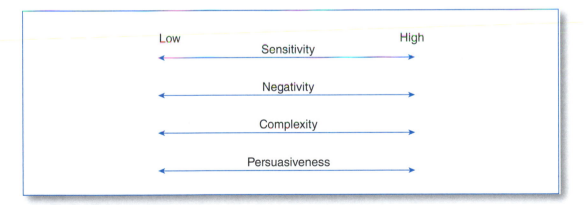

Message Sensitivity

When considering technology, managers must determine the extent to which the message is sensitive. A sensitive message is one that evokes an emotional reaction from the receiver. Neutral messages convey information that readers process and respond to intellectually but not emotionally. Receivers will not become upset with neutral messages, but neither will they become ecstatic or pleased.

Sensitive messages should usually be communicated in face-to-face settings to increase the personal element. An extreme example is when a US soldier is killed in battle. A military representative first informs relatives in a personal meeting. Telephone calls are not considered an option. An example at the other end of the sensitivity continuum is that a regular meeting's agenda could be circulated by e-mail, and a meeting reminder could be posted on employees' calendars using Microsoft Outlook. Face-to-face interaction would be an inefficient channel for this routine purpose.

What if it is not possible to communicate a sensitive message face-to-face? Here, the technology with the widest bandwidth should be used. Also, an interactive system with an opportunity for feedback should be supplementally used if possible. Symbolically, this may indicate a high level of concern. For instance, a company with offices in several states was forced to restructure. The grapevine was rampant with concerns about layoffs, loss of benefits, and forced relocations. It was not possible for the CEO to visit all the locations in a timely manner, so she chose to announce the general plan for the restructuring via an interactive video teleconference. All the employees met in various conference rooms and lunchrooms throughout the company. After the CEO announced the restructuring, the telephone lines were opened for questions.

This technology had one distinct advantage even though it may not have been as personal. It allowed the message to be sent throughout the company concurrently so all the employees received the same message at the same time, thus controlling rumors and minimizing anxiety. This is an advantage that would not have been possible without the technology.

Message Negativity

Messages extend along a continuum from positive to negative. When sending a negative message, managers should generally think about the receiver's reaction. Consequently, the extent to which a message is negative and the extent to which it is sensitive are highly related. Some of the same generalities exist for the other categories.

Another important consideration exists when communicating negative messages via technology, however. A person receiving bad news via a technological channel may believe the manager was hiding behind the technology rather than facing the receiver directly. Or it may appear that the manager did not want to be responsible for the message.

Almost everyone has complained to a company about poor service or an incorrect billing. Frequently, the response to the complaint is an impersonal form letter. The reaction was probably increased frustration and even hostility. In short, technology often depersonalizes. Contemporary organizations are making efforts to balance high tech with "high touch." Addressing customers by name in mass mailings (a process made possible by technology)

STOP AND THINK

Consider a time when you complained to a company about their service or product.

1. How personalized was the company's reply message?

2. If the response was negative and you did not get what you asked for in your complaint, how did it make you feel? Are you a repeat customer? Why or why not?

is one example. Other strategies for softening the blow when sending negative messages are presented in Chapter 7. Managers can successfully influence receivers' reactions to bad news.

Message Complexity

Guidelines for using technology are somewhat clearer when considering message complexity. As the complexity of the message increases, managers should attempt to use (1) wider bandwidth, (2) the medium that will add to psychological closeness, (3) the technology that provides for the greatest amount of feedback, and (4) symbolism consistent with the complexity.

Discussion of a complex team-project schedule involving a series of dates and figures provides an example. Assume seven managers at four locations are a "virtual team." A number of viable solutions exist for communicating complex messages, without getting everyone together face-to-face. Fax, e-mail attachments, shared databases, and conference software that allow file sharing are common technologies for team communication. A relatively wide bandwidth is used; feedback is provided, and the sophisticated technology symbolizes the seriousness of the task.

Research shows the communication of complex, detailed information is not necessarily improved by face-to-face interaction.[22] An explanation of a complex engineering formula, for instance, can be just as effective with audio and graphic communication as when the person doing the explanation is physically present. Interactive computer conferencing via local area networks (LANs) can facilitate the communication of complex messages because it may stimulate better concentration from the receiver.

Message Persuasiveness

Persuasive messages involve an effort to induce a receiver to take a particular action. Persuasion is not an effort to coerce, fool, seduce, or manipulate the receiver. Rather, it is an attempt to get employees to comply with behaviors that will meet the goals of the organization. When thinking of persuasion, salespeople probably come to mind; however, managers frequently use persuasion, influence tactics, or compliance-gaining strategies to affect employees' performance. Efforts to introduce new work procedures, increase teamwork, or change corporate culture require persuasive communication. Suggestions for delivering persuasive business presentations are found in Chapter 5.

The topic of persuasion has been of interest since Aristotle's time. But a leading researcher more recently wrote: "Despite the vast number of pages written and the countless studies undertaken about persuasion, it is difficult to shake the uneasy feeling that we have precious little reliable, socially relevant knowledge about it."[23] Our understanding of persuasion is further complicated when considering technologically mediated communication. Little research has been conducted in this area; consequently, it is necessary to generalize about what we know from nonmediated communication.

A popular book, *Influence: The New Psychology of Modern Persuasion,* presents three conclusions about persuasion that are particularly pertinent to our discussion.[24] First, managers can more easily persuade those who like them. Second, people are more easily

STOP AND THINK

Consider a project team you participated in, either at school or at work.

1. Did your team meet in person or virtually?

2. To what extent did you develop positive feelings about the other team members?

3. If you have worked in teams both virtually and face-to-face, compare the intensity of the team spirit you developed in each environment. Which was stronger? Why?

persuaded when they perceive the persuader as an authority. Third, it is easier for managers to persuade others as they get psychologically and physically closer to them.

Persuaded by the One You Like

Few would be surprised to learn that we most prefer to say yes to the requests of someone we know and like. In addition, we like people with whom we spend more time, even if we are forced to spend this time together.

This research finding is important to our discussion because the quality of the time we spend with people via technology is generally not the same as if the person were physically present. In other words, no matter how much time we spend with people in teleconferences, it cannot substitute for personal presence.

Persuaded by the One You Believe

The second principle is not overly surprising either. We listen and are persuaded by those who appear to be authorities on the topic. This point is important among television news executives, because newsreaders and reporters must be believable if they are going to be watched. According to a recent *Reader's Digest* poll, the most trusted American journalists are ABC's Robin Roberts and Diane Sawyer, followed by NBC's Brian Williams, and CNN's Anderson Cooper[25]; they succeed partly because they look and sound like authorities.

But what about average managers who must use video or telephonic technology in an attempt to persuade? It would seem they are at a disadvantage. Again, these technologies should be used for persuasion only when necessary due to time or cost restrictions.

Another point adds to this caveat: It is more difficult to say no when looking a person directly in the eye. Even when we like a person or believe she is an authority, it is easier to say no from a distance. Technology seems to buffer the importance of trust that has been built into the communicators' relationship, diminishing its prominence as an element of the environment.

Persuaded by the One Who Is Close

Much sophisticated work has gone into preparing persuasive audiovisual presentations. But these presentations are not as effective as personal exposure of the one attempting the persuasion. If possible, it is best to have the person physically present. When physical presence of an authority is not possible, a well-organized presentation by a somewhat less credible source may be a good substitute. Often, the PowerPoint slide show is circulated electronically to audience members. What is the balance between physical presence and credibility? These questions must be addressed. When considering persuasive managerial communication, however, one principle must always be considered. A person physically present is more persuasive than one who is present only via technologically mediated communication. That is why, despite the recent dramatic increase in online automobile sales, dealers continue to make an effort to lure online shoppers into their showrooms. And a test drive remains the best way to close a sale.

A LOOK TO THE FUTURE

E-mail, online dashboards, conferencing software, intranets, smartphones—all of these systems are with us today and are being used more and more frequently in the workplace. If one were to speculate about what developments would affect managerial communication in the future, any number of possibilities would exist. However, several safe projections can be made (Table 3–1). The first is that technology will simply be used more. Second, technology use will be monitored and regulated. Third, decision making will be affected. Fourth, job and organizational design will be altered. Fifth, mediated collaborative writing will be common. These trends are discussed next.

Table 3–1   Predictions for Technological Communication
Technology use in business environments will continue to increase.
Monitoring of employee technology use will become more extensive.
Technology will affect decision-making processes.
Technology will alter job and organizational design.
Mediated collaborative writing will be common.

Technology Proliferation

So far, this chapter has described the advantages and disadvantages of technology for communication in organizations. Problems with technology include the danger of sensory overload with useless cues (jamming), narrow bandwidth, diminished feelings of personal closeness, and reduced opportunities for feedback. Despite these disadvantages, however, networked organizations are the norm, mostly because they increase productivity. The strategic decision for managers, therefore, is not *whether* to use technological channels but *which* digital channel will best suit the situation and *how* to maximize its capabilities. In the following paragraphs, we will examine the strengths and weaknesses of four communication technologies commonly used in today's workplace—e-mail, instant messaging, texting, and blogging—and offer guidelines for best practice.

E-mail

An estimated 247 billion e-mails are sent each day worldwide, with the number expected to increase to 294 billion by 2010.[26] According to a recent White Collar Productivity Index survey of time spent in the workplace, the average US executive receives two hundred e-mails per day after spam is extracted. Administrative and newer staff receive an average of fifty e-mails per day.[27] Nearly one in ten workers say they would need two or more days to catch up on e-mail if they went on a two-week vacation.[28] E-mail's influence has likewise grown. Fifty-six percent of workers surveyed by *USA Today* believe that e-mail increases their productivity. And one-third of chief information officers say losing an e-mail system for a week would be more traumatic than getting divorced, according to a survey by computer storage company Veritas.[29]

The risk of sensory overload, rather than motivating managers to ignore technological media, has stimulated managers to develop a variety of coping skills. They may use an assistant to sort and redirect the crush of messages. Features in most e-mail programs also are useful for coding and filtering messages according to sender or topic. Some companies try to help their managers cope with e-mail overload by enforcing "e-mail-free Fridays" or at least banning the use of the Reply All feature. The French have taken it a step further—labor unions and corporate representatives have agreed on "an obligation to disconnect from remote communication tools" that would apply to 250,000 employees. The accord proposed to the French Labor Ministry would require employers to verify that all workers receive eleven uninterrupted hours of daily "rest" time away from e-mail.[30] But managers most often are turning to IM and text messaging to avoid the crush of e-mail. That strategy, described earlier in this chapter, cuts e-mail traffic but does not diminish the amount of time spent interacting with technology or the level of resultant anxiety.

There are exceptions to today's technology-oriented executives. John Scully, the former CEO of Apple Computer, was infamous for not allowing employees to send him e-mail messages. Colleen Barrett, president emeritus of Southwest Airlines, is proud that throughout her presidency, until 2008, she did not have an e-mail address, did not use a PDA or surf the web, and only recently acquired a smartphone. She thinks e-mail is "very impersonal . . . a horrible way to communicate."[31] These examples of managerial nonuse of technology are the obverse of executives and employees in a company such as Colruyt, the Belgian discount food chain. Colruyt uses technology to maximize both vertical and horizontal information sharing. Secrecy is minimized, empowerment for decision making is maximized, and power no longer equates with access to information in such postmodern organizations.[32]

In response to the problems caused by overreliance on e-mail, best practices have emerged. Here are a few guidelines (see Table 3–2):

- Keep e-mails short so readers see the entire message on one screen and do not need to scroll. Recipients will not read long e-mails.[33]

- Do not use e-mail for urgent messages that call for immediate response. Many business professionals check their e-mail only once or twice per day.

- Do not use e-mail for dialogues. Discussions will be slow and inefficient.[34] Use the Reply All function sparingly.

- Push company-wide announcements to the intranet and simply e-mail the link to everyone. Focusing on the company's intranet as a source of routine information will relieve e-mail overload.[35]

- Create a code of conduct, train all employees about it, and periodically remind employees to follow it. The policy should address issues such as spam, message retention, records management, privacy, and non-work-related use.

Table 3–2 Best Practices for E-mail

Keep the message short.
Do not use e-mail for urgent messages that call for immediate response.
Do not use e-mail for dialogues.
Push company-wide announcements to the intranet.
When deciding what to include in your message, think of e-mail as a public forum.

Instant Messaging

Instant messaging is the informal name for service systems released by software developers in the 1990s. This communication method allowed users to communicate immediately through a common messaging program. America Online was the first company to successfully attract a strong instant messaging customer base. The majority of AOL's customers were young and technologically savvy. These young consumers quickly made AOL IM a success.[36]

The first generation of IM consumers who flocked to these early IM programs has since entered the workforce. They brought with them a level of technological comfort that has changed the face of modern business communication. Instant messaging has several unique advantages over other communication methods. International communication, message archiving, improved communication efficiency, and ease of implementation are the primary advantages of instant messaging.

Communication can be very expensive for multinational corporations. International phone calls are expensive, as is video conferencing hardware; in addition, videoconferencing requires a fixed location. Most free instant messaging programs have conferencing features that allow team members around the world to collaborate instantly using smartphones and tablets. They can also access these chat functions from any Internet connection in the world without IT support. Thus, IM improves international collaboration without increasing expenses.

Maintaining accurate records of communication improves employee efficiency and is beneficial during legal proceedings. Referring to transcripts of a conversation allows employees to retain and understand the intent of the conversation. During legal discovery, these archives may protect an organization from false accusations. Most free instant messaging programs have message archiving options. These archives are easy to set up and require significantly less server space than e-mail archives.[37] Instant messaging archives provide the same level of legal documentation as e-mail archives, but at a lower cost.

Instant messaging greatly improves communication efficiency compared to traditional electronic communication. Instant messaging programs allow users to immediately ask clarifying questions, converse at a comfortable pace, and also have a transcript of the conversation for review. Finally, instant messaging programs are very easy to implement because many employees already use them.

There are several disadvantages to instant messaging that must be identified in order to minimize their impact. Effectively managing these disadvantages will protect your organization. Instant messaging can establish legally binding contracts, distract workers, and expose companies to legal jurisdiction in other states.

The legal elements of a contractual agreement are offer, consideration, and acceptance. E-mail or instant messenger conversations that include these elements can be legally binding even if the specific details of the deal need further negotiation. The following IM exchange could be considered a legal contract:[38]

Buyer:	How's it going? Hope to see you and the family on the lake Friday.
Supplier:	We should be there.
Buyer:	Could you get me six of those new widgets by the end of the month? Got a project coming up, the boss is pushing hard.
Supplier:	Those systems are pricey.
Buyer:	They would make the job go a lot easier.
Supplier:	No problem. We've got plenty in stock, so I'll deliver them on the 20th.
Buyer:	Great and see you Friday.[39]

Any specific details that are not included would be negotiable, but the supplier could be forced to deliver six widgets to the buyer on the 20th. Breaching a contract can expose a company to legal liability and hurt its reputation. Employees must be educated on safe use of electronic communication, whether e-mail or instant messaging, to protect the organization.

Instant messaging can also disrupt workplace productivity. Instant messaging as well as e-mail are often used for personal communication, thereby reducing time on task. Instant messages can easily be archived and reviewed if managers believe this is a problem in their organization. Company policies for e-mail should be adapted to manage instant messaging. Ignoring this easily corrected disadvantage to instant messaging can reduce company productivity.

Another disadvantage of IM is that it can expose companies to legal jurisdiction liability in other states. In 2006, the New York Court of Appeals ruled that a Montana business could be sued in a New York court. The Montana business entered into and later breached a contract using instant messages. Conducting business over instant messenger was sufficient contact for New York courts to have jurisdiction over the Montana business. Employees using instant messaging to conduct business with outside parties must understand the legal implications.[40]

Clearly there is great potential for growth in instant messaging by businesses. Many companies are already utilizing instant messaging in their daily operations. Managers cannot ignore the growth of instant messaging communication. Table 3–3 lists some best practices for instant messaging communication.

A recent study by research company Radicati Group indicated that IM accounts are expected to grow to over 4.4 billion worldwide by 2017. With this increased personal and professional use of instant messaging, companies are responding by providing workers with enterprise-grade IM accounts, which have functionality and security that cannot be attained with public IM accounts, thereby overcoming concerns, especially when they are communicating with customers or business partners.[41]

Billions of dollars in commodities, stocks, bonds, and commercial goods are traded every day using instant messaging technology. The strong international communication, easy message archiving, high level of efficiency, and easy implementation will lead more organizations to use instant messaging. The contract formation issues, employee distraction, and legal jurisdiction concerns associated with instant messaging can be easily managed. The productivity and cost reduction benefits of instant messaging far outweigh the potential negatives to businesses.

Table 3–3	Best Practices for Instant Messaging Communication
Archive all incoming and outgoing messages.	
Develop an instant messaging policy and circulate it among employees.	
Do not use instant messaging for highly sensitive communication.	
Educate employees about the potential legal liability they expose the company to through instant messaging.	
Do not ban instant messaging, but provide guidance on how to use it.	

Text Messaging

Text messaging, also known as Short Message Service (SMS), quickly became the new way for business people to communicate in the 21st century. It permits the sending of short messages between mobile phones, other handheld devices, and even landline telephones.[42] Young people in the United States seem to have adopted texting as their primary means of communicating with each other. Their typical attitude is that e-mail is old-school technology, useful only for exchanging messages with parents, grandparents, and professors. On the other hand, contemporary business professionals are being encouraged to use this channel together with e-mail. Although two-thirds of business professionals are using text messaging for business-related communications,[43] it does not appear that e-mail will be replaced anytime soon in business and industry.

Text messaging has many advantages. The most commonly identified benefits of text messaging are its speed, access, and discretion. Texting is fast because the message you send travels instantaneously, like a live conversation in person or by telephone. By contrast, e-mail is asynchronous and interaction is not expected to be real time. There is a lag, especially when servers accumulate e-mails before delivering them to members of the network.

Accessibility is another advantage of text messaging. An SMS can be sent to anyone, anytime, anywhere. For this reason, many companies are using it to communicate with employees as they travel or to send important announcements to everyone in the company. Text messages, unlike e-mail, can be delivered directly to someone's desktop so that it can receive immediate attention.[44]

Finally, sending an SMS is a discreet way to get in touch with someone. Most text messaging devices have a setting that will permit the device to vibrate when a new message hits, preventing disruptions and intrusions. One handy application is when an employee urgently needs to communicate with the boss while she or he is in a meeting. Because it is less disruptive than a phone call while remaining more "personal" than e-mail, texting is handy for dual communications.

The most commonly listed disadvantages to text messaging are its lack of security, structure, and formality. Security is a major issue because texting is instantaneous, and it does not allow enough time for virus scanners to check completely for viruses, thus leaving computers unprotected. No matter how fast virus scanners become, they will always be able to protect against e-mails better than SMSes.[45]

Lack of structure is another disadvantage of instant messaging. Unlike e-mails, which are set up in memo format, text messages do not have a set form. Most are sent as very short messages by using a shorthand code that users must learn to decipher.

For example, a synopsis of the classic novel, *Pride and Prejudice*, sent as a text message, might look like the following:

5SistrsWntngHsbnds.NwMenInTwn-Bingly&Darcy Fit&Loadd

This mysterious string of letters and symbols translates to this:

Five sisters are wanting husbands. They have their sights set on two new men in town—Bingley and Darcy. They are handsome and wealthy.[46]

This type of message can be difficult for new users to understand. Perhaps more importantly in business settings, a cryptic text message may lead to serious misunderstandings and costly errors. It may encourage employees to take more care when crafting text messages if you remind them that texts can be archived and are discoverable in a court of law.

Finally, managers may be reluctant to allow texting technology because they fear that employees will abuse it. Texting was designed for recreational "chatting," and it is easy to get involved in personal exchanges that take up valuable work time. Additionally, from a distance, an employee who is typing messages may appear to be on task. A flood of nonurgent or personal text messages can be distracting to busy workers as well.

After reviewing the advantages and disadvantages, a business can decide whether using SMS technology will be beneficial to them. Many companies that have already adopted this technology have been increasing their usage of this communication channel, but they are not abandoning e-mail. Instead, they are using texting in tandem with e-mail to send reminders or announcements that need to be communicated immediately.[47] For example, an employee might send an important e-mail to his boss and then send a reminder SMS, letting her know that the e-mail was sent.

Best practices for text messaging in business are still evolving. At the current time, the principles for effective use of instant messaging are considered applicable to text messaging use and are summarized in Table 3–4.

Overall, it appears that business professionals will continue to increase their use of text messaging. With its many advantages, including mobility, convenience, and immediacy, more companies will use it to stay in touch with employees and bosses as they travel or when a message needs to be received quickly. Beyond convenience, this technology offers business people the competitive advantages of increased productivity and efficiency. However, with the security problems and other disadvantages it is unlikely that SMS will replace e-mail anytime soon, at least for business purposes.

Table 3–4   Best Practices for Text Messaging Communication

Remember that texts are generally not secure, so limit proprietary information.
Be concise, but be sure your shortcuts (acronyms, abbreviations, jargon) are familiar to all.
Use punctuation for clarity and accuracy.
Avoid emoticons and formatting for emphasis (all caps, multiple exclamation points).
Develop a text messaging policy and circulate it among employees.

Blogging

The use of blogs (short for web logs) as a technological communication tool is a growing trend among Internet users today. The very first blogs were online "diaries."[48] Blogs can be updated at any time from any place. Unlike most Internet pages, blogs are dynamic. An individual can easily update the information in her blog, add more information, or start a completely different train of thought.[49] Blog composition requires no knowledge of web-programming languages, such as HTML.[50] Blogs are made available via Really Simple Syndication (RSS), the technology that allows blogs to reach audiences worldwide.[51]

Blogs are proliferating in the business environment because they open up new internal and external channels.[52] Although the technology is the same, the ways that blogs are used internally and externally differ.

The most common use for blogs within businesses today is as a project coordination tool. A team working on a project can use a blog to share information or provide progress updates. This information can be seen by the team members, managers that wish to "check in," or any other individuals within the company that are allowed access. Instead of spending the time to have a meeting with the team to discuss the team's progress on a project, the manager can simply take a look at the group's project blog. The benefit of blogs as a project coordination tool is amplified for teams that include members located in different geographic locations.

Blogs can also be used internally as a means of sharing information and collecting feedback from stakeholders.[53] If a company is looking for feedback from employees about a new policy, for example, they could start an internal blog about the issue. Previously, a series of meetings, reports, letters, memos, or "town-hall" gatherings may have been necessary. Blogs allow everyone to participate in the discussion at their convenience and keep a permanent record of all the thoughts, comments, and input that can be reviewed and considered at the convenience of the decision maker.

Blogs can be used externally to accomplish a variety of tasks. Companies can begin blogs to communicate with customers, potential customers, or even external vendors and supply chain members.[54] Communication using blogs or similar technology is viewed as more genuine, credible, and "real" compared to the rote and often boring language of mission statements and press releases. Blogs are written in a conversational tone, which external stakeholders view more favorably.[55] Companies can use external blogs to obtain feedback from their customers about current or future products. Companies can use blogs to respond to criticism or crisis in the market. Companies can use blogs to gather new ideas about changes or new products that they should consider offering.[56] The sum of a customer-focused blog is that it allows companies to build and maintain relationships with their public, strengthening their brand and positioning in the marketplace.[57]

Another external use for blogs is to advertise. Many companies operate in niche markets and are constantly looking for new ways to reach their target market.[58] With over 112 million blogs online to choose from, chances are good that a blog focused on any given industry exists. Companies can capitalize on this opportunity by running banner ads on these blog sites, virtually guaranteeing that the people that come to read the blog are in their target market.

Blogs offer companies a chance to learn of criticisms, crises, or information much more quickly. In return, blogs also offer an avenue to respond to such criticisms, crises, or information quickly.[59] Previously, corporations relied on press releases, industry trade publications, or time-intensive website upgrades to announce new products or services. Blogs provide a means for corporations to communicate with consumers before, during, and after new products are brought to market.

Blogs also offer some challenges in managing external relations. Corporate blogs, although maintained by individual employees, do represent the "voice of the corporation." Without proper monitoring, it is possible that the company could get a bad reputation.[60] Companies must also remember that most blog posts are permanent. There is

Table 3–5   Best Practices for Blog Communication

Internal Blogs	External Blogs
Use instead of meetings for simple and quick progress updates, information sharing, and gathering of feedback.	Use for quick release of information during crises.
To encourage honesty, do not censor bloggers.	Be sure that company-sponsored postings are consistent with the company's brand, mission, and image.
Write in a conversational tone.	Monitor blogs daily to keep abreast of public sentiment.
Maintain a professional writing style, remembering that posts are permanent records.	Respond quickly to publicly posted blog comments, whether positive or critical.

little companies can do after the fact to remedy situations such as releasing information in a blog that was not meant to reach the general public and/or competition.

Since blogs are seen as another "voice" of a company, it is important to ensure that the voice speaking in external blogs agrees with the voice speaking in mission statements, press releases, advertisements, websites, and other forms of external communication. One way to ensure this continuity of voice is to create guidelines that employees must follow when writing blogs for external audiences. Guidelines may also help avoid legal troubles that could result from improper blog usage. Table 3–5 offers a summary of best practices for corporate blogs.

In summary, e-mail, IM, text messages, and blogs are contemporary communication technologies that are integral to networked organizations, and with their use, the hierarchical culture is dissolved. Rank does not matter as much to workers who are on the network and who know what everyone is doing. Today's managers no longer manage information; they manage networks of people. Teams use technology to collaborate, overcoming geographic barriers among team members. In addition to increasing efficiency, technology reduces groupthink, defuses emotional issues, and enhances the creativity of decisions. Clearly, these advantages outweigh the risks and costs of using technology for workplace communication.

Monitoring Technology Use

A second prediction about technologically mediated communication in business is that monitoring mechanisms will become increasingly sophisticated. Surveillance methods are developing hand in hand with innovations in communication technology. These efforts are exemplified by federal law enforcement and national security officials' sweeping regulations that allow surveillance of Internet communications, including encrypted e-mails, social networking websites, and peer-to-peer software, such as Skype. In the United States, phone and broadband networks are already required to have interception capabilities, under a 1994 law called the Communications Assistance to Law Enforcement Act. These capabilities apply to companies that operate from servers abroad and that conduct international business.

The business sector is following the example of governmental surveillance policies by developing technologies that allow eavesdropping on employees. Electronic monitoring systems allow employers to gather very detailed information about how their employees spend their time at work.[61]

Companies monitor employees for many reasons. These include the following:

- Mitigating legal liability
- Reducing the misuse of company resources
- Protecting intellectual property[62]

First, companies monitor in order to prevent lawsuits. Companies can be held liable for any and all communication that uses their computer systems.[63] In fact, a sexual harassment suit was brought against Chevron when an employee sent an offensive e-mail over the company system. This seemingly incidental e-mail ended up costing the company $2.2 million.[64]

Second, companies monitor to catch employees who are misusing the company's resources. For example, employers want to know if an employee is spending valuable work time surfing the Internet, playing computer games, or planning a vacation online.

Third, many companies have intellectual property and trade secrets that they need to protect. Monitoring employees is one way to keep tabs on their property and make sure it is not leaked out to a competitor. All an employee would have to do is accidentally or even purposefully send an e-mail to the wrong person, and it could end up out of the company's control.

Companies now have various ways to monitor employees in the workplace. They range from programs that block access to certain Internet sites to ones that record every key stroke ever typed on the worker's computer (even ones that have been deleted).

Secret monitoring by employers is widespread and supported by the courts.[65] Some employers automatically send copies of every e-mail to the sender's supervisor.[66] They can also use global positioning systems on employees' badges to allow them to record workers' movements.[67] In addition, 32 percent of employers use video surveillance to watch employees, and of these organizations, 20 percent do not inform workers that they are being taped.[68]

The monitoring of individuals has enabled employers to prevent problems and to reprimand workers who have disobeyed corporate policies. *The New York Times*, Xerox Corp., and First Union Bank have apparently terminated employees after discovering improper use of company-provided Internet.[69] A *CIO Magazine* survey stated that 90 percent of chief information officers reported they would fire an employee if the individual used the company e-mail to sexually harass someone else.[70] Eighty-four percent stated they would

STOP AND THINK

1. How do you feel about the courts' decisions to support secret monitoring of employees' technology use?

2. How can these limitations on employees' constitutional rights to privacy and freedom of expression be justified?

fire someone for sending pornography to coworkers, and 80 percent would fire an employee for compromising trade secrets.[71]

Employees should realize that any time spent using technology at work should be limited to work-related activities. Further, any communications being sent or received to a work e-mail address, pager, smartphone, or tablet should be considered appropriate for anyone to read. In 2010, in its first ruling on the privacy rights of employees who send messages on the job, the Supreme Court unanimously agreed that supervisors may read through subordinates' text messages if they suspect that work rules are being violated. Since employers are not required to let employees know when they are monitoring, it is up to the employees to be on their best behavior and to think twice before doing something even slightly inappropriate while on the job.

Decision Making

A third major prediction about the future of communication technology in business is that it will significantly affect business decisions. Managerial decision making may be defined as the process of identifying and solving problems. Decision making requires that managers scan for pertinent information. Most discussions on this topic generally contain two major stages. One is the problem identification stage. Information about relevant conditions is monitored both to determine whether performance is meeting expectations and to diagnose the cause of any shortcomings. The other stage involves solution identification. Alternative actions are considered, and one alternative is selected and implemented. A more thorough explanation of the rational problem-solving process is presented in Chapters 4 and 12. In both stages of the process, the more information available, the greater the probability that effective decisions will be made. And more and more information is available with increased technologies.

Burger King provides an example of the effect of communication technology on decision making. Each Burger King restaurant is networked via computer to a central office where each sale is transmitted and recorded. When one store is running low on a product, even without the store manager placing an order, the central facility is aware of the shortage and can send supplies. This is comparable to e-mail except the messages are automatically prepared and transmitted. Thus, stage one in the decision process, the problem identification stage, is more easily accomplished because of communication technology.

As organizations become larger and as more sophisticated information systems are designed, the probability becomes greater that technological communication systems will be used for decision making. For instance, Intel, the world's largest microchip maker, has several manufacturing and research facilities in Arizona and Northern California. Attempts to resolve complex technological problems frequently require input from various experts. Assume that highly technical information is needed to analyze a unique problem. This information may be available only in the Science Library at Arizona State University. An engineer in California can access the information through a special terminal in her office that is connected to the library in Tempe, Arizona. A copy of the document can be available to the engineer within seconds.

This quick access to information has three apparent implications. First, anyone who wants to remain competitive must know where and how to access the information. Information sharing is a key to good business decision making, and successful contemporary organizations strive for transparency.

Second, managers who are bombarded with masses of information find the odds of making an effective decision greatly diminished. If managers receive large quantities of both relevant and irrelevant information, the important facts and figures may be overlooked and can create problems, because the human mind can process only so many data. As noted earlier in Figure 3–1, a point develops at which the mind blocks out any additional, though valuable, information. As technology allows for rapid acquisition of greater amounts of information, poorer rather than better decisions may result.

Third, communication technology allows managers to quickly change their decisions. Say a manager writes an analytical report comparing the acquisitions of two pieces of property for a retail outlet. The report's recommendation is finalized and ready for submission to an executive committee. At the last minute, new information is made available through a database to which the company subscribes. This allows the manager to alter the report's recommendation at the last minute. As presented in Chapter 2, the manager's challenge is to know where to get information, when and how to present it to others, and how and when to use it. In some ways, information technology makes the decision-making process easier, but in other ways, it becomes more complex.

Job and Organizational Design

A fourth trend in business communication technology is that it will allow managers to monitor more closely the standards expected from a job performance. Take a simple example of a sales representative responsible for calling on furniture stores. The objective is to obtain cooperation in setting up a special display within the stores. The standard of performance is to make two calls per day and obtain three displays per ten calls. The formal agreement is to report the day's activities to the central office at the end of each day. This is done via smartphone, tablet, or laptop. E-mail and text messages are exchanged continuously.

In this example, even more emerging technologies could be used, such as photo messaging. Snapchat, Instagram, Kik, Wickr, and other apps let users exchange images, either plain or with virtual scribbles, of people and projects. In fact, snapping photos has become the most widely used function of smartphones, and not just among teenagers. Snapchatters sent 350 million photos and videos each day in 2013, up 600 percent from the previous year.[72] It is logical to assume that many of these exchanges supported business functions.

Without sophisticated technology, such an intensive level of interaction among employees and their managers would not have been possible. It would have been necessary to mail reports to the central office, so feedback may not have been obtained for several days. Interaction via technologically mediated communication allows managers to maintain control over their direct reports and allows employees in the field to stay connected.

In addition to improved control of specific jobs, organizational relationships may change with mediated communication. We generally think of jobs being connected by means of either horizontal or vertical integration. Horizontal communication or integration occurs between people at the same hierarchical level. Managers may meet horizontally to coordinate activities, solve problems, resolve conflicts, or just share information. Regardless of the purpose, more horizontal communication can occur as a result of technology.

Consider this example. The board of directors of a hospital system with eight locations directed the human resources managers to implement a safety training program in each hospital. The managers want to share ideas with each other on the most efficient way to implement the program. Technology makes travel for a meeting unnecessary—a videoconference, satellite downlink, or teleconference would meet the purpose. In this case, technology allows for greater integration at lower expense.

Vertical integration is the coordination among higher and lower levels within the hierarchy. Unfortunately, it often seems that different levels of the organization typically do not communicate well with each other.[73] But as noted when discussing formalization, mediated communication should assist this process. Managers and subordinates are more accessible with technology. Distance and time are less troublesome.

This improved vertical and horizontal integration is resulting in dramatically different job and organizational structures. Recent research indicates that, in an effort to create competitive advantage, managers' jobs have become more information oriented, while the number of layers of managers has decreased.[74] And technology facilitates this trend toward networked information exchange.

Collaboration

The fifth prediction about the future of business technology is that it will play a major role in work collaboration. Picture five managers, each sitting at a computer in five different locations around the country. Special software allows the managers to edit the same document simultaneously. Any changes made to the document are visible to all members as changes occur. Furthermore, protocols built into the software allow group members to alter or even delete each other's work.

Most business documents require more than one person to be involved in the writing process. Examples include proposals, reports to regulatory agencies, annual reports to shareholders, policy manuals, operating procedures, newsletters, directives, user manuals, training materials, mission/vision and strategic goal statements, progress reports, and personnel reports. Technology allows collaborative writing of such documents to be performed concurrently, not just sequentially. Unfortunately, collaborative writing too often means one person writes part of the report and then sends it to another person for revision. This person then passes it on to another and so forth. This is extremely time consuming, and coordination is difficult.

STOP AND THINK

Recall a team project you participated in, either at work or at school.

1. What communication tools did you use to expedite team collaboration?

2. How well did they work?

3. What could the team have done better to ensure that everyone's input on the deliverable was maximized?

Today's technology allows managers to do more than relay documents; it allows managers to develop synergy that accompanies true collaboration. Groupware is a family of software that supports group tasks in various levels of shared electronic environments. Groupware provides computer-mediated communication systems, allowing different viewpoints and ideas to be compared and discussed in real time. As versions of the text are compared, a better product results without bruising egos. Because collaborative writing is becoming so important, it is discussed more extensively in Chapter 6.

Group Decision Support Systems (GDSSs) are software and associated processes that have been designed to advance coordination of group projects. The fundamental goal of a GDSS is to support collaborative work activities, such as idea creation, message exchange, project planning, document creation, copyediting, and joint decision making.[75] A commonly used example is wikis. Group Decision Support Systems provide a platform for groups to collaborate when members are dispersed, working in their separate offices, homes, or client locations. Other systems support face-to-face meetings that occur in one physical setting, such as a conference or boardroom. With these, it is possible to instantaneously display ideas on large screens, vote on individual preferences, compile the anonymous input of ideas and preferences, and electronically exchange ideas between members. GDSS programs include various quantitative analysis techniques. The most sophisticated systems include expert advice in the selecting and arranging of rules to be applied during interpersonal communication.[76]

THE MANAGEMENT CHALLENGE

What does all this mean for managers? It means they must become sensitive to the correct type of communication channel to use in different situations. It means managers must learn to use these new technologies. It means another dimension has been added to managerial communication.

Let us expand on each of these points. Several studies have indicated a strong correlation exists between a manager's media sensitivity and managerial performance. When a task involved complex information or was highly emotional, for instance, effective managers were more inclined to use communication channels with a broad bandwidth than were ineffective managers.[77]

Innovations in communication technology have added a whole new dimension to the manager's job: understanding and selecting the correct communication channel. A corollary to this requirement is that managers must guide their subordinates in the proper, ethical use of the technology. For instance, instant messaging is an official corporate communication tool for approximately 26 percent of US companies. Employees use IM on their own in another 44 percent of companies, sometimes for personal as well as business-related use. Yet 35 percent of companies do not have an official IM policy, risking breaches of confidentiality, viruses, and copyright infringement.[78] New communication tools are constantly becoming available, requiring strategic decisions. It is clear that business is committed to investing in technology, and companies expect managers to make this investment pay off.

The technology payoff could be increased if managers had a guidebook summarizing when each technology is best used, but such a resource is not possible. Too many contingencies must be considered to say categorically which technology should be used when. This chapter, however, has attempted to raise some of the important questions managers should ask themselves as they choose a channel for their message. Figure 3–3 illustrates the question process that managers should follow when selecting a technology.

Figure 3–3   Technology Choice Contingencies

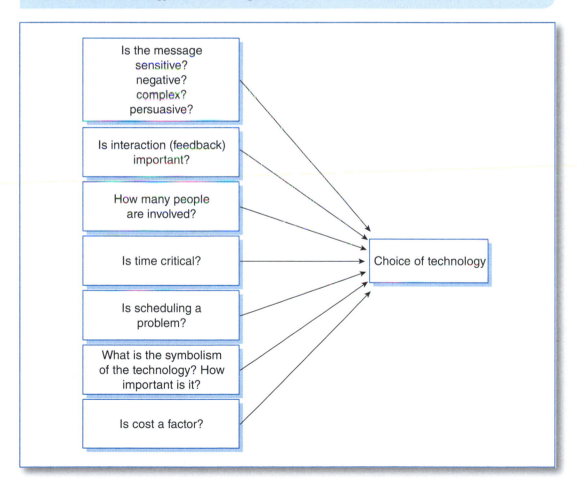

SUMMARY

To understand better how technology affects managerial communication, four concepts are discussed. First, bandwidth is affected because one channel is generally omitted when technologically mediated communication is used. Perceived closeness, or propinquity, is a consideration because electronic media affect the extent to which people feel close to each other. The feedback cycle is much shorter with technology, so this is also a consideration. Finally, the symbolic interactionist perspective is considered because the use of various communication channels has different symbolic values.

When matching technology to the message, four message factors are considered. First is message sensitivity. Greater bandwidth should generally be used with sensitive messages. The second category is message negativity. Managers must be careful not to hide behind technology when presenting negative messages. The third category is message complexity. Two ways to effectively transmit relatively complex messages are teleconferencing and computer conferencing. The fourth category is message persuasiveness. The extent to which the receiver likes the sender and the extent to which the sender is perceived as an authority must be considered. In general, persuasion is less effective when the communication is mediated by technology.

Going forward, technology will continue to proliferate, and so will surveillance mechanisms. Best practices are emerging for the most common technologies, including e-mail, texting, instant messaging, and blogging. Technology will continue to affect managerial communication in decision making, job and organizational design, and collaborative writing. All these technologies will challenge future managers as they make strategic decisions and as they monitor and guide their employees' technologically mediated communication.

Cases for Small-Group Discussion

CASE 3–1

Communicating with Technology on Friday Afternoon

Colleen cheered as she completed the last of her attachments for the report, which had been a last-minute request on a fair weather Friday. She was eager to begin the weekend, since she had made plans with her roommate to spend it at the seashore. She saved the interactive PDF file, which linked to eighteen ancillary files, and attached all nineteen files to her e-mail to her boss.

Colleen pressed Send and logged off. She rushed from her office to catch the 5:15 p.m. uptown bus. If she missed it, she would have to wait about a half hour for the next one. As she jumped on the bus before the doors closed and grabbed a seat in the back, she opened her purse. She quickly turned off her phone, which had only a small charge left, to preserve the battery. She brushed her hair and put on some lip gloss in preparation for dinner at a nice uptown bistro. Brian, her date, had made reservations for outdoor dining on the bistro's balcony overlooking the bustling street below.

At the same moment, Colleen's boss was opening Colleen's e-mail. As he downloaded the files, error messages began popping up. Six of the files had been corrupted in electronic transit. He called Colleen's extension; it went immediately to voicemail. He called her cell phone and heard a familiar message—the recipient was not receiving calls. He e-mailed her, hoping that she would somehow still be available, to no avail. Panic quickly set in—the report had to be delivered at a meeting in one hour, and the other four functional area managers would be present.

QUESTIONS

1. Do you perceive any possible repercussions from the failure of the electronic transfer of the six files?

2. What would you suggest as a one-hour plan for Colleen's boss?

3. How could problems like the one in this scenario be avoided (a) by Colleen, (b) by Colleen's boss, or (c) by company policies?

CASE 3–2

Reply to All?!

Jamal Wright arrived at the office a bit late on Monday morning, around 9:45. He had been invited to speak at the Miami Chamber of Commerce breakfast as the chief operating officer for InterWorld Traders, an international shipping service. His topic, ironically, was communication efficiency. His speech was well received, and he was in a good mood as he logged in for the day. As he opened his e-mail, he was instantly struck by the incredible number of internal e-mails he had waiting in his inbox. Normally about 20 messages, today the tally was 21,291! The e-mail messages were from all over the world, and were short messages in reply to others' messages. Thousands of them!

Jamal scrolled down the list until he got to the last ones he had read on Friday afternoon. The culprit soon surfaced. It was a message from Sue Knowles, a manager in charge of distribution analysis. Her job focused on the efficiency of logistical matters concerning the shipping of parcels and the organization of the firm's headquarters warehouse. Sue had sent out a call asking for input concerning any efficiency issues that had been noticed in any of the areas within the firm. Unfortunately, the question was open ended, and her delivery method had created a monster. She had sent the message to all of the 546 supervisory-level managers or higher within the company. She had not used a mail merge process to send the messages; instead, she had listed a group with all of the e-mail addresses included in the recipients line of her message. The result was disastrous. As several well-meaning recipients responded with their observations and suggestions, they had unfortunately selected Reply All. Apparently, the recipients were under the impression that only two or three people had received the initial e-mail. Unfortunately, as others also hit Reply All in their responses to the responses, millions of e-mail messages flooded the firm's servers.

Jamal returned to the more recent messages. They were noticeably aggressive messages, like "Remove me from this e-mail list" and "I wish you people would learn to use e-mail properly!" and "You idiots stop e-mailing me!" There were even some who obviously realized what was going on—they had replied to all saying, "Everyone stop pressing Reply All!"

The tumult of messages was growing greater minute by minute. The company was bogged down in its inability to function by e-mail, and there seemed to be no end in sight.

QUESTIONS

1. How could blunders like the one described above be prevented?

2. Since it was not prevented, what should Jamal do now?

CASE 3–3

The Potential for Technology

Bill Emory is the operations vice president of a banking firm in California that has forty-eight branch operations. These operations vary from drive-in facilities with ten employees to larger facilities employing as many as 150 people. Employee turnover has always been a major problem in these branches, and no employment strategy has been effective in reducing this problem. The high turnover has made employee training a special problem.

The human resources department is responsible for employee training, but HR charges branch operations for the expenses incurred. The recent expansion in training due to ever-changing services offered by the bank has become extremely costly. Emory has decided it is time to attempt to reduce these costs by implementing some new training strategies. He believes that many of the new communication technologies could be used to save training expenses. In particular, savings could be realized for the branches that are more than 400 miles from the corporate office. (In the past, the training representatives would travel to the branch site, stay overnight, present a one- or two-day training session, and then return. Emory would like to reduce these travel and lodging expenses.) Emory has casually asked the HR manager, Joan Tyson, to investigate communication technology possibilities in training, but no action has been taken; consequently, Emory has decided to write a persuasive letter to Tyson encouraging Tyson's staff to investigate this subject.

PROJECT

Write a memo to the HR manager, Joan Tyson, which could be used for this purpose. Include one or two specific technologies that might be appropriate, their advantages, and the communication impact that could be expected. Special attention should be given to training for the tellers. For instance, the procedures for recording the various transactions and customer communications should be part of the training.

CASE 3–4

Improvements at ServeNow

ServeNow is a grocery store chain that has seven stores in the southeastern United States. ServeNow's strategy is to target smaller towns (under 50,000 population) so it can become the dominant store in the area. The chain is headquartered in the largest town (population 75,000) in which it has a store. Each store is at least 50 miles from another store within the network.

The owner of the stores, Edward Bushley, has found that it is extremely difficult to monitor store activities because of travel logistics. As a result, the manager of each store has traditionally had a lot of latitude. Many of the pricing and inventory decisions are made at the individual locations. However, most purchasing is made through a central purchasing office in the headquarters city.

But during the past two weeks, three managers left ServeNow to start an online grocery brokerage service. This took Bushley by surprise, but being an entrepreneur himself, he understands their desire to start their own business. In addition, another manager is nearing retirement. Bushley has found that it is extremely difficult to find qualified replacements for these energetic, creative managers.

Bushley had hoped that potential managers would be available among his present employees, but he discovered the company is weak in its succession planning. Current staff members do not seem to have the capabilities or desire to become store managers. It has become obvious that managers have to be found outside of the present staff.

Bushley has retained a small-business consultant, Solange DePeres, who specializes in personnel problems. DePeres agreed that no potential managers were on the present staff. The assistant store managers would be able to manage during the transition, but ultimately new personnel would have to be hired. She stated that Bushley would have to hire managers who were not familiar with the stores' operations and simply spend more time with them than he had with the previous managers. In particular, Bushley would have to spend time training them and answering operational questions.

Bushley asks DePeres, "How can I possibly spend more time at the individual stores? It seems that I am already too busy to maintain a balanced lifestyle."

PROJECT

Assume you are the small-business consultant, Solange DePeres, and make several recommendations to help Bushley stay in touch with his stores and develop his managerial force. Consider especially the technological communication tools on the market. Explain your recommendations.

Student Study Site

Visit the Student Study Site at **study.sagepub.com/hynes6e** for web quizzes, video links, web resources, and cases studies.

Notes

1. C. Cherry, *On Human Communication,* 3rd ed. (Cambridge, MA: MIT Press, 1978), pp. 3–5.
2. Benjamin van Loon, "Productivity Is Money," *Profile Magazine*, April-June, 2013, http://profilemagazine.com/2013/productivity-is-money/.

3. Selection of these variables is partially based on C. Heeter, "Classifying Mediated Communication Systems," in *Communication Yearbook,* vol. 12, ed. James A. Anderson (Newbury Park, CA: Sage, 1988), pp. 477–486.

4. Felipe Korzenny and Connie Bauer, "Testing the Theory of Electronic Propinquity," *Communication Research* 8, no. 4 (1981): pp. 479–498.

5. For further discussion, see Larry R. Smeltzer and Charles M. Vance, "An Analysis of Graphics Use in Audio-Graphic Teleconferences," *Journal of Business Communication* 26, no. 2 (1989): pp. 123–142.

6. Steven H. Chaffee and Charles R. Berger, "What Communication Scientists Do," in *Handbook of Communication Science,* eds. C. Berger and S. Chaffee (Newbury Park, CA: Sage, 1987), pp. 99–123.

7. "Radio Shack Uses Email to Fire 400 Employees," *Huntsville Item*, September 1, 2006, p. 1.

8. N. L. Reinsch, Cam Monroe Steele, Philip V. Lewis, Michael Stano, and Raymond W. Beswick, "Measuring Telephone Apprehension," *Management Communication Quarterly* 4, no. 2 (1990): pp. 198–221.

9. N. L. Reinsch, Jr. and Raymond W. Beswick, "Voice Mail versus Conventional Channels: A Cost Minimization Analysis of Individuals' Preferences," *Academy of Management Journal* 23, no. 4 (1990): pp. 801–816.

10. Larry R. Smeltzer, "An Analysis of Receivers' Reactions to Electronically Mediated Communication," *Journal of Business Communication* 23, no. 4 (1986): pp. 37–54.

11. Jim Louderback, "IM's: No Longer Just a Teen Thing," *USA Weekend,* January 3, 2003, p. 4.

12. Jennifer Tanaka, "You Pinging Me? IM Has Already Arrived at the Office," *Newsweek,* May 12, 2003, p. E12.

13. Jill Colvin, "You've Got Voice Mail, But Do You Care?" *Houston Chronicle*, April 5, 2009, p. G6.

14. Aviva Musicus, Aner Tal, and Brian Wansink, "Eyes in the Aisles: Why Is Cap'n Crunch Looking Down at My Child?" *Environment and Behavior,* April 2, 2014. doi: 10.1177/0013916514528793.

15. Earl C. Gottschalk, Jr., "Firms Are Cool to Meetings by Television," *The Wall Street Journal,* July 26, 1983, p. 1.

16. Sharon Begley, "Will the BlackBerry Sink the Presidency?" *Newsweek*, February 16, 2009, pp. 37–38. See also Gail Thomas and Cindy King, "Reconceptualizing Email Overload," *Journal of Business and Technical Communication* 20 (2006): pp. 252–287.

17. Maggie Jackson, *Distracted: The Erosion of Attention and the Coming Dark Age* (Amherst, NY: Prometheus Books, 2008).

18. R. L. Daft and K. E. Weick, "Toward a Model of Organizations as Interpretation Systems," *Academy of Management Review* 9, no. 2 (1984): pp. 284–295.

19. M. S. Feldman and J. G. March, "Information in Organizations as Signal and Symbol," *Administrative Science Quarterly* 26, no. 1 (1981): pp. 171–186.

20. R. L. Daft, R. H. Lengel, and L. K. Trevino, "Message Equivocality, Media Selection, and Manager Performance: Implications for Information Systems," *MIS Quarterly* 11, no. 2 (1987): pp. 355–366.

21. This categorization was largely drawn from Ronald E. Dulek and John S. Fielden, *Principles of Business Communication* (New York: Macmillan, 1990).

22. R. E. Rice, "Evaluating New Media Systems," in *Evaluating the New Information Technologies: New Directions for Program Evaluation,* ed. J. Johnson (San Francisco: Jossey-Bass, 1984), pp. 53–71.

23. Gerald R. Miller, "Persuasion," in *Handbook of Communication Science,* eds. C. Berger and S. Chaffee (Newbury Park, CA: Sage, 1987), pp. 446–483.

24. Robert B. Cialdini, *Influence: The New Psychology of Modern Persuasion* (New York: Quill, 1984).

25. Joe Kovacs, "Reader's Digest Poll of Americans Has Eye-Opening Results," May 7, 2013, WND Media, http://www.wnd.com/2013/05/fox-news-anchor-ranks-dead-last-for-trust/#sJUBumFVCBuPeHQV.99.

26. Yuki Noguchi, "Make It Stop! Crushed by Too Many Emails," NPR, *Morning Edition,* E-radio, June 16, 2008, http://www.npr.org/templates/story/story.php?storyId=91366853.

27. Bary C. Sherman, "More Proof That Email Wastes Time and Money," *BusinessWeek,* December 19, 2005.

28. Kevin Maney, "How the Big Names Tame Email," *USA Today,* July 24, 2003, p. 1A.

29. "She Hates Email," *Newsweek,* May 12, 2003, p. E18.

30. Scott Sayare, "Accord Would Cap Off-the-Clock Email," *Houston Chronicle*, April 12, 2014, p. A14.

31. Maney, "How the Big Names Tame Email," p. 2A.

32. Dubravka Cecez-Kecmanovic, Marius Janson, and Ann Brown, "The Rationality Framework for a Critical Study of Information Systems," *Journal of Information Technology* 17, no. 4 (December 2002): pp. 215–227.

33. D. Shipley and W. Schwalbe, *SEND: The Essential Guide to Email for Office and Home* (New York: Alfred A. Knopf, 2007).

34. "Choosing a Communication Channel," *Strategic Communication Management* 16, no. 2 (2012): pp. 38–39.

35. D. Dick, "Designing a Web Site for a Corporate Intranet," *Intercom* 51, no. 2 (2004): pp. 12–13.

36. Jeff Tyson and Alison Cooper, "How Instant Messaging Works," n.d., *How Stuff Works,* http://communication.howstuffworks.com/instant-messaging1.htm.

37. Nancy Flynn, *Instant Messaging Rules* (New York: AMACOM, 2004), pp. 145–155.

38. Stephen Yoch, "When 'You've Got Email' Means 'You've Got a Deal!'," *FCA Contract Insight* 4, no. 1, March 2010, http://www.finishingcontractors.org/uploads/media/CI_Mar.10.pdf.

39. Ibid.

40. Kenneth Rashbaum, "A Single Instant Message Can Land Your Company in a New York Court: The Deutsche Bank Case," *The Privacy and Data Security Law Journal* 10 (2006): pp. 889–896.

41. Sara Radicati, "Instant Messaging Market 2013–2017," September 2013, http://www.radicati.com/?p = 8801.

42. *Wikipedia*, the Free Encyclopedia, "Text Messaging," n.d., accessed January 8, 2007, http://en.wikipedia.org/wiki/Text_messaging.

43. K. A. Frenkel, "The Rise of Business Texting," *CIO Insight,* 2014, pp. 1–16.

44. Joshua Brost, "You've Got (Less) Mail: CIOs Surveyed Say Workplace Communication Will Favor Real-time Tools," press release, August 25, 2011, http://rht.mediaroom.com/index.php?s = 131&item = 1201.

45. Allan Pratt, "Texting Security Concerns—AWTTW," *Tips4TechsBlog*, June 20, 2013, http://tips4tech.wordpress.com/2013/06/20/texting-security-concerns/.

46. Barack, *School Library Journal* 52, no. 1 (January 2006).

47. D. Shinder, "Instant Messaging: Does It Have a Place in Business Networks?" (November 2, 2004), accessed January 3, 2007, http://www.windowsecurity.com/articles/Instant-Messaging-Business-Networks.html.

48. *Wikipedia*, the Free Encyclopedia, "Blog," (n.d.), accessed February 23, 2008, http://en.wikipedia.org/wiki/Blog.

49. S. Baker, "The Inside Story on Company Blogs," *BusinessWeek Online*, February 14, 2006, accessed February 21, 2008, http://www.businessweek.com/technology/content/feb2006/tc20060214_402499.htm.

50. *Wikipedia,* "Blog."

51. S. Baker and H. Green, "Social Media Will Change Your Business," *BusinessWeek Online*, February 20, 2008, accessed February 21, 2008, http://www.businessweek.com/stories/2008-02-20/social-media-will-change-your-businessbusinessweek-business-news-stock-market-and-financial-advice.

52. L. Rosencrance, "Blogs Bubble into Business," *ComputerWorld Online*, January 26, 2004, http://www.computerworld.com/softwaretopics/software/story/0,10801,89283,00.html.

53. Baker, "The Inside Story."

54. Ibid.

55. P. Blackshaw and M. Nazzaro, "*Consumer-Generated Media (CGM) 101: Word-of-Mouth in the Age of the Web-Fortified Consumer*," Nielsen BuzzMetrics White Papers, Spring 2006, accessed March 8, 2008, http://www.artsmarketing.org/marketingresources/files/Consumer-Generated%20Media.pdf.

56. Baker and Green, "Social Media."

57. Baker, "The Inside Story."

58. Ibid.

59. C. Catalano, "Megaphones to the Internet and the World: The Role of Blogs in Corporate Communication," *International Journal of Strategic Communication* 1, no. 4 (2007): pp. 247–262.

60. Ibid.

61. H. J. Wen, D. Schwieger, and P. Gershuny, "Internet Usage Monitoring in the Workplace: Its Legal Challenges and Implementation Strategies," *Information Systems Management* 24, no. 2 (2007): pp. 185–196.

62. D. Elmuti and H. H. Davis, "Not Worth the Bad Will," *Industrial Management* 48, no. 6 (2006): pp. 26–30.

63. R. L. Wakefield, "Computer Monitoring and Surveillance," *The CPA Journal* 74, no. 7 (2004): pp. 52–55.

64. Ibid.

65. G. S. Alder, M. L. Ambrose, and T. W. Noel, "The Effect of Formal Advance Notice and Justification on Internet Monitoring Fairness: Much about Nothing?" *Journal of Leadership and Organizational Studies* 13, no. 1 (2006): pp. 93–108.

66. J. Lloyd, "Management Email Monitoring Brings 'Big Brother' to Mind," *The Receivables Report for America's Health Care Financial Managers* 21, no. 1 (2006): pp. 6–7.

67. A. D. Moore, "Employee Monitoring and Computer Technology: Evaluative Surveillance v. Privacy," *Business Ethics Quarterly* 10, no. 3 (2000): pp. 697–709.

68. American Management Association, "2005 Electronic Monitoring and Surveillance Survey: Many Companies Monitoring, Recording, Videotaping—and Firing—Employees" (2005), accessed July 1, 2007, http://www.amanet.org/press/amanews/ems05.htm.

69. A. M. Everett, Y. Wong, and J. Paynter, "Balancing Employee and Employer Rights: An International Comparison of Email Privacy in the Workplace," *Journal of Individual Employment Rights* 11, no. 4 (2004–2005): pp. 291–310.

70. Ibid.

71. Ibid.

72. Victor Luckerson, "Oh, Snap! How Photo Messages Could Make Texting Obsolete," *Time*, December 30, 2013, pp. 18–19.

73. Gerald M. Goldhaber, *Organizational Communication* (Dubuque, IA: Wm. C. Brown, 1983), p. 156.

74. Jeffrey Pfeffer, "Producing Sustainable Competitive Advantage through the Effective Management of People," *The Academy of Management Executive* 19, no. 4 (2005): pp. 95–108.

75. Paul Benjamin Lowry, Aaron Curtis, and Michelle Rene Lowry, "Building a Taxonomy and Nomenclature of Collaborative Writing to Improve Interdisciplinary Research and Practice," *Journal of Business Communication* 41, no. 1 (January 2004): pp. 66–99.

76. Marshall Scott Poole and Geraldine DeSanctis, "Understand the Use of Group Decision Support Systems: The Theory of Adaptive Structuration," in *Organizations and Communication Technology,* eds. J. Fulk and C. Steinfield (Newbury Park, CA: Sage, 1990), pp. 173–193; and "Smart Programs Go to Work," *BusinessWeek*, March 2, 1992, pp. 97–105.

77. Gail S. Russ, Richard L. Daft, and Robert H. Lengel, "Media Selection and Managerial Characteristics in Organizational Communications," *Management Communication Quarterly* 4, no. 2 (November 1990): pp. 151–175.

78. "The Present (and Future) of Business Communications," Accounting Web (n.d.), accessed July 25, 2005, http://www.accountingweb.com.

PART II

Group Communication Strategies

Managing Meetings and Teams

Groupthink leads "to weak and faltering decisions, or rather, indecisions. When you take the most gallant soldier, the most intrepid airman or the most audacious soldier, put them at a table together, what do you get? The sum total of their fears."

—Winston Churchill, describing meetings during World War II

Meetings are an important organizational communication process that continues to be useful for coordination of work functions. The American Management Association concluded that collaboration and team building (which are primarily accomplished during meetings) are among the most critical workforce skills today and will be even more so in the future.[1] In fact, 90 percent of all US businesses and 100 percent of the Fortune 500 companies use some form of group structure. Their need lies in the complexity and interdependence of tasks, which make it difficult for one person to have the knowledge to make decisions and solve problems in today's organizations. The contemporary regulatory environment illustrates this interdependence and the high cost of decisions. Governmental regulations on how and what an industry can do often require that lawyers, industrial relations managers, tax specialists, accountants, and governmental experts discuss ideas before a decision is made.

From a broader perspective, it is easy to see why teams have been adopted as a key personnel configuration in the postmodern business environment. As discussed in Chapter 1, today's workplace is fast paced. The traditional management hierarchy has been replaced by flexible, cooperative, mission-driven managers who expect their subordinates and associates to participate fully in the task or project at hand.

Managing teams—and the meetings that teamwork requires—calls for special skills. Just because a work group is labeled a team doesn't mean it automatically functions as a team. As a team leader, you must use a variety of communication strategies to maximize your team's effectiveness. This chapter describes those key strategic considerations. But first, we briefly review the range of functions that meetings and teams perform.

Managers use meetings for several functions: informational, fact finding, problem solving, decision making, and coordinating (see Table 4–1). While a meeting may be labeled team, staff, marketing, committee, ad hoc, or something else, any meeting should allow members to share information, obtain ideas, solve problems, coordinate efforts, make decisions, and build working relationships. A gathering of workers who simply sit and hear the manager make announcements is not a true meeting.

STOP AND THINK

1. What kinds of teams and groups have you been a part of, either at work or in your personal life?

2. To what extent has working with others in those groups made it easier to accomplish the task?

Managers use informational meetings to explain important new decisions or company activities to employees, answer questions, or help them to understand how to perform a desired task. The essential aim is to communicate a company point of view and have it accepted by employees. Such meetings succeed when they get the employees to examine, articulate, and align their own interests with the company's.

Managers conduct fact-finding meetings to tap the expertise of several employees and at the same time obtain facts for planning and decision making. For example, a sales manager may call in all the sales representatives to find out about such matters as business conditions, competition, customer desires, and complaints. A production manager having trouble with a specific operation might meet with all the key people who have knowledge of a situation.

In a problem-solving and decision-making meeting, team members pool their specialized expertise with the objective of developing a solution. This meeting goes beyond simply finding facts; it seeks to identify the issues and discuss the probable gains and losses resulting from alternate actions.

In coordination meetings, project teams keep each other informed of their progress and plan each stage of their joint efforts. Whatever their purpose, meetings are a way of managerial life; however, managers must use meetings prudently to maximize their benefits and minimize their costs.

An outstanding example of meetings that accomplish the goals described above was the Katrina Working Group sessions led by the mayor of Houston, Texas, Bill White, following the devastation of Hurricane Katrina in September 2005. Every morning, he presided over a session of community leaders, corporate executives, church leaders, emergency services staff, and elected officials to determine how to serve the thousands of evacuees from New Orleans and other Gulf Coast areas who were seeking shelter in Houston. Forty people sat at long tables arranged in a square in a large room, with dozens of others sitting in rows behind the tables. Mayor White refused to allow speeches or grandstanding. Instead, he asked participants to raise issues and helped them formulate response plans. As a result of the efficient methods that the mayor's team used to handle the crisis, ensuring

Table 4–1   Functions of Meetings

| Share Information |
| Find Facts |
| Solve Problems |
| Make Decisions |
| Coordinate Tasks |

humanitarian aid to evacuees while maintaining the city's normal functions, Houston reelected Bill White in November 2005 with 91 percent of the vote.[2]

ADVANTAGES AND DISADVANTAGES OF WORKING IN TEAMS

Whether participating in a team or leading one, managers should be aware of advantages and disadvantages of group work, as summarized in Table 4–2.

Advantages of Teams

One advantage is that a group decision may be of a higher quality than that made by an individual. But before using a team, you must analyze the nature of the problem. Teams are better at solving problems for which there is no single correct solution or for which solutions are difficult to verify objectively.[3] Such problems require decisions that cannot be programmed. Nonprogrammed decisions are the result of infrequent situations that require creativity, insight, and the sharing of ideas and perspectives regarding a problem.[4] Groups, especially heterogeneous groups, bring a greater variety of information and a wider choice of solutions.

A second advantage to a team is that when members have had an opportunity for discussion, they are more likely to be committed to the information presented or the decision made. In other words, they become "owners" of the decision. A classic study conducted by Coch and French over fifty-five years ago investigated workers' resistance to technological changes in their jobs. During team or employee meetings, they noted that when workers participated in discussions regarding implementation of the changes, significantly less resistance resulted than that which occurred among workers excluded from participation.[5] Each employee who participated in the meeting had increased ownership of the outcome, and the responsibility felt for making the solution or program work was enhanced.

Table 4–2   Advantages and Disadvantages of Teams

Advantages	Disadvantages
Higher-quality decisions	Low-quality or premature decisions
Increased productivity	Wasted time
Increased commitment, loyalty, retention	Costly
Fewer communication breakdowns	Overused
Increased motivation	Risk of groupthink

A more recent study of employee retention factors found similar results. When asked which improvement would make the biggest difference in their organization's ability to retain employees, 42 percent of the executives surveyed chose empowering workers to participate in decision making. By contrast, only 6 percent cited more attractive compensation packages as an effective tool for lowering turnover.[6]

Another advantage of a team meeting is that it may reduce the chance of communication problems. When a group of people hears the same message at the same time, the possibility of misinterpretation declines. Participants' questions can clarify the message, and each participant has the opportunity to hear the answer and ask additional questions. Feedback is increased and timing is reduced as a barrier to communication.

An old tale illustrates yet another benefit of working in teams. A man was lost while driving through the country. As he tried to read a map, he accidentally drove off the road into a ditch. Though he wasn't injured, his car was stuck deep in the mud. So the man walked to a nearby farm and asked for help.

"Warwick can get you out of that ditch," said the farmer, pointing to an old mule standing in a field. The man looked at the haggard mule doubtfully but figured he had nothing to lose. The two men and Warwick made their way back to the ditch.

The farmer hitched the mule to the car. With a snap of the reins he shouted, "Pull, Fred! Pull, Jack! Pull, Ted! Pull, Warwick!" And the mule pulled the car from the ditch with very little effort. The man was amazed. He thanked the farmer, patted the mule, and asked, "Why did you call out all of those other names before you called Warwick?"

The farmer grinned and said, "Old Warwick is just about blind. As long as he believes he's part of a team, he doesn't mind pulling."[7]

> ### STOP AND THINK
>
> 1. What advantage of working in teams does this fable exemplify?
>
> 2. To what extent do you agree that teammates influence your own efforts?

Disadvantages of Teams

We have seen that working in teams can improve quality, productivity, creativity, loyalty and commitment, and even retention. But there is a downside. Richard Hall put it well when he noted, "Time spent on meetings is time not spent on other activities."[8] While the hourly cost of a meeting in terms of the base pay of the participants is already high, to determine the real cost, one must add payroll taxes, fringe benefits, and general overhead. To cover meeting costs, participants' base pay would probably need to be doubled to determine the actual cost. Meeting costs often go unnoticed because they are not budget line items. Meetings are a hidden cost that can either impede or improve the effectiveness of a work group.

In addition to the high cost, the team may develop low-quality decisions. Pressures to conform, premature decisions, hidden agendas, extensive conflict, disruptive and dominant individuals, lack of planning, and poor leadership can easily reduce effectiveness.[9] Later in the chapter, we detail these factors and techniques for managing them.

A common disadvantage of meetings is their frequent overuse. Organizations often develop a *meeting style* of management. Management must meet for every little thing. Meetings generally are not necessary for routine or repetitive programmed decisions that can be handled by an established procedure. Unfortunately, meetings are held too frequently just because "we always have a meeting at this time." Overuse of meetings may cause employees to find them a nuisance, so they avoid them. Consequently, employees may miss truly important meetings or be unable to distinguish between a critical and a useless meeting.

Another problem is that the weekly team meeting might be a waste of time if members are not required to gather facts before the meeting, make decisions at the meeting, or present information. The manager must analyze each meeting to determine need. Still another often useless meeting pattern finds the manager telling a group about a new event or presenting a progress report without providing an opportunity for questions or interactions. Clearly, it may be more efficient to share information through a memo or e-mail rather than a meeting.

Groupthink

After extensive analysis, Irving Janis wrote a book titled *Victims of Groupthink*.[10] Groupthink is the tendency of a group to conform to ideas simply because the general sense of the group has moved in a particular direction and the members of the group feel committed to continue in the same line of thought. Although the group may be pursuing an incorrect conclusion, the group does not alter direction for fear of offending a group member. It is the extreme form of cohesiveness and is especially likely when a group has a high sense of teamwork and desire for consensus or harmony.

Groupthink is especially important because of its potential for disastrous effects. Some say the disaster of the space shuttle Challenger was a result of groupthink.[11] The night before the space shuttle's launch in 1986, engineers urged managers to delay because they were worried about failure of the O-rings in the cold weather. Their concerns were overruled, the Challenger was launched, and the O-rings failed, causing the deaths of seven astronauts. Subsequent investigations indicated that, despite evidence of the potential risks being presented in meetings, the meeting members kept redefining what they considered risky to downplay the problem. Unfortunately, dissenters and whistle-blowers are too often ignored, and many other disasters have been at least partially attributed to groupthink.[12]

Based on Janis's concept, Von Bergen and Kirk describe symptoms of groupthink that managers should watch for:[13]

1. The illusion that everyone in the group holds the same viewpoint with an emphasis on team play

2. The belief that the group can make no mistakes

3. The belief that disagreements are to be avoided, faulty assumptions are not questioned, and personal doubts must be suppressed in favor of group harmony

4. The tendency to comfort one another and to ignore or at least discount warnings that an agreed-on plan is either unworkable or highly unlikely to succeed

5. The tendency to direct pressure on any dissenting group member who expresses strong challenges to the consensus opinion of the group

6. The presence of inordinate optimism that predisposes members to take excessive risks

When in a decision-making meeting, the effective manager is alert to groupthink symptoms and takes appropriate action. Or more appropriately, she takes actions to ensure that groupthink does not develop. Three actions help to avoid the tendency toward groupthink:

1. *Do not make an early decision.* Do not commit early or become locked into a position early in the problem analysis. When a manager begins a discussion by saying "This is what I would like to see" or "This is the best solution . . . but I would like your comments," he is probably preventing an open discussion and is setting the stage for an early unanimous decision.

2. *Be open to criticism.* This is easy to say but difficult to do. It is natural to defend one's idea, but a wise manager will encourage employees to "push back." Criticism of an idea should not be taken as criticism of another's self-worth. When criticism cannot arise within the group, it may be solicited from an outsider who will generally be less susceptible to status and conformity pressures.

3. *Use a "devil's advocate."* If one member of the group is asked to provide opposition to any ideas expressed, this will ensure alternatives. This procedure works best when other members know that the dissenter is playing the devil's advocate role; otherwise, they may consider the person to be an agitator who should be ignored. In addition, the same person should not play the devil's advocate in every meeting. Not only does constantly stating opposing viewpoints put pressure on the person, but it may also result in a negative image of the individual. By rotating the "voice of doom," everyone will practice identifying what could possibly go wrong, an extremely useful skill for combating groupthink.

> **STOP AND THINK**
>
> 1. What are the primary reasons that doubters keep quiet during meetings?
>
> 2. Why do we need laws to protect whistle-blowers from retaliation?

STRATEGIC CONSIDERATIONS FOR MEETINGS

As we have seen, meetings have advantages as well as disadvantages, and groupthink adds to their complexity. The following discussion of ten strategic considerations, which are listed in Table 4–3, is provided to assist managers when considering the various contingencies. Strategic considerations 1–6 apply to any meeting, whether in-person or electronic; strategic consideration 7 applies when groups are meeting face-to-face; and strategic considerations 8–10 apply when groups are meeting virtually.

Table 4–3   Strategic Considerations for Meetings

Consideration	Applies to Face-to-Face Meetings	Applies to Virtual Meetings
1. Whether to meet	✓	✓
2. Attendees	✓	✓
3. Agenda and materials	✓	✓
4. Leadership style	✓	✓
5. Management of disruptions	✓	✓
6. Follow-up	✓	✓
7. Physical facilities	✓	
8. Technology support		✓
9. Team relationships		✓
10. Cultural differences		✓

Strategic Consideration 1: Should We Meet?

There are good reasons to have a meeting, and poor reasons to do so. As we have seen, the best reason is to get everyone's input on a complex problem or task. A poor reason to meet is to show others that one has the power to call people together or to be the center of attention. Another wrong reason is social or recreational—a meeting is an opportunity to get away from the desk, to visit with Bill from Accounting about the football game, or to be seen with some influential decision makers. Often, a brief informal group conversation may be better than a formal meeting. A good way to handle the former is to hold the meeting with everybody standing up.[14] This strategy ensures involvement, attention to the meeting's purpose, and brevity.

If you have decided to have a formal meeting, you next must attend to the premeeting arrangements.

Strategic Consideration 2: Who Should Attend?

Once you have decided to hold a meeting, you need to select the meeting participants. Among the criteria to consider are (1) how many people to invite, (2) who the members will represent, (3) the members' functions in the meeting, and (4) their team-ability.

First, choose a manageable group size. Remember the guideline that increasing the size limits the extent to which individuals want to communicate. Research shows that as a group grows, communication becomes distorted and stress between members increases. However, a decrease in group size may also be dysfunctional. Thus, small groups may engage in superficial discussion and avoid controversial subjects.

But what is the ideal size? Filley, who has conducted extensive research on work groups, believes the optimum size is generally about five. But when the problem is more complex, relatively larger groups—as large as twelve to thirteen members—have proved more effective. Smaller groups are often faster and more productive, on the other hand. Generally, the larger the group, the less inclined an individual group member is to participate.

Sometimes, it may not be possible to limit the size of the group to five or seven employees. In such cases, a manager could break the large group into smaller subgroups. The improved decisions or more accurate sharing of information may justify the time and effort required to coordinate several groups.

Second, when selecting members, an important thing to remember is that the team should reflect the organizational members the problem affects. For instance, if the concern is a departmental one, then members of the department should be involved. If two departments share the problem, team membership obviously should be drawn from both areas. When possible, membership should also include people with authority to follow through on the chosen action with time, personnel, and financial resources. But salience of the meeting's topic should be considered more important than organizational status when selecting participants.

Third, consider participants' potential functions within the team. When scheduling a problem-solving meeting, include people who are familiar with the different aspects of the problem. Also, include people who will actually carry out the solution to ensure implementation of the decision. In short, subject-matter expertise should be a prime criterion for membership in a team or work group.

Finally, consider participants' team-ability. Task knowledge is an insufficient qualification for meeting participation. Ability to work with others may become even more of a concern for cross functional teams and virtual teams because of the special communication challenges they involve. Members of teams may be too passive, tactful, or constrained to work together in a satisfying manner. They fear alienating one another.[15] On the other hand, members may be too passionate, stubborn, and aggressive. They might be unable to cooperate and compromise in a team setting. Clearly, your group must have the needed team skills to function in a meeting and resolve the problem.[16]

If a manager has difficulty finding employees with team-ability, training may be called for. Teamwork is a skill that can be acquired, not a gift one is born with. Understanding group dynamics comes with study and practice. Parts IV (Strategies for Understanding Messages) and V (Interpersonal Communication Strategies) of this book offer guidelines for developing some of the process skills required for meeting participation, including collaborating, listening, giving constructive feedback, negotiating, compromising, and other conflict resolution strategies.

Strategic Consideration 3: Agenda and Materials

Premeeting arrangements include preparing the agenda and other appropriate materials. The agenda may be the first thing that comes to mind when considering materials for a meeting. More than a list of the meeting topics, the agenda is the script or working paper from which the meeting operates. As the cliché says, "What gets scheduled gets done." Consequently, the agenda deserves the manager's special consideration. Careful planning is half the battle. However, be sure to follow the agenda during the meeting. When others try to introduce new elements during the meeting, refer to the written agenda.[17]

Regardless of the type of meeting, the agenda needs to communicate the *what, why, when*, and *who* (the Ws) of a meeting. Frequently, one or several of the elements of an agenda are often omitted, yet each is important. For instance, if time frames for each agenda topic are included, the meeting is less likely to run long and more likely to address all the topics. And if expected outcomes for each topic are specified, the meeting participants are more likely to reach the stated goals. An agenda template is shown in Figure 4–1.

What. People first need to know the *what,* the topic under discussion, so they may understand exactly what is to be discussed. Let the agenda make this clear. A topic listed as "Maintenance" will not communicate as fully as one that reads "Maintenance Status of the Emergency Generator." A more complete description enables participants to gather any special information or prepare questions relevant to the discussion.

Figure 4–1   Meeting Announcement and Agenda Template

MEMORANDUM

DATE:
TO:
FROM:
SUBJECT: Meeting Notificaton and Agenda

DATE:

START TIME: END TIME:

LOCATION:

AGENDA:

	Topic	Time	Leader	Expected Outcome
A				
B				
C				
D				
E				

Everyone knows that agendas are important, but half of all business meetings are held with no agenda. Maybe the extra effort of an agenda seems unjustified, or the lack of an agenda may merely reflect a lack of planning. It may also be that agendas are not the common practice in many companies. Agendas are often not needed in small informal meetings where two or three employees get together or when one obvious topic is the only point for discussion. However, some managers assume agendas are never needed for small meetings. Agendas require planning time—an asset that ineffective managers rarely possess. Many managers would rather spend additional time in a poorly conducted meeting than take the time to plan. In many cases, a manager may wish to solicit input on the agenda from members. In these cases, it should be done in a systematic way to ensure orderly input. Few leaders like surprises at meetings.

Why. People attending a meeting need to know the goal for each agenda item. Describe this clearly, so participants can work toward it. Failure to clarify a group discussion's goal leads to circular talk and anxiety among participants. When people do not know why they are attending a meeting, apprehension arises.

When. Setting the time involves several strategic factors. First, what time of day is best for all the participants? A quick review of the organization may indicate that the first thing in the morning is bad if many other activities are competing for attention, whereas immediately after lunch may be a difficult time for people to stay alert.

Second, how long should the meeting last? If a meeting schedule does not allow sufficient time, critical issues may receive superficial coverage. But remember that people value time highly and resent its waste or misuse. Be sure to list both the start time and the end time on your meeting announcement to allow participants to plan their day.

A standard time limit that applies to all meetings is impossible to set. However, some ground rules on length are possible. The most effective meetings last no longer than one and a half hours. After this long, people need to break for coffee or fresh air. Short, single goals can be met in less than an hour, and this should be the time span a manager aims for. Individual agenda items should also be assigned a time limit. Too often, meetings go on and on because no one has established definite time parameters.

When applies to the appropriate time to send out the agenda as well. The purpose of the agenda and any supporting material is lost if none of it arrives until the last minute. Neither should one send the materials with so much lead time that the participants forget about it. A rule of thumb is that the longer a meeting is (and, consequently, the more scheduling and preparation required by the participants), the greater the lead time required for the agenda and supporting materials. But avoid too long a lead time, which could bring about forgetfulness. Generally, participants need two or three days' notice to prepare for a meeting.

Who. It is not a mere courtesy to inform the participants about the others who will be at the meeting. This knowledge allows the participants to complete their own audience analysis. Knowing who else will be present lets the participants prepare any material or information that others in the meeting may request.

A list of participants also forces the meeting manager to think about possible group dynamics. For instance, will a verbally dominant person attempt to control the group? Will the correct mix of expertise be present? Answers to these questions can influence meeting outcomes.

Strategic Consideration 4: Leadership Style

The problems facing organizations are so varied and complex that no one style of leadership suits all situations. Consequently, a manager must be flexible and diagnose the situation to determine the appropriate leadership behavior from one situation to another.

When diagnosing the situation to determine the most effective style, managers need to consider three factors: the group, the objective of the meeting, and the type of leadership behavior with which the manager personally feels most comfortable.[18] Figure 4–2 shows how these three factors operate together.

Each group differs but needs a leader with some degree of interpersonal orientation; therefore, tight control is generally inappropriate. Less control is required when the group is mature and knows the topic, whereas a new or immature group needs a leader who provides more control and direction.

A routine or structured meeting may call for more leader control and task orientation, but a democratic or more laissez-faire approach may be required for a solution to an abstract problem or one requiring a creative solution. A highly emotional task requires less control, while more control may be best for a nonsensitive objective.

Finally, a manager must be aware of the type of leadership behavior with which she is personally most comfortable. This awareness helps a manager to monitor her own behavior and remain flexible rather than use the same behavior repeatedly. Increasing one's repertoire of management tools is a requirement for today's fast-paced, constantly shifting workplace.

Figure 4–2   Determining Leadership Style

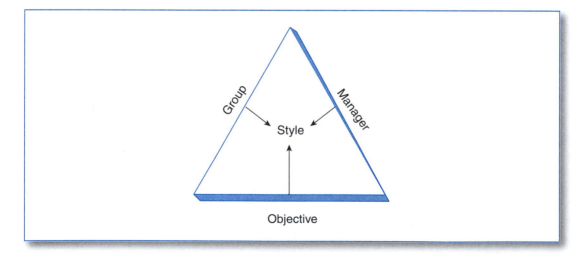

Leading Project Teams

Managing project teams calls for special leadership skills. Among them is the ability to select team members who communicate information freely and honestly. One nontraditional tool for objectively evaluating project team members is social network analysis (SNA). SNA begins with a survey about who respondents go to for advice or information, whom they communicate with most frequently, and who is their most valued contact in the organization.

Survey results are analyzed and "sociograms" are designed that reveal employees' social network and connections. From these sociograms, a project leader can identify people with *centrality*. Centrality is a measure of a person's relative importance based on their location in the social network. Thus, when putting together a project team or when analyzing a dysfunctional team, a manager should consider whether individuals have high degrees of centrality. These people control the flow of information and collaboration, bridging potential communication gaps in the team and in the organization.

One manager who uses SNA to evaluate project teams is Steve Randle, vice president of IT Operations for XO Communications. Headquartered in Virginia, XO Communications is one of the United States' largest communications service providers to businesses and government. Randle reports, "Teams with members who show high centrality will be able to more effectively access needed resources across the organization and will more readily share information with other groups who need to be involved with a project in a timely manner. With better planning I can expect better results."[19]

The following are some other strategies that will help you maximize your project team's effectiveness.

> **STOP AND THINK**
>
> Consider a person in your organization who exhibits high centrality.
>
> 1. What are some of the ways this person develops a social network?
>
> 2. To what extent can you adopt these behaviors to strengthen your own centrality?

- *Be a facilitator.* Managing teams is less about supervising than it is about motivating members to do their best. Avoid the tendency to micromanage once the team's objectives and responsibilities have been defined.

- *Support the team.* Provide resources, run interference, and resolve internal conflicts. Give them all the information they need, and more, to encourage trust. Remember that people cannot work in a vacuum.

- *Delegate.* Managers occasionally have trouble admitting that they cannot do it all. Instead of trying to manage every aspect of a meeting or project, trust members to perform their tasks. This also engenders respect for you as a leader and maintains morale.

- *Seek diversity.* As discussed later in Chapter 12, heterogeneous groups experience more conflict but often produce higher-quality results than homogeneous groups. Stress the importance of collaboration, flexibility, and openness toward unfamiliar viewpoints and work styles.[20]

Strategic Consideration 5: Managing Disruptions

One of the most aggravating behaviors is when a team member continually disrupts the communication flow. This person may be unskilled in group dynamics or may be coming to the meetings with a hidden agenda (that is, private objectives) that conflicts with the stated agenda. Disruptive behavior may include continuous clowning, dominating the conversation, attempting to change directions, or making accusations. These disruptions need resolution; otherwise, teams can quickly deteriorate.

Before the Meeting

A manager can minimize disruptions by taking a preventive point of view. John Jones suggests seven tactics that managers may use ahead of time when they believe a person will disrupt a meeting:[21]

1. Before the meeting, ask for the disrupter's cooperation.

2. Give the person a special task or role in the meeting, such as posting the viewpoints of others.

3. Work out your differences before the meeting (possibly with a third-party facilitator) to present a united front to all other members.

4. Structure the meeting to include frequent discussion of the meeting process itself.

5. Take all the dominator's items off the agenda.

6. Alert the person to the consequences of disruption. For example, say, "I have learned that a number of people are angry with you, and plan to confront you in the meeting."

7. Arrange for allies to support you in dealing with the disruptive behavior of the individual.

During the Meeting

While prevention is preferred, a manager also needs to have options for controlling disruptive behavior during a meeting. The following are some strategies:

1. When dealing with an emotional conversation, make sure only one person speaks at a time, paraphrase each statement to ensure accuracy before allowing anyone else to speak, and be sure that everyone takes turns. One surprisingly effective technique is to move on to the next agenda item. One can return when tempers cool.[22] You might also stand and move to the flip chart or screen or casually stand near the parties involved. This will help keep control in a nonverbal manner.

2. A less obvious disruptive influence occurs when participants do not get involved in the discussion. One way to ensure that participants become involved is to use the Delphi technique (discussed later). When the participants need to have

answers prepared for specific questions before the meeting, ask for these answers during the meeting.

3. Ask participants to jot down answers on a notepad when sensitive issues are discussed. Ask the participants to submit their written reactions anonymously to you; then, read them to the group. Participants thus have an opportunity to present viewpoints in a "safe" manner.

4. Ask questions throughout the meeting to help keep the participants involved. When worded correctly and addressed to the right audience, questions develop a participative climate. Questions have the greatest chance of soliciting participation when they are open ended, brief, unbiased, easily understood, and immediately pertinent to the topic.

A manager needs to consider four possible alternatives when asking a question.[23] When an *overhead question* is asked, anyone in the group may answer. A good idea is to begin with an overhead question and continue until forced to change. Either domination or nonparticipation by certain individuals may require a *direct question,* simply one that is directed to an individual. With direct questions, keep a balance instead of continually asking a verbal person or an assumed expert.

A *reverse question* is one originally asked by a group member. The leader then directs it back to the person who asked it. Do this when it is apparent that the participant really wants to make a statement but is not quite sure it would be appropriate. A final alternative is the *relay question,* which is asked by a group member and is relayed by the leader to the group: "Mary's question is interesting. What is a good answer?" The relay question gives you an opportunity to keep the communication moving among all the members of the group.

Strategic Consideration 6: Follow-Up

At meeting's end, reanalyze the original goals to ensure you have met them, make appropriate follow-up assignments, and evaluate the meeting process to determine if and how future meetings could be improved. One way to determine if the goal has been met is to review the rational problem-solving process to ensure each step was followed. If the group has defined the problem and has reviewed alternative solutions to this problem, it can be assumed the original objective has been met.

Another easy way to determine if the objective is met is to write out the decision or summarize the discussion in a few sentences. This clear statement allows the participants to review it and make sure they understand it. A summary of the decision reached will bring to the surface any individual misunderstandings or disagreements.

A good idea is to point out differences that exist at the end of the meeting. This recognizes that disagreement is not always bad; also, the disagreements will probably be vital to future discussions. A clear understanding of differences at the end of that meeting should make future meetings go more smoothly and help to prevent unnecessary meetings.

Appropriate post-meeting follow-up is also an important component of team management. Before closing the meeting, clearly set out the next steps each member is to take.

Also, announce the next meeting, if necessary. Written confirmation of the decisions reached and any future actions to be taken by the participants is a good practice. Such a memo or e-mail serves as a reminder of the results and informs other personnel who are interested but did not attend the meeting.

Stress the positive when writing the follow-up memo so the participants can see the fruits of their labor. A follow-up memo or e-mail becomes a record of the meeting, ensures follow-up, and establishes accountability for future action. Some companies have a standard form for the follow-up memo (shown in Figure 4–3) that helps to keep it short, simple, and accurate.

In a meeting, much happens that is lost forever. A manager may need to provide more detailed minutes. Minutes are particularly valuable as a starter for future meetings on the same topic. Traditional minutes should capture a summary of the meeting that includes action items, decisions, and open issues.

- *Action items.* Action items are to-dos assigned to meeting participants. Record the task, the person responsible, and the date agreed upon to complete the task.

- *Decisions.* All decisions that may affect future choices of the group should be recorded.

- *Open issues.* New issues raised at the meeting but not resolved there should be recorded so they can be carried over to a future meeting.[24]

The minutes should record these three results for each topic on the agenda. In addition, any significant comments about that topic should be recorded. Participants appreciate

Figure 4–3   Meeting Follow-Up Memo

Subject of meeting _____

Name of sender _____

Where and when held _____

Present _____

Major conclusions _____

Future actions _____

Next meeting _____

Figure 4–4   Evaluation Sheet

Listed below is a series of statements about a meeting. Circle the number of the scale that best describes the meeting in which you just participated.

1. The objective of the meeting was clearly defined.

Strongly agree   5   4   3   2   1   Strongly disagree

2. A systematic approach was used to solve problems.

Strongly agree   5   4   3   2   1   Strongly disagree

3. All the participants were involved in the meeting.

Strongly agree   5   4   3   2   1   Strongly disagree

4. Disruptions were effectively managed.

Strongly agree   5   4   3   2   1   Strongly disagree

5. An appropriate format was established for the meeting.

Strongly agree   5   4   3   2   1   Strongly disagree

6. Appropriate premeeting details (agenda, room, etc.) were arranged.

Strongly agree   5   4   3   2   1   Strongly disagree

7. Time was well managed.

Strongly agree   5   4   3   2   1   Strongly disagree

8. The stated objectives could have been met without a meeting.

Strongly agree   5   4   3   2   1   Strongly disagree

9. The objective of the meeting has been met.

Strongly agree   5   4   3   2   1   Strongly disagree

having their comments displayed in a way that is visible to everyone. Conventional minutes are often distributed to all meeting members. For political or corporate culture reasons, a manager may want to summarize the information for larger distribution and post it to an intranet site.

The final step in the management of a meeting is the evaluation of the meeting itself, an important self-development activity. One extreme form of evaluation is audio recording of the meeting and evaluating it step-by-step. This may be especially worthwhile for project teams that meet regularly over extended time periods. In fact, your organization may require this of all project managers when they begin a project with a new team of specialists.

The evaluation sheet in Figure 4–4 represents one tool that can be used to evaluate a meeting.

STRATEGIC CONSIDERATION FOR FACE-TO-FACE MEETINGS

In addition to the previous six strategic considerations, leaders of face-to-face meetings have another unique concern: they need to consider the physical arrangements. The following section offers guidelines for arranging a room that will maximize the meeting's effectiveness.

Strategic Consideration 7: Physical Facilities

Once the participants have been selected and the agenda, along with any supporting material, has been prepared, meeting leaders should choose an appropriate location. Physical surroundings are important. A few simple guidelines will help to make a meeting productive:

- Use a room where the chairs and tables can be arranged to meet group needs.

- Match the size of the room with the size of the group. Meetings held in close, cramped rooms with the members jammed together around narrow tables make for an unpleasant conversational climate and hamper decision making. Tension, a prime breeder of conflict, builds in a close and uncomfortable meeting room. At the same time, however, a room seating forty-five can be cold and overwhelming to a group of five.

- Check for comfortable chairs, ventilation, and lighting. Remember, though, that soft, overly comfortable chairs can affect concentration and even prolong the meeting.

- Make sure space exists for visual aids if they are to be used. If you know you will be needing equipment, writing materials, and so on, be sure they are available. Keep the audience in mind. Thus, providing place cards may be useful if the participants are strangers.

- Above all, arrange to have the meeting in a meeting room rather than the meeting leader's office. It will create an environment that emphasizes the participants are coming together for specific purposes at a specific time on neutral turf. The atmosphere created is one of urgency and seriousness, which helps keep the meeting on the topic.

Seating Arrangements

After designating the appropriate facility for the meeting, managers should consider which of several possible seating arrangements to use. Depending on the situation, more than one arrangement may be possible; however, a few arrangements should be avoided. The first arrangement to avoid is the long, narrow table that makes it nearly impossible for all participants to see one another. A manager can use eye contact to gain attention or control a participant; consequently, such a seating arrangement works against the manager's attempts to use all the nonverbal techniques available.

A second arrangement to avoid is one that divides up sides. For instance, if two groups are in natural opposition they should not sit across from each other. Similarly, one should keep two hostile participants apart or in such a position that they cannot easily see each other.

Several seating arrangements lend themselves to effective meetings: the table with the leader at one end, the round table or circle, and the U shape.[25] When the leader sits at one end of the table, control of the meeting is easier because all communication will tend to flow toward the head person. However, this arrangement loses effectiveness with a group larger than six or seven participants. As groups get larger, sidebar comments tend to increase and eye contact is difficult to maintain.

When the size of the meeting becomes larger than ten to twelve members, a U-shaped arrangement is preferred. The manager sitting in the middle of the U can maintain eye contact with all the participants; at the same time, communication among subunits of the group is less likely. A variation is the oval-shaped table. When the president of the United States meets with his/her Cabinet (most senior appointed officers), for instance, everyone sits at an oval table, with the president at the middle, directly across from the vice president. Other members are seated according to the order of precedence, with higher ranking officers sitting closer to the center of the table.

STOP AND THINK

Recall the legend of King Arthur and the Knights of the Round Table. What was the king's motivation for his choice of seating?

The manager using the round table or circle arrangement has less direct control of the group than with other arrangements. Because the manager has a less dominant position, participants tend to address each other rather than the leader. A table is, in a sense, a kind of communication line, as the contour of the table establishes the flow of communication. Thus, the round table is best when seeking a true participative form of decision making and trying to minimize status differences. Figure 4–5 illustrates the different arrangements.

Managers might consider the advice of Dennis Crowley, chief executive of Foursquare, the location-based social networking site, regarding seating. When he conducts regular meetings, he mixes up the arrangement so everyone sits next to everyone else occasionally. Crowley believes in the importance of his staff getting to know each other, which is reflected in the company's relaxed, open culture.[26]

In review, three major types of premeeting arrangements require analysis: what materials to prepare, what physical setting to use, and how to arrange seating. These factors do not guarantee an effective meeting, but strategic analysis in these areas will increase effectiveness.

Figure 4–5   Seating Arrangements

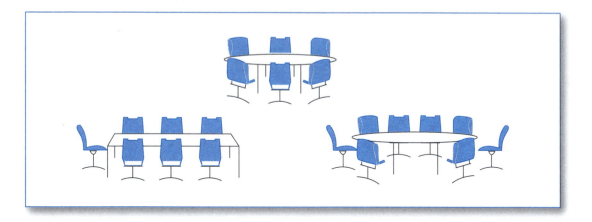

STRATEGIC CONSIDERATIONS FOR VIRTUAL MEETINGS

Companies operating in the global marketplace require their employees to connect and collaborate no matter where they are. From the employees' perspective, working in a virtual environment has widespread appeal. The number of US employees who work from home has grown by 80 percent since 2005, and by 2016, telecommuting is expected to increase another 21 percent to nearly 4 million.[27] For this model to be successful, flexibility, responsiveness, cost-effectiveness, and rapid response time are imperative. Clearly, managing virtual meetings calls for additional strategic considerations.

The seven strategic considerations described in the previous sections apply primarily to groups that are meeting face-to-face. However, the first six are also relevant to virtual meetings. The exception is Strategic Consideration 7—arrangement of the meeting room. When group members are geographically dispersed, this point is obviously moot. Although physical facilities and furniture do not affect the outcome of virtual meetings, technology does; electronic meetings can be derailed if the tech support is inadequate. Therefore, Strategic Consideration 8 addresses technology adequacy. Meeting leaders should do all they can to ensure that everyone will be able to hear and see each other during the conference.

Strategic Consideration 8: Technological Adequacy

In addition to building team relationships by emphasizing similarity, managers should ensure that technological channels connecting virtual team members are stable and strong. E-mail is a lean channel and usually asynchronous; minimal information can be transmitted, even when emoticons are used to indicate emotion. Teleconferencing is a richer channel, efficient, and relatively cost-effective, but it can be impractical when meeting members are in different time zones.

Online videoconferencing tools are proliferating. Among the more popular are Skype, GoToMeeting, WebEx, Adobe connect, Microsoft Lync, Team Hangout, and RingCentral. All are low cost and have even higher bandwidth than teleconferences, allowing participants to observe nonverbal behaviors. Some web conferencing software has capabilities for desktop sharing, encrypting, meeting through mobile devices, and even recording. On the other hand, video and audio quality may be problematic, and the technology may break down more frequently as sophistication increases. Managers must ensure that the technology is well supported so that their virtual teams can develop rapport and their meetings can achieve the work goals.

Managers should regularly check that cross team communication systems are working. During every virtual meeting, they should address this aspect of the project, discuss productive methods for interaction, and consider the latest technologies for team collaboration.

Strategic Consideration 9: Team Relationships

As described in Chapter 2, the outer layer of the strategic communication model consists of the organization's culture and climate. A trusting open climate makes it much easier to communicate freely. But when groups and teams "meet" only through technology, the hardware can form a barrier, making it more difficult to establish trust. In organizations where the cultural norm is to communicate exclusively through technological channels, as in a multinational corporation or a workforce of telecommuters, developing relationships among team members becomes even more of a challenge.

Today's cross functional work teams may never physically be in the same room. Members may work at home, in different offices, even in different parts of the world. Yet in order to accomplish their assignments, they must be able to communicate smoothly and freely. Wise meeting leaders will help their people to overcome geographical and technological barriers in order to develop trusting relationships. As you have learned, interpersonal communication builds relationships, relationships build trust, trust builds commitment, and commitment expedites productivity (Figure 4–6).

Understanding that virtual teams will become more productive when members have strong affiliation with each other, managers should encourage relationship building by applying the similarity-attraction principle. That is, team members will be more attracted to each other if they perceive that they are similar. In what ways can members of a team

Figure 4–6   Effects of Interpersonal Communication

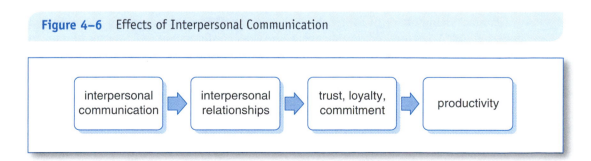

who work off-site possibly find similarity? Well, at a minimum, they have similar work values and goals. When virtual teams recognize that they are working toward common objectives with similar payoffs, then they will find it easier to work together. The manager should carefully and consistently communicate these common objectives and provide opportunities for frequent communication among the team members, thereby encouraging relationship development. The result will be increased productivity.

Strategic Consideration 10: Cultural Differences

Being culturally aware in a virtual environment, where people are based around the world, is even more important than in face-to-face settings. Cultural diversity has both positive and negative aspects. Diversity fosters increased creativity, innovation, and flexibility but may cause communication difficulties, misunderstandings, decreased cohesion, and increased conflict.[28] Managers must be aware of the cultural differences in their teams and promote cultural training for all members.

Once team members have learned the importance of cultural sensitivity, they can put teammates at ease by respecting the conventions of that culture. Writing styles, for example, vary from culture to culture. A direct, concise e-mail may be standard in the United States, but Japanese recipients will consider it rude and vulgar. In the Japanese culture, a more indirect, wordy, polite style is preferred. American business writers can easily show their awareness of these stylistic differences by adding -san or -sama when addressing Japanese teammates, much like Americans may address someone as sir or ma'am.[29]

When transnational team members are interacting orally rather than in writing, their fluency in English may be problematic. Sensitive managers should build in more time during teleconferences and perhaps hire translators. Nonverbal behavior, as will be discussed in Chapters 10 and 11 of this book, also varies from culture to culture. For example, direct eye contact is important in US meetings, but in many Eastern cultures, it is considered disrespectful. Therefore, when managers use videoconferencing tools in an attempt to allow their team to see each other's nonverbal cues of posture, facial expression, and voice tone, the risk of misunderstanding remains strong. Managers must decide whether these more expensive methods of communication are worth reducing the assumptions and barriers involved. Again, cultural diversity training can reduce the likelihood of misunderstandings and blunders in communication practice.

In summary, the skill sets required for success in managing effective virtual meetings are more complex than the skill sets required for success in managing face-to-face meetings. In addition to Strategic Considerations 1–6, managers of virtual teams must provide appropriate technology (Strategic Consideration 8), and training must be available to support the development of team relationships and cross-cultural communication competencies (Strategic Considerations 9 and 10). Participants in virtual meetings struggle to reach shared understanding, to coordinate perspectives, and to establish a sense of social presence, and these need to be acknowledged and dealt with by management.[30]

GROUP DECISION-MAKING FORMATS

One additional factor needs a meeting leader's attention. Whether a team or work group meets virtually or face-to-face, its leader should identify and follow a formal decision-making plan. This section describes three standard processes for reaching a group decision and explains which processes work best for virtual meetings and which work best for in-person meetings.

A diagnosis of the environment, task, group, and leader's personal preference will help to determine the appropriate decision-making format for the meeting. A formal plan is essential. Do not fall into the trap of believing that once the participants know the goal, everything will automatically fall into place. Both experience and research suggest group members are haphazard and unorganized in their discussion and decision attempts when managers fail to use organizing formats.[31]

Three approaches to decision-making are shown in Table 4–4 and are explained in the next sections. The appropriateness of each of these is determined by the objective of the meeting, the participants in the meeting, the leader's style preference, and whether the meeting is held face-to-face or electronically.

Rational Problem-Solving Process

The first decision-making format we will describe works well when the group meets face-to-face. Its validity is rooted in the fact that it is "rational"; that is, the process is how we think. In 1910, John Dewey described the steps that rational individuals use to solve a problem.[32] Most know these as the six stages to problem solving: (1) defining the problem, (2) analyzing the problem, (3) brainstorming the possible solutions, (4) determining the criteria that must be met to eliminate the problem, (5) selecting the best solution, and (6) implementing the solution (see Table 4-5). This process is an excellent conflict-resolution strategy.

Table 4–4 Decision-Making Formats

Type of Format	Applies to Face-to-Face Meetings	Applies to Virtual Meetings
Rational Problem-Solving	✓	
Nominal Group Technique	✓	✓
Delphi Technique		✓

Table 4–5   The Rational Problem-Solving Process

| 1. Define the problem |
| 2. Analyze the problem |
| 3. Brainstorm the possible solutions |
| 4. Determine the criteria that must be met to eliminate the problem |
| 5. Select the best solution |
| 6. Implement the solution |

When using this process in a meeting, it is critical to follow the sequence. People tend to begin to discuss solutions or even implementation of a solution before the problem has been precisely defined. However, it is critical to get everyone to agree on the problem being discussed before addressing solutions. One way of doing this is to write the problem on a flip chart or whiteboard so everyone can see it. This same procedure can be followed for each step to ensure progress and focus.

After agreeing on the definition and scope of the problem, the group must spend time analyzing it fully. Again, you may meet resistance, especially if the members are intimately familiar with the problem. However, exploring causes, effects, extent, and history of the problem may help the group avoid solutions that address mere symptoms rather than root causes of the problem.

The third step, brainstorming possible solutions, has received much attention in business literature. Alexander Osborn, an advertising executive, first described brainstorming as a special technique for facilitating the idea-generating portion of the decision process.[33]

The objective of brainstorming is to generate ideas rather than evaluate or analyze those ideas. A group can brainstorm successfully and produce a maximum number of ideas by adhering to three rules:

- Ideas are expressed freely without regard to quality. All ideas, no matter how unusual, are recorded.

- Criticism of the ideas produced is not allowed until all ideas have been expressed.

- Elaborations and combinations of previously expressed ideas are encouraged. The major strength of brainstorming is that one idea will create another. The ratio of high-quality ideas to the total number is not high, but often only one creative idea is needed for the solution.

Groups allowed to produce for longer work periods typically produce more ideas under brainstorming instructions than do individuals. Most groups continue to produce indefinitely, whereas individuals taper off.[34]

The fourth step is also important. The group must understand and honor required criteria for a "good" solution. Upper management sometimes imposes these criteria, or standards, on the group. Other times, the decision-making team may develop its own. Typical criteria are that a solution must be cost-effective, legal, timely, practical, and consistent with the organization's mission and/or values.

Step 5 in the rational decision-making process, selecting the best solution, is automatic in that it is a matter of comparing the list of criteria or standards with the list of brainstormed solutions. The idea from step 3 that best fits the criteria developed in step 4 now becomes the best solution. Following this process prevents groups from choosing a solution that is favored by someone with authority or someone who dominates the discussion. Rather, the best solution is chosen rationally.

As a final step, the group considers implementation of their solution. In today's business environment, where continuous quality improvement is stressed, it is important to put systems in place that will monitor how well the new solution is working. The monitoring systems can detect weaknesses and shortcomings before they create major damage and wipe out the good work of the problem-solving team.

Two other decision-making formats widely used in business are based on Dewey's classic process. They are the nominal group technique and the Delphi technique.

The Nominal Group Technique

Sometimes face-to-face meetings experience an imbalance of participation among the members. That is, some people dominate the discussion, and others are relatively silent. Common causes include unequal organizational status and varying interest levels among the group members. For whatever reason, the meeting leader can overcome such unbalanced input by applying the nominal group technique for decision making. This process may be adapted for virtual meetings, as well, if unbalanced participation is a symptom.

When using the nominal group technique (NGT), the meeting leader directs each participant to create separate lists of the advantages and disadvantages associated with the problem and solutions under discussion. After a predetermined time, the participants present their advantages and disadvantages, which are posted so everyone can see them, either in the room where the group has gathered or in a "virtual room," such as an electronic bulletin board. Then, members are directed to work alone again to rank all advantages and disadvantages from highest to lowest priority. After this, a master list is compiled. The participants can then discuss the issue based on the information presented in the master list. When groups follow this procedure, they generate a basis for group discussion that reflects all the participants' views that were individually developed by working alone.

The NGT has several advantages that a manager should consider when planning a meeting. One is that all participants can express their views without intimidation from more powerful or vocal group members. The procedure also ensures that each step in the rational problem-solving process is followed. Finally, it can save time because the meeting participants can generate their initial lists before the meeting. The NGT thus integrates the advantages of both group and individual creativity, whether or not the participants are ever physically together.[35]

The Delphi Technique

The Delphi technique is a unique group problem-solving process that does not require physical proximity of group members. This technique has been beneficial when team members are geographically dispersed or their schedules preclude a common meeting time. It is generally used with an ad hoc meeting of experts and with virtual teams who meet only electronically.

Delphi uses an initial questionnaire that elicits the participants' expert opinions on a topic. Once these opinions have been collected, all group members receive a second questionnaire listing others' contributions, and all are asked to evaluate each idea using several specified criteria. This step is then followed by a third questionnaire that reports the second-round ratings, a mean rating, and any consensus. The participants then revise their earlier ratings considering the average or consensus. A final questionnaire includes all ratings, the consensus, and remaining problems.

The advantages of the Delphi technique are that it does not require physical proximity and that it controls some of the possible disadvantages of face-to-face group decisions. The most vocal or highest-status person does not have an opportunity to control the group because everyone's comments are pooled. Also, the coordinator can guarantee the decision-making process does not omit any critical steps or ignore important comments.

In summary, managers should follow a pre-selected decision-making format to maximize the efficiency of the group meeting. A number of factors, including whether the meeting is face-to-face or electronic, will help the manager to determine which format is best. You may wonder which of the three formats described above yields a superior decision. Some research has been done in an attempt to answer that question, but the results indicate that the quality of decisions is generally higher with any of the three—Dewey's rational problem-solving process, the nominal group technique, or the Delphi—than when no particular format is followed and the discussion wanders freely.[36] Managers should consider decision-making formats to maximize group effectiveness.

SUMMARY

The team is a common personnel configuration today. Team meetings have advantages and disadvantages, including groupthink, with which managers should be familiar. To make effective use of meetings, a number of contingencies need to be reviewed. The first and most obvious consideration facing a manager is the stated objective. If the objective is a programmed decision or if a commitment does not present a special problem, a meeting may not be required.

Once it is clear that a meeting should be conducted, it is important to consider who should attend. Criteria for selecting meeting members include how many to invite, whose interests they represent, their knowledge and authority, and their team-abilities.

Next, a manager must make the premeeting arrangements. These involve deciding what should be on the agenda and which additional materials should be attached to the agenda. If the meeting will be face-to-face, the manager should decide on the physical arrangements (including seating) for the meeting. Overlooking any one of these questions may cause an omission that reduces meeting effectiveness.

After the arrangements have been prepared, managers need to select the appropriate leadership style for the situation, group, and objective. The selection of the appropriate leadership style will assist in the format choice. Project team leadership calls for special skills.

This chapter presents three decision-making formats for a meeting: the rational problem-solving approach, the nominal group technique, and the Delphi technique (which can be used for virtual meetings or geographically dispersed group members). Each of these approaches has inherent strengths and challenges.

Regardless of the format selected, disruptions can occur during a meeting, but they can be prevented if a manager takes precautions, including talking to potential disrupters ahead of time or planning special activities for them during the meeting. Once a disruption occurs, strategic communication can control it.

Finally, a manager's responsibility as the leader of a meeting includes the post-meeting follow-up. This follow-up may take the form of traditional meeting minutes, a short memo, or an e-mail and an effort to ensure that various commitments have been met. Also, formal evaluation of the meeting helps to determine ways a future meeting could be improved.

When virtual teams meet via technology, three further strategic considerations become relevant. First, managers must make extra efforts to build team relationships, which will pay off in increased trust, commitment, and productivity. Second, managers must provide training in cultural diversity to build their virtual teams' awareness of communication style differences in writing and speaking. Third, managers must maximize the technological platforms upon which their virtual teams must perform. Whether the teams meet by e-mail, teleconference, or web conference, adequate technology support is imperative.

Cases for Small-Group Discussion

CASE 4–1

Teams and Technology

Team Green was ecstatic. Their analysis of the firm's latest investment projects had been chosen over the Blue and Red teams yet again, for the sixth time in a row. The competition, the brainchild of CEO Roger Cannon, had been going on for three years, once every quarter. The teams were to analyze the projects under consideration and present their analysis and recommendations to the top management and any board members that wanted to attend. Managers and directors were all together for quarterly corporate retreats in remote locations, so the presentations were accomplished via videoconference from the company to the location of the retreat. For the first year and a half, the teams were fairly competitive, but then Team Green had dominated the competition and the reward: time off and three-day paid vacations at a Destin, Florida, resort.

The members of the other two teams had become disgruntled, and Team Red seemed to have given up, turning in a marginal analysis and a short, minimal presentation. Rather than foster a cooperative and edifying mood, the competition had taken a turn for the worse, creating hostility and suppressing communication among the groups. Roger had noticed the trend away from the analysts debating and negotiating with each other, but he did not want to fail in his rewarding of excellence. The competition, he felt, had greatly enhanced the quality of the firm's capital investment decisions.

Prior to the establishment of the competition, the analysts had been one big group, arguing back and forth about the best way to analyze the firm's projects and about the best decision. Roger wanted to enjoy the benefits of both systems but wondered if that was possible given the current state of affairs.

QUESTIONS

1. Was the competition a good idea? What are the benefits and drawbacks?

2. How does the use of videoconferencing technology affect participants' attitudes toward the other teams and teamwork in general?

3. Suppose you are hired as a communication consultant, with the task of coming up with a system to reward excellence but avoid hard feelings and discouragement. What would you change?

CASE 4–2

The Regional Relationships

Jerry Blaire is the regional manager of a national electronics franchise retail store. This franchise has over two hundred locally owned stores throughout the eastern United States. As the regional manager, Blaire is responsible for an urban area in which there are eight stores plus the remainder of the state, which has another six stores.

The regional manager is the liaison between the manager-owner of the stores and the corporate offices in Boston. Responsibilities include monitoring the individual stores to ensure the provisions of the franchise agreement are maintained, dealing with any complaints from managers, taking product orders, introducing new products, and managing the regional advertising program.

Blaire has been with this company for seven years, and before that, he worked with a home entertainment retail store for three years after he earned his degree in marketing.

Blaire is responsible for coordinating the advertising campaign for all fourteen stores in the region. A major part of the campaign involves store hours, which had traditionally been from 10 a.m. to 8 p.m., Monday through Saturday. The minimum number of hours required by the national office is 40 per week. However, several of the managers have been pressuring lately to change the store hours, especially those from downtown areas. They maintain that their business is minimal after 6 p.m., so they would like to close earlier. Meanwhile, the suburban stores want to stay open later because they do more business in the evening. According to the provisions of the franchise agreement, all the stores in a region must maintain the same store hours.

The problem is getting more attention from the store managers and is a frequent topic of discussion as Blaire makes his visits. Blaire has decided to have a meeting for all the managers, so he can systematically analyze the problem of store hours.

QUESTIONS

1. What type of leadership style should Blaire use in this meeting? Why?

2. What meeting format would you recommend?

3. What special problems would you anticipate for this meeting?

4. What preliminary arrangements are particularly important for this meeting?

5. Do you think it is a good idea for Blaire to have a meeting, or should he make this decision about hours himself?

CASE 4–3

Keeping the Meeting on the Topic

Waith Manufacturing Company's data processing department was preparing to implement a new computerized production information system at its new Madison plant. The project was divided into two parts. One consisted of the installation of a new computer network at the plant and the development of new database programs. The second involved hooking the plant's network into the company intranet so all departments had access to the production reports.

Alonzo Mendoza was the systems analyst responsible for the development and implementation of the project. Janet DeLaura was a lead programmer under Mendoza working on the plant side of the project. Bill Synge was the other lead programmer responsible for the intranet. Mendoza scheduled a series of weekly status meetings with DeLaura and Synge to ensure the project was moving along as scheduled and to allow for discussion of critical problems. One month before the scheduled implementation of the project, Mendoza called a special meeting to develop the actual series of tasks needed for the final system conversion. During this meeting, Mendoza outlined the major tasks concerning the whole project that had to be done on that last day.

He then solicited input from DeLaura and Synge. DeLaura spoke up immediately and began talking about several new problems that had surfaced on her side of the project. Mendoza interrupted her, saying those problems would be discussed at the regular status meeting since this meeting had been called to develop final conversion tasks only. DeLaura became irritated and was silent for a few minutes. Synge said he had a few items to add to the conversion list and covered the first two tasks. Then he said the last task covered reminded him of a current problem he had in the interface program. Mendoza replied brusquely that only conversion tasks would be discussed at this meeting. Neither DeLaura nor Synge had much to say during the rest of the meeting.

QUESTIONS

1. What would you have done to keep the meeting on the right topic?

2. What technique might Mendoza have used to avoid interfering with the flow of ideas?

3. What might DeLaura and Synge have done to improve communications?

Student Study Site

Visit the Student Study Site at **study.sagepub.com/hynes6e** for web quizzes, video links, web resources, and cases studies.

Notes

1. American Management Association, *AMA 2012 Critical Skills Survey*, accessed August 25, 2014, http://www.amanet.org/uploaded/2012-Critical-Skills-Survey.pdf.
2. Rick Casey, "The Katrina Coffee Klatch," *Houston Chronicle*, September 14, 2005, p. 1B.
3. H. Simon, *The New Science of Management Decision* (New York: Harper and Row, 1960).
4. P. S. Goodman, E. Ravlin, and M. Schminke, "Understanding Groups in Organizations," in *Research in Organizational Behavior,* vol. 9, eds. I. B. M. Staw and L. L. Cummings (Greenwich, CT: JAI Press, 1987), pp. 121–173.
5. Lester Coch and John R. P. French Jr., "Overcoming Resistance to Change," *Human Relations* 1, no. 4 (1948): pp. 512–532.
6. "Korn/Ferry International Executive Quiz," n.d., accessed April 9, 2006, www.ekorn-ferry.com.
7. Adapted from James W. Moore, *Some Folks Feel the Rain: Others Just Get Wet* (Nashville, TN: Dimensions for Living, 1999). Used by permission. All rights reserved.
8. Richard H. Hall, *Organizations,* 5th ed. (Englewood Cliffs, NJ: Prentice Hall, 1991), p. 180.
9. M. E. Gist, E. A. Locks, and M. S. Taylor, "Organizational Behavior: Group Structure, Process, and Effectiveness," *Journal of Management* 13, no. 2 (1987): pp. 237–257.
10. I. L. Janis, *Victims of Groupthink* (Boston: Houghton Mifflin, 1972).
11. G. Moorhead, R. Ference, and C. P. Neck, "Group Decision Fiascoes Continue: Space Shuttle Challenger and a Revised Groupthink Framework," *Human Relations* 44, no. 4 (1991): pp. 539–550.
12. T. Hensley and G. Griffin, "Victims of Groupthink: The Kent State University Board of Trustees and the 1977 Gymnasium Controversy," *Journal of Conflict Resolution* 30, no. 4 (1986): pp. 497–531.
13. C. Von Bergen and R. J. Kirk, "Groupthink: When Too Many Heads Spoil the Decision," *Management Review,* March 1978, p. 46.
14. Robert Towensen, *Up the Organization* (Greenwich, CT: Fawcett, 1970), p. 171.
15. P. Slater, "Contrasting Correlates of Group Size," *Sociometry* 21, no. 1 (1958): pp. 129–139.
16. J. M. Levine and R. Moreland, "Progress in Small Group Research," *Annual Review of Psychology* 41 (1990), pp. 585–634.
17. K. G. Stoneman and A. M. Dickinson, "Individual Performance as a Function of Group Contingencies and Group Size," *Journal of Organizational Behavior Management* 10, no. 1 (1989): pp. 131–150.
18. N. Shawchuck, *Taking a Look at Your Leadership Style* (Downers Grove, IL: Organizational Research Press, 1978).
19. Brad Johnson, "Secrets of Successful IT Teams: Socially Connected Employees," *CIO*, May 9, 2008, The Playoff Push section, http://www.cio.com/article/2436381/staff-management/secrets-of-successful-it-teams--socially-connected-employees.html.

20. Liz Hughes, "Do's and Don'ts of Effective Team Leadership," *WIB, Magazine of the American Business Women's Association,* January–February 2004, p. 10.

21. John E. Jones, "Dealing with Disruptive Individuals in Meetings," *1980 Annual Handbook for Group Facilitators,* ed. J. William Pfeiffer and John E. Jones (San Diego, CA: University Associates, 1980), p. 161.

22. D. J. Isenberg, "Group Polarization: A Critical Review and Meta-analysis," *Journal of Personality and Social Psychology* 50, no. 4 (1986): pp. 1141–1151.

23. Lawrence N. Loban, "Question: The Answer to Meeting Participation," *Supervision,* January 1972, pp. 11–13.

24. "3M Meeting Network: Articles and Advice," n.d., accessed June 12, 2006, http://www.3m.com/meetingnetwork/readingroom/meetingguide_minutes.html.

25. J. R. Hackman and C. G. Morris, "Group Tasks, Group Interaction Process and Group Performance Effectiveness: A Review and Proposed Integration," in *Advances in Experimental Social Psychology,* vol. 8, ed. I. L. Berkowitz (New York: Academic Press, 1975), pp. 1–50.

26. Adam Bryant, "If You Don't Know Your Co-Workers, Mix Up the Chairs," *The New York Times,* July 29, 2012, Sunday Business section, p. 2.

27. Global Workplace Analytics report, September 2013, http://www.globalworkplaceanalytics.com/telecommuting-statistics.

28. Rathtana V. Chhay and Brian H. Kleiner, "Effective Communication in Virtual Teams," *Industrial Management*, 55, no. 4 (2013): pp. 28–30.

29. Ibid.

30. G. R. Berry, "Enhancing Effectiveness on Virtual Teams," *Journal of Business Communication*, 48, no. 2 (April 2011): pp. 186–206. doi:10.1177/0021943610397270.

31. David R. Weibold, "Making Meetings More Successful: Plans, Formats, and Procedures for Group Problem-Solving," *Journal of Business Communication* 16, no. 3 (Summer 1979): p. 8.

32. John Dewey, *How We Think* (Boston: D. C. Heath, 1910).

33. Alexander F. Osborn, *Applied Imagination* (New York: Scribners, 1957).

34. Marvin E. Shaw, *Group Dynamics,* 3rd ed. (New York: McGraw-Hill, 1981), p. 57.

35. Andrè L. Delbecq, Andrew H. Van De Ven, and David H. Gustafson, *Group Techniques for Program Planning* (Glenview, IL: Scott, Foresman, 1975).

36. Robert C. Erffmeyer and Irving M. Lane, "Quality and Acceptance of an Evaluative Task: The Effects of Four Group Decision-Making Formats," *Group and Organizational Studies* 9, no. 4 (December 1984): pp. 509–529.

CHAPTER 5

Making Presentations

It usually takes me more than three weeks to prepare a good impromptu speech.

—Mark Twain, American humorist and author

Managers today find that presentation skills are important for a multitude of situations. At any time, they might be called on to present a product report, a marketing status report, a persuasive report to convince upper management to accept a new product design, a financial report, or an after-dinner speech to honor the winner of a cost-saving campaign.

For several reasons, the value of competency in presentational speaking is likely to grow.[1] First, as organizations become more complex, managers are often called on to present proposals and make explanations to large numbers of people. Second, products and services also are becoming more complex. The public may require detailed explanations of their function and/or design.

No matter what the topic, a formal presentation is a critical form of communication. It is generally given to a group of decision makers on an important topic. It is essential that these decision makers have timely and understandable information.[2] To be effective in making such presentations, managers need to understand essential strategies. To assist you in meeting these challenges, this chapter describes steps in planning, organizing, and delivering formal presentations.

After offering general strategies for formal presentations, this chapter describes ways to succeed in two special situations: media speaking and team presentations. The chapter concludes by identifying strategies for organizing and delivering informal, impromptu presentations. Whether in a meeting, on stage, or at a quasi-social event, if you find yourself in the spotlight, you need to shine. Knowing how to analyze the audience, organize your thoughts, and deliver your message with confidence will not only ensure that you have made your point but will also enhance your professional image.

PLAN YOUR PRESENTATION

When beginning to think about your formal presentation, consider your purpose, length of time to speak, and audience.

Purpose

The first step in planning an effective presentation is to determine the purpose. The purpose of business presentations is generally to inform, convince, or cause action. Some presentations have multiple purposes. When, for example, an engineering sales representative presents a product design to a client's engineering management group, he might have two purposes in mind. He will want to inform the audience of the product's technical features, and he will want to persuade the group to order the product.

In some situations, the exact purpose is easy to determine, but in others, the purpose may be complex because the speaker and the audience have two different goals. For instance, the audience may want to know the most cost-effective location for a new manufacturing plant. The speaker, however, may want the audience to accept a certain location that has a special need for economic development. That is, the audience wants to be informed, whereas the speaker wants to persuade.

The purpose may also vary within the group. Consider an audience that consists of five people: a vice president, a production superintendent, a director of finance, a marketing manager, and a personnel director. Suppose they were all attending a presentation comparing the *relative success* of two products introduced in a test market three months ago. What is relative success to each audience member? Each will look at the products from a different perspective because of differing functional responsibilities. The marketing manager may think in terms of market share, whereas the finance manager may look at only the cost factor. What type of information should the speaker emphasize?

The power and status of the different audience members can also influence the overall purpose. One member's viewpoint may initially differ from that of another member, but the more powerful person can quickly influence the less powerful member. In the previous example, the vice president may simply say that the most important consideration is the expansion of production facilities required by the two new products. Suddenly, the definition of relative success has changed again. Though the goal of informing the audience has remained the same, the information required to meet this goal has been shaped by the audience.

The best way to ensure clarity of purpose is to write out a purpose statement. Not only does this act force you to think about the purpose, but the written statement can then also be presented to an associate or to likely

STOP AND THINK

1. Think of a public service message you recently saw on television or heard on the radio. While the primary purpose may have been to inform, can you identify any other purposes?

2. What do you think the sponsor of the message was trying to accomplish?

Figure 5–1   Your Presentation Purpose

I want to tell you _____

(content)

So you will _____

(purpose)

audience members for their reaction. The feedback will help you define the purpose clearly and accurately. Figure 5–1 will help you write out your purpose statement. Just fill in the blanks.

Once you have clearly established your purpose, you are ready to consider cost and time to determine what expense can be justified. One five-minute presentation might involve hundreds of work hours and cost thousands of dollars; another might require a minimum of effort. As with any managerial communication, a manager must make strategic decisions.

Length of the Presentation

Sometimes, managers have no choice here, as when they are given a set amount of time to speak during a meeting or conference. In such cases, it is crucial to stay within the assigned time limit. The audience is probably listening to a number of such presentations. When many speakers exceed their time limits, the audience becomes less and less receptive to the proposals of the transgressors. All they can think about is escape.

Even when speakers are given some choice on the length of the presentations, most make them too long rather than too short. Remember that it is difficult to hold adults' attention beyond twenty minutes. When a presentation goes beyond fifteen minutes, divide it into major segments by using reviews, questions, or graphics. One of history's most inspirational public speakers, President Franklin Delano Roosevelt, advised that when presenting one should "be sincere, be brief, be seated."

Audience understanding does not necessarily last as long as the speaker's. Just because a speaker is eloquent for an hour does not mean others are listening and understanding. To improve effectiveness, watch the audience for nonverbal and verbal feedback to evaluate comprehension.[3] This feedback will probably indicate it is best to keep the presentation short. If they want to know more, they will ask for it.

Audience Analysis

At the same time that effective managers analyze their speaking purpose, they begin to analyze the audience. In any communication process, people naturally tend to become self-centered. Thus, a speaker may concentrate on his or her interests and forget about the audience. One group of consultants on oral presentations noted that managers often prepare messages that fail to tell the listeners what they want and need to hear but instead focus on the speaker's interests.[4]

The most successful presentations are prepared with a particular audience in mind and are organized to suit their knowledge, attitudes, likes, and dislikes. Many presentations are technically well delivered, but they fail because the speakers do not anticipate audience reaction.

Though audience analysis is part of the *pretalk* preparation, a speaker should also be ready to analyze on the spot. During delivery, the presentation may be modified to reflect audience factors not available in advance. For instance, you would need to alter your presentation if you found that a critical decision maker needing special information decided at the last minute to attend the presentation. Nevertheless, when a thorough audience analysis precedes a presentation, few last-minute adjustments should be required.

The Audience Analysis Worksheet provided at the end of this chapter is designed to assist you in analyzing audiences. Once all the questions have been answered, it might be beneficial to ask another person to answer them as well, to compare answers. This feedback is especially important when the presentation is critical but little is known about the audience.

If you already know the audience well, say, for an internal presentation, a thorough analysis is not necessary. For instance, an internal auditor who gives a quarterly report to a bank's board of directors may not need a separate analysis each quarter. However, a periodic review of the audience may remind the speaker about some of its special characteristics. It may be easy to forget that the interests, technical knowledge, or attitudes differ from one board member to another; thus, a quick audience analysis will help to reorient the speaker.

> ## STOP AND THINK
>
> Recall a time when you had to deliver the same message to two different audiences. For example, you might have just had a collision while driving your car, and you now had to tell both your mother and your insurance agent. How would you tailor the message to each listener?

ORGANIZE YOUR PRESENTATION

The second step is organizing the presentation. Every presentation has a beginning, a middle, and an ending. These three main parts are described next. However, to a great extent, your purpose and audience will determine how you structure your presentation.

Introduction

The most crucial part of a presentation is the introduction. A presentation should begin with a statement that captures the audience's attention. Quite often, a speaker will begin with humor or trite remarks. Depending on the gravity of your message, these timeworn openings may not be appropriate.

Though common, a speaker should rarely begin with an apology. Beginning with "I know that you do not want to be here," or "I realize that it is late in the day," or "I am not much of a speaker" does little to enhance speaker credibility and may detract from the audience's perception of the meeting. Instead, begin the presentation with a positive statement that has impact. Strategies for getting the attention of business audiences are listed next:

- *A startling statement:* If our costs continue to increase over the next five years at the rate they have in the past five, we will have to charge over $150 for our lowest-priced shirt. Today, I will present four strategies for reducing costs in . . .

- *A hypothetical statement:* What would happen if we could no longer obtain the silver we need to produce XY 115? I am going to show you a viable substitute for that metal.

- *Some historical event or story:* Just eight years ago this week, we purchased the Bordin division, our first major acquisition. This presentation will review the progress of our purchases.

- *A rhetorical question:* What will the inflation rate be in 2018? Will the energy problem continue? This presentation will outline the reasons why we need a market projection plan.

- *Reference to some current event:* On Tuesday, February 19, Millville had a chemical fire that killed five people and injured fifteen. To avoid that kind of disaster in our operations, we need to increase our budget for safety training.

- *A quotation:* The national director of the health department has stated, "The number one health problem today is alcoholism. One in ten Americans has a drinking problem." This serious problem is one of the many reasons we need an employee assistance program.

- *A personal anecdote:* The other day I was talking to one of our longtime customers when she said the reason she keeps banking here is that nothing ever changes. That got me thinking about our reputation for stability in a chaotic economy. But I also began to wonder whether we've become stagnant.

Whatever strategy is selected, a speaker's first goal is to develop a dynamic, attention-getting opening.[5] Its success will set the tone for the rest of the presentation. Next, the speaker should clearly state the purpose (inform, convince, cause action, inspire, introduce, congratulate, and so on) and the topic. Even if your purpose and topic were disclosed on the agenda or by your meeting moderator, it is a good idea to restate them in your introduction to avoid any confusion.

The discussion of listening in Chapter 9 indicates the difficulty of maintaining attention for a long period. By telling your listeners what is to come and why, you encourage them to make an effort. Thus, the third part of your introduction should establish the audience's motivation to listen. The speaker explains the significance of what the audience is about to hear and how it pertains to their interests and needs. A common error is to focus instead on the significance of the content to the *speaker*. While statements such as "I care deeply about this" might increase speaker credibility, they do not always lead to the listeners' agreeing to care, too. The best word to use at this point is "you," as in "After hearing my presentation, *you* will be able to . . ." Focusing on audience benefits will also help build the speaker's credibility, which is especially critical in persuasive speaking.

In some situations, it may also be appropriate to give the audience some directions regarding interruptions. For instance, you may ask them to jot down their questions and raise them after your remarks are finished. Unfortunately, in small meetings, the listeners will often feel free to interrupt with questions. It is important not to let the audience take control of your presentation. On the other hand, you can ask meeting members for their reaction and maintain a dialogue throughout the presentation. Effective speakers usually stay away from the "I talk, you listen" syndrome, which often loses the interest of the group.

One optional subsection of the introduction is the establishment of the speaker's credentials. Obviously, if the audience knows the speaker well, this can be omitted. For external or new audiences, however, it is important that they perceive the speaker as an expert on the topic. It is risky to rely on the meeting moderator's introduction to achieve this goal. Instead, during your opening remarks, you might describe the research you conducted, the extent of your involvement in the topic, your position title, or even an anecdote that will enhance your credibility.

The final subsection should be a preview of the main points you will cover. Forecasting your main points will clarify the structure of the presentation and help your audience stay on track. You might even enumerate the points so your audience can "count down" as they listen. This preview acts as a transition between the introduction and the body of your presentation.

Table 5–1 summarizes the parts of a presentation introduction: an attention-getting opening, a purpose statement, motivation to listen, any ground rules regarding questions/participation (optional), establishment of speaker credibility (optional), and a preview of the main points. Next, we will describe strategies for organizing the body of your presentation. Since organization is determined by the speaker's purpose, organization of persuasive presentations is discussed in a separate section from organization of informative presentations.

Persuasive Presentations

As mentioned above, the purpose of a business presentation is generally to inform or to persuade, and the body of your presentation should be organized according to your purpose. This section shows you some basic organizational structures for the body of a persuasive presentation.

Table 5–1   Parts of the Introduction

Attention step
Purpose statement
Motivation to listen
Directions about interruptions (optional)
Speaker credibility (optional)
Preview of main points

Howell and Bormann discuss three patterns that provide meaningful strategies for persuasive situations: the problem-solving pattern, the state-the-case-and-prove-it approach, and the psychological-progressive pattern.[6]

The first pattern, *problem solving,* is most often effective in the discussion of a relatively complicated problem, especially if the audience is largely ignorant of the facts or is likely to be hostile to the message. With this approach, the speaker leads the audience through a series of steps, beginning with a definition of the problem, then moving to an exploration of the problem (which includes an examination of causes and effects), then enumerating and evaluating representative solutions, and, when appropriate, recommending the best solution.

The manager using this plan must be especially well prepared on all aspects of the situation. The audience may not be familiar with the problem, its causes, and potential remedies or an objective and logical solution. It is the most common pattern of argument in business presentations.

The second pattern of organization for persuasion, *state the case and prove it,* is relatively simple. It entails the straightforward development of a central thesis with supporting arguments. Normally, each supporting element begins with a contention or topic sentence followed immediately by substantiation. Typically, the pattern consists of an introduction followed by a thesis statement; then, each supporting contention has appropriate elaboration and support. The presentation closes with a summary repeating the proposition.

Whereas the problem-solving pattern is an inductive organizational approach, the state-the-case-and-prove-it approach is deductive. It begins with a general conclusion and then justifies it. This second approach is appropriate for organizing discussions of familiar much-argued topics. The audience familiar with a topic has no need to explore it gradually and comprehensively. It is also used in advocacy, such as courtroom settings.

The third organizational strategy, the *psychological-progressive pattern,* involves five steps: (1) arouse, (2) dissatisfy, (3) gratify, (4) visualize, and (5) act. Applying this pattern, a manager first uses an appropriate attention-getter. The next task is to demonstrate the nature and urgency of the problem in a way that sets out the difficulties, tensions, or pathos of a specific situation of immediate concern. Then, the speaker links his/her recommendation with the problem so the decision-making audience can understand the proposal as a viable solution.

The accepting audience usually needs to be moved both rationally and emotionally. Thus, the manager should focus on helping the audience to visualize how the recommendation will remedy the situation. Demonstrating the solution's implementation, or providing a "free sample," often will clinch the audience's decision to comply. Finally, the speaker should state specifically and concretely what the audience must *do* or *believe* after listening to the presentation. Basically, the psychological-progressive pattern is a problem-solving approach that is ideally suited to presentations designed to innovate or effect change. It is the typical structure of television commercials.

A city manager asking the city council for an additional $300,000 in the budget for snow-removal equipment gives a clear example of the psychological-progressive approach. The request was made during June because the new budget began July 1.

Remember last February when we had to cancel our city council meeting because of the snow and ice on the streets? Besides that some of us couldn't get to work, children couldn't get to school, and in some cases, it was even difficult to buy groceries (**arouse**).

This was not only an inconvenience; it was a potentially dangerous situation. Emergency health care could have been a problem. Fortunately, no emergencies developed. Furthermore, it cost employees lost work time, and it made our city look inefficient. Our city works manager, who has been with us more than fifteen years, was extremely demoralized at the inability to do anything about the situation due to the shortage of equipment (**dissatisfy**).

This problem can be solved with the purchase of four additional plows. These plows have been offered at a special price from Kast Manufacturing in Minneapolis, which has more than twenty years of experience with snowplows. They also provide free delivery of the plows and a three-year warranty on all the hydraulic systems and an eight-year warranty on the main blade and all structural components. In other words, this purchase will take care of our needs for a long time.

With this addition and the resolution of the snow-removal problem, this council will be identified as a group with vision and the ability for long-range planning rather than short-term reactions (**gratify and visualize**).

I am asking you to approve an additional $300,000 for next year's budget so that we can purchase four more snowplows. This could then become part of the city works equipment budget (**action**). This action will resolve our snow-removal problem next year and for many years in the future.

Persuasion Variables

As the preceding discussion indicated, different persuasive approaches are suited to different occasions or circumstances. To be a truly strategic attempt at persuasion, however, your efforts and ultimately your success should be moderated by a number of variables. These variables are categorized under the labels of sender, message, receiver, and context (see Figure 5–2).[7] The strategic communication model discussed in Chapter 2 provides background information about each of these variables. Context is described as a factor in the model's first, outermost layer. Sender and receiver variables are described in the second layer of the model. And message variables appear in the third layer.

Among variables associated with the *sender* of a persuasive message, probably the most significant variable is the speaker's credibility. Dimensions of speaker credibility include competence and trustworthiness; education, occupation, and experience; the citation of evidence; and the position advocated (in other words, how much of a change in attitude the speaker is asking for). Whether or not the speaker is liked will probably affect success

Figure 5–2   Persuasion Variables

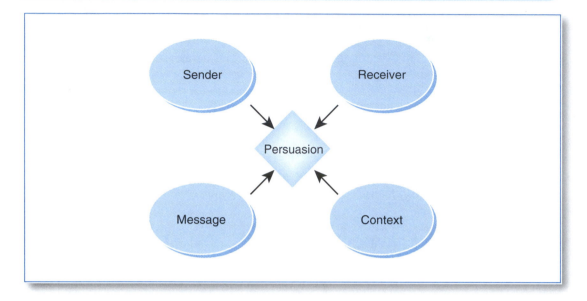

in persuading. Also, the degree of similarity between the speaker and the audience frequently affects success. Even physical attractiveness has been linked to persuasiveness in some studies.

A number of *message* variables can contribute to the success of a persuasive effort. The order of the information is one variable. Should a persuader be direct or indirect? Research indicates that the indirect approach is generally best for hostile audiences. Another factor involves whether a person should be explicit or implicit in stating what is desired. Though most studies indicate that being explicit is generally best, some evidence supports being implicit for audiences that are highly intelligent and educated and/or familiar with the subject.

Another issue relevant to message content is whether a persuader should ignore or refute opposing arguments. Usually it is best to refute them. Business audiences typically expect the persuader to address relevant obstacles. Finally, most studies conclude that concrete examples are more persuasive than statistical summaries, because they are more vivid and bring the evidence to life. Business presenters often believe that "the numbers" are automatically persuasive. However, specific cases, stories of dissatisfied customers and the like can be far more convincing due to their emotional impact.

Among *receiver* variables, one might consider the general persuasibility of the person. Some people are simply more susceptible to persuasion than are others. Are there personality traits related to ease or difficulty with which a receiver is persuaded? Research provides inconsistent answers to that question. For example, some studies show self-esteem positively related to persuasibility, whereas others show a negative relationship. One possible explanation is that some personality traits provide effects that both enhance and prohibit persuasion. For example, intelligent receivers would be better able to understand persuasive messages, but they would also be better able to see weaknesses in a message and think of counterarguments.

Receiver readiness to accept appeals is a complex factor. Successful persuasive speakers conduct extensive audience analyses and plan to present appeals that are most likely to move their listeners. Audience demographics, knowledge levels, and attitudes all must be considered when choosing material for presentation. For example, a manager persuading an audience of factory workers to adopt a new process should explain the benefits of the process to the workers, such as improved safety, rather than benefits to the company, such as increased profitability or productivity. Hourly employees may interpret management buzzwords, such as *efficiency* as "layoffs" or *quality* as "more work."

Context variables include primacy/recency effects, media, and persistence effects. In general, the order of points in a persuasive message (first or second) is not related to success. There is, however, some evidence that primacy effects are more likely to be found with interesting, controversial, and familiar topics, so begin with your strongest reason when persuading a hostile audience. Recency effects are more common with topics that are relatively uninteresting, noncontroversial, and unfamiliar, so build toward your strongest reason when persuading an apathetic audience.

With regard to the many media available today, research shows that audiences are more easily persuaded in face-to-face situations than when the message is filtered through media such as teleconference or video. One exception is the written word—audiences tend to believe what they read, either in books, onscreen, or online. But electronic, visual, and auditory media appear to act as a buffer. A disembodied voice or a televised image can be dramatic, but the most powerful speakers prefer to look directly at their listeners as they present their case. This phenomenon helps to explain the amount of time, money, and effort that political candidates expend traveling and speaking to voters instead of relying solely on media coverage.

The last context variable is the persistence of the persuasive message. Generally, persuasive effects will decline over time. Thus, for maximum effectiveness, persuasive messages should be delivered as temporally close as possible to the point of decision or action. Thus, politicians usually spend the bulk of their advertising budget in the week before the election.

Though no one can prescribe a guaranteed plan for persuading people, managers should consider the variables earlier described as they develop their persuasive strategies. To the extent that you do, you should find that your rate of persuasive success increases appreciably.

STOP AND THINK

A job interview is a high-stakes persuasive situation. Analyze your communication strategy during your latest job interview by answering these questions about the four persuasion variables.

1. How did you enhance your credibility? (sender)

2. When answering questions, did you use direct or indirect order? Why? (message)

3. In what ways did you adapt your message to the receiver? (audience)

4. Were you one of the first or last applicants interviewed? How do you think that affected the hiring decision? (context)

Ethical Persuasion

Before turning to the topic of informative presentations, it is appropriate to consider the importance of taking the high road in persuasive speaking. Ethical persuasion calls for the speaker to tell the truth, the whole truth, and nothing but the truth. A persuasive speaker who misleads the listeners, whether deliberately or purposefully, will lose credibility and lose business.

Dr. Anne Bradstreet Grinols, a business professor at Baylor University who specializes in ethics, suggests strategies for ethical persuasion that are based on audience analysis. Using terms from force field analysis, she recommends beginning by identifying the "driving forces" behind the change in belief or behavior that the speaker is advocating. What do the listeners need to know? What do they care about? Driving forces are good reasons to say yes.

Second, she recommends identifying the "restraining forces" that are roadblocks to the advocated change in belief or behavior. What will prevent the listeners from acting? What arguments against the change will listeners find compelling? Restraining forces are reasons to say no.

Third, Grinols recommends that persuasive speakers tell the story that listeners need to hear by reinforcing the benefits of making the advocated change and removing the barriers to making the advocated change. The story, of course, must always be truthful and respectful of the listeners.[8]

Informative Presentations

We have seen that managers generally use three organizational patterns to develop the body of their persuasive presentations: the problem-solving pattern, the state-the-case-and-prove-it pattern, and the psychological-progressive pattern. But what if the purpose of the presentation is to describe or inform rather than to persuade? In informative speaking situations, it is best to organize the information in a definite sequence. Clarity may demand that a subject be presented one way as opposed to another, or the subject itself may suggest the best pattern or arrangement. Some arrangement possibilities and examples of appropriate topics for each sequence are listed next.

- *Spatial or geographic:* Description of our new facility's layout

- *Political and economic categories:* Sales of our product line for various social groups

- *Importance:* Changes to employees' benefits package

- *Chronological:* History and future of our company

- *Advantages and disadvantages:* Various models of fax machines on the market

- *Comparison and contrast:* Where we stand among competitors in our industry

- *Structure and function:* New management layer being added to our company

A typical informative speaking situation is when a manager must explain new work procedures or processes. Giving instructions can be a challenge. The wrong strategy is simply telling employees once what to do, ending with "Do you have any questions?" Listeners may hesitate to ask questions for fear of seeming uncooperative or unintelligent. So instead, they return to their tasks, try out the new procedure, and make mistakes. Rather than risk the boss's criticism, they may ask a coworker for help, thus often compounding the problems and errors.

A better strategy for giving instructions is to use *tell—show—do*. First, the manager explains the steps in the new procedure, contrasting it with the current one. If the task is complex, the manager should cluster the steps into groups or stages. For example, instead of describing a twelve-step procedure, the speaker could describe three stages, with four steps per stage. Dividing a body of information into smaller gulps makes it less daunting to listeners. After telling the audience about the new procedure, the manager shows the audience how to do it, either demonstrating it personally or using a model. More audiences are visual learners than auditory learners, so a demonstration is often very effective. Finally, the manager lets the employees try the new procedure themselves. The manager should offer liberal feedback and encouragement as she observes their efforts, since positive reinforcement is a powerful motivator for learning.

Whatever the division of the topic or the order in which it is to be presented, it is important to have a definite, logical, and strategic plan for the body of an informative presentation. Adding smooth transitions is the key to the clarity of the plan's organization. A bridge or link must exist between units so the audience can follow the organizational plan. As the speaker moves to a new unit, this link may take the form of a simple announcement that a new unit will now be discussed. More helpful to the audience, however, is a transition that explains how the next point will compare with the previous one. A transition that begins with a review and follows with a preview is sometimes known as a *Janus statement*, after the god in Roman mythology, Janus, who had two faces. Another device is the repetition of key words or phrases for emphasis. Examples of transitions at four levels of complexity appear in Table 5–2. A wise informative speaker will use transitions liberally to keep the audience on track.

Table 5–2 Types of Transitions

Function	Example
Show relationship between ideas	and, in addition, also, or, however, on the other hand, by comparison, furthermore
Enumerate ideas	first, to begin, my second point is, finally, in conclusion
Summarize ideas	Now that we have discussed its features, let's turn our attention to its benefits
Emphasize ideas	If you remember nothing else, please remember this—

Evidence

Whether your purpose is to inform or persuade, your business presentation must include evidence. The type of information and corresponding research required largely depend on which of the two types of evidence is required: fact or opinion. Evidence of *fact* is an objective description of something using empirical evidence without interpretation or judgment. A fact can be proven—that is, it is either true or untrue. Evidence of *opinion* is the application of interpretation and judgment rather than truth.

Business speakers often are expected to present facts, especially statistics, as evidence for their main points. Audiences respect speakers who "deliver the numbers." However, research consistently shows that product facts, such as the features of a product, are not persuasive in themselves. Audiences may value rational thought but instead make decisions on the basis of their emotions.

STOP AND THINK

Think of the last time you made a major purchase—a car, a house, a vacation package, and the like. What kinds of evidence (facts or opinions) were the most important when making your decision?

A body of recent research in neuroscience and psychology highlights the important role that emotions play in decision making.[9] In particular, empirical studies of investor decision making support the belief that individuals do not act rationally and consider all available information when trading stocks. Both professional and amateur investors let emotions drive their investment decisions instead. Whitney Tilson, a highly successful US money manager and founder of Tilson Capital Partners, suggests that overconfidence is the emotion that most often trumps rationality. Moreover, the more difficult the task (such as predicting the price of a stock), the greater the degree of overconfidence. Overtrading is one example. Tilson reports a study of 78,000 investors at a large US discount brokerage whose average annual turnover was around 80 percent. The least active quintile, with an average annual turnover of 1 percent, scored a 17.5 percent annual return. Standard & Poor's return was 16.9 percent over the same period. The most active 20 percent of investors, with annual turnover of greater than 100 percent, scored just a 10 percent annual return. Tilson concludes that investors habitually chase performance irrationally, although it does not work.[10] The take-home point here is that business speakers who rely on factual evidence should be aware of its limitations in convincing people to behave in certain ways.

Turning to opinions as a form of evidence, three types of opinions may be used in a presentation: personal, lay, and expert. While all managers probably support their presentations with personal views from time to time, success in using personal opinions for support largely depends on the manager's credibility with the audience. A manager uses lay opinion when citing the opinions of ordinary people (nonexperts), such as customers, workers, or the public. This source is prevalent in presentations on marketing or personnel problems.

A manager uses expert opinion when citing an authority to provide evidence. This form of evidence works well when objective facts are difficult to find or when the speaker is unknown to the audience. However, the expert chosen must be respected, objective, and possess actual expertise. For instance, a baseball player may be an expert in baseball but not on the quality of paint, advertising notwithstanding.

Different presentation strategies require different evidence. In persuasive presentations, the psychological-progressive pattern generally requires less factual information and more emotional appeals. Consequently, it places more emphasis on opinion than on empirical information. The state-the-case-and-prove-it and problem-solving patterns call for extensive facts in most situations. Opinion is advisable in the latter cases when the manager has a high degree of credibility, and expert opinion is valuable when there is no doubt about the authority of the expert.

Audiences judge evidence, whether fact or opinion, according to its timeliness and its source. Personal opinion is the weakest type of evidence, unless the speaker has high credibility—authority, power, dynamism, trustworthiness, and expertise. Thus, a manager is wise to cite details about the research conducted, including when and from where the evidence was retrieved. In situations where the audience does not know the speaker, the credibility of the evidence becomes crucial to speaker credibility.

To summarize, the body of any presentation is the longest and most complex part. It must be carefully organized, and the organizational pattern must be made apparent to the audience. Speakers' options for organizing the main points in the body of their presentation are determined by their purpose (informative or persuasive). After the main points have been selected and arranged in a logical sequence, they each must be supported and developed by evidence (opinions or facts). The most common organizational patterns for the body of persuasive and informative presentations appear in Table 5–3.

Table 5–3   Sequencing Options for Main Points

Persuasive Purpose	Informative Purpose
Problem-solving	Spatial/geographic
State-the-case-and-prove-it	Political/economic categories
Psychological-progressive	Importance—chronological advantages/disadvantages; comparison/contrast; structure/function

Closing

The end of the presentation is relatively easy to prepare yet crucial to the presentation's final impact. It should contain a brief summary of the purpose and the main points covered in their appropriate order. Once the presentation is finished, make sure it is finished. Do not present

Table 5–4   Parts of the Closing

Purpose statement
Main points
Significance of the message
Call to action (optional)
Final thought/challenge

any new information or leave a question unanswered. Repeat the significance of the message to the audience, as stated in the introduction, to ensure retention. If some action is to be solicited from the audience, make the expectations clear. And leave the audience with a powerful *final thought* or challenge. Whatever the specific nature of the ending, it should strongly and clearly communicate that the speaker is ending. Too often, speakers just trickle off with a "Well, that's it; thanks for listening" ending. Your audience is listening closely at this point. They will be affected by your final impression as well as your first impression.

Table 5–4 summarizes the parts of a presentation's conclusion.

Questions

Speakers solicit questions after the presentation to allow for appropriate additions and clarifications. In a situation where the group may be inhibited, but questions are important to open the dialogue, the speaker may want to ask one member of the audience to be ready with a question to stimulate further questions.

Several suggestions are helpful when answering questions:

- If the original question was not audible to everyone, repeat it.

- Select questions from all areas of the room, not just from one section or person.

- Do not evaluate a question by saying, "That's a good question." Such a response could be inadvertently telling others that their questions are not good.

- Do not answer with responses such as "as I said earlier," or "well, obviously," or "anyone would know the answer to that." Such responses can be quite demeaning.

- Look at the whole group when answering a question, not just the person who asked it.

- When you have finished, do not ask, "Does that answer your question?" because that makes you seem tentative. If you did not answer their question satisfactorily, they will likely let you know.

- Do not point a finger to call on a questioner. It is a scolding pose and may appear authoritarian. Instead, invite the question by extending an open hand, palm up.

- If you have no answer to a question, it is best to admit it. Consider telling the questioner where else they might find an answer.

- Allow sufficient time to answer all questions.

PREPARE YOUR VISUAL AIDS

Visual aids are a must for all but the most informal business presentations. They represent another way of maintaining audience attention and involvement. Since the spoken word is, at best, limited in communication, and since its sound is transitory, the listener may miss the message, and the opportunity to hear it again may never arise. However, visual support can help to overcome these limitations. Additionally, visual aids can clarify complex information. You can successfully use visual aids in the introduction, body, and closing of a presentation.

Criteria

Good visual aids make a positive impression on the audience and justify the time spent in their preparation. An effective aid is one designed to fit the speaker, the audience, and the room. Four criteria make for an effective visual aid:

1. *Visibility.* The visual aid must be easy to read. Some speakers attempt to make visual aids from printed material; these are generally poor because lettering on visual aids must be larger and bolder than normal printer lettering. Also, technical drawings cannot easily be used; lines on many of the drawings are lost because they are so faint. Little is more irritating to an audience than to be told there is something important on the visual aid that they cannot see. Have the artwork drawn to eliminate unnecessary lines and to make essential lines heavier on the drawing. Use a readable and consistent font, especially when using PowerPoint. Generally, a sans serif font is appropriate, such as Calibri, Arial, or Helvetica. Be careful not to overuse uppercase, bold, and italics, all of which are harder to read than regular font in sentence case.[11]

2. *Clarity.* Clarity refers to what an audience understands from a visual. Make the main points easy to identify. Color is a good way to focus the audience's attention on the important parts of the visual. Though statistics show that audiences remember only 20 percent of what they hear but remember 80 percent of what they see, they must be able to understand what they see to remember it.[12] When designing a PowerPoint slide, use basic, dark, solid background colors. Choose light colors for text. Avoid busy backgrounds, distracting color combinations, and low-contrast color combinations, such as black on red or medium blue on dark blue.[13]

3. *Simplicity.* After determining the content of a visual aid, look for ways to simplify it. Nothing should appear on the visual aid except the content relevant to the specific ideas to be communicated. Decorating a PowerPoint slide with clip art, borders, even the company logo, can be distracting. Most templates for computer slide shows include extra design elements that may be colorful but are irrelevant to the speaker's message. Additionally, overused templates can communicate a lack of originality.

4. *Relevance.* Do not use a graphic or sound effect just because it is handy or pretty when it was originally prepared for some other purpose. Impressive special effects can backfire if used merely to impress. For example, in *Guide to PowerPoint*, authors Mary Munter and Dave Paradi suggest not using any of the three-dimensional (3-D) chart or graph effects in a PowerPoint presentation because they are unnecessary and confusing for the audience.[14]

Keep several rules in mind when designing your visual aids. These are not magic formulas, but they are helpful guidelines. First, no textual visual aid should contain more than six lines. Second, no line should contain more than six words. To meet these first two rules, a speaker may need to use more than one visual aid or design overlays to build a more complex visual. In a PowerPoint presentation, overloading a slide with too many lines of text will divert the audience's attention from listening to reading. Avoid full sentences, unless you decide to quote an entire passage. Think of the slide as a billboard; just because you have the space does not mean you have to fill it. With PowerPoint, less is more.

Third, rows or columns of data should be shown on a single line at a time by using an accentuation technique to keep the audience's attention on the point of discussion. Simple accentuation techniques include pointing with a pencil or laser pointer, cutting a window on a sheet of flip chart paper to reveal only the items under discussion, or using the Build feature of PowerPoint. During a PowerPoint presentation, you can change the cursor from an arrow to a pen by hitting Control [(Ctrl) + P] on the keyboard. Then, you can use the cursor to circle or underline data or words for accentuation. Hitting Ctrl + E changes the cursor to an eraser. Hitting Ctrl + A brings back the arrow.

STOP AND THINK

Recall a business presentation you listened to where the speaker used visual aids.

1. To what extent did you find the visual aids helpful? Distracting? Confusing?

2. What elements of the visual aids had the biggest effect, either positive or negative, on the impression the speaker made on you?

3. What elements of the visual aids had the biggest effect on your retention of the message?

Along with the design elements of visibility, clarity, simplicity, and relevance, the timing of the visual aid contributes to its effectiveness. Since the visual aid is a graphical message intended to complement the verbal message, both messages should be presented at the same time. An aid should not be visible until it is used, and it should be removed from sight after it has been discussed so it does not distract the audience. A common mistake of many speakers is to leave a flip chart open or keep a slide on screen after the need for the visual has passed.[15] An easy way to hide a PowerPoint slide while you are presenting is to hit B on the keyboard—the screen goes to black. Hitting B again brings back the slide. Similarly, the W key makes the screen go white.

Types

The criteria for effective visual aids are universal, but a speaker's choice of visual aids will be influenced by the size and type of audience and by the type of equipment provided in the presentation room.

Most business conference rooms are equipped with whiteboards and/or flip charts. These are impromptu speaking tools to be used only when there is insufficient time to prepare anything else. A right-handed speaker writing on the board or flip chart should stand to the right of the chart or wall, facing the audience. If the speaker's back is turned and eye contact is lost, the audience's attention may dwindle. Handwritten visuals are rarely professional looking. However, spontaneous diagrams and flowcharts can sometimes be a dramatic way to clarify complex processes under discussion. They also can be effective during brainstorming sessions.

The most common type of visual aid used for business presentations, of course, is *computer-generated graphics,* such as Microsoft PowerPoint and, more recently, Prezi. Introduced by three Hungarian media designers in 2009, Prezi is a cloud-based presentation software tool for presenting ideas on a virtual canvas. The product employs a user interface that allows speakers to zoom in and out of their presentation media and navigate through information within a 3-D space. Panning, zooming, and rotating objects can be very effective, but overuse of such visual stimulation may risk inducing nausea in the audience.

In the twenty years or so since it was introduced, PowerPoint has become the standard presentation software. One writer compared delivering a presentation without PowerPoint slides to serving french fries without ketchup. In busy corporate settings, absent audience members have been known to request copies of the slides, assuming that the visual aids contain all relevant information from the presentation. Another reason for its popularity is that the software is very user friendly and, perhaps most importantly, almost universally available. One survey found over 90 percent of responding firms making presentations in-house use PowerPoint graphics.[16] In fact, companies are now incorporating presentation graphics software into their day-to-day internal communications and into their decision-making process.[17]

Recently, however, there has been a backlash against PowerPoint use, or more accurately, its abuse, in business presentations. Edward Tufte, one of the world's leading authorities on the presentation of visual information, condemns the software because it reduces the analytical quality of a presentation. Because only about thirty-five to forty words fit on each slide, and because a typical slide is viewed for only about eight seconds, he argues that audiences cannot adequately link information together in a cohesive argument. Tufte criticizes the style-over-substance approach of the PowerPoint design guidelines and points out that the bureaucracy of bullets and multilevel lists not only oversimplify ideas for the audience but also damage the credibility of the presenter. There is growing concern that presenters have come to rely on PowerPoint as a crutch and use it in place of detailed, technical reports.[18]

A tragic example of PowerPoint's misuse is the 2003 crash of the space shuttle Columbia. The Columbia Accident Investigation Board (CAIB) reported that NASA engineers, tasked with assessing possible wing damage during the mission, presented their findings in a confusing PowerPoint slide so crammed with bulleted items that it was almost impossible to analyze. The CAIB report noted, "It is easy to understand how a senior manager might read this PowerPoint slide and not realize that it addresses a life-threatening situation."[19]

One alternative to the traditional list of bullet points on PowerPoint slides is gaining popularity. The design strategy calls for placing an "assertion" as a complete sentence in the title or headline space at the top of a slide. Then, images, equations, or charts that provide evidence supporting the assertion appear in the body of the slide. Callouts with arrows are sometimes added to explain the images (see Figure 5–3). This *assertion-evidence* (AE) design at least partially assuages Tufte's challenges because it graphically displays relationships between ideas on the slide. Research by Michael Alley and his team at Penn State University shows that audiences understood and retained more information from presentations accompanied by AE-designed slides than from presentations accompanied by standard bullets-designed slides.[20]

Another point of controversy Tufte has called attention to is the lack of plagiarism controls included in the PowerPoint software. He believes the presentation software should be held to the same standards as any other scholarly paper or research report.[21] For better or worse, PowerPoint is the standard in American business presentation graphics. As such, managers need to learn to use computer-generated slide shows properly, following the principles outlined here.

Handouts are another form of visual aid. These written materials are different from the other visual aids because each member of the audience receives a copy, which may be used for reference during and after the presentation. Handouts are particularly valuable when the subject calls for complicated charts and graphs, detailed regulations, points of law, company policy, and the like. Often, the material can be distributed to the participants before the meeting, so less time is spent during the meeting for review. It is then possible to go directly to the discussion phase of the presentation.

Figure 5–3   Sample PowerPoint Slide Design

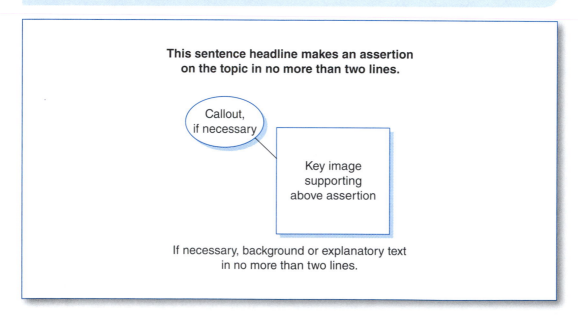

When planning to distribute materials during the meeting, limit the information to what is required and do not distribute it until it is needed. Too many materials in front of the audience may distract them from the verbal message. The audience will be tempted to review the handout for one topic while you are discussing a different one. Naturally, this reduces the impact of the message.

DELIVER YOUR PRESENTATION

Now is the time for the real test: delivering the message. Thorough preparation will allow concentration on a number of elements that require attention during the delivery. A well-prepared speaker will have analyzed the audience and will have an idea of what to expect from the various members. The purpose and audience have been analyzed, the opening statement is ready, the message is organized, the closing is prepared, and visual aids are created.

Speaking Anxiety

What about stage fright? It might be consoling to know that about 60 percent of all speakers experience anxiety to some degree before speaking. A survey of three thousand Americans revealed that the prospect of giving a speech brings forth people's greatest fear; they fear it even more than dying.[22] On this very subject, George Jessel, the late entertainer, once said, "The human brain is a wonderful organ. It starts to work as soon as you are born and doesn't stop until you get up to deliver a speech."

The best solution to anxiety is preparation. As you become better prepared to perform a task, your confidence generally increases, which, in turn, reduces anxiety. Rehearsal of the entire presentation is advisable when anxiety is particularly high. You should become more comfortable with each rehearsal.[23]

STOP AND THINK

Athletes, actors, and musicians know the difference between eustress and distress. It is the difference between helpful stress and harmful stress. Think of a time when you had to perform before an audience. Did the level of your anxiety make you perform better? Or did it work against you?

But no matter how well prepared you might be, some anxiety may remain. A small amount of tension or anxiety is good because it keeps a speaker alert; however, several techniques may be used when anxiety is so great that it may interfere with the presentation's effectiveness.

First, consider the value of the presentation and remember that the material is important. Believe that the audience is there to listen and that you have an opportunity to provide a valuable service. Carly Fiorina, former CEO of Hewlett-Packard, explains her poise and persuasiveness when before an audience thusly: "It doesn't matter whether I'm talking to two people, ten people, or thousands of people. I think about it as though I'm talking to just one person. Every communication is a conversation."[24]

Second, it helps to sit with your eyes closed and to take a few deep breaths. With hands relaxed and dangling to the side, rotate your head slowly while you concentrate on an especially pleasing thought (a mountain valley with beautiful flowers; soothing, fluffy clouds floating across the sky; waves breaking on a beach).[25] Deep breathing oxygenates your brain, thus increasing alertness. It also relaxes tense muscles in your throat and neck. As a bonus, increasing the amount of air in your lungs ensures that your voice will project farther. One minute of relaxation can be worth an hour of frantic preparation.

A third way to reduce anxiety is to memorize the first few remarks in the presentation. By the time these memorized comments have been presented, some of the initial anxiety should have subsided. Even though this part of the presentation has been memorized, it may be a good idea to have notes available just to increase confidence.

Fourth, planned bodily activity can help reduce anxiety. Strategic movements during the delivery can be used to control the higher level of energy produced by the anxiety. This movement may take the form of appropriate gestures or of walking to a laptop, flip chart, or screen.

Speaker Notes

How can notes be best arranged and used to support a business presentation? Traditionally, some people have advocated a precise outline following all the "proper" rules; others have maintained that 5-by-8-inch cards are essential. The Notes Pages feature in PowerPoint is handy. It gives you a printed sheet for each slide, with a representation of the slide at the top of the sheet and your notes about that slide appearing below it. Many speakers just use their PowerPoint slides as cues. Each person must find what works best for him or her.

Good speaker notes will help you channel your efforts toward effective delivery. Notes written clearly and concisely make it easy to maintain eye contact with the audience. The need to maintain eye contact with the audience supports the recommendation that speaker notes rather than graphics be used. Standing with your back to the audience while you read the speech off the screen is an all-too-common, unprofessional speaking style.

Although notes can be a valuable source, they can easily become a psychological crutch. To make sure they do not become so, keep the following *do nots* in mind.

- Do not twist, bend, smooth, roll, or fold the notes in an aimless way because of nervousness. This behavior does nothing to relieve a speaker's anxiety, and it may increase the anxiety of the audience.

- Do not gaze at the notes out of a feeling of insecurity. Looking down to keep from looking at the audience can get to be a bad habit that physically and psychologically separates you from the audience.

- Do not write out your notes (or slides) in full sentences. You will be tempted to read the presentation aloud rather than speak extemporaneously from key points.

- Do not try to hide from the audience the fact that you are using notes. Why play games with the audience? The best procedure is to use notes openly, but only when necessary.

Nonverbal Aspects

Several nonverbal aspects of communication need to be considered during the delivery of a presentation, including eye contact, facial expressions, posture, gestures, and movement. Speakers are integral parts of the messages they convey, so how they present themselves affects the message directly.

As you will see, the nonverbal components of communication discussed in Chapters 9 and 10 can apply to the speaking as well as to the listening role. For instance, just as eye contact is important when listening for the total message, eye contact can be used to complement the delivery of a message. By looking at different members of the audience, effective speakers use eye contact to involve the audience in the presentation. Speakers can also use the rest of their faces to show concern or excitement about the message. A smile, a puzzled frown, a grimace—all complement the verbal message.

Preview Chapter 10 to learn how a speaker's posture, gestures, and body movement may also add to the spoken word. A forward-leaning posture may emphasize or show involvement, and walking toward a member of the audience may psychologically draw that person and others into the message. The most important thing to remember is that body movements have meaning, and they should be used to enhance the message, not distract from it.

Another aspect of nonverbal communication is proximity. Few would question the speaker's need to stand when the audience includes more than seven or eight people; however, many managerial presentations involve audiences of fewer than seven people in a conference room. This latter situation calls for managers to analyze the group, the purpose, and themselves to determine whether to stand or sit.

Voice Quality

Other nonverbal aspects important to the delivery of a presentation reside in the quality of your voice. Among the major vocal considerations of nonverbal communication discussed in Chapter 10 are rate, pitch, and volume.

The best speaking rate depends on your material. Generally, present ideas that are potentially difficult to comprehend at a slower rate than ideas that are easy to understand. Slow down to emphasize an important and/or primary point and speak faster when presenting secondary information. If you are feeling nervous, make a special effort to slow down, since nervousness usually speeds up a speaker's speech rate, and you do not want to seem out of control. Also, out of consideration, you might slow down for an audience that may have difficulty understanding your dialect or terminology. On the other hand, if your regional dialect is a drawl, make an effort to increase your rate for more liveliness and energy. Vary your rate to keep the attention of the audience; a voice that never changes speed becomes boring.

Speakers who talk at a constant pitch will also find it difficult to hold the audience's attention. Use wide variations in pitch for emphasis and interest. Usually, failure to vary pitch is a habit, commonly known as monotonal speaking. Read the following sentence aloud three times, raising the pitch on the italicized word each time. It is easy to see that understanding can be drastically affected by pitch.

I never said he promoted *her*. (Give him some credit. He has better insight than that.)

I never said *he* promoted her. (I just said she got promoted, not by whom.)

I never *said* he promoted her. (But I might have implied it in a number of ways.)

The third voice quality, volume, can add to a presentation by making it lively and easy to follow. The correct volume depends on group size and the physical surroundings; however, regardless of the situation, changes in volume improve emphasis and add variety. A speaker who is difficult to hear may be perceived as incompetent and shy. Keep in mind one special warning about volume: A speaker does not gain attention or make stronger emphasis merely by being loud. In fact, an effective speaker may lower her voice during distractions, so her audience is forced to quiet down to hear her.

You can use several exercises to prepare your speaking voice. One simple but effective technique is to read aloud a few paragraphs from the editorial or sports section of the newspaper as though you were giving a presentation. This tactic draws attention to your voice quality. You should pay attention to the way professional speakers, such as TV newsreaders and announcers, use their voices to convey information and emotion.

In summary, research shows that 55 percent of your impression is the result of how you look, 38 percent is the result of how you sound, and just 7 percent is the result of what you say. So when you announce, "I'm delighted to be here tonight," while your voice shakes and your eyes dart to the door and you fumble with your notes, the audience is more likely to believe that you are *not* delighted to be here.

STOP AND THINK

1. In addition to rate, pitch, and volume, what other aspects of voice affect your impression of the speaker? How about regional accent?

2. When you listen to a presenter who speaks in a different dialect, how does that influence your impression?

3. Do you listen more carefully or does your attention wander?

Practice

The cliché "Practice makes perfect" definitely applies to presentations. Practice is essential for managerial presentations because in US business, you should speak extemporaneously, not give memorized recitations or verbatim readings, as is the custom in other cultures. Unfortunately, many managers skip practice because they believe either that they are too busy or that practice is not important.

Even in the case of busy executives, however, practice is essential. It allows you to increase self-confidence and poise and to improve wording so the speech flows smoothly. Additionally, practice permits you to identify any flaws or gaps in the presentation, to deal with distractions, and to make sure the visual aids are smoothly integrated.

Lee Iacocca, an American business leader who was CEO of Chrysler and Ford motor companies, once said that perfect practice makes perfect.[26] Practice does not mean simply reviewing the basic outline or slide show while sitting at a desk. Rather, it means rehearsing it aloud in a situation that simulates the actual situation as nearly as possible. Also, it means applying all the guidelines available for good presentation development and delivery.

Look for a speech ally among your coworkers who can play the role of the audience and ask questions. Generally, whatever effort is expended in practice could make the difference between a mediocre presentation and an outstanding one.

Whenever possible, use the actual room and all the planned visual aids during the practice session. Doing so allows you to arrange the room properly. For example, though a semicircular arrangement would permit easy eye contact with all the participants, the room may dictate a theater-style arrangement. Knowing such things ahead of time allows you to make adjustments and avoid last-minute anxieties.

A practice session with the visual aids also helps you evaluate timing and get used to the remote. You can also determine such simple things as where to plug in the computer projector and where a light dimmer is located. Taking precautions can help to prevent disaster after hours and hours have gone into preparing a presentation.

Finally, practice will help you arrange notes for maximum benefit. Managers who are completely familiar with their subject and feel they do not need notes may wind up embarrassing themselves, their audience, and their organization. A rehearsal helps to settle the number of notes required and how detailed they should be. Also, additional notations can be made for clear transitions or ideas that need to be spoken more slowly, loudly, or clearly. And you will not be tempted to read from your PowerPoint slides during the presentation.

MEDIA PRESENTATIONS

The camera and microphone appear everywhere. A manager needs to learn to use these devices to maximize their potential. Unfortunately, many managers still take a defensive posture toward these audio and video presentation possibilities. Most people do not want to get involved in games for which they do not know the rules; thus, they shy away from the camera or microphone.

But the media offer many possibilities, from public service announcements to internal informative or motivational messages to employees. Managers sometimes receive requests from local radio or television stations for informative or persuasive presentations. While television and radio are different forms of communication, they can be rewarding and valuable media for your message.

To take advantage of these media, managers need to know the special rules that apply to the microphone and the camera. The first rule is to speak as though the audience is right there. Think of the microphone or camera as a friendly, trusting person. This approach reduces the likelihood of insincere, overly dramatic, inappropriate communication styles.

A second rule is to use the face, hands, and body as in ordinary conversation to keep the presentation as natural as it would be in person. Normal gesturing helps to communicate honesty, and it can complement the ideas being expressed. Some caution, however, should be exercised. Grins, frowns, grimaces, and sweeping gestures are magnified by the camera and are seldom appropriate. Keep gestures close to your upper body so they can be seen in close-up shots.

A third rule is to use a script. What may seem to be an ad-lib presentation by a professional performer is probably the result of an extensive script. A script is a means of coordinating the audio, visual, time, content, and human variables. In addition to the words, it also contains instructions about production matters for crew members, enabling them to visualize how to integrate their responsibilities with the overall show. It helps establish the occasion's structure, organization, and timing. In other words, the script helps all parties know the sequence—how it will begin, move, and conclude.[27]

A fourth rule is closely related to the third: prepare and practice. We have already seen the importance of practice in relation to the face-to-face presentation; however, practice is even more important for a television or videoconference presentation. All the new stimuli make it difficult to concentrate on the task, so be prepared for distractions.

Another reason for the extra practice is the strict time limitations. Media presentations have to be implemented in terms of seconds. In reaction to the tight scheduling, the novice media speaker should resist the tendency to speak rapidly and thus appear nervous.

Extensive practice is called for because of the higher level of refinement required for a media presentation. The audience expects polished, professional speakers on the air. Remember, too, that every detail becomes a permanent record when captured on tape.

Table 5–5 Delivery of Media Presentations

Vocal Impact	Nonverbal Impact	Visual Image Impact
Maintain normal volume (do not shout into the microphone)	Avoid white, black, and stripes—patterns that vibrate on TV	Design clean, uncluttered visuals that can be read in thirty seconds
Use a conversational rate (approximately 110 words per min.)	Maintain eye contact with the camera	Keep all text at 40 points or larger
Project extra vocal enthusiasm and energy	Stand tall and straight	Avoid textual lists of bullet points
Articulate clearly	Use natural but slower chest-high gestures	Label chart columns, rows, and parts to help speed understanding (avoid legends)
Maintain fluency; avoid filled pauses (uh, ok, so)	Move slowly and stay within microphone and camera range	Keep right side of visuals empty so presenter picture in picture (PIP) won't mask visual image
Pause before important points for drama	Use natural facial expressions and head movements	Point to visuals on document camera or draw on computer slides

A fifth and final rule relates to the clothing appropriate for a media appearance. The obvious recommendation is to wear what you want others to see you in, but you'll also want your outfit to be unobtrusive. The following are some tips:

- Do not wear large patterns. They have a stroboscopic effect and appear to be moving.

- Do not wear clashing or loud colors (especially red). They can be easily distorted on-screen.

- Avoid wearing black and white. Black absorbs too much light and white reflects it.

- Avoid large, glittery, or moving jewelry.

Professor Tom Hajduk, director of the Center for Business Communication at Carnegie Mellon University, developed a communication audit form for evaluating TV/videoconference presentations.[28] The audit provides a useful checklist of the unique delivery requirements for media presentations, as summarized in Table 5–5.

These rules should help managers take full advantage of the opportunities presented by the camera and microphone. Such appearances can be challenging but enjoyable experiences that provide a valuable service to your company while offering a tremendous opportunity for professional self-development.

TEAM PRESENTATIONS

Not all presentations will be planned and presented by an individual. When the stakes are high and the situation is complex, a single presenter may not be able to accomplish the task. For example, an architecture firm is bidding on a contract to design a new science complex for a university. The firm sends a team of experts to make a presentation to the potential customer. The team consists of the principal in charge of the project, a design principal or project manager, an interior designer, a laboratory designer, and a mechanical engineer. Each team member will speak about his/her area of expertise, and each will help achieve the goal, winning the bid. Team presentations allow shared responsibility, but they are difficult to do well. Clearly, presenting as a team requires advanced communication, organization, and planning skills.

Team presentations can be divided into the following three phases: planning, design, and delivery.

1. The first phase is the *planning* phase. The team defines its purpose and analyzes the occasion of the presentation, selects a moderator, establishes channels of communication among themselves, and assigns segment speakers.

2. During the second phase, the *design* phase, each speaker on the team makes his/her individual presentation plans then shares them with the other team members. The team creates appropriate visual aspects (a single slideshow,

coordinated outfits, handouts, and demonstrations), rehearses once or twice together, and brainstorms how they will handle the questions and answers (Q & A) session.

3. The third phase is the *delivery* phase. During this phase, the team delivers the presentation, each speaker staying within time limits. Each speaker uses previews or summaries to smooth the seams. The team presentation begins and concludes with the moderator. All team members appear to listen closely to the others when not presenting. After the team's presentation, each member is prepared to answer audience questions according to his/her individual expertise.

Here is a summary of the characteristics of successful team presentations:[29]

Content: Organized, supported, and relevant to audience

Visuals: Creative, professional, and effective

Delivery: Consistent, polished, and dynamic

IMPROMPTU SPEAKING

So far, this chapter has focused on strategies for planning, organizing, and delivering formal presentations. In addition, business professionals frequently are expected to offer a brief statement when they have not had time to prepare. As a manager, you will suddenly be invited to "make a few remarks" in business and quasi-social settings. What should you do? The natural reaction is to blurt out the first idea that pops into your head then hope that another idea occurs to you so you can say it as well. This approach is called "stream of consciousness" speaking, and it will suffice in ordinary conversations. However, in business settings you will need to know how to deliver informal, *impromptu* presentations with style.

An impromptu is a brief oral presentation of opinions and facts with minimal preparation. It is commonly experienced during meetings, employment interviews, events such as celebrations, and informal gatherings. Your performance during such occasions can have a major impact on your professional image. While no one expects you to say something profound off-the-cuff, you do not want to disgrace yourself in the presence of your colleagues, bosses, and clients when called upon for a comment.

Here are some techniques for making informal presentations and brief impromptu remarks:

1. Get mentally ready. Use nonverbal communication tools (vocal style, body language, appearance) to look and sound confident. Nonverbal communication is discussed in Chapter 10. As you will see, 93 percent of the impression you make is determined by nonverbal elements.

2. Work the question/subject around to fit your knowledge and interests. Restate the question as you plan a response. If you cannot talk and think at once, stall for time by asking the person who has called on you to repeat the question. In most impromptu speaking situations, you will be allowed to tailor the subject to suit your expertise.

3. Begin with a main point. Your opening sentence should be a generalization or a statement of opinion or belief. In writing, the main point is called the topic sentence or thesis, and it usually appears at the beginning of a paragraph. Similarly, in speaking, you should begin with a broad, sweeping statement.

4. Support your main point by developing it with facts, statistics, examples, analogies, reasons, illustrations, or personal stories. Supporting ideas are more specific, concrete, and narrow than main ideas. They help the listeners to understand your opening statement.

5. Come back to your main point. By restating the main idea, you will reinforce it and aid the listeners' retention.

6. Stop talking. A common mistake during impromptu speaking is to babble on for too long, repeating yourself or talking in circles. A brief, well-organized comment will make a stronger impression than a long-winded speech consisting of random, scattered thoughts.

Table 5–6 summarizes impromptu presentation techniques.

Table 5–6   Impromptu Presentation Techniques

1. Get mentally ready. Look confident. Breathe.
2. Work the question/subject around to fit your knowledge and interests. Restate the question as you plan a response.
3. Pick a main point.
4. Support your main point by developing it with facts, examples, analogies, reasons, et cetera.
5. Come back to your main point.
6. Stop talking.

SUMMARY

To ensure an effective presentation, a manager should thoroughly analyze the purpose, time restrictions, and audience; complete all necessary preparations; and use appropriate delivery techniques. A thorough analysis of the purpose means the speaker should determine if everyone involved has the same goal for the presentation.

Once the goal has been clearly established, the necessary preparations must be completed. Preparation includes the development of an introduction, a sequence of main points that is appropriate for an informative or persuasive purpose, and a strong closing. The sequence of main points should be determined by the speaker's purpose. Support for each main point takes the form of evidence, which can be facts or opinions. Transitions must be added to bring unity and coherence to the completed presentation plan.

In addition, visual aids must be prepared. Visual aids help to maintain interest and accurately communicate the key ideas. Visibility, clarity, simplicity, relevance, and timing are important to ensure that the visual aids complement the verbal communication.

Both nonverbal and verbal characteristics of the speaker are important for an effective, professional delivery. Eye contact, facial expressions, posture, gestures, and movement all need to be considered. Voice rate, pitch, and volume affect the impact of the presentation.

A speaker should schedule sufficient time for questions and answers at the end of the presentation. When this part of the presentation is well managed, feedback and two-way communication develop.

A special presentational situation that more and more managers face today is speaking before a camera and microphone. Most of the rules that apply to a traditional face-to-face speaking situation apply also to this form of a presentation. However, several additional rules dealing with nonverbal cues and the use of a script will help a manager to present an effective message via the electronic media.

A second special speaking situation is the team presentation. Together, team members should plan, design, and deliver their message. Successful team presentations are well-organized, supported, and relevant to the audience. Visuals are creative, professional, and effective. The team members' delivery style is consistent, polished, and dynamic.

AUDIENCE ANALYSIS WORKSHEET

1. How many do I expect in the audience?

2. Who are the most powerful or influential members?

3. What is their knowledge of the content area?

_____High, may be higher than mine

_____About the same as mine

_____Less than my knowledge of the subject

_____Probably do not have even basic knowledge

_____Varies

4. What types of evidence will most impress this group?

_____Technical data

_____Statistical comparisons

_____Cost figures

_____Historical information

_____Generalizations

_____Demonstrations

_____Stories and examples

_____Opinions of the speaker

5. What is the group's attitude toward the subject?

_____Exceptionally positive

_____Somewhat positive

_____Neutral

_____Somewhat negative, reluctant

_____Definitely negative

_____Group varies, some positive and some negative

6. What is the group's attitude toward me as the presenter?

_____See me as credible and knowledgeable

_____Neutral, probably do not have an opinion

_____See me as having little knowledge and credibility

7. What is the group's attitude toward the organization I represent?

_____See the organization as reliable and trustworthy

_____Neutral

_____Might question its capabilities and reliability

(Continued)

(Continued)

8. What will be the group's disposition at the time of my presentation?

_____Will have listened to many other presentations similar to this one, could be tired

_____Will have been sitting for a long time, may need a minute to stretch

_____This presentation will be unique, so it should be easy to grab their attention

_____This is an early item on the agenda; they should be fresh

9. What are the *most important* audience characteristics to consider in the presentation?

Case for Small-Group Discussion

CASE 5–1

Presentations and Technology

Jessica Dunham paced as she spent the last few moments before her board presentation trying to calm down. She had prepared a PowerPoint presentation and had practiced many times. It was no different than many PowerPoint presentations she had done in college, but this time it was on the job and in front of her boss's boss!

She walked into the room. Everyone was seated and ready. Jessica had started the projector earlier and made sure everything was working properly. "Good morning, everyone," she began. Just then, the lights flickered. She looked at the projector in horror. It had shut down. She quickly restarted the machine, and it warmed up within one minute . . . of silence. Jessica was embarrassed and even more anxious now.

"Let's try this again," she said with a smile. "Good morning, everyone," she said. "I have a presentation prepared for you today summarizing our port logistics." Jessica pushed the slide advance button on the remote. Nothing happened. She pushed the button again and again, frantically. "Well, this doesn't seem to be working." Jessica stepped in front of the projection. The projector blinded her temporarily, but she was able to advance the slide with the arrow buttons on the keyboard of her laptop computer. "This exhibit shows our historical traffic patterns prior to the opening of dock 43." Jessica looked at the screen in horror; the exhibit had shrunk to the size of a page of typing paper. When the power had surged, the projector had reset at its highest resolution! Jessica turned beet red. "Excuse me just a moment, folks," she said. Jessica spent the next minute and a half scrolling though the menus to reset the resolution setting for the display. "OK, now let's review the traffic patterns . . . the blue lines indicate the traffic prior to the opening of dock 43, and the red lines show the traffic patterns after the opening."

Jessica looked at the screen again. The red lines were absent from her display. For the next four minutes, she apologized for the delays as she reopened her linked data file that had also closed when the power had flickered.

For the remainder of the presentation, no mishaps occurred, but Jessica felt the damage had been done. She returned to her office and hung her head in her hands. Her boss showed up two minutes later. "Builds character, huh, Jess?" she said. "Same thing happened to me about a year after I started. I learned quickly that one of the hazards of counting on technology is that technology can let you down. Ever since then, I have a paper handout backup, just in case."

"That was so embarrassing! I'm surprised I wasn't fired!" Jessica replied.

"No, you didn't show the board anything they hadn't seen before, Jess. Don't worry about it. Learn from it! Take a deep breath, go get a latte, and then get back to work!"

QUESTIONS

1. What can we learn from Jessica's negative experience?

2. How would you structure a "paper backup plan" as Jessica's boss suggested?

Exercises for Small Groups

EXERCISE 5–1

Prepare a five-minute informative presentation for your class on the latest developments in office ergonomics. Begin by analyzing your audience and selecting your topics and their order of presentation. Your discussion should address the following elements:

- How will you introduce your subject so that you grab the audience's attention?
- What type of supporting information will most impress your audience?
- What kind of closing should you use?
- How will you encourage questions at the end of your presentation?
- What would be the best type of visual aids to maintain the audience's attention?

EXERCISE 5–2

Pick a computer presentation graphics package or multimedia package with which you are familiar. Assume you are a new sales representative for the company that developed this software. For instance, PowerPoint is a Microsoft product. In three days, you will be making a sales presentation on the latest version of this software to a group of executives at a large company. Obviously, you will want to inform them of all the features offered by your software and its advantages over the competition and previous versions. You will also want to persuade them to purchase the software. How would you accomplish your goals?

EXERCISE 5–3

Pick one of the following topics to use in the development of a five-minute persuasive presentation:

- Lie detectors should (or should not) be used in the hiring process.
- Lie detectors should (or should not) be used by businesses in attempting to deter employee theft.
- Businesses should (or should not) be permitted to subject employees to random drug testing.
- Top executives should (or should not) be held criminally liable for their companies' illegal (or unethical) actions.
- Social responsibility should (or should not) be a major concern of today's CEOs.
- A manager should (or should not) be concerned about the personal problems of his or her employees.
- An international code of ethics should (or should not) be developed.
- Unionization is (or is not) appropriate for today's white-collar workers.

After picking a topic, visualize an audience to whom you would speak on the subject. Of the three persuasive presentation patterns described in this chapter, which would be most appropriate for your presentation? Given the topic you have chosen and the audience you have visualized, what type of evidence would you use to persuade them to accept your point of view?

EXERCISE 5–4

Pick one of the following scenarios and develop a ten-minute informative presentation:

- For an audience of graduating seniors in business administration, discuss the topic of appropriate dress for employment interviews.
- For an audience of business executives, discuss the topic of appropriate dress for television interviews.

Student Study Site

Visit the Student Study Site at **study.sagepub.com/hynes6e** for web quizzes, video links, web resources, and cases studies.

Notes

1. S. Clay Willmington, "Oral Communication for a Career in Business," *Bulletin of the Association for Business Communication* 52, no. 2 (June 1989): pp. 8–12.
2. Robert J. Olney and Anita S. Bednar, "Identifying Essential Oral Presentation Skills for Today's Business Curriculum," *Journal of Education for Business* 64, no. 4 (January 1989): p. 161.
3. Carol A. McFarland, "Teaching Students the Elements of Oral Business Presentations," *Bulletin of the Association for Business Communication* 43, no. 1 (March 1980): pp. 15–17.

4. Ernest G. Bormann, William S. Howell, Ralph G. Nichols, and George L. Shapiro, *Interpersonal Communication in the Modern Organization* (Englewood Cliffs, NJ: Prentice Hall, 1982), p. 197.

5. Lawrence L. Tracy, "Taming the Hostile Audience," *Training and Development Journal* 44, no. 2 (February 1990): p. 35.

6. William S. Howell and Ernest G. Bormann, *Presentational Speaking for Business and the Professions* (New York: Harper & Row, 1971), pp. 122–130.

7. Daniel J. O'Keefe, *Persuasion Theory and Research,* 2nd ed. (Thousand Oaks, CA: Sage, 2002), pp. 181–264.

8. Anne Bradstreet Grinols, "Ethical Persuasion: Taking the High Road in Compelling Communication." (Paper presented at the Association for Business Communication Southwestern United States Regional Conference, March 12, 2013).

9. Baba Shiv, George Loewenstein, Antoine Bechara, Hanna Damasio, and Antonio R. Damasio, "Investment Behavior and the Negative Side of Emotion," *Psychological Science* 16, no. 6 (2005): pp. 435–439.

10. "Human Behavior: The Greatest Barrier to Trading Success," *Australasian Investment Review,* n.d., accessed January 20, 2006, www.aireview.com.

11. Mary Munter and Dave Paradi, *Guide to PowerPoint* (Upper Saddle River, NJ: Pearson Prentice Hall, 2007), pp. 65, 94.

12. Donna Barron, "Graphics Presentations at Your Fingertips," *The Office,* July 1990, p. 32.

13. Robert P. Sedlack, Jr., Barbara L. Shwom, and Karl P. Keller, *Graphics and Visual Communication for Managers* (Mason, OH: Thomson South-Western, 2008), p. 71.

14. Munter and Paradi, *Guide to PowerPoint.*

15. James Wyllie, "Oral Communication: Survey and Suggestions," *Bulletin of the Association for Business Communication* 43, no. 2 (June 1980): pp. 14–17.

16. "The Pros and Cons of High-Tech Presenting," *Presentations* 13, no. 4 (April 1999): p. 34.

17. Patricia L. Panchak, "Capitalizing on the Graphics Edge," *Modern Office Technology,* June 1990, p. 63.

18. Edward R. Tufte, *The Cognitive Style of PowerPoint: Pitching Out Corrupts Within* (Cheshire, CT: Graphics Press, 2006).

19. "Over-Reliance on PowerPoint Leads to Simplistic Thinking," *The New York Times,* December 14, 2003, accessed January 12, 2006, http://partners.nytimes.com/2003/12/14/magazine/14POWER.html.

20. Joanna K. Garner and Michael Alley, "How the Design of Presentation Slides Affects Audience Comprehension: A Case for the Assertion-Evidence Approach," *International Journal of Engineering Education* 29, no. 6 (2013): pp. 1564–1579. See also: Michael Alley, *The Craft of Scientific Presentations,* 2nd ed. (New York: Springer-Verlag, 2013).

21. Tufte, *The Cognitive Style.*

22. David Wallechinsky and Irving Wallace, *The Book of Lists* (New York: William Morrow, 1977).

23. Kenneth R. Meyer, "Developing Delivery Skills in Oral Business Communication," *Bulletin of the Association for Business Communication* 43, no. 3 (September 1980): pp. 21–24.

24. Dave Clarke Mora, "Carly, Reconsidered," *Continental,* September 2003, pp. 31–33.

25. Mary Ellen Murray, "Painless Oral Presentations," *Bulletin of the Association for Business Communication* 52, no. 2 (June 1989): pp. 13–15.

26. Lee Iacocca, *Lee Iacocca Talking Straight* (New York: Bantam Books, 1988).

27. Evan Blythin and Larry A. Samovar, *Communicating Effectively on Television* (Belmont, CA: Wadsworth, 1985), pp. 92–96.

28. Tom Hajduk, "Communication Audit: TV/Videoconference Presentation," vol. 11.1, accessed August 11, 2014, Communication Consulting Group, www.ccg-usa.com.

29. T. Leech, *How to Prepare, Stage, and Deliver Winning Presentations*, 3rd ed. (New York: AMACOM, 2004).

PART III

Managerial Writing Strategies

CHAPTER 6

Contemporary Managerial Writing

If writing must be a precise form of communication, it should be treated like a precision instrument. It should be sharpened, and it should not be used carelessly.

—Theodore M. Bernstein, editor, *New York Times*

Managers spend about 75 percent of their time communicating,[1] and the higher managers go in their organizations, the more time they spend communicating. While much of this communication involves oral, face-to-face interaction, some requires writing e-mails, memos, letters, and reports. All have the potential to play a critical part in the success of the manager and the organization.

Given the time and effort required to put things in writing, readers may wonder why managers would prefer to write a message rather than communicate it orally. Written managerial communication offers several strategic advantages: economy, efficiency, accuracy, and official permanence.

Writing is usually more economical than long-distance phone calls and much more economical than long-distance travel. Furthermore, it provides immediacy, in that the manager can write the message whether or not the receiver is immediately available to receive it.

Writing is efficient because the manager can work independently and use words selectively. Additionally, e-mail allows receivers to read messages at their convenience and thus avoids the time wasted in telephone tag.

Accuracy is another advantage of writing; writing permits greater control of words and message organization than does oral communication. Accuracy, in turn, often eliminates confusion, ensures clarity, and further contributes to economy and efficiency.

Finally, writing provides an official record that can be retained for recall and review. In our increasingly litigious society, the importance of documentation cannot be overstressed. Managers must understand that all documents generated by their organization are "discoverable." That is, attorneys can compel their disclosure as part of pretrial procedures. This fact implies that all official records must be accurate and clear, able to stand up to scrutiny.

The difference between a legal judgment for or against organizations and their managers is becoming more often a matter of adequate documentation.

Once a manager has decided to capitalize on the benefits of writing as a communication channel, the manager should consider two unique characteristics of writing in a business context: collaboration and the uniqueness of managerial writing. Collaboration and the unique roles of business writing are examined in the next sections of this chapter.

COLLABORATIVE WRITING

A major development in the modern corporate world is the emergence of collaborative writing. It is becoming more prevalent because of the increased emphasis on teamwork. Also, these teams frequently consist of people with unique specialties that they bring to bear toward the successful completion of major projects.

Though it may assume any of many forms, collaborative writing is entrenched in contemporary professional writing. In personal interviews with two hundred businesspeople in two states, one team of researchers found that 73.5 percent of respondents routinely collaborate with at least one other person in writing.[2] Another research team found that 87 percent of respondents sometimes wrote as members of a team or group.[3] At America West Airlines, most of the reports are collaboratively written. The same is true at Accenture.

Collaborative writing comes in a number of different guises. Sometimes a supervisor has a staff member research and write a document, after which the supervisor edits it. Sometimes the collaboration comes in the planning of the document, which is composed and revised by an individual. Other times, an individual does the planning and composing of work that is revised collaboratively. Peers often critique one another's work. And there are times when the collaboration pervades the entire writing process from start to finish.[4] Recent research indicates that a typical document cycles through three to five revisions before it is sent to the intended readers.

STOP AND THINK

1. Why do you think that businesses typically cycle documents so thoroughly before releasing them?

2. How important is it that business documents generated by a business have a clear and consistent "voice" or style?

Advantages of Collaborative Writing

Collaborative writing is becoming more popular largely because of the advantages of group decision making. It often works better than an individual effort because of the additional minds and perspectives being applied to creating the document. Furthermore, the understanding of, and the motivation to carry out, the directives of the document are greater among those who actually contributed to its development.

Collaborative writing is also thought to be particularly advantageous when the size of the task and/or time limits call for the labor of more than one person, when the scope of the job calls for more than one area of expertise, or when one of the task goals is the melding of divergent opinions.[5]

Gebhardt notes that the theoretical underpinnings of collaborative writing are "the rhetorical sense of audience; the psychological power of peer influence; the transfer-of-learning principle by which (people) gain insights into their own writing as they comment on the works of others; and the principle of feedback through which (people) sense how well their writing is communicating."[6]

Terry Bacon has found that collaborative writing socializes employees in several fundamental ways. It helps to acculturate newcomers by teaching writers about the corporation's capabilities and history and by modeling the corporation's values and attitudes in the actions of the experienced members. It also helps break down functional barriers, and it fosters the informal chains of communication and authority through which the corporation accomplishes its work.[7]

Finally, and perhaps most importantly, collaboration can improve writing quality.[8] People, without outside direction, can respond to each other's drafts with sharply focused and relevant comments.[9] Recent developments in technology facilitate collaborative writing. New online environments, such as Google Docs, allow groups to compose, revise, and edit documents synchronously and asynchronously, resulting in better messages. Aspects and Lotus Notes have been shown not only to result in better documents but also to avoid emotional conflict among collaborators.

Disadvantages of Collaborative Writing

Some disadvantages of collaborative writing are also those associated with group decision making. Some members do not do their fair share. Coordinating schedules for meetings can be complicated and vexing. Personality conflicts can all but stall the group's progress. And some people believe that one person acting alone could probably complete the chore in much less time than it takes a group to do so. Finally, though one person may do a poor job on part of the project, everyone is held responsible for the entire end result.

Respondents in one study noted that the two major costs of collaboration were time and ego. One commented that in collaboration you had to "check your ego at the door," you had to be "confident in your own abilities and yet able to take criticism."[10]

Another surveyed group of professional writers cited several problems associated with collaborative writing. They spoke of difficulty in resolving style differences, the additional time required to work with a group, the inequitable division of tasks, and the loss of personal satisfaction, ownership, or sense of creativity.[11]

Probably the most serious problem associated with collaborative writing is ineffectively dealing with conflicts that arise. Some people see all conflicts as bad and try to ignore them or sweep them under the carpet. They do not realize that some conflicts are functional and can help the group to come to a more creative resolution of its problem.

Guidelines for Effective Collaborative Writing

In their extensive research into the collaborative writing of people in a number of professions, Lisa Ede and Andrea Lunsford came up with the following profile of effective collaborative writers:

They are flexible; respectful of others; attentive and analytical listeners; able to speak and write clearly and articulately; dependable and able to meet deadlines; able to designate and share responsibility, to lead and to follow; open to criticism but confident in their own abilities; ready to engage in creative conflict.[12]

Generally, this profile depicts people who are able to work with others, people who are going to be in greater demand as collaboration becomes more the norm than the exception.

In addition to the advice implicit in the preceding characterization of effective collaborative writers and groups, there are other ways to achieve successful collaborative writing experiences. One basic guideline is to make sure the work is divided equitably among group members. Nothing is surer to destroy a person's morale than to begin feeling overworked compared to others in the group.

Second, writing teams should use electronic technology for collaboration; the media appear to buffer emotions while increasing efficiency.

Third, all collaborative writing groups should have a team leader, even though the person may not have any formal authority. The leader should be responsible for coordinating the team's collaborative efforts, shaping the team's vision, and resolving conflicts among individuals and functional departments. The latter task usually requires good interpersonal skills if the leader has no formal authority.[13]

Though no one can guarantee that all collaborative writing experiences will be problem free, we are confident that anyone who follows the preceding guidelines will encounter fewer insurmountable problems and will attain greater success in group writing projects.

THE UNIQUE ROLE OF MANAGERIAL WRITING

In recent years, the various fields addressing composition have given much attention to discourse communities. A *discourse community* is a group of people who think in similar ways about how to communicate subjects to be dealt with and how to approach them, as well as what makes up legitimate knowledge. These communities may be large or small, and any organization may contain a number of discourse communities.

Managers serve in sufficiently common roles and work in sufficiently common contexts to make them members of a unique discourse community. Managers are people who plan the organization's objectives, organize the functions of the organization, lead people in the accomplishment of those objectives, and control activities to make sure they are proceeding in the right direction.

Equally important in defining the discourse community of managerial writers is the context in which they do their work. Context may be the most powerful variable affecting what writers in organizations do and how these writers perceive, interpret, and value their own activity. The following paragraphs examine several aspects of the unique context in which managerial writing occurs.

STOP AND THINK

What are some other discourse communities that you have participated in?

One of the most critical aspects of the context of managerial writing is the fragmented nature of a manager's workday. Most people think of managers, especially higher-level executives, as having meticulously organized days overseen and protected by assistants. Henry Mintzberg found the opposite to be true. As he and colleagues recorded the activities of a number of managers, he found their days to be filled with interruptions. On the average, they had a full half hour of uninterrupted time only once every four days.[14] More recently, Gloria Mark observed employees at two high-tech firms and found that the average worker spends only eleven minutes on any given project before being interrupted. IT workers have it worse, getting interrupted every three minutes.[15] Most people faced with a writing task like to go somewhere quiet and work in sizable blocks of time. Such luxury is rarely available to managers.

Another aspect of the managerial writing context is the extent of collaboration and delegation that occurs. As was noted earlier, collaboration is becoming more common in business and requires managers who can work well with others. Additionally, managers have the option of delegating some of their more routine writing chores.[16] This delegation, however, presupposes the manager's knowledge of various subordinates' abilities and willingness to handle the assignment.

The size and culture of the organization are also important elements of the context of managerial communication. Small companies can communicate many things orally, but the larger a company gets, the greater is the need to put things in writing for the record. With size also comes a tendency for greater formality in many written documents. With regard to culture, bureaucracies thrive on formality, while more participative organizations lean toward informality.

Authority and politics play a significant role in the context of managerial writing. Max Weber described three types of authority: traditional, charismatic, and legal.[17] How managers communicate messages is greatly influenced by the type of authority they are perceived to have. Also, business organizations must be viewed as political systems.[18] Managers who forget to consider the political forces at work in the company may soon find they no longer work at the company.

In our increasingly litigious society and given the ever-increasing role of government in business, legal concerns represent another important element of the managerial writing context. Managers are considered legal agents of the organization in many types of writing they do. They must be conscious of such things as libel, slander, privacy, and equal opportunity.

For managers, the phenomenon of a discourse community means they face a unique writing environment (see Table 6-1). They must carefully analyze the organizational culture in which they work, they must find the best time and place to write, and they must always remember that writing has a unique role in the manager's job.

A manager who has committed to using the written communication channel and who has considered the

Table 6–1 Elements of a Manager's Discourse Community

Fragmented workday
Extensive collaboration
Option to delegate
Organization's size and culture
Lines of authority
Political forces
Legal concerns

unique characteristics of writing in an organizational environment, as described in the previous sections of this chapter, is now ready to begin the writing process. This process consists of three stages: planning, composing, and revising. If the manager follows this process, the resulting document is more likely to be successful in reaching its goal.

STAGE ONE: PLANNING

The planning process for a managerial writer is a lot like the one journalists are trained to use. The parallel is logical since both might be characterized as professional writers. Both spend a significant amount of time writing at work, and both write for readers who are in a hurry. Thus, both might be expected to determine the five Ws—what, why, who, when, where—and how.

What?

The *what* question deals with the nature of the message. A manager should have a fairly clear idea of what needs to be communicated early in the planning stages. Does he need certain information? Is she granting or rejecting a request? Is he informing subordinates of a policy change? Is she trying to secure the cooperation of workers in implementing certain procedures?

Any time readers see a message that seems to bounce from one side of an issue to another, any time readers are forced to wade through a message that rambles on endlessly and incoherently, any time readers wonder, "What is this person trying to say?" the chances are good that the writer *did not know* exactly what he was trying to say or what purpose he was trying to accomplish.

Why?

The answer to the *why* question is probably just as important as the answer to the *what* question. Furthermore, the answer should be just as clear to the reader as it is to the writer. Unfortunately, many miscommunications occur because the sender does not know why a message is being sent or does not bother to share with the reader the reason for the message.

Many corporate policies, procedures, and rules, for example, are imposed on employees without any accompanying justification. Personnel would probably be much more receptive to these directives if they understood why the directives were necessary. Humans are complex creatures who like to deal with cause and effect. When an effect is imposed and the cause is withheld, one likely result is resistance.

Who?

One of the most important elements of the planning that should precede any managerial communication is the answer to the *who* question—who is receiving the message?

Demographic characteristics, such as age, sex, education, political affiliations, and job title, may provide some indication as to how the reader will interpret a message. Within an organizational setting, however, these characteristics fall short of telling us about the writer-reader relationship and about the characteristics of the organization and the department that may be pertinent to successful message transmission.

To engage in a truly thorough reader analysis and to be fully attuned to the reader's likely reception of a message, a writer should consider the following points:

- The relative power position between the writer and the reader
- The communication requirements the organization exerts on the reader and the writer
- The business functions the writer and reader work in
- The frequency of communication between the writer and the reader
- The reader's reaction to past messages from the writer
- The relative sensitivity of the message

The time spent on reader analysis may vary with the relative importance of the message. For very important messages, a writer may scrutinize all the information available to determine the best wording, the most appropriate organization, the right medium, the best timing, and the best source and destination for the message. However, even routine messages will improve as a result of audience analysis and adaptation.

When?

The importance of the answer to the *when* question may vary according to how routine the information being conveyed is. Many routine messages, such as sales reports, are distributed periodically. No actual decision has to be made as to when they are sent because dates have already been set. Likewise, trivial information is likely to be received in the same way regardless of timing.

For a nonroutine message, however, the decision on when to send it may directly affect how the message is received. For example, the managers of a textile mill had to tell employees they were not going to get a pay raise even though the company had shown a profit the preceding quarter. Management chose to convey this message in letter form just before the employees went on vacation. Not only did this timing likely ruin the vacations of many employees, but it probably encouraged as well a number of them to spend their vacations looking for another job.

On the subject of timing, managers need to keep in mind that it is possible to send messages too early as well as too late. For example, the agenda for a meeting and supporting material could be sent so early that the recipients forget the meeting by the time it is scheduled to occur. But if the material is sent too late, participants might not have time to get fully prepared for the meeting. Two to five days' notice is a generally safe range; but the longer the meeting and the greater the amount of supporting material to be distributed, the longer the lead time needed.

Where?

The *where* question sometimes has to be addressed at both ends of the communication spectrum: From where should the message come and to where should it be directed? Should the message come from a manager at a particular level, or should it come from a person higher in the organization, so as to carry the additional weight of authority?

At the other end of the spectrum, we may have to decide where the reader should be while receiving the message. To illustrate, some companies have grappled with the problem of newsletter distribution: whether to send it to employees' homes or distribute it at work. Sending it to the homes might get the families interested, but it might also be viewed as an infringement of employee privacy or personal time.

How?

The *how* question is largely a matter of media selection. Even when managers decide to put it in writing, they are still faced with a number of written media options: letter, memo, report, e-mail, brochure, newsletter, manual, or even bulletin board. The choice of medium is determined at least in part by how personal the message needs to be, how widespread its distribution, and how quickly it needs to reach the audience.

> ### STOP AND THINK
>
> Think of a situation other than business writing where planning is the key to success. Try to answer the five Ws and H for that situation. Then decide to what extent going through that process will help you to reach your goal.

Additionally, managers should remember a rule of thumb that applies to media selection in general. Specifically, if a manager regularly uses one particular medium, the choice of a different medium might communicate a sense of urgency or importance. For example, if a manager regularly communicates with subordinates in person, a memo might suggest something unusual and worthy of extra attention.

Though the preceding planning concerns were discussed separately and in a particular order, they are all interdependent and should not be treated in isolation. The good managerial communicator learns to see the interrelationships and to treat the five Ws and H as a decision package.

STAGE TWO: COMPOSING

Once the planning stage has been carried out satisfactorily, the manager is ready to begin building the message that will accomplish the purpose to be served. More specifically, the manager must compose a message. Words need to be chosen with care and organized in a clear, comprehensive, and coherent fashion. The manager should follow the guidelines described next when selecting words and composing them into sentences and paragraphs. The result is a document written in contemporary style.

Selecting Words

Words are symbols that define the content of a message; thus, words should be carefully selected so the overall content will accomplish the communication's goal. Each word carries the potential for contributing to the effectiveness of the message, and each carries the potential for causing misunderstanding. Great care should be taken to ensure message effectiveness and avoid misunderstanding. The following principles will help writers accomplish their goals.

Principle One: Choose Words Precisely

While some business documents (contracts, job offer letters, performance appraisals) may call for high levels of precision, managers would be wise to exercise care in choosing words in all their writing. And as they strive for this precision, they should remember that words can have both denotative and connotative meanings.

Denotative meanings are objective; they point to; they describe. Most people think of dictionary definitions as denotative meanings because these definitions are compiled from the common usages associated with a word. Most people agree on the denotative definitions of terms—that is, they agree as long as there are no words similar in sound or appearance to confuse the issue. For example, can you pick out the correct word in each of the following sentences?

- The advertising agency that we just bought should profitably (complement, compliment) our manufacturing and distribution interests.

- My computer printer has operated (continually, continuously) for the last five years.

- The manager assured us that he had (appraised, apprised) his superior of the shipping problem.

- The secretary made an (illusion, allusion) to what had taken place in the cafeteria.

- To persuade upper management to take this action, we will need the testimony of an expert who is completely (uninterested, disinterested).

Along the same lines, consider the following excerpts from letters written to a government agency.

- "I am very much annoyed to find that you have branded my son illiterate. This is a dirty lie as I was married a week before he was born."

- "Unless I get my husband's money pretty soon, I will be forced to lead an immortal life."

In business writing, wrong word choices can produce embarrassing humor at best and considerable confusion at worst. Neither is likely to provide a boost to a manager's career.

Connotative meanings, on the other hand, are subjective. They can be different for different people because they are determined largely by a person's previous experiences or associations with a word and its referent.

Though connotations are subjective, people can manipulate the language to bring forth either positive or negative connotations. An expression with intended positive connotations is called a *euphemism*. The words *slim* and *slender* are much more euphemistic than are words such as *skinny* and *scrawny*.

As advertisers and other interested parties try to portray life in the most pleasant way possible, euphemisms have become a part of American life. When, however, euphemisms are used in an effort to veil or gloss over major human and environmental tragedies, we must recognize the language abuse and the feeble cover-up. When *collateral damage* is used to describe the deaths of innocent civilians in war, for example, we must wonder at the value assessed to human lives by the people using these descriptions.

Managers, as well as people in other careers, bear a responsibility to their audiences to use the language as accurately as possible. Managers should strive to communicate precisely and honestly and to avoid insulting the reader's intelligence. Additionally, they should try to act as responsibly as they can in using words as control tools and instruments of change.[19]

Principle Two: Use Short Rather Than Long Words

Winston Churchill once said, "Big men use little words and little men use big words." People who are genuinely secure generally feel quite comfortable using simple words that are easy to understand. Short words are usually less confusing than long words. Long words, especially when strung out with several other long words, can produce a communication barrier between writer and reader.

Written business communications should be economical and efficient. The boxed lists on the following pages provide alternatives for some of the many longer words used and abused in business writing.

We are not suggesting that the use of any words in the left-hand column will condemn a message to ambiguity and obscurity. The caution here refers to the unnecessary use of long, difficult words. When overused, they tax a reader's understanding—and patience—and create a barrier to effective communication.

The US Congress has recognized the importance of "plain language" in government forms, benefits applications, reports, regulations, and other documents. Beginning in 2007, Congress considered bills mandating that government agencies use language that is clear and well organized and that follows best practices of writing. The Plain Language in Government Communications Bill of 2007 (S.2291), cosponsored by ten Senators,

Instead of Using	Use
advise	tell
ameliorate	improve
approbation	approval
commence	begin
demonstrate	show
encounter	meet
expectancy	hope
explicate	explain
locality	place
modification	change
perspicacity	sense
subsequent to	after
terminate	end
usage	use
utilize	use

failed by just one vote in the fall 2008 session. One opponent, Utah's Senator Robert Bennett, voiced concern that such legislation would cause legal terms to become lost in translation, though he agreed that the measure would improve Americans' access to their government. Another Plain Language bill (HR 946) was introduced in February 2009 and was signed into law by President Barack Obama in October 2010. The Plain Writing Act mandates that federal employees be trained to write clear, concise, well-organized documents to the public regarding their benefits or services or regarding filing taxes. Documents include (whether in paper or electronic form) letters, publications, forms, notices, and instructions. At the state level, more than twenty-two states now have Plain Language statutes on their books, notably New York, Connecticut, Pennsylvania, Florida, Minnesota, California, Oregon, and Washington.

Principle Three: Use Concrete Rather Than Abstract Words

In discussing a topic, a writer can choose from a range of words. This range, or continuum, might be thought of as a ladder that the writer can climb. This ladder (see Figure 6–1) moves from concrete (specific) words on the lowest rungs to the more abstract (general) words on the highest rungs.

Concrete words tend to be specific; they create clear pictures in the reader's mind. Abstract words are less specific and produce wider, more general interpretations of meanings. The ladder moves from something easily visualized to something that is more abstract, even vague, as shown by the examples in Figure 6–1.

The level of abstraction or concreteness depends in part on the reader's background, needs, and expectations. Abstract words and phrases threaten some readers and generate mistrust and confusion. They give rise to questions that the text may or may not answer: When? How many? Who? How much? Which one? Notice the differing amount of information in the following pairs of expressions:

Concrete words and phrases frequently create sharp, vivid images and stimulate reader interest. Forming concrete phrases may take more time and thought, but they are more efficient and stay with the reader longer than do abstract phrases.[20] Additionally, concrete writing takes less time to read, produces better message comprehension, and is less likely to need rereading than abstract writing.[21]

Abstract	Concrete
a good student	student earned the highest semester total grade point in a class of sixty-eight students
in the near future	by Friday, June 19
a significant profit	a 28 percent markup
a noteworthy savings	50 percent off the normal price
at your earliest convenience	by the close of business this Friday

Principle Four: Economize on Words

The scientist Pascal wrote a twenty-page letter to a friend in 1656. In a postscript, he apologized for the letter's length, saying, "I hope you will pardon me for writing such a long letter, but I did not have time to write you a shorter one." Pascal was testifying to the fact that conciseness, or economy of word choice, takes time and effort.

A practical, bottom-line reason exists to write concisely. Wordiness costs companies money. Unnecessary words take valuable time to compose and read; they waste paper and resources. Consider the following two versions of a business message.

- Enclosed please find a check in the amount of $82.56. In the event that you find the amount to be neither correct nor valid, subsequent to an examination of your records, please inform us of your findings at your earliest convenience.

- Enclosed is a check for $82.56. If this amount is incorrect, please let us know.

The second version takes fifteen words to say the same thing said by the first version in forty-one words—a reduction of over 63 percent.

Figure 6–1 Abstraction Ladders

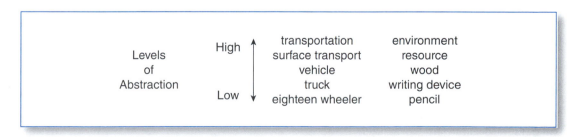

Wordy/Redundant Phrases	Alternatives
due to the fact that	because
for the purpose of	for
for the reason that	since, because
in order to	to
in the event that	if
with reference to	about
pursuant to your request	as requested
subsequent to	after
along the lines of	like
true facts	facts
necessary steps required	requirements
basic principles	principles
enclosed herein please find	here is
look forward with anticipation	anticipate
consensus of opinion	consensus
from the point of view of	from
inasmuch as	since, because
in accordance with	as
on the grounds that	because
at a later time	later (or a time)
within a period of one year	within one year
take into consideration	consider
a check in the amount of	a check for
for which there was no use	useless
that could not be collected	uncollectible
notwithstanding the fact that	although

Why do people in business continue to be wordy when such reductions are possible? Two likely reasons stand out. One is that writers often use wordy phrases out of habits that developed when they had to write long essays in school. In evaluating students' work, quantity is sometimes as important as quality to teachers.

The other reason is that untrained business writers often look to the files for a model when faced with a writing assignment on the job. When the files are filled with jargon and wordy expressions and when the novices mimic these writing patterns, the tradition of verbal waste continues. Note in the examples that follow how the wordy/redundant expressions on the left can be replaced by the more economical alternatives on the right.

If today's emphasis on controlling costs is to be applied to business writing, the expressions illustrated in the left-hand column will have to be replaced by the alternatives in the right-hand column.[22] Though writing concisely is time-consuming at first, it eventually becomes a relatively easy habit.

A good example of economy in writing is text messaging. Students and workers alike have learned to extract main ideas from chunks of information and experiences and to communicate these ideas in cryptic messages. As discussed in Chapter 3, texting has replaced e-mail in many organizations as the channel of choice, because of its simplicity and immediacy. Living in the era of information overload, readers ask, "What do we need to know? Why do we need to know it?" And texters limit their messages accordingly.

One might argue that economy in writing necessarily causes meaning to be lost. However, Larry Smith and Rachel Fershleiser have shown that messages can be short on words while deep in meaning. Founders of the online magazine *SMITH*, they asked the world to send in six-word memoirs. They used Ernest Hemingway's example as a model. According to legend, when asked to write a novel in only six words, Hemingway came up

STOP AND THINK

1. Which of the two following statements is more powerful?

   - "Well, please stop me if you've heard this before, but I've been giving this matter a lot of thought, and I'm concerned about whether the solution we're considering is actually going to help us to achieve our goals, don't you agree?"

   - "That won't work."

2. If you selected the second statement, what conclusion should you draw about the importance of conciseness?

with "For sale: baby shoes, never worn." Over 15,000 people responded to the challenge. Some notable examples posted on *SMITH* include these:

- "My second-grade teacher was right."—Janelle Brown

- "Secret of life: Marry an Italian."— Nora Ephron

- "Took scenic route, got in late."—Will Blythe

- "Became my mother. Please shoot me."—Cynthia Kaplan

- "It's pretty high. You go first."—Alan Eagle[23]

Principle Five: Avoid Clichés and Jargon

Trite expressions or clichés have an accepted meaning; however, these words yield dull messages that lack creativity. Readers may understand what is written, but the message appears impersonal since the writer has injected nothing original into it.

Additionally, trite phrases often go out of style quickly, so the writing (and writer) may seem timeworn. The following lists present some overused phrases to avoid and their alternatives:

Overused Phrases	Alternatives
white as a sheet	pale
busy as a bee	busy, working
smart as a whip	intelligent
follow in the footsteps of	pursue the same career
get it all together	get organized, resolve the problem
stretches the truth	exaggerates, lies
clean as a whistle	sanitary, clean
rock of Gibraltar	reliable, dependable
really down to earth	realistic, honest, sincere
as luck would have it	unfortunately, luckily

The last of the preceding examples illustrates a significant shortcoming in the use of these hackneyed phrases. They can have more than one meaning. Furthermore, sometimes they are simply vague, and sometimes their logic can be questioned. These weaknesses are illustrated in the following examples:

"at an early date" or "at your earliest convenience"

Such phrases usually follow a request for information or for a favor of some sort. They are normally used by people who do not want to appear pushy. Such people do not realize two things. One is that the reader's "earliest convenience" may end up being something quite different from what the writer had in mind. The second is that businesspeople deal with deadlines all the time. They are not likely to take offense when asked for something within a range of time if the writer concisely and courteously states the reason for the time range, as in the following example:

> "So that we may fill your order as quickly as possible, please send us this information by March 21."

Some readers interpret these two clichés as presumptuous:

> "Thanking you in advance . . ." and "Permit me to say . . ."

Besides being timeworn, mechanical, and impersonal, the first expression seems to say, "I expect you to comply with my request, but I don't want to have to take the time to thank you later, so I'll do it now." The second expression seems to seek permission, but the writer says what he or she wants to say before getting that permission. The second expression should be dropped, and the first might be replaced by,

> "I appreciate any help you can give me in the matter."

Jargon is the technical language or specified terms that become part of the everyday vocabulary of an organization or discipline. Insiders know what the words mean, but outsiders/customers may not. Jargon includes technical terms, acronyms, and terms used in special ways. When writing to readers outside the organization, managers should avoid using jargon. Rather, they should choose the layperson's version whenever possible to reduce the likelihood that the reader will misunderstand the message.[24] Additionally, some organizations are so large that the people in one functional unit may not understand the jargon of other units. The following lists illustrate how some jargon used in business might be simplified:

With only one exception, the descriptions on the right are wordier than the jargon on the left. If these wordier versions ensure understanding and prevent inquiries aimed at clarification, then the extra effort and words used will have been worthwhile. This is a decision managers must make when writing.

Acronyms can be particularly troublesome. In some situations, an acronym may be perfectly appropriate, while in other situations, it may cause a problem. For instance, in one division of Exxon, a DHR is the director of human resources, but in other divisions it is a by-product of the chemical scrubbing process.

Finally, a word of caution about *business-ese*. Expressions and terms can quickly become popular in business circles and then become obsolete just as quickly. A Texas entrepreneur, Ron Sturgeon, captured 1,200 examples of "biz jargon" in his book, *Green Weenies and Due Diligence.* Some are funny and colorful ("herding cats," "circling the drain," "mouse milking"), while some are more sober ("dilution," "FTE," "synergy").[25] Sometimes, in a misguided

Jargon	Layperson's Version
TQM	Total quality management
Accounts receivable	Firms or people owing money to the company
Amounts payable	Amounts owed by the company
HVI bonus	Extra pay for selling high-volume machines
Maturity date	Date that final payment is due
Feedstock	Raw materials used for manufacturing in the petrochemical industry
Fuplexing	Photocopyist's term meaning copying on both sides of a sheet of paper
FAA	Federal Aviation Administration
Abstract	History of the property
Per diem	Daily
Assessed valuation	Value of the property for tax purposes
Current ratio	Ratio of current assets to current liabilities
CRM	Customer relations management

attempt to sound professional, business-ese makes longer words out of short ones, such as *functionality* for "functions" and *objectivality* for "objectives." When deciding whether to use business-ese in your message, be guided by your receiver's expectations, the communication climate, and the cultural context (see Chapter 2).

Principle Six: Use Positive Words That Convey Courtesy

As stated earlier, written communications present stimuli and generate responses. Generally, the more positive the stimuli, the more positive the response. Conversely, the more negative the stimuli, the more negative the response. Behavioral scientists, for example, tell us that subordinates will live either up or down to the expectations communicated by their managers.[26]

Whether a manager is dealing with subordinates, superiors, peers, customers, suppliers, or others, she is likely to want her message to be well received. The positive wording of a request, of information, or even of bad news should increase the probability of a positive or at least neutral reaction by the receiver.

The difference between positive and negative wording is not a matter of content but of emphasis. Negative messages emphasize the least desirable aspects of a situation. As such, they are likely to arouse defensive or antagonistic responses from the reader.

The sender of an effective communication must establish credibility and goodwill with the receiver, and positiveness and courtesy aid the manager in developing these aspects. The following examples illustrate the different impacts that can be generated by positive and negative wordings of messages:

I cannot have the report ready by tomorrow morning.
I can have the report completed by 3:30 p.m. Wednesday.

You should not use Form A to file the weekly sales report.
Form B is the weekly sales report form.

We regret to inform you that we must deny your request for a promotion because you haven't earned enough continuing education credits.
As soon as you earn six more continuing education credits, we can process your request for a promotion.

In each of the alternative statements in the preceding examples, the writer states what can be done or what has been done rather than what cannot be done or what has not been done.

Let's look at a real-life example. In the hospitality management industry, theft of hotel-room amenities is a major cost of doing business. Guests routinely steal towels, pens, even furniture from their hotel rooms. Instead of posting warnings or threats, Holiday Inn Express takes a positive approach. A notice placed on the bathroom countertop reads,

Is that not better than saying, "Don't steal items from the room"?

Dear Guest,

Due to the popularity of our guest room amenities, our Housekeeping Department now offers these items for sale:

Irons: $40.00

Ironing boards: $30.00

Blow dryer: $30.00

Bath towels: $15.00

Hand towels: $10.00

Each guest room attendant is responsible for maintaining the guest room items. Should you decide to take these articles from your room, instead of obtaining them from the Executive Housekeeper, we will assume you approve a corresponding charge to your account. Thank you.

Some phrases, because they seem discourteous, are likely to irritate readers. Avoid them to ensure a positive and courteous climate. Although we should not totally avoid negatives, we can minimize them. Words and phrases like "inexcusable," "you claim that," "your insinuation," "you failed to," and "obviously you overlooked" should be avoided if possible. The next chapter on messages will explain this point further.

Being positive and conveying courtesy in word choice also involves using gender-neutral language. Rarely is it necessary for writers to identify people as male or female.

Today, we use gender-neutral terms to describe jobs. Also, pronouns and nouns that refer to one sex when both are being described *(manpower)* are unacceptable. Likewise, expressions that belittle the behavior or qualities of one gender should be avoided. The following listings present unacceptable and acceptable terms.

TERMS TO AVOID

man (when referring to the species)	man hours
man-made	steward, stewardess
manpower	homemaker
grow to manhood	fairer sex
businessman	weaker sex
cameraman	old man, breadwinner
fireman	career woman
foreman	lady doctor/lawyer/realtor
salesman	workman's compensation

ACCEPTABLE TERMS

business executive	work hours
state career (e.g., doctor, lawyer, editor)	camera operator
humanity, human beings, humans, people	firefighter
human power, human energy	supervisor
workers, work force, employee	sales representative, salesperson, salesclerk
flight attendant	workers' compensation

On the subject of sexism in writing, one particularly thorny problem is the generic or universal pronoun *he*. Until about thirty years ago, the standard practice had been to use *he* in impersonal constructions where both sexes were to be included: "Each person has his own problems to resolve." Authorities have noted that such constructions can make women feel ignored in the business world.

Fortunately, managers have several options available for avoiding such pronoun use. One is the use of plural nouns and pronouns. Instead of "A manager should motivate his employees," one could write "Managers should motivate their employees."

Another option is the use of "he and she," "his or her," "s/he," or "his/her." Though not entirely graceful, this option is considered acceptable. Writers should be careful, however, not to use this option too often, for it could hinder style and readability.

Another technique, one used widely in this book, is to alternate masculine and feminine pronouns. One paragraph may use *she* as the generic pronoun, while the next might use *he*. While this technique avoids the generic *he*, it does not sacrifice style the way *he or she* sometimes does. Furthermore, traditional usage is spared, at least in part.

A fourth nonsexist technique is one that is not satisfactory to strict grammarians. It uses plural pronouns for traditionally singular antecedent references, such as *each, every, everyone, everybody,* or *anybody.* For example, "Everyone has their problems to resolve." This technique legitimizes popular use.

The last, and best, suggestion is to replace third-person pronouns *(he/she)* with second person *(you)*. Not only does this avoid the gender issue, it directly engages the reader too. Thus, "If you are going to be late, call your supervisor" is better than "If an employee is going to be late, he/she should call his/her supervisor."

Principle Seven: Use a Conversational Style

Sentences communicate effectively when they use everyday language; that is, when the words are those that would be used in face-to-face communication. A conversational style involves writing with words from a person's speaking vocabulary. Usually, the words should not include colloquialisms, slang, or jargon; they should be the language most people would use in conducting everyday business.

The most successful business professional who exemplifies writing in a conversational style is billionaire investor Warren Buffett, chairman of Berkshire Hathaway, Inc. In 2005, The National Commission on Writing honored Buffett's folksy annual report. "No annual report has had a greater impact on American business," said Bob Kerrey, the commission's chair and president of The New School, A University in New York.[27]

Buffett's 2013 annual letter to shareholders, while maintaining his trademark style, communicated his strategy for investing. He advocates keeping cool in a chaotic environment and taking a long-term view. "Games are won by players who focus on the playing field—not by those whose eyes are glued to the scoreboard," he wrote."[28]

Buffett's conversational writing style is not an aberration. Other successful executives, such as Bill Gates, openly admire it. In an interview with Maria Bartiromo in February 2009, Gates admitted that writing an annual letter about his foundation's activities was Buffett's idea—and Gates "ran a few drafts by him. . . . His advice is very helpful."[29]

A conversational style is particularly important in business letters since it aids in developing the "you viewpoint." The you viewpoint involves consideration of the reader's point of view. It helps a writer personalize letters, something most readers appreciate in business correspondence.[30]

Before writing, the sender identifies who will receive the information; the reader's need for the information; and as much as possible, her knowledge, expertise, interests, culture, and value system.

Even form paragraphs and letters can be written with a category of reader in mind, people who might have certain common concerns that have to be addressed. Form paragraphs and letters can be written in a conversational style, as though they were composed by a human being rather than a jargon-stuffed computer. And technology makes it easier than it has ever been to personalize a form paragraph or letter.

These first seven principles have focused on the selection of words. Since each word can influence the total message, each word deserves attention. The manager also needs to analyze the combination and organization of words strategically to ensure effective communication. The remaining principles will address the ways in which words might be grouped for best effect.

Organizing Words for Effect

The next four principles discuss organizational guidelines for putting words together to convey a message. Comprehension is largely determined by the extent to which the writer uses these principles.

Principle Eight: Keep Sentences Short

We sometimes encounter long-winded sentences in business writing. These seemingly never-ending constructions stem from several possible causes. One cause mentioned earlier is the need to impress. Consider the following example from a government report:

It is obvious from the difference in elevation with relation to the short depth of the field that the contour is such as to preclude any reasonable development potential for economic utilization.

One would have to study the preceding message long and hard to figure out that the writer was, in fact, saying:

The field is too steep to plow.

On the other hand, some people write these lengthy, roundabout sentences to avoid appearing forward or pushy, as in the following example:

During the past two weeks, we have been wondering if you have as yet found yourself in a position to give us an indication of whether or not you have been able to come to a decision on our offer.

Most businesspeople who face deadlines daily would not be offended if they were asked a question more to the point:

Have you decided on the offer we made you two weeks ago?

Another possible cause for unnecessarily long sentences is the need to say everything that can be said about a topic in one sentence. Note the confusion created by the following example and the improvement in the alternative version.

Although seventeen people from our department (purchasing) attended the workshop, nine of them, including Jerry Stoves, had no background for the topic of the workshop (advanced negotiating technique) offered by the Purchasing Association of Chicago.

Last week seventeen people from our purchasing department attended a workshop on advanced negotiating techniques. The Purchasing Association of Chicago offered the workshop. Of the seventeen who attended, Jerry Stoves and eight others lacked the necessary background.

One way to shorten sentences is to avoid expletive constructions: "It . . . that" and "There is . . ." or "There are . . ." An expletive has no grammatical antecedent in a sentence, and it often diffuses the focus of the message by displacing or even eliminating people in the sentence. For example, in the sentence "It is thought that interest rates will fall," the word *it* has no antecedent, yet *it* gets the main emphasis. The person who holds this opinion is unknown. A better wording would be "I think that interest rates will fall." Instead of "It is suggested that you rewrite this proposal," say, "Please rewrite the proposal." Generally, "there is" and "there are" constructions merely add length and waste time. Rather than saying, "There are three options from which you can choose," say, "You can choose from three options."

Unnecessarily long sentences require readers to spend too much time trying to understand the message. And the more time and patience required to understand a message, the less likely the reader is to understand the purpose.

Effective writing is easy and quick to read. Studies show that good business sentences are fifteen to twenty words long. They also use no more than ten long (three-or-more-syllable) words in every one hundred words.

Effective sentences express one main point. Any connected phrases or clauses should explain that point. When we place two or more important ideas in the same sentence, we reduce the importance of each and often confuse the reader.

Principle Nine: Prefer the Active to the Passive Voice

The active voice presents the parts of a sentence in the normal order expected by English-speaking people. The subject of the sentence is the actor, who is acting in a way portrayed by the verb, and the action is directed toward the object. The following sentences illustrate the active voice.

- David Lopez directed the meeting.

- Donna Hebert enforced the policy.

- Ridley Gros promoted the university.

The passive voice reverses the order of the parts so that the subject is being acted on by the object in a way depicted by the verb.

- The meeting was directed by David Lopez.

- The policy was enforced by Donna Hebert.

- The university was promoted by Ridley Gros.

Besides the reversed order and the slight additional length, the passive voice weakens the sentence construction by making the doer of the action the object of the "by" phrase. Furthermore, the passive voice carries the hazard of luring the writer into longer, more roundabout expressions.[31] For example, instead of writing,

The new president reorganized the administration,

we see:

A reorganization of the administration was effected by the new president.

Though managerial writers should favor the active voice in the majority of the sentences they construct, they may occasionally prefer the passive voice. Passive voice is more diplomatic. Notice that by eliminating the *by* phrase from a passive-voice sentence, we eliminate the doer of the action. In sensitive matters, or when addressing people of higher authority, this may be appropriate. Note the following diplomatic transformation.

Active: The director of purchasing has been soliciting bids from unauthorized vendors.

Passive: Bids from unauthorized vendors have been solicited by the director of purchasing.

Passive minus the by phrase: Bids from unauthorized vendors have been solicited.

Principle Ten: Organize Paragraphs Logically

Paragraphs bring separate thoughts together and arrange them to convey a single important idea. A paragraph is a device to combine sentences to form messages. Alone, these sentences might seem illogical and would not make the same point.

Five guidelines can help writers develop effective paragraphs (see Table 6–2). First, present one major idea in a paragraph, along with whatever support is necessary for the development of that idea.[32] This paragraph quality is called *unity.*

Table 6–2 Developing Effective Paragraphs

1. Present one major idea in a paragraph.
2. Decide if a deductive or an inductive pattern is appropriate.
3. Use a variety of sentence structures in a paragraph.
4. Structure paragraphs to emphasize important points.
5. Keep paragraphs relatively short.

Second, determine if a deductive or an inductive pattern is appropriate. Deductive paragraphs present the main idea in the first sentence and the supporting ideas in the sentences that follow. Inductive paragraphs begin with the details or the support and end with the main idea. The deductive pattern is the most commonly used, but the inductive pattern is useful for persuasion.

Third, use a variety of sentence structures in a paragraph. A paragraph that contains all simple sentences can be tedious; interest builds when a combination of sentence structures is used.

Fourth, structure paragraphs to emphasize important points. Emphasis can be accomplished in a variety of ways:

- Repeat key concepts.

- Use attention-getting words, such as action verbs, and the personal pronoun *you*.

- Use typographical devices, such as bullets, text boxes, italics, boldface, or numbers.

Be sure that bulleted lists, repeated phrases, and compound structures are in *parallel* form. That is, sentence elements that are alike in function should also be alike in construction.[33] Look at the following examples:

Parallel: The company has *a* mission statement and *a* code of ethics.

Not parallel: Citizens are concerned whether the president *has lied* under oath or *looking* directly into the cameras.

Excellent examples of parallel structure can be found in the words of great orators. Look at this excerpt from the Rev. Dr. Martin Luther King's famous I Have a Dream speech: "So let freedom ring from the prodigious hilltops of New Hampshire. Let freedom ring from the mighty mountains of New York. Let freedom ring from the heightening Alleghenies of Pennsylvania. Let freedom ring from the snowcapped Rockies of Colorado." Notice how the repetition and parallel structure of these sentences add rhythm, balance, and a buildup of emotion.

Fifth, keep paragraphs relatively short. Short paragraphs are easy to read and give more emphasis to the information they contain. Readers need visual and mental breaks so they can assimilate the message; short paragraphs help to achieve these breaks. In business letters and short memos, paragraphs usually average four to six lines in length; in reports, they average eight to ten lines. Exceptions, however, will sometimes be justified by the need for emphasis (shorter paragraphs) or by the complexity of the material (longer paragraphs).

These guidelines for composing short, strong, clear messages are followed by prominent leaders in fields other than business. One example is Lieutenant General Gus Pagonis, who was the officer in charge of logistics during the Persian Gulf War of 1991. His book *Moving Mountains: Lessons in Leadership and Logistics from the Gulf War* tells how he delivered meals, fuel, ammunition, and other supplies to 541,000 US military forces in Kuwait during the 100-hour lightning ground war. Pagonis wrote that his operating principle was KISS– Keep It Simple Stupid. An important application of that principle was his communication patterns. He limited paperwork to an amazing 3-by-5-inch index card per report. Furthermore, he limited all e-mail messages to just six lines. Apparently no one could take time to scroll. Under harrowing wartime conditions, Pagonis's insistence on good writing contributed to his success.

Principle Eleven: Be Coherent

With coherent writing, the relationship between sentences is clear. Sentences flow from one to another easily and smoothly. This movement from one thought to another is accomplished through transition, which is sometimes described as a bridge that connects thoughts. Transitions may be natural or mechanical.

Natural transition occurs when the content of the thoughts is such that the second flows naturally and smoothly from the first. Note the smooth movement from the first thought to the second in the following opening paragraph to a job application letter.

> Now that the Dillon Pharmaceutical Company is expanding its Western region, won't you need trained and experienced sales representatives to call on accounts in the new territory? With a degree in marketing and eight successful years in pharmaceutical sales, I believe that I am well qualified to be one of those representatives.

The first sentence introduces the ideas of training and experience, and the second sentence builds on that introduction.

Often, however, a writer cannot rely on the content of thoughts to show a clear connection between them. The writer may have to show that connection with mechanical *transitions*. A writer can (1) repeat key words, to show the reader that the same subject is still being addressed, (2) use pronouns and synonyms, to avoid being too repetitious, or (3) use transition words, words that are used to connect thoughts and show a particular type of relationship between them. Table 6–3 lists some frequently used transition words.

In addition to making sure the thoughts within a paragraph flow smoothly, writers should be concerned that this quality of coherence pervades entire documents. More specifically, paragraphs, like sentences, need to be clearly related. Sometimes this relationship is shown through the use of transitional devices such as those previously discussed. At other times, an entire sentence at the beginning or end of a paragraph will be used to show the relationship of that paragraph to the one that precedes or follows it.

As we move into longer and more complex documents, such as reports, the task of ensuring coherence becomes more involved. For example, a five-page section of a twenty-five-page report may need an introductory paragraph to show what is included in that

Table 6–3 Frequently Used Transition Words

but	accordingly	even so
next	again	on the other hand
thus	consequently	furthermore
then	otherwise	in summary
finally	besides	similarly
hence	conversely	as a result
still	to illustrate	in contrast
also	in addition	subsequently
and	however	for example

section. It may also need a concluding paragraph to tie up the section and show how it relates to the larger purpose of the report. A simpler kind of transitional device is a "Janus statement," named for the Roman god with two faces—one looking backward and one looking ahead. The writer can accomplish both a review and a preview with a Janus statement, such as "Now that we have described X, let us turn our attention to Y."

A final way to build coherence in long documents is by using headings and sub-headings. Chapter 8 addresses report and proposal writing in more detail, including heading use.

Before we leave the subject of coherence, a word of caution may be in order. Though the transitional devices discussed here can show relationships to readers, logical organization is the foundation of coherent writing. Writers must clearly understand why information is being arranged in a certain way. They must have a logical plan of presentation, for transitional devices cannot show relationships that do not exist.

STAGE THREE: REVISING

The third stage, revising and editing, is perhaps the most important to practice. Few writers possess the skill to write clear copy in one sitting.[34] The multitude of writing principles, approaches, and grammatical rules requires all writers to check their work. Revising is a service to the reader. Thus, the writer should begin stage three by shifting perspective, distancing himself from the writing, and assuming the role of the reader. It is difficult to objectively examine the message from the reader's viewpoint; however, the following questions can help systematize the revision process:

- What is my purpose?

- Have I included all the information the reader wants or needs to know to understand my message?

- Does my message answer all the reader's questions?

- Is there any information nonessential to the reader that I can delete?

- Have I included reader benefits?

Next, revising involves (1) reading what has been written for clarity, concreteness, and conversational tone; (2) determining factual accuracy; (3) organizing to ensure coherence;[35]

Table 6–4 The Seven Cs of Good Business Writing

Completeness	Answer all reader questions
	Include the five Ws and H
Conciseness	Shorten or delete wordy expressions
	Avoid repetition
Consideration	Focus on "you," the reader
	Show reader benefits or interests
	Emphasize the positive
Concreteness	Use specific facts and data
	Use active, not passive, voice
	Rely on vivid, image-building words
Clarity	Use short, familiar words
	Avoid jargon
	Follow a logical sequence of points
Courtesy	Be tactful and appreciative
	Avoid discriminatory language
	Respond promptly
Correctness	Maintain accurate writing mechanics
	Avoid "wrong word" errors

(4) rewording awkward sentences and phrases; and (5) rearranging content and adding illustrations and transitions. Writers should not assume their prose is satisfactory after only one or two drafts. Few people write that well.[36]

The final step is to edit the document for correctness. Running a spell-checker and grammar checker will catch most surface errors. However, these devices are insufficient since (so far) they do not always predict intended meanings. An amusing, well-known case where punctuation significantly changes a sentence's meaning is the following:

A woman, without her man, is nothing.

A woman: without her, man is nothing.[37]

The amount of revising and editing necessary will depend on the individual writer's skill. However, all good writers rewrite. They even sometimes have someone else read their work before finalizing it. Others can often detect errors or confusing statements that writers miss because writers read into their messages what they want to communicate. At the very least, a writer should set aside a draft and let it "cool off" for a while before revising. When e-mailing, a writer can queue messages to be reread rather than composing and immediately clicking the Send button. Hastily sent e-mails can be embarrassingly incomplete or inaccurate.

Though revising and editing may seem time-consuming and tedious, the results are worth the effort. By making the message clearer and easier to understand, revising benefits the reader and reduces the likelihood of requests for later clarification. In the long run, it saves time and money while enhancing the writer's image.

When revising and editing, an easy way to keep your goal in sight is to remember the "Seven Cs" of good business writing. Table 6–4 presents these guidelines.

SUMMARY

Written managerial communication has several strategic advantages: economy, efficiency, accuracy, and official permanence.

In addition, managerial writing has two unique characteristics: (1) Collaboration is used quite often when creating documents, and (2) managers work in an environment that makes special demands on their documents. First, collaboration is a fact of modern organizational life. In addition to the advantages of group decision making, it also socializes employees in several ways and can improve the quality of the writing. In addition to the disadvantages associated with group decision making (e.g., domination, reluctant contributors), time, potential ego damage, style differences, and conflicts can work against effective collaboration.

Despite the potential pitfalls, we can identify effective collaborative writers. Good writers are flexible, respectful, attentive, articulate, responsible, and confident people who work well with others.

Guidelines for effective collaboration include dividing the work equitably among members. Conflict should be viewed as potentially constructive. The group's leader should coordinate efforts, shape the team's vision, and resolve conflicts.

Second, managers are members of a discourse community. Among the aspects of their managerial writing context are the fragmented nature of their time at work, the extent of collaboration and delegation, the size and culture of the organization, the authority and politics they must deal with, and the legal considerations of which they must remain aware as they write.

Once a manager recognizes these unique aspects, she is ready to write. The writing process consists of three stages: planning, composing, and revising. In the planning stage, the manager identifies what, why, who, when, where, and how. In the composing stage, the writer selects words and arranges them for proper effect, keeping certain strategic concerns in mind. The following principles guide the selection and arrangement of words for message clarity, comprehension, and coherence:

Selecting Words:

1. Choose words precisely.
2. Use short rather than long words.
3. Use concrete rather than abstract words.
4. Economize on words.
5. Avoid clichés and jargon.
6. Use positive words that convey courtesy.
7. Use a conversational style.

Organizing Words:

1. Keep sentences relatively short.
2. Prefer the active to the passive voice.
3. Develop logically organized paragraphs.
4. Be coherent.

In the revising stage, the writer examines the message for ways to improve on these eleven principles. Additionally, the manager edits for correctness of expression. Surface errors affect the success of a document in reaching its goals and also can damage the reader-writer relationship.

EXERCISE: PLAIN ENGLISH AT A GLANCE

One of the goals of the US Securities and Exchange Commission (SEC) is to help potential investors make good financial decisions. Therefore, in 1998, the SEC published a plain English guide that was designed to help writers create clearer business prospectuses and other disclosure documents. As a result, disclosure documents have become more informative and easier to read. The SEC's *Plain English Handbook* is found at this website: https://www.sec.gov/pdf/handbook.pdf. The handbook reinforces the principles that you have read in this chapter for plain writing.

Follow the SEC's plain English principles to improve the sentences below:

1. *Change the following sentence from the passive voice to the active voice:*

   A decision was made by the board to wear polo shirts when voting on important matters.

2. *Change the nominalizations (buried verbs) in the following sentence:*

   I came to the realization that the Fund's performance is a reflection of the maximum sales charge of 5 percent.

3. *Directly address the reader (use the you viewpoint) in the following sentence. Change any nominalizations into verbs. Change any passive voice constructions into active voice:*

   The volatility of the market should be taken under consideration by short-term investors in the selection and purchase of stocks.

4. *Rewrite the following sentence into plain English.*

   Your financial adviser should not be held accountable in the event you experience a decline in investment income or a net loss in total assets.

5. *Eliminate the unnecessary words in the following sentence:*

   In order to make progress in improving your writing skills, it is imperative that you devote yourself to the study of the principles of good writing.

6. *Improve the tone of the following sentence by changing the negative words to positive:*

   We were sorry to learn of the disappointing service you had from our sales force, which we are afraid will not improve until the current personnel are fired.

7. *Put the following sentence into parallel structure:*

   If you want to find out more about our offerings, visit our website after calling our toll free number with a request for a password.

8. *Rewrite the following sentence into shorter units:*

According to Nancy Smith, Director of the Office of Investor Education, three people, Ann Wallace, from the Division of Corporate Finance, Carolyn Miller, of the SEC, and William Lutz, Professor of English at Rutgers University, poured their hearts and minds into the *Plain English Handbook* that inspired me to create these exercises, which you are enjoying as well as finding informative, I hope, and so all of the credit and none of the blame goes to them.

9. *Revise the following sentence to directly address the reader (you attitude).*

We take pleasure in announcing that, effective today, the company will give a 20 percent discount on all purchases made by employees.

Case for Small-Group Discussion

CASE 6-1

Back to School

Because you are known to be a good writer, the director of human resources has asked you to put together a seminar on written communication for employees in your company who need help. The seminar would cover basic principles of written communication, letters, memos, and formal business reports. Managers have complained to the HR director that their employees do not write well. They produce as evidence sloppily proofread e-mails. The employees, on the other hand, are grumbling that having to attend a writing seminar would be like going back to high school, where a fussy old English teacher berates them over minor punctuation concerns.

QUESTIONS

1. How would you determine who should attend the seminar?

2. How would you market it so that participants of the seminar would attend willingly rather than through coercion?

3. How would you organize the seminar? What materials would you use?

4. What topics would you address in the seminar?

Exercises for Small Groups

A. Rewrite the following sentences to eliminate confusing, long words.

1. Bill received excessive remuneration for his promulgated work according to his professional colleagues.

2. What form of personal conveyance shall we solicit between the airport and the hotel?

3. The best operative unit for this interaction is the computer-assisted storage system.

4. Extel, the computer company, has an inordinate influence on your purchasing agent.

5. The company terminated their contract with the city as a consequence of their ineffectual payment procedures.

6. The audience was demonstrating engrossment with the audio-visually mediated presentation.

7. We received approbation from the executive committee.

8. This antiquated procedure could be liquidated with a new word processing system.

9. Last year's profits were exorbitant in that division.

10. Our assets cannot be utilized to the maximum due to the unavailability of trained human resources.

B. Rewrite the following sentences using concrete words.

1. We received a lot of responses to our survey.

2. The personnel department has expanded in the last several years.

3. Profits are up throughout the industry.

4. If we don't receive the order pretty soon, we will have to cancel it.

5. Please send your reply as soon as possible.

6. We would like to receive as many bids as possible.

7. We need the shipment by sometime next month.

8. Extel is a large company.

9. Is it possible to meet next week?

10. We are expecting a rapid rate of inflation.

C. Reduce the length of the following sentences.

1. Record sales were set by the top division, from $48.2 million to $51.4 million; the home appliance division decreased from $67.2 million to $58.4; the big shock was in the electronic division, which saw a drop from $17.2 million to $14.9 million; but all in all, top management was generally pleased.

2. Management attributed the decline to several significant business environment economic factor conditions including higher borrowing interest rates.

3. At this point in time pursuant to your request, we find it difficult to meet your stated requests as made in your letter.

4. The task force has been given the special responsibilities to accomplish the goals as stated in the letter sent yesterday by the executive vice president to the task force chairperson who was assigned the position.

5. On the grounds that this action could be completely finished in a period of one year, it was not seen as a totally practical action to take.

6. The past history of the new innovations indicates that the product innovation department should be terminated and ended.

7. We received your recent inquiry of last week regarding our new products we just came out with.

8. For the reason that all the information was not completely available, no immediate decision could be made then.

D. Rewrite the following sentences to eliminate trite expressions and improve clarity.

1. Enclosed please find a check in the amount of $40.

2. Please be advised that your order will be shipped within a short period of time.

3. I enclose herewith an order to which you will please give your earliest attention and forward, with as little delay as possible, as per shipping instructions attached.

4. Your letter dated July 25 has been duly received and noted.

5. Referring to your letter of the fifth, we wish to state that there has been an error in your statement.

6. With reference to your letter of the tenth, permit me to state that there will be no interference with the affairs of your department.

E. Change the negative tone and use more courteous words in the following sentences.

1. We cannot deliver all one hundred units by Friday, March 6.

2. We don't provide second mortgages.

3. We are sorry that your total deposit on the trip cannot be refunded.

4. No. An extension will not be permitted.

5. We do not feel that you qualify for the excessive request that you made.

6. You are not qualified for this position.

7. The competition provided a much more favorable bid, and they have a reputation for fine service.

8. Sorry, but the product you requested is no longer available.

F. Clarify the following message by using paragraphs and transitions and by generally following the guidelines presented in this chapter.

Most managers would agree that there are advantages to both the telephone and letters. Letters are more effective in some situations whereas the use of the telephone is best in others. So now the question is, "What are the advantages of each?" The telephone has the advantages of speed, immediate feedback, consuming less time, and cost. An advantage of the business letter is that a hard copy is available. Also, future reference can be made to it for legal reference. Also, enclosures can be included. One of the disadvantages of the telephone is that the conversation cannot be filed for future reference. Another advantage of the letter is that it can be circulated to other people who may be involved with the topic involved. Another disadvantage of the telephone is that you may not know if you are disturbing the receiver at a busy time during the day. The letter can be read when the receiver is ready to read it. All of these advantages and disadvantages must be considered when strategically determining the most effective communication tool. The greatest mistake may be to communicate via the most "convenient" media without considering the alternatives. Analysis of the situations is required to ensure that the most effective technique is used.

Student Study Site

Visit the Student Study Site at **study.sagepub.com/hynes6e** for web quizzes, video links, web resources, and cases studies.

Notes

1. Henry Mintzberg, *The Nature of Managerial Work* (Englewood Cliffs, NJ: Prentice Hall, 1980), pp. 38–39.
2. Lester Faigley and Thomas P. Miller, "What We Learn from Writing on the Job," *College English* 44, no. 6 (October 1982): p. 567.
3. Lisa Ede and Andrea Lunsford, *Singular Texts/Plural Authors* (Carbondale: Southern Illinois University Press, 1990), p. 60.
4. Nancy Allen, Dianne Atkinson, Meg Morgan, Teresa Moore, and Craig Snow, "What Experienced Collaborators Say about Collaborative Writing," *Journal of Business and Technical Communication* 1, no. 2 (September 1987): p. 71.
5. Ibid., p. 85.
6. R. Gebhardt, "Teamwork and Feedback: Broadening the Base of Collaborative Writing," *College English* 42, no. 1 (September 1980): p. 69.
7. Terry R. Bacon, "Collaboration in a Pressure Cooker," *The Bulletin,* June 1990, p. 4.
8. A. M. O'Donnell, D. F. Dansereau, T. R. Rocklin, C. O. Larson, V. I. Hythecker, M. D. Young, and J. G. Labiotee, "Effects of Cooperative and Individual Rewriting on an Instruction Writing Task," *Written Communication* 4 (1987): pp. 90–99.
9. Rebecca Burnett, "Benefits of Collaborative Planning in the Business Communication Classroom," *The Bulletin,* June 1990, p. 10.
10. Allen et al., "What Experienced Collaborators Say about Collaborative Writing," pp. 82–83.
11. Ede and Lunsford, *Single Tests/Plural Authors,* p. 62.
12. Ibid., p. 66.
13. Bacon, "Collaboration in a Pressure Cooker," p. 5.

14. Henry Mintzberg, *Mintzberg on Management: Inside Our Strange World of Organizations* (New York: Collier Macmillan, 1989), p. 8.

15. Sharon Begley, "Will the BlackBerry Sink the Presidency?" *Newsweek*, February 16, 2009, p. 37.

16. Marie Flatley, "A Comparative Analysis of the Written Communication of Managers at Various Organizational Levels in the Private Business Sector," *Journal of Business Communication* 19, no. 3 (Summer 1982): p. 40.

17. Max Weber, *The Theory of Social and Economic Organization,* trans. A. M. Henderson and Talcott Parsons, and ed. Talcott Parsons (New York: The Free Press, 1947), pp. 324–386.

18. James G. March, "The Business Firm as a Political Coalition," *Journal of Politics* 24 (1980): pp. 662–678.

19. Barbara Czarniawska-Joerges and Bernward Joerges, "How to Control Things with Words: Organizational Talk and Control," *Management Communication Quarterly* 2, no. 2 (November 1988): pp. 170–193.

20. Sarah Ellen Ransdell and Ira Fischler, "Effects of Concreteness and Task Context on Recall of Prose among Bilingual and Monolingual Speakers," *Journal of Memory and Language* 28, no. 3 (June 1989): pp. 278–279.

21. James Suchan and Robert Colucci, "An Analysis of Communication Efficiency between High-Impact Writing and Bureaucratic Written Communication," *Management Communication Quarterly* 2, no. 4 (May 1989): pp. 454–484.

22. "Weak Writers," *The Wall Street Journal,* June 14, 1985, p. 1.

23. Larry Smith and Rachel Fershleiser, "Not Quite What I Was Planning: Six-Word Memoirs by Writers Famous and Obscure" (2008), accessed February 11, 2008, www.smithmag.net.

24. Peter Crow, "Plain English: What Counts Besides Readability," *Journal of Business Communication* 25, no. 1 (Winter 1988): pp. 87–95.

25. Ron Sturgeon, *Green Weenies and Due Diligence: Insider Business Jargon* (Lynden, WA: Mike French, 2005).

26. Sterling Livingston, "Pygmalion in Management," *Harvard Business Review,* September–October 1988, pp. 121–130.

27. Associated Press, "Billionaire Buffett Gets an Award—For Writing," February 4, 2005, accessed February 8, 2005, http://msnbc.msn.com/id/6913932/print/1/displaymode/1098/.

28. Berkshire Hathaway, Inc. *2013 Annual Report* (2014), www.berkshirehathaway.com.

29. Maria Bartiromo, "Facetime: Melinda and Bill Gates on Making a Difference." *BusinessWeek*, February 16, 2009, pp. 21–22.

30. Kitty Locker, "Theoretical Justification for Using Reader Benefits," *Journal of Business Communication* 19, no. 3 (Summer 1982): pp. 51–65.

31. Pamela Layton and Adrian J. Simpson, "Deep Structure in Sentence Comprehension," *Journal of Verbal Learning and Verbal Behavior* 14 (1975): pp. 658–664.

32. Thomas L. Kent, "Paragraph Production and the Given-New Contract," *Journal of Business Communication* 21, no. 4 (Fall 1984): pp. 45–66.

33. For a comprehensive explanation of parallel structure, see Gerald J. Alred, Charles T. Brusaw, and Walter E. Oliu, *The Business Writer's Handbook,* 8th ed. (New York: Bedford/St. Martin's Press, 2006).

34. Larry Smeltzer and Jeanette Gilsdorf, "How to Use Your Time Efficiently When Writing," *Business Horizons,* November–December 1990, pp. 61–64.

35. Larry Smeltzer and Jeanette Gilsdorf, "Revise Reports Rapidly," *Personnel Journal,* October 1990, pp. 39–44.

36. Jeanne W. Halpern, "What Should We Be Teaching Students in Business Writing?" *Journal of Business Communication* 18, no. 3 (Summer 1981): pp. 39–53.

37. Lynne Truss, *Eats, Shoots and Leaves: The Zero Tolerance Approach to Punctuation* (New York: Gotham Books/Penguin Group USA, 2003).

Writing Routine Messages

And, of course, you have the commercials where savvy businesspeople get ahead by using their Macintosh computers to create the ultimate American business product: a really sharp-looking memo.

—Dave Barry, humorist and columnist

As earlier chapters have emphasized, written communication is an important part of a manager's job. One study of 837 business school graduates with varying years of experience found that they spent over one-fourth of their time at work writing.[1] And of all the different types of writing they do, e-mail, letters, and memos are certainly the workhorses of written managerial communication.[2] Another study (of 188 participants in a writing seminar) revealed that 63.1 percent of the managers surveyed wrote letters daily and 76.3 percent wrote memos daily.[3]

E-mail, letter, and memorandum are probably the forms of written communication that benefit most from the strategic considerations we discuss in this text. The conciseness of these messages and the relatively detached atmosphere in which managers usually write them can help ensure that the principles of reader adaptation and strategic analysis are used.

Unfortunately, too many managers take routine writing tasks for granted. Perhaps because managers write so many of them, e-mails, letters, and memos frequently can become impersonal things that convey information in a lifeless manner. Rather than being responses to a specific communication situation, many messages merely respond to types of situations. Thus, some managers write stock answers to claims and ignore, or at least discount, the factors making the claim unique and calling for adaptation.

Additionally, because e-mails, letters, and memos are such common and relatively informal media, managers often become lax regarding the quality of their messages. One study of correspondence in thirteen industries found punctuation errors in 43.7 percent of the correspondence surveyed, word usage errors in 52.2 percent, and sentence construction mistakes in 45.3 percent.[4]

Perhaps because routine correspondence is so bound by conventions of format, the language used in them poses another problem. These media can easily become choked with stock phrases and clichés that turn the message into a ritual utterance: "as per your request," "reference your letter," "herewith acknowledge receipt," and "please do not hesitate to contact me." Such documents often communicate very little except a negative impression of a stuffy, impersonal author.

This chapter takes a strategic approach to e-mail, letter, and memo writing, emphasizing ways in which a writer can adapt correspondence to fit as nearly as possible to the needs of the intended reader. The chapter also offers two general patterns for correspondence situations you are likely to face as a manager and specific types you can use for guidance in certain cases. Of course, use these models as a foundation only; as suggested in Chapter 2, each message a manager writes needs to be adapted to fit the audience and the situation.

AUDIENCE ADAPTATION

In many writing situations, a writer may not know the reader of the message very well. Indeed, the writer may not know the reader at all. Thus, managers must carefully consider the strategies of messages they send in order to achieve the maximum benefit. Fortunately, we can recognize some writing strategies that suit most correspondence situations.

The "you" attitude is the basis for the organizational strategies this chapter details. Writers who have this attitude prepare messages matching their readers' interests. They do this by putting themselves in the reader's place. A writer with the you attitude begins by asking herself, "How would I feel if I were this person in this situation? What would I want to read in this message?"

The you attitude requires empathy, the ability to understand another's feelings; we show empathy when we say to a colleague who is having trouble solving a problem, "I know what you mean," or "I know what you're going through."

Basis of the You Attitude

The great American film director Billy Wilder said, "An audience is never wrong." Furthermore, every audience is unique. Just as you would not give the same birthday gift to every member of your family, you should not give the same message to every employee. Audiences want to know that you understand their specific needs and concerns, so you must address them personally.

> **STOP AND THINK**
>
> 1. When you are thumbing through a magazine, what makes you stop and read an article?
>
> 2. Why does a particular billboard message or TV commercial catch your attention?

The you attitude, which is reader oriented, grew out of an awareness that most people, especially when they are involved in business matters, are likely to be looking after their own interests. In reading a message, they want to know how they can gain, or at least how they can minimize a loss. Thus, when communicating in a positive situation, good writers seek to increase the positive impact of the news. In a negative situation, writers seek to reduce negative impact while stressing reader benefits.

Few people have trouble using the you attitude in positive situations, but some balk at using it in negative ones, fearing that the you attitude shows weakness. This view is a misperception.

Anticipating Questions

To be effective, writers should anticipate the questions a reader might have. Thus, as they write, they ask themselves just what the reader might be uncertain about and then answer the uncertainties so no additional correspondence is needed. Remember the five Ws: who, what, when, where, and why.

Stressing Reader Benefits

Arguably, the most likely audience question is "What's in it for me?" or WII-FM. With the you attitude, the writer always strives to show the reader how she benefits. This is not to say that the writer gives in to the reader. Rather, the writer designs the message to either capitalize on or overcome the reader's attitudes about the writer as well as the issue at hand. Thus, a businessperson trying to collect on a past-due account might stress that the reader needs to pay the account balance to retain credit privileges at the store as well as an overall good credit rating. The potential for success in this case is far greater than if the credit manager had stressed only the company's interest by writing of its need to receive payment.

Avoiding Negatives

A writer should avoid negatives and words with negative connotations, especially in negative situations. These words have a way of jumping off the page and putting the reader on the defensive. Watch, especially, words such as *unfortunately, claim, allege, problem, damage,* and *regret.* A negative word can affect a reader's perceptions so much that he will not be able to read the rest of the message objectively. Stressing the positive, on the other hand, will improve the writer-reader relationship and make it more likely that the writer's goal will be reached.

An easy way to find positive words for a negative message is to say what *will* happen rather than what *will not* happen. So instead of telling a customer, "Unfortunately we can't meet Friday's deadline," one could say, "Your shipment will arrive on Monday." As described in the previous chapter, Holiday Inn Express uses this strategy well. Instead of warning hotel guests not to steal the towels from the rooms, a written note simply announces, "Should you decide to take these articles from your room . . . we will assume you approve a corresponding charge to your account."

Note the positive terms in the message: "take," "approve." Guests are not likely to be offended or insulted by this announcement.

Here is another example of a negative message couched in positive words. In July 2013, Chevron announced that it would build a fifty-story office tower in downtown Houston, Texas. The project was predicted to bring about 1,700 new jobs to the city. Six months later, Chevron announced that the project, along with several other real estate projects around the United States, would be delayed, and the company would "focus its resources elsewhere." The news release stated, "Chevron continues to maintain a strong balance sheet and operating cash flow, but the company is in a unique, capitally intensive period that will drive peer-leading production and value growth."[5] The language in this message put a positive spin on bad news for the city of Houston.

Nonverbal Elements and the You Attitude

The you attitude shows itself in a variety of ways, some more obvious than others. One of these ways is metacommunication. Without reading a word, an individual receiving a message can tell a lot about the sender and the sender's attitude toward the reader.

Both the stationery chosen for correspondence and the keying job send messages to readers. A positive letter marred by smeared or pale print, typos, stains, or hand corrections or a cheap grade of paper creates static in the communication channel. While the written message says the writer cares, the physical elements of the medium suggest indifference at best. On the other hand, error-free letters with crisp black print on white, high-rag-content bond paper suggest professionalism and concern for the reader's feelings.

Similarly, the nonverbal elements of e-mail can make a positive or negative impression on the reader. A writer implementing the you attitude will send concise e-mails. How concise? Most readers prefer them limited to one screen in length so they do not have to scroll. Brief paragraphs with spaces between them improve readability. If the e-mail is a reply, or the latest in a series of exchanges, the writer should delete all but the most recent message being responded to. Formatting is often lost when a reader opens an external e-mail, so the writer should limit the use of tabs and other design and formatting elements.

Diction

The you attitude also influences a message's wording. If the reader's interest is of central concern, show this by making the reader central as well. If the reader is asking, "What's in it for me?" she will have a hard time determining that if you write exclusively about yourself, using *I, me, mine,* or *we, us, our, ours.* A better focus is on *you, your, yours.* Thus, rather than saying, "We are sending the samples of the ads we worked up for Reality Industry's new pumps," a writer should substitute, "You will soon receive three samples of the magazine ads for your new pumps." The revision makes the reader rather than the writer the focus of attention.

STRATEGIES

Thus far, we have looked at a variety of ways in which a manager can personalize messages to make them better understood and received by readers. However, one key element remains: overall strategy. The suggestions given so far for signaling concern for the reader will fall short if you do not organize the message in a manner that anticipates reader reaction. Let us look at two basic strategies that, when used properly, can appropriately address reader reaction. The strategies deliver the message while promoting a positive image of the writer.

Direct Strategy

The direct strategy is used for messages conveying good news or neutral information. Someone receiving good news is pleased after reading it and appreciates having the good news as quickly as possible. However, if the message's main idea is buried in the middle or is located near the end, the reader, who probably began with some enthusiasm, loses interest and becomes frustrated at wasting valuable time searching for the main point. This frustration can affect the reader's attitude toward the writer: "Why can't she come right to the point?" Thus, such a message in a positive situation with lots of potential for building goodwill can instead weaken and even destroy the positive impact.

Opening

A better strategy is to put the main point first. A brief introduction might be needed to orient the reader, but this introduction should not delay the presentation of the main point. An easy way to remember this principle is the acronym BIF, or big idea first.

Body

A message using the direct strategy next provides the necessary supporting details: the reasons for the decision, background or history, specifics about the situation, or the procedures the reader needs to follow. Of course, these details promote the writer or the company she represents, especially when the message grants a favor.

> ### STOP AND THINK
>
> In addition to routine business messages, where else have you seen messages organized according to the direct strategy, which puts the big idea first?

Close

A direct message has a positive ending. Among the choices can be an offer to help, a statement of gratitude, or a call for any further action the reader needs to take.

Indirect Strategy

Unfortunately, not all messages communicate good news or even neutral information. Often, requests are denied, proposals are rejected, and job applications are turned down. The readers are naturally not pleased, but the documents need to be written. The effective bad news message conveys its information while creating a minimum of resentment. If possible, it should help build goodwill for the company since the reader may be desirable as a customer, client, or future employee.

A good strategy for negative situations is the indirect one. Using this strategy, a writer leads the reader logically to the bad news. Successfully developed, the message minimizes the reader's negative reactions and builds goodwill. A comparison between the direct and the indirect approaches is presented in Table 7–1. Not all indirect messages convey bad news. The persuasive message is a specialized type of indirect message that will be detailed later in the chapter.

Table 7–1 The Direct Approach
Compared to the Indirect Approach

DIRECT	INDIRECT
Opening	**Opening**
Main point	Neutral buffer
Body	**Body**
Supporting information	Explanation and negative news
Close	**Close**
Positive statement	Goodwill

Opening

Instead of BIF, big idea first, the writer should use the BILL formula—big idea a little later. The indirect message begins with a buffer, some neutral or positive statement that clearly relates to the purpose that both reader and writer agree on. The beginning might be agreement with the reader; it might express appreciation for the reader's candor in writing; or it might be a compliment.

A good opening begins to let the reader down gently. Ideally, it would subtly set up the explanation that follows in the body of the message. As we saw with the good news strategy, the reader expects things to go his way. When the indirect beginning fails to reinforce that expectation, the stage is set for the denial or bad news to follow.

Body

Next, the message analyzes the circumstances or provides details about the facts that led to the bad news being conveyed. The challenge here is to be convincing. The tone of this part is cooperative. The writer does not have to say, "Let's look at the facts," but the reader should have that feeling. A large body of research summarized by Professor Kitty O. Locker of Ohio State University shows that you can improve the reader's response to the bad news when you (1) offer a reason for the outcome and (2) provide an alternative or a compromise whenever possible.[6]

Next, one implies or directly expresses the negative information in as positive a tone as possible. Naturally, a writer should not be so subtle in implying the negative news that the reader is left hanging. But any direct statement should be tactful and not blunt. The best approach is to subordinate the actual point where the bad news is stated in the middle of a paragraph, rather than allow it to appear at the beginning or end.

Close

The next step is important: At the end, strive to rebuild goodwill. Depending on the situation, several options are available. One is to suggest another course of action open to the reader. In response to claims for goods, suggest others that are more durable or appropriate for the reader's use. A letter rejecting a proposal, for example, might give another outlet for the idea.

STOP AND THINK

In addition to negative business messages, where else have you seen messages organized according to the indirect strategy, or BILL?

Close the indirect message on a positive, friendly note. Often, the effort at building goodwill is enough. Sometimes a little more is necessary. A manager might want to offer services or information. For example, a letter written to an old customer might have a catalog enclosed and end by looking forward to the reader's next order.

Handling Negatives

Since an indirect message conveys bad news, it is potentially very negative. To minimize the damage to a company's goodwill, good writers generally avoid negative words. Although the task is a challenge, avoiding negatives pays off in the long run because the practice helps to keep the overall tone positive. The following three rules hold the key:

- Place negative information at points of low emphasis.
- Avoid *no* or *not* when possible.
- Avoid words with negative connotations.

De-emphasize negative facts by placing them in a subordinate structure (a dependent clause, a parenthetic expression, or a modifier) rather than in a main clause or a sentence. In a paragraph, negative information should not be placed in a prominent position. Compare the following two short paragraphs telling a job applicant that the company has no job openings in his area.

> We do not anticipate any openings in the Baytown Company anytime soon since we have been laying off people in your field. You might apply at Rumfield and Company or Bennington, Inc., since they are adding to their staffs.

The writer could easily have softened the negatives by placing them in a less prominent position, as you see below.

> Please consider applying for one of the engineering positions now open at Rumfield and Company or at Bennington, Inc. rather than at Baytown Company. Currently Baytown's personnel needs are in other areas.

The second suggestion for avoiding negative writing (avoiding *no* and *not*) is easier to follow than it seems. Recall the Holiday Inn Express example described earlier in this chapter, which asks guests not to steal items from the rooms but uses positive words. In the revision in the following examples, the writer emphasizes what she *can* do, not what she *cannot* do.

We cannot fill your order until you tell us what size grill your restaurant currently uses.

We can fill your order as soon as you let us have your restaurant's grill size.

Please specify your grill size so that we may fill your order as quickly as possible.

allege	argue
failure	mistake
claim	damage
regret	error
careless	broken

The third suggestion (avoiding words with negative connotations) is one of the most important. Whereas *claim* and *state* might have very similar denotations, their connotations are widely separated. Writing to a person and saying, "You next claim that . . ." makes it sound as if the reader is wrong. Numerous words are likely to irritate or even inflame when they appear in bad news messages. (See examples of such words in the box at left.)

SPECIFIC TYPES: DIRECT MESSAGES

The direct and indirect strategies are useful for most writing situations managers face. Nevertheless, because some situations are so frequent (for example, the inquiry) and because some are so sensitive (for example, negative responses to claims), several specialized versions of the direct and indirect patterns have developed. Table 7–2 lists seven specific versions reviewed here.

The patterns suggested here are not absolute. After strategic analysis, a manager may determine that a different approach is appropriate. That kind of adaptation is to be encouraged because it helps to prevent following a mechanical pattern. First, we look at correspondence using the direct pattern; then, we consider those following the indirect. Remember to use a direct approach for good news and neutral, informative messages.

Inquiries and Requests

Perhaps the most common direct correspondence is the inquiry. Managers in all areas of business routinely need information to conduct their affairs. A manager might need to know about the performance of a product; another might want credit information about a client or wish to know about the qualifications of a job applicant. Since most readers see these requests as routine and reasonable, they are likely to respond to them willingly.

If you project yourself into the position of a reader receiving an inquiry, you'll see why the direct approach is so appropriate. You are probably busy with other matters and need to know quickly what is required of you. When you receive an inquiry, you appreciate the reader's efforts to be direct and to let you know from the start what she wants.

Table 7–2   Types of Direct and Indirect Messages

Direct	Indirect
Inquiries and requests	Negative responses to inquiries and requests
Positive responses to inquiries and requests	Refused claims
Claims	Persuasive messages
Positive responses to claims	

Opening

Make the inquiry clear from the start. One effective method is to begin with a question that summarizes the writer's objective. For example, an inquiry about a potential employee could begin with "Would you please comment on Mary Keynes's qualifications to become a management intern? We at Infovend are considering her for the position, and she has given your name as a reference." The question beginning the inquiry makes the purpose immediately clear.

Body

In many cases, the next step in the inquiry is an explanation of the inquiry's purpose. In the example just given, you quickly made it clear that you are considering Keynes for a job. The amount of information a writer gives depends on the situation. In an inquiry about the potential employee, you also probably would want to assure the reader that her response will be kept confidential.[7]

The body of the inquiry needs to be efficiently organized; it cannot simply be a "fishing expedition" for information. Even after the purpose is clear, the reader usually needs guidance to answer the inquiry satisfactorily. Given as much of the sample letter about Mary Keynes as we have so far, it might be answered several ways depending on how the reader projected your needs—or it might not be detailed at all. Thus, the next part of the inquiry should set out the areas requiring information, plus any necessary additional information. Numbering the questions may also help the reader respond.

Close

The close of the inquiry is friendly and builds goodwill. In some cases, it is appropriate to offer similar services. In situations where a purchase might follow, you might ask for a speedy reply.

Let us look at the complete inquiry about Mary Keynes. Note that in this inquiry about a person, you emphasized confidentiality, an advisable practice in this kind of correspondence.

Dear Professor Renton:

Would you please comment on Mary Keynes's qualifications to become a management intern? We at Infovend are considering her for the position, and she has given your name as a reference. Of course, whatever information you give us will be held in confidence.

1. How well does Keynes manage time? Is her work punctual?

2. Did you have a chance to observe her under pressure? If so, does she manage well or does pressure adversely affect her performance?

3. How well does she relate to her peers? Please comment on her relationship with them: Is she a leader or a follower, gregarious or shy, and so on?

I look forward to hearing your comments on Keynes's qualifications and will appreciate whatever insights you can share with us.

Sincerely,

Tim Inman

Human Resources Manager

Positive Responses to Inquiries and Requests

Inquiries naturally need answers. The favorable response to an inquiry is a direct one, as the reader is pleased to get the requested information or item.

Opening

You begin by identifying the request you are responding to. This identification appears in the first sentence of the message. The opening also makes it clear the reader's request is being granted.

- I found Mary Keynes, the subject of your June 5 inquiry, to be one of the most promising students I have ever taught.

- As-Best-As Filing Cabinets have all the features you mentioned in your March 4 letter and several more you might be interested in knowing about.

- Here is my response to your September 14 inquiry about our experiences with the M-102 Security System.

You can begin by directly answering the most general of the questions originally asked (as in the first two examples) or by agreeing to respond to the question originally posed (as in the third example).

Body

The way in which you organize the body of the message varies depending on the original inquiry. For an inquiry that asked one question, the details in response appear in order of importance. If you are responding to a series of questions, normally answer them in the order asked. If the original is really a request (for example, "May we use your facilities for a club meeting?"), the body gives necessary conditions for use.

Not all responses to inquiries are completely good or bad news. Thus, although a manager is willing to answer most questions, some topics are confidential. In these cases, the denial is subordinated and appears after the writer explains why. For example, the response to the inquiry about a company's experiences with the M-102 Security System may withhold some details for security reasons.

Close

The positive response to an inquiry continues to be positive in the close. Note the following closings to the messages whose beginnings we gave earlier.

- If I can help you with any other information about Mary, please contact me.

- If you need any other information on how As-Best-As Filing Cabinets can meet your storage needs, please let me know.

- I'd be delighted to answer any further questions about our experiences with the M-102 Security System. I think you'll be pleased with the system.

Claims

A third type of direct message is the claim. Usually, a dissatisfied customer writes about a problem and requests a solution or claim. Project yourself as manager and consider how you would feel receiving a claim letter. Customer dissatisfaction leads not only to a loss of goodwill and revenue but also reflects badly on your ability as a manager. Naturally, you would want to find out quickly what the problem is and resolve it.

Opening

Even though the claim deals with something negative, it is written directly. From your perspective, directness strengthens the claim. In fact, some readers may interpret indirectness as lack of confidence in the claim being made. Indirectness would thus be a strategic error.

Early in the claim, you should include details about the faulty product, service, or sale. Which details to incorporate depend on the situation, but they may include invoice numbers, dates, and the product identification or serial number.

Another good tactic that makes the message convincing is to include the significance of the problem to you or your business. For example, a warehouse manager whose new intercom system failed might write,

> The new intercom system you sent us (Invoice #16789) has broken, thus considerably slowing the processing of orders in our company warehouse.

Body

The next step is logical: the facts of the case need detailing. In the intercom example, you discuss how the system broke down and the possible cause. Naturally, you do not need to be an expert analyst, but the more facts you include, the more convincing your argument. If appropriate, you may also wish to detail the damage that resulted.

Of course, detailing the problem requires tact and forbearance. You feel justified in writing about the problem, but you do not attack the person who sold or installed the product or its manufacturer. Name-calling or accusations do little, if any, good and may create reader resentment, which usually precludes a favorable settlement. Abusive messages are best left unsent.

The next part of the letter states what you want: What will set things right? Unfortunately, some letters end before this point. An unhappy writer complains and then forgets to say what he wants. Specifying the action or amount of money needed for satisfaction is usually preferable. Occasionally, the settlement can be left up to the reader if the situation is routine.

You may also wish to include a deadline for action on the matter. Naturally, a deadline needs something to back it up. One authority recommends that the writer make a threat or ultimatum that she is willing and able to carry out if the situation is not resolved.[8] Weigh threats carefully. They can be counterproductive.

Close

Once again, avoid negativity in the close. If you threaten to take your business elsewhere, the reader may lose any motivation for cooperation. End by expressing confidence in the good faith of the reader or by expressing intended gratitude for the early resolution of the problem.

Let us look at the rest of the claim about the faulty intercom and see how it illustrates these points.

Dear Mr. Packard:

The new intercom system you sent us (Invoice #16789) has broken, thus considerably slowing the processing of orders in our company warehouse.

Although the system worked fine immediately after installation, we began to notice problems with it during stormy weather. When it rained, static garbled many of the messages. Finally, during one heavy downpour, the main transmitter stopped working and began smoking.

We are shipping the transmitter to you via Brown Express. We would like it either repaired or replaced. Your prompt attention will help our warehouse to return to normal.

Sincerely,

Patricia Muranka

Purchasing Manager

In this message, the manager detailed the problem her department faced, yet she resisted accusatory language. She set out her experience with the system and provided enough information for the manufacturer to diagnose the problem. The ending is positive yet assertive.

Positive Responses to Claims

The fourth type of direct message is the positive response to a claim. While the use of the direct order is unquestionable, this type still challenges the writer who is aware of the unpleasantness the reader experienced. The reader may have lost sales or may have been uncomfortable or inconvenienced. The challenge here is to rebuild goodwill and, in many cases, restore faith in the product. The reader who does not believe in the product will buy elsewhere next time. Occasionally, especially when dealing with angry customers, you respond to a very unpleasant or accusatory letter. You must not rise to the bait.

Opening

Begin the adjustment grant with the good news. The reader needs a reminder to recall the situation, but this reminding should be done quickly. Thus, the letter responding to the claim about the faulty intercom might begin in the following manner:

> Your transmitter is now in working order and should arrive in Cedar Rapids by truck in the next few days.

Body

After the good news, the development of the body depends on the situation. Routine cases need little explanation. In many cases, however, the reader needs more. It is usually necessary to explain what went wrong, and it is often a good idea to stress that the problem is corrected and will not recur.

Occasionally, you will need to explain the proper use of the product to a reader who unintentionally misused the product. In such cases, the reader's goodwill is worth the cost. This explanation needs to be tactful and is most effective when presented impersonally, as in the second example that follows:

- You left the valves open on the unit. As a result, your heater was on constantly and wore out.

- The valves leading out to the unit must be kept tightly closed to reduce the demand on the heating unit.

In the explanatory material and the close, keep the tone positive. Common courtesy seems to dictate an apology, but it often serves to open old wounds. Instead, look to the future with a confident, positive approach:

You can expect many more years of trouble-free service from your transmitter.

Close

The closing of an adjustment grant is positive. It anticipates continued good relations with the customer and may include information on other products or services the company offers. You build goodwill by discussing the advantages of the product. You also refrain from stating the fault was the electrician's rather than the manufacturer's, although you have taken steps to protect the equipment in the future.

Dear Ms. Muranka:

Your transmitter is now in working order and should arrive in Cedar Rapids by truck in the next few days. Please call your electrician when it arrives so his installation will protect the warranty.

You reported that the system had static in it during rainstorms and that it smoked when the system stopped working. I've checked the new patented fusible ground lead and found that it had melted, as it was designed to do, and protected the transmitter and you from electrical shock.

When your electrician installs the transmitter, have him check the unit's grounding. At present, when it rains, the unit is shorting out because of incomplete grounding.

You might be interested in our new security alarm system that hooks into the existing intercom system. The enclosed pamphlet gives you the details. We will be glad to discuss its installation with you.

Sincerely,

Robert Packard

Customer Service Manager

SPECIFIC TYPES: INDIRECT MESSAGES

Most managers cannot comply with all the requests made of them. In those situations, the response is best organized according to the indirect plan.

Negative Responses to Inquiries

The strategy for constructing negative responses to inquiries requires thought and planning. When requests need denying, use a bad news strategy. Reasons appear first, followed by the refusal.

Opening

The opening should remind the reader of the request. This initial statement should also serve as a buffer that does not imply either a positive or negative answer. Furthermore, the opening should lead logically into the body.

Suppose, for example, you received a letter from a researcher inquiring into the population sample used to determine your company's marketing strategies. Since such questions deal with proprietary information that the company keeps confidential, you must deny the request. At the same time, you do not want to refuse directly. Your request might begin with one of the following buffers:

- Thank you for your inquiry about our marketing research and strategies.

- The results of your study of population samples should prove interesting.

This introduction gives no false hope for a positive reply, but it does not deny the request yet. However, it lays the basis for that rejection. The rest of the letter develops the approach.

Body

From this beginning, you move into a discussion of why the request cannot be granted. You consider the reader and choose examples or reasoning likely to convince the reader that yours is the only viable solution. For example, in the preceding letter, you could appeal to the reader's own experience as a researcher who has spent hours developing ideas. Similarly, after great expense, your company had developed ideas that it applies to its own needs.

Once you have given the reasoning, you can state the refusal. Occasionally, writers refuse requests so vaguely that the reader still sees hope for the request. The well-written refusal reasons the reader out of the original request. However, the reasoning does not suggest the original request was ill advised or misdirected.

Close

Close positively to build goodwill. The close can look to the future, such as a wish for success in the reader's work or a suggestion for some other sources of information the reader could use.

In the letter refusing the request for information on marketing strategies, note how you imply the refusal rather than state it. Note also that you make no apology for refusing.

Dear Ms. Leeper:

The results of your study of population samples should prove interesting, as most companies protect these data because they are so central to their marketing strategies.

At Flo-Sheen Fabrics, we develop our marketing strategies only after our test market has had a chance to examine our new fabrics. As a researcher, you can surely appreciate the countless hours that go into any marketing campaign.

We keep the population sample used for our marketing analysis confidential both to protect their privacy and to help us keep our competitive edge. Our competition would have an unfair advantage over us if they were able to know in advance what products we planned to introduce or what strategies we would use.

You might look into any text on statistical sampling to learn the considerations managers must take in selecting population samples.

Sincerely,

Sheila Hebert

Vice President

Refused Claims

A greater challenge than the negative response to an inquiry is the refused claim. In most cases, the person making the claim believes she is justified; her interests have been damaged by what she sees as bad products or services. However, for whatever reason, you have determined that you must reject the claim.

In doing so, you must maintain a positive tone and build goodwill. The key is empathy. Imagine how you would want to be treated in this situation—probably reasonably. To respond in an authoritarian or a condescending fashion would be foolish. The language must be positive and selective. Most likely, the reader will be sensitive to any possible nuances.

Opening

The claim refusal must begin as most negative messages would: with a buffer. This buffer can refer to the reader's original claim as its subject, or it can be an expression of appreciation—some opening that brings the reader and writer together neutrally.

The effective opening also indicates the line of reasoning to be followed. Take, for example, the opening sentence, "Whitlow Co. does guarantee its sump pumps for eighteen months in normal operation under normal circumstances." The reader is reminded of the original claim and is introduced to the line of reasoning in "normal operation" and "normal circumstances." Another opening might be the following:

Your recent letter shows that you are a person who appreciates being treated fairly and openly. You will be interested in what we have found in our investigation into your questions.

Body

The body details your findings. This explanation should be objective and convincing, but it should avoid a my-side, your-side dichotomy. One effective tactic in some situations is to describe the effort that went into investigating the matter. For example, a negative response to a warranty claim may emphasize the laboratory tests made on the broken part. This detail is useful because it projects a caring image; the decision made is not just some automatic response.

Give the refusal once the reasons are clear. Of course, the refusal should appear at a point of low emphasis. If the refusal is based on company policy, the policy should be clearly explained. But remember that customers generally resent managers "hiding behind" company policy. Use logic whenever possible instead.

Close

Most claim refusals close with an effort at resale. If the customer has been treated fairly in a reasonable manner, she may stay with the product since the company was not at fault. Frequently, it is a good idea to get off the immediate topic by mentioning an upcoming sale or by sending a recent catalog.

Dear Ms. Clark:

Whitlow Co. does guarantee its sump pumps for eighteen months in normal operation under normal circumstances. After your recent letter, we looked closely into the questions you raised.

Our laboratory examined the returned pump and found that the entire unit had been submerged for some time. This submersion was in keeping with the newspaper accounts of heavy flooding in your town last month. Apparently the area where your unit was located was also inundated. While the pump is designed to take care of normal seepage, it is mounted at least 18 inches above the basement floor to protect the housing and pump. Like most motor-driven appliances, the pump must be kept totally dry, as it is in normal circumstances.

You might be interested in another model pump we offer, the SubMerso. Its waterproof housing withstands even prolonged immersion. The enclosed pamphlet details its capacities. We'll be glad to answer any questions you might have on it.

Sincerely,

Lionel Naquin

Customer Service Representative

Apologies

When composing a bad news message such as a negative response to an inquiry or a refusal to a claim, you may be tempted to include an apology. This decision is controversial. Corporate attorneys have traditionally warned against apologizing because it implies responsibility for wrongdoing and even guilt, inviting legal action against the writer and her organization. Public relations professionals agree that apologies can be interpreted as an admission of error or carelessness, damaging a company's image. In a 1997 study titled "Liability Means Never Being Able to Say You're Sorry," the author concluded that our present legal system discourages apologies.[9]

Recently, however, the trend has been changing due to evidence that an apology can help rather than hurt, in terms of both image and legal judgments. In the field of medicine, malpractice-reform advocates say an apology can help doctors avoid being sued and can reduce settlements. This approach seems to be working. For example, since 2002, the hospitals in the University of Michigan Health System have been encouraging doctors to apologize for mistakes. The system's annual attorney fees have dropped by two-thirds, and malpractice lawsuits have fallen by half.[10] As of 2014, thirty-six states have enacted apology laws; they are designed to protect health care providers who want to talk to patients and families when an adverse outcome occurs without fearing litigation.

The United States has witnessed a remarkable rise in the number of public corporate apologies. During the 2000 "summer of apologies," company executives begged pardon for unreliable flights, bad phone service, and tire blowouts. Since then, the pattern has continued. In January 2014, after a massive data breach that affected up to 100 million shoppers, the CEO of Target quickly issued a public apology. "Our top priority is taking care of you and helping you feel confident about shopping at Target. . . . We didn't live up to that responsibility, and I am truly sorry."[11] CEOs have even apologized for sins to which they had no connection, as in 2005, when Ken Thompson, CEO of Wachovia, announced that two of its acquired companies had owned slaves. He stated, "On behalf of Wachovia Corporation, I apologize to all Americans."[12]

If a manager makes the strategic decision to apologize, either individually or on behalf of the organization, what are some guidelines? A good apology is genuine and timely. It should consist of four parts:

- An acknowledgment of the mistake or wrongdoing
- The acceptance of responsibility
- An expression of regret
- A promise that the offense will not be repeated[13]

Perhaps the most critical issue is acceptance of responsibility or fault. A partial apology, where the manager expresses sympathy or regret without admitting guilt, softens the blow and may be wise when there is significant damage or injury. Partial apologies can also resolve disputes when the extent of fault is unclear or difficult to establish. In other circumstances, when a manager or company has clearly committed an egregious act, a more complete apology may be appropriate.

In either situation, the focus should be on the future and on making amends.[14] An excellent example of a corporate apology occurred in February 2006. Hallmark's website crashed under the volume of traffic on Valentine's Day. An e-mail went out the next day to all customers who had attempted to send an e-greeting. It began, "We owe you an apology." It continued with a description of what had happened and its consequences—"We cringe at the disappointment we caused." It ended with a positive look to the future: "We are now challenging our team to reevaluate every step." More recently, in the Target identity theft case described above, the retailer offered all of its customers—whether or not they were directly affected—a year of free credit monitoring to compensate for their risk of data breach.

Persuasive Messages

The indirect strategy is appropriate for persuasive messages. A manager uses the indirect persuasive strategy when trying to persuade others to do things they might not ordinarily wish to do. You might need to write a persuasive letter to convince a reluctant client to pay his bill. Or you might write a persuasive e-mail to gain a colleague's support on a project.

Opening

The persuasive message opens by catching the reader's interest.[15] One effective way of doing this is to show the reader that her goals are your goals. The best way to show this identity of goals is to show her that the message deals with matters she is interested in. At the same time, since the message must catch the reader's interest, the opening must be brief.

Body

The body consists of several parts. First, it must set out the problem that you and the reader share. Then, it must reveal the solution to the problem—the solution that you want the reader to embrace. This section reflects careful strategy since the reader's possible objections must be anticipated and answered. In this section (which can consist of several paragraphs), you must stress the benefit accruing to the reader as a result of the solution.[16]

Close

The ending is important. The effective persuasive message does not end after the proposed answer is revealed. At the end, after the reader's interest has been aroused, the interest must be channeled into action. Otherwise, interest will decline, with nothing resolved. The action item should be specific: a meeting, an order, a payment, an interview, a change in procedure. An action must be prompt. Delay only lessens the probability of action.[17]

The following job application letter illustrates the implementation of the persuasive strategy.

Dear Mr. Harris:

Now that Lynch's is about to open its third department store in Jonesboro, won't you need a sufficient staff of part-time employees to supplement your full-time workers? I believe I have the background and motivation necessary to become one of your most productive part-time workers.

As a junior marketing major at State University, I am currently taking marketing courses. I could apply what I learn over the next two years to my sales work at Lynch's. The job references listed on the attached résumé will all attest to the fact that I am very energetic and enthusiastic about my work.

Another reason I think I would make a good part-time employee for you is that I am very interested in pursuing a career with Lynch's after graduation. I would see these two years as a testing period to prove myself, and you would have the two years to decide whether or not you would be equally interested in me.

If I have described the kind of part-time salesperson you want at Lynch's, may I have an interview to further discuss the position? I can be reached at 992-8403, and I can be available at a time convenient to you.

Sincerely,

John Morris

LETTER FORMATS

Thus far, we have discussed two strategies for organizing routine messages—direct and indirect—and showed how to use them when sending messages to external audiences such as customers, clients, regulatory agencies, and other stakeholders. Typically, these messages are in letter or e-mail format. Good writers know that the appearance of a document can affect the reader's reaction to its content, much the same way a speaker's appearance affects the listeners' response to her message. A word about contemporary letter format is therefore appropriate.

Many routine business messages are sent electronically, either as e-mails or as e-mail attachments. Formatting elements, such as tabs (indents) and centering, can change or even disappear according to the technology used to open the message. So the appearance of a message should be simple, plain, and as easy to read as possible. A standard contemporary style is to begin every part of a business letter at the left margin (left justified, ragged right).

Reliance on the concept of white space makes sense, too. Standard business letter style calls for single spacing within paragraphs, and double spacing between paragraphs and between elements of the letter. This line spacing format eliminates the need to indent when you begin a paragraph. Keeping paragraphs short, as discussed in Chapter 6, also builds white space. The persuasive letter in Figure 7–1 exemplifies excellent strategies for both content and format.

Figure 7–1   Sample Persuasive Letter

LaSalle Senior Center

1111 N. Wells St., Suite 500, Chicago, IL 60610

312-573-8840 Fax 312-787-1212

Gerry Hynes
3780 Copperfield Dr., Unit 1018
Bryan, TX 77802

Dear Gerry,

As the year moves to an end, I think about two of our seniors who died this year. They were each exceptional in their own way; each had a key role at the LaSalle Senior Center and each benefited from the services we offered just as we benefited from their gifts. They were like many of the seniors we work with, both a client and a volunteer.

Marc Stuart was a regular volunteer at both the Wednesday and Sunday meals. Having management experience, he was inclined to supervise both clients and volunteers. He was part of the fabric of the Senior Center and showed his support by his presence and by his care for other seniors. The Senior Center provided Marc with a place to serve and live out his faith. He told me on several occasions that his first priority was LaSalle Street Church followed by the Senior Center.

Allene Hales was exceptional by any standard. With little formal education, very modest means, and compromised health, she brought people together at the Senior Center and in her community. She knew erveryone. And she was always helping others, offering a kind word, sharing money or food. The Senior Center recognized her for her gifts and provided her some real help with day-to-day matters.

Marc and Allene found a home at the Senior Center. They found a place that offered them help, a place where they could serve and a place to belong. Thanks to your support, the LaSalle Senior Center continues to be that place for over 200 local seniors every month.

Please consider making a gift* to help continue our ministry to our neighborhood's older friends.

Sincerely,

Keith Chase-Ziolek
Director

*A generous donor will match the first $5,000 in gifts.

Source: Chase-Ziolek. Reprinted by permission of the author.

Regarding typography, the best typeface for business correspondence depends on whether the message will be read on paper or on a monitor (see Table 7-3). For hard copy documents, *Times New Roman*, 12 points, is standard in the business world. TNR, released in 1932, has a traditional, professional, formal look. It is a *serif* font, with projections at the edges of the letters that make the type easier to read, especially in the smaller sizes. Other popular serif fonts are *Garamond* and *Cambria*. In addition to business letters, paper documents, such as newsletters, brochures, and manuals, should use a serif font.

For electronic messages, *Calibri*, 11 points, is standard. Calibri is a contemporary *sans serif* font; sans serif fonts do not have projections on the edges of the letters. Sans serif fonts are easier to read onscreen and are often used for websites, posted announcements, and signs. Headlines and headings, which are usually in larger type size than the accompanying text, also may be in a sans serif font. PowerPoint slides, as you discovered in Chapter 5, typically are in *Arial* font, one of the most popular sans serif fonts. Other sans serif fonts popular for business writing are *Verdana* and *Helvetica*.

If you are thinking that typeface is a trivial matter, consider the case of Ikea, the Swedish retail giant. In 2010, the company's home furnishings catalog switched from a customized version of Futura to Verdana, a style invented by Microsoft and intended to be used for messages read on screens rather than on paper. This change touched off an uproar across the world. Design specialists as well as customers complained that the new font was plain and ugly, especially when enlarged to the size of a catalog headline or a billboard. Ikea defended the change by pointing out that Verdana is used in all countries and with many alphabets. "It's more efficient and cost-effective," said Ikea spokeswoman Monika Gocic. "Plus, it's a simple, modern-looking typeface."[18]

Table 7–3 Font Styles for Business Messages

Font	Category	Uses
Times New Roman	Serif	Hard copy documents and business letters
Garamond	Serif	Hard copy documents and business letters
Cambria	Serif	Hard copy documents and business letters
Calibri	Sans serif	E-mail, websites, posted announcements, headings, and signs
Arial	Sans serif	PowerPoint, e-mail, websites, posted announcements, headings, and signs
Verdana	Sans serif	E-mail, websites, posted announcements, headings, and signs
Helvetica	Sans serif	E-mail, websites, posted announcements, headings and signs

INTERNAL CORRESPONDENCE

The writing strategies described in this chapter apply to internal as well as external correspondence. While letters are the most frequently used medium of communication between firms, memos and e-mail are the most frequently used within an organization.[19] The memo is an efficient, straightforward kind of communication. Often, memos are sent electronically, as e-mails. E-mail is becoming more commonly used for routine external communication as well. A hybrid format is a business letter or memo sent as an e-mail attachment, a practice that allows the sender to stabilize design and format elements when the document is opened.

Because the reader of a memo is human, the writer needs to adapt strategically. This is especially true when one is writing to employees at a different level within the organization, or who possess a less specialized knowledge of the subject, or when the memo deals with sensitive matters. While internal messages are often routine, informal exchanges of information, they should be composed carefully.

Memo Format

Memo formats differ from one another in minor details, but they generally have four standard headings: *To, From, Subject,* and *Date.* In e-mails, these headings are automatically provided. The From line offers few problems. However, if needed, a writer can add to her authority by including her job title after her name. She can add the names of others here as well—assuming she has their agreement.

The Subject line has obvious value in directing the reader's attention. Be specific about your topic and purpose. For instance, "Subject: Request for Vacation Schedules" is more likely to stimulate reader response than the vaguer "Subject: Schedules." Using key words in the Subject line will often aid in the memo's later retrieval from computer files as well.

Just as with face-to-face interactions, memos sent within an organization typically have a set protocol one should respect. This means paying attention to the format generally used, as well as noting any subtleties related to whom the memorandum or its copies (cc:) are sent.[20] Often, by noting at the cc: line that the memo is being sent to a boss, one is also sending the message of one's easy access to that boss. Similarly, be sure that you copy your immediate supervisor when contacting his bosses. In general, copy your supervisor to keep him aware of what is going on. Even in cases where that individual is not immediately involved, he appreciates knowing about events. However, the proliferation of e-mail "copies" and Reply to All in most organizations is a caution not to flood people with excessive messages that are merely for your information, or FYI.

Another format element to note is the need for either your initials or signed name on the From line of the paper memo. This authenticates the document just as a signature does on a letter. However, adding your name at the end of a memo or e-mail is redundant if it appears on the From line. Pithy quotations, illustrations, and similar "signature" elements at the bottom of e-mails add clutter and can be annoying distractions to business readers. Remember that short, simple messages have the most impact.

Finally, remember that design elements such as tabs and bullets may not be preserved in e-mail at the receiving end. Instead, rely on double spacing between sections to frame your paragraphs with white space.

E-mail Format

Standard e-mail format varies from organization to organization, and often from writer to writer. You have probably noticed differences in the following style categories:

- Forms of address—greetings and sign-offs
- Linguistic novelties—emoticons, jargon, and acronyms
- Punctuation and capitalization
- Spelling—conventional or "IM shorthand"
- Endings—thought of the day, slogans, images

Rules have emerged for e-mail style, or *netiquette*, but they are often ignored. For instance, some writers begin an e-mail with a salutation or Dear line, despite the To line at the top. *Dear* was born about a thousand years ago, meaning "honorable, worthy," and took on the sense of "esteemed, valued" and "beloved." In the age of the quill pen, according to William Safire, *Dear* was used as a polite form of address for anyone—friends, business acquaintances, or strangers. Today's e-mails are as likely to begin with Good afternoon, Hello! or Hi as with Dear. Occasionally, managers address multiple audiences as All or even Folks.

Judith Martin, author of *Miss Manners' Guide to Excruciatingly Correct Behavior, Freshly Updated,* suggests that you may begin an e-mail "with almost anything civil. Or even nothing, because an e-mail is like a memo and doesn't require a salutation. . . . But that is presuming informality is understood not to be a euphemism for rudeness or sloppiness."[21] Good advice for e-mail writers, then, is to be courteous but concise. Overly formal formatting is as inappropriate as overly casual formatting.

Memo and E-mail Uses

Memos and e-mails serve a variety of uses within an organization. We have listed the most common below. You may see other practices where you work as well.

Communicating to Groups

Managers find memos and e-mail useful for communicating the same information to several individuals at once. Not only does the memo or e-mail save time over talking, but it ensures as well that each person has the same information.

Fixing Responsibility

The memo or e-mail can be a valuable management tool in other ways. For example, it can fix responsibility for actions. A manager who uses memos for giving assignments has a written record if questions of responsibility arise later.

Communicating with Opponents

Managers quickly learn to appreciate the memo and e-mail as a way of communicating with those they cannot get along with. Personal dislikes crop up in any organization from time to time, but memos and e-mails bridge the gaps that may ensue. The message gets delivered without bringing the two factions together. However, it is never appropriate to "flame" a reader with an emotion-packed e-mail. Remember the permanency of all memos, whether paper or electronic. Never write something you could not defend in a meeting or courtroom.

Communicating with the Inaccessible

Memos and e-mails are handy for dealing with people (especially supervisors) who are hard to reach. Those who are busy or absent can be reached by memo or e-mail, or increasingly by text message. A series of memos can also be proof of past attempts to contact a boss if problems arise.[22]

An example of a clear, concise, informative memo follows.

MEMORANDUM

TO: All Salaried Employees

FROM: Alan Reynolds, Director of Human Resources

DATE: October 3, 2014

SUBJECT: Changes in Payroll Practices

We've made a couple of changes in the payroll procedures to alleviate some of the bottlenecks that have delayed paychecks in the past few months.

1. Paychecks will no longer be mailed out. You will receive your check for the month on the last working day of that month. Direct deposits will still be made to your checking or saving account provided you use direct deposit for only one account.

2. All travel and expense reimbursements received before the twentieth of each month will be included in that monthly paycheck. Requests for reimbursement will no longer be paid by individual checks as in the past. Of course, these expense reimbursements are not taxed.

These changes in payroll should help to guarantee timely paychecks.

Types of Internal Correspondence

Memos and e-mails tend to fall into two groups: announcements and requests. Both these general types can be directed to large groups within a firm (especially announcements), and both can be directed to individuals.

Announcements

Announcements concern policy changes, meetings and conferences, new procedures, and personnel changes (including promotions). By nature, they are informative messages and follow the direct order strategy. Other types of notifications include status reports, such as progress and periodic reports. The informative memo appearing in the previous section is an example of an announcement.

The goodbye e-mail announcement has recently emerged as a new genre, due to massive layoffs. During the 2008 economic crisis, more than 45 million Americans lost their jobs. Rather than notify colleagues by phone or memo, workers sent blast e-mails. Some were understandably sad, angry, or bitter in tone, but experts warn that negativity in these permanent messages could hurt a job search. Donna Flagg, a New York business and management consultant, suggests staying professional and upbeat, simply announcing you are leaving and how to reach you. A goodbye e-mail can even help with the job search.[23]

Requests for Action

The nature of the request-for-action memo dictates its organization. When a manager requests action that typically falls under her jurisdiction, direct order is appropriate and the memo or e-mail begins with a clear subject line. When the requested action may meet with resistance, a less specific Subject line and a more persuasive strategy (indirect order) are appropriate. Direct or indirect, these memos and e-mails often require listing steps and careful wording for successful action. Remember, concrete language is always preferable to vague expressions, such as "please give your attention to this matter" and "reply at your earliest convenience," when requesting behavior change (see Chapter 6).

Political Uses in Business

Recall from the previous chapter that managers belong to a discourse community with unique characteristics and uses for their writing. The memo and e-mail are an example of a strategic tool for managers. In fulfilling their ostensible task of communicating announcements and requests for action within an organization, they are often put to other strategic uses. The uses are detailed next.

One political device is the copy list. Managers can protect themselves, publicize alliances, and show favor by including—and not including—certain people as cc: recipients.

Another practice that is widely used is to write a memo or e-mail summarizing a meeting. While the message is ostensibly "for the record," its recording of the meeting or conversation can affect perceptions. The meeting minutes become the reality and may, for example, prove ownership of an idea.

Still another political tactic is to attach a cover memo to that of a colleague. If the original memo reflects badly on the writer, the practice serves to offer another viewpoint.

Managers sometimes use memos to shape employees' opinions. A prominent example is Donald Rumsfeld. As US secretary of defense from 2002 until his resignation in 2006, he composed some twenty thousand memos and e-mails to his staff. That averages out to 20–60 per day. Rumsfeld poured out his thoughts about the Iraq War in the memos, often referred to as "snowflakes." He argued the need to "keep elevating the threat," "link Iraq to Iran," and develop "bumper sticker statements" to rally public support for the increasingly unpopular war.[24]

A valuable lesson for managers is that putting anything in writing makes it permanent. Think twice about how you commit yourself to paper or e-mail in controversial situations. "Routine" documents can have an important impact on a manager's effectiveness.

SUMMARY

Letters, e-mails, and memos can benefit greatly from strategic considerations. However, they are frequently mere impersonal messages written automatically. One key consideration for audience adaptation in routine messages is the you attitude. The writer with this attitude projects himself into the reader's position and prepares messages to suit that reader.

The you attitude also influences the organization of ideas: Direct order is appropriate for good news and neutral information; indirect is for bad news messages and persuasive messages. Direct order places the main point first; indirect, later.

Common types of direct messages are the inquiry, the positive response to an inquiry, the claim, and the positive response to a claim.

Indirect messages include the negative response to an inquiry, the refused claim, and the persuasive message.

Negatives must be handled carefully in correspondence. A writer should de-emphasize the negative by using subordination, by avoiding terms such as *no* and *not,* and by avoiding negative wording or words with negative connotations. Apologies are a strategy that can improve a manager's and organization's image. They can also create the impression of guilt and liability.

Memos and their electronic equivalent, e-mails, are the most frequently used internal written communication. E-mails and memos are efficient, straightforward messages that require some strategic considerations in their writing. They have several uses for a manager, including communicating to groups, fixing responsibility, communicating with opponents, and communicating with the inaccessible. They fall into two categories: announcements and requests for action.

Memos and e-mails are frequently used in office politics.

Cases for Small-Group Discussion

CASE 7–1

Claim Refusal Letter

You are the sales manager for a furniture manufacturer and have just received a strongly worded claim letter from Hyram Blalock, who owns a large hotel in a nearby city. Blalock has been refurbishing his hotel and had placed a special order with you for 115 headboards to fit specifications he sent.

He ordered headboards an inch and a half narrower than for conventional king-size beds. He also specified a finish different from that normally used in this grade of headboard. Finally, he wanted his hotel's logo imprinted on each headboard. You completed this order and shipped it to him about a week ago.

He ordered the mattresses directly from a manufacturer that has since gone out of business. They did, however, deliver his mattresses before going bankrupt, just a week before your headboards arrived. The problem is that all these mattresses were manufactured in the conventional dimensions, rather than the narrower ones for which the headboards were designed.

Blalock is asking you to take back the current shipment and either change the dimensions to fit the conventional mattresses or send a different set (which would, of course, have the finish he specified and his hotel's logo on them).

Obviously, you cannot comply with his request. Write an appropriate strategic claim refusal. The facts are on your side—he ordered the headboards in the size and finish that he received. However, the challenge is to tell him so without lecturing or using negatives. If you do choose to alter the headboards in the original order, feel free to do so—but be sure to charge him. Most importantly, you want to keep Blalock as a customer.

CASE NOTE

This case tempts the writer to respond to Blalock with the same kind of letter he sent. Those using the appropriate indirect negative response will avoid lecturing to the reader as they remind him of his role in the problem. The suggested option (remodeling the headboards) is one strategy, but it should not be presented as if the writer feels guilty. If the letter suggests guilt, then the writer can expect more problems.

CASE 7–2

Inquiry Letter

You are the assistant human resource manager for an insurance company whose territory includes your state and three surrounding states. Your company has recently revamped its retirement and employment benefits packages, and you have been assigned the task of communicating these changes to all employees.

Since some of the changes are complex, you will be traveling to four sites in your region to meet with the company's agents and their personnel. You need to arrange hotel accommodations for the personnel at each of the sites, and you will need a meeting room with a screen and equipment for projecting your PowerPoint slide show. Since the company has had a very good year, management wants the employees to enjoy their stay at the hotels. So you also need to inquire into the recreational and banquet facilities available.

Write a letter of inquiry to the Hotel Beacon in a major city in one of your surrounding states. The letter should elicit the information you will need to decide if the hotel is the right one for your meeting. Make it clear that you will be looking at other hotels, seeking the best rate for services required.

CASE NOTE

The most common pitfall in this case will be the lack of clarity. The letter is actually more complex than it seems. The temptation for some will be to write a brief letter, which the hotel marketing manager will be unable to answer in proper detail. In addition to being thorough, the letter should also build goodwill; the writer may be interested in doing more business in the future with the reader.

CASE 7–3

Request Refusal Letter

You are the administrative assistant to R. D. Spenser, president of Flo-Sheen Fabrics. Flo-Sheen employs over three hundred people in its mill and corporate offices. Each year, these employees contribute generously to the city's annual fund-raising drive. Spenser also has developed a volunteer program that allows some employees to work on charitable projects on company time.

On your desk today, you found a letter that was sent to Spenser from a statewide youth organization requesting permission to conduct a fund-raising drive in your plant for a new project it is developing. The organization wants to establish a scholarship fund for its brightest members.

Spenser jotted a note at the bottom of the letter asking you to deny the request. Do so, but build up goodwill. Be positive yet assertive; do not leave the organization wondering if the request is denied.

CASE NOTE

Since the letter must build goodwill, the writer must use tact in denying the request. One option would be holding out the possibility of putting the youth organization on next year's list. But do not leave the reader feeling that another letter might get the results that the first one missed. The letter also needs to explain why the president of the company is not responding.

Exercise for Small Groups

Exercise 8-1

As you prepare to revise the memo at the top of the next page, consider purpose, audience, organization, and tone. Change the headings to standard format. Consider using design elements such as bullets, headings, or a word table to clarify the information in the memo's body.

Student Study Site

Visit the Student Study Site at **study.sagepub.com/hynes6e** for web quizzes, video links, web resources, and cases studies.

Chapter 7 Memo

INTEROFFICE CORRESPONDENCE

St. Louis, Missouri

To: Purchasing   **From:**

Date: January 21

Subject: Schedules

Well we had our team meetin just like usual this week. We talked about alot, but I thought I should remind you of a few things that are pressing. Don't forget that we are supposed to send our schedules for the week to Buffi. These should be transmitted by EMail each Monday or Friday if you can get it done early. It'r really helpful to know where you are when we can't find you.

Your vacation schedules should be estimated by now so please give them to me by the end of next week.

cc:

Notes

1. Gilbert C. Storms, "What Business School Graduates Say about the Writing They Do at Work," *Bulletin of the Association for Business Communication* 46, no. 4 (December 1983): pp. 13–18.
2. JoAnne Yates, "The Emergence of the Memo as a Managerial Genre," *Management Communication Quarterly* 2, no. 4 (May 1989): p. 486.
3. Mary K. Kirtz and Diana C. Reep, "A Survey of the Frequency, Types, and Importance of Writing Tasks in Four Career Areas," *Bulletin of the Association for Business Communication* 53, no. 4 (December 1990): pp. 3–4.
4. Edward Goodin and Skip Swerdlow, "The Current Quality of Written Correspondence: A Statistical Analysis of the Performance of 13 Industry and Organizational Categories," *Bulletin of the Association for Business Communication* 50, no. 1 (March 1987): pp. 12–16.
5. Nancy Sarnoff, "Chevron Puts Office Tower on Hold," *Houston Chronicle*, December 20, 2013, p. 1.
6. Kitty O. Locker, "Factors in Reader Responses to Negative Letters: Experimental Evidence for Changing What We Teach," *Journal of Business and Technical Communication* 13, no. 1 (January 1999): pp. 5–48.
7. Stephen B. Knouse, "Confidentiality and the Letter of Recommendation," *Bulletin of the Association for Business Communication* 50, no. 3 (September 1987): pp. 6–8.

8. Marlys Harris, "Gaining through Complaining," *Money,* May 1982, pp. 174–175.

9. Lisa Tyler, "Liability Means Never Being Able to Say You're Sorry: Corporate Guilt, Legal Constraints, and Defensiveness in Corporate Communication," *Management Communication Quarterly* 11, no. 1 (August 1997): pp. 51–73.

10. Stuart Shapiro, president and chief executive of the Pennsylvania Health Care Association, letter to the editor, *The New York Times,* June 6, 2013, p. A22.

11. Excerpt from a full-page advertisement, "Open Letter to Target Guests," from Gregg Steinhafel, chairman, president, and CEO of Target, Inc., published in the *Houston Chronicle,* January 13, 2014, p. A9.

12. Barbara Kellerman, "When Should a Leader Apologize—And When Not?" *Harvard Business Review,* April 2006, pp. 73–81.

13. Ibid., p. 76.

14. Ameeta Patel and Lamar Reinsch, "Companies Can Apologize: Corporate Apologies and Legal Liability," *Business Communication Quarterly* 66, no. 1 (March 2003): pp. 9–25.

15. Mohan R. Limaye, "The Syntax of Persuasion: Two Business Letters of Request," *Journal of Business Communication* 20, no. 2 (Spring 1983): pp. 17–30.

16. Chadwick B. Hilton, William H. Motes, and John S. Fielden, "An Experimental Study of the Effects of Style and Organization on Reader Perceptions of Text," *Journal of Business Communication* 26, no. 3 (Summer 1989): pp. 255–270.

17. Jeanette Gilsdorf, "Write Me Your Best Case for . . . ," *Bulletin of the Association for Business Communication* 54, no. 1 (March 1991): pp. 7–12.

18. Lisa Abend, "The Font War: IKEA Fans Fume over Verdana," *Time,* August 28, 2009, http://content.time.com/time/business/article/0,8599,1919127,00.html

19. Marie E. Flatley, "A Comparative Analysis of the Written Communication of Managers at Various Organizational Levels in the Private Business Sector," *Journal of Business Communication* 19, no. 3 (Summer 1982): pp. 35–50.

20. Gerald J. Alred, Charles T. Brusaw, and Walter E. Oliu, *Business Writer's Handbook,* 8th ed. (New York: St. Martin's Press, 2006), p. 327.

21. William Safire, "To Whom It May Concern: Here's How to Address E-mail," *Houston Chronicle,* October 22, 2006, p. E6.

22. Max Rose, "A Memorandum about Memos," *Supervisory Magazine,* March 1980, pp. 6–8.

23. Kelly Dinardo, "Laid-Off Workers Let E-Mails Fly," *Houston Chronicle,* March 6, 2009, p. A11.

24. Robin Wright, "Rumsfeld's Blunt Style on Display in 'Snowflakes,'" *Houston Chronicle,* November 1, 2007, p. A17.

CHAPTER 8

Writing Management Reports and Proposals

No one who has read official documents needs to be told how easy it is to conceal the essential truth under the apparently candid and all-disclosing phrases of a voluminous and particularizing report.

—Woodrow Wilson, twenty-eighth US president

Reports are among an organization's most important communication tools. They appear in a variety of forms, carry out a number of functions, and ensure the efficient transfer of data. Data transfer takes place within an organization and between an organization and its stakeholders. Managerial reports should be well organized and objective. They carry verifiable information that addresses some purpose or problem.

Evidence indicates the importance of reports in business is not likely to diminish soon. In one study of recent business graduates, 65.6 percent of respondents noted that they frequently wrote informational reports, while 31.3 percent replied that they sometimes wrote these reports. In the same study, 40.6 percent responded that they frequently wrote analytical reports and 43.8 percent replied that they sometimes wrote these reports.[1]

In another, larger study of recent business graduates (837 respondents), 74 percent either sometimes, often, or very often wrote short reports. In that same study, 42 percent of the respondents either sometimes, often, or very often wrote long reports.[2] Another researcher found that report writing in private-sector firms differed by level—middle-level managers write a bit less than lower-level managers, and upper-level managers write less than middle-level managers.[3]

Report audiences can be both internal and external to the organization. In their role as report writers, managers appreciate how internal reports can contribute to the management functions. Reports are essential to managers' ability to control organizational actions.

Managers are required to plan, organize, execute, evaluate, and improve, and they need some medium for carrying out these tasks. Internal reports are a means to those ends. While some internal reports depict current status or progress toward a goal, others convey the results of previous management decisions; still others relay a manager's evaluation of results and performance and give suggestions (or orders) for change in current policies and procedures to bring about greater effectiveness and efficiency.

Managers also write reports to external audiences. For example, corporate annual reports are read by shareholders and other stakeholders. Government regulatory agencies often require companies to file reports periodically. Common to all these diverse report writing settings is that managers must have the know-how to approach problems, solve them, and communicate the findings to internal and external readers.

THE REPORT WRITING PROCESS

Typically, managers write reports for one of three reasons. The most common is simply that someone has asked them to. A higher-level manager who sees an area where information is lacking or a problem that needs solving will ask a subordinate to fill that gap or solve that problem. A report may also be part of a company's regular business. Thus, writing progress or periodic reports may be one of a manager's regular duties. Finally, a manager may write reports spontaneously, perhaps to fill gaps he has found on his own or to share information with the rest of the staff or to propose changes.

Groundwork

Of course, managers do not just sit down and write reports one after another. Typically, they must lay the groundwork for the report. The prewriting process mirrors the "Stage One: Planning" section on routine documents that is discussed in Chapter 6. This preliminary effort often takes more time than actually writing the report and can intimidate some writers.[4]

Defining the Problem or Objective

After accepting a report writing assignment, a manager must make sure the process leading up to the report will yield optimum results. The writer's time is valuable not only to the company but to the writer as well. Valuable hours spent following blind leads waste personal energy and resources.

First, the report writer must determine the problem under study or the objective. What does the person who authorized this report want from her effort? The problem may be nothing more than an information gap—someone needs data or demographics on sales, for example. The problem may also be one requiring analysis. Thus, the report writer must choose from among several options and recommend a plan of action.

STOP AND THINK

1. How does thinking about a report's purpose compare with the prewriting strategies you read about in Chapter 6?

2. When considering a report's audience, how does the WII-FM concept ("What's in it for me?") apply?

Developing Recommendations

Once the problem and purpose have been determined, the next step before gathering data is to develop solutions or action items. The manager must analyze the need for change and determine the best plan for improvement. For example, productivity in a plant has dropped, and a manager needs to determine the cause (or causes) and propose a solution. Possible causes might be raw material shortages, equipment malfunctions, abuse of sick leave, or a host of combinations. Once these causes are analyzed, the researcher develops solutions and considers constraints such as resources and time frames in identifying the most reasonable plan.

Seeking Data

Once the manager has done the problem analysis and determined the information needed for the report, she gathers data to support her ideas. Most of the data needed for business reports are primary data, that is, data the writer collects from interviews, surveys, experiments, and observation. Occasionally, writers draw from secondary research data—that is, material already published.

The next step is to gather and analyze the data. Finally, the manager transforms the results into a format that will clearly and easily be understood by the report readers. Supporting data must be carefully selected and described so that they enhance the writer's purpose. Helpful tips for presenting data in easy-to-read formats, including tables and graphs, are presented later in this chapter.

Classification of Reports

Knowing what form the final report will assume helps writers gauge the effort needed to prepare the report and thus helps in the budgeting of time and resources.

Various systems exist for cataloging groups of reports. Probably the most effective classification system is according to level of *formality*. This continuum starts with the most informal routine reports, which may resemble forms. The manager simply fills in several blank spaces and, in some cases, provides a brief narrative or description. Examples are the trip report, the expense report, and the attendance report.

Next on the formality continuum is the letter or memo report. Either of these may be several pages long (ten-page letter reports are not unheard of). As explained in the preceding chapter, letter reports are addressed to external audiences, while memo reports go to internal audiences. Detailed descriptions of letter and memo reports, along with example reports, are presented later in this chapter.

Next on the continuum, the report becomes more formal, and front matter appears. Thus, for example, the writer may precede a report with a transmittal document, title page, and table of contents. Back matter, such as appendixes and glossaries, may be added as well. Later in the chapter, we describe what goes into those elements of a formal report, and you will see an example of a formal report with front and back matter.

Another useful classification system for reports is according to their frequency. *Regularly scheduled* reports must be written at certain stages of a project or as the calendar dictates. Thus, a corporation produces annual reports, quarterly reports, monthly reports, even daily reports that are read by various audiences. On the other hand, a manager may perceive a unique need for a document. In these cases, onetime-only paperwork, known as *special* reports might need to be composed. Problem analysis reports, proposals, and evaluations are the most common special reports that fall under the onetime-only umbrella. Problem analysis reports can be crucial for a company and are necessary when an issue becomes more complex and requires objective, unbiased facts. The goal is to define or clarify a problem and explore solutions.[5] Proposals suggest changes in organizational policies or procedures. They can be directed to internal or external audiences. Evaluations present assessments of how well or how poorly a current policy or procedure is working. Evaluation reports may trigger proposal reports.

Companies may classify special reports according to their level of formality. For example, an informal proposal might recommend staff changes, new product ideas or methods, and procedural or departmental changes. When proposals are more complex, and involve more time and money, a more formal approach is in order. Formal proposals are typically directed toward senior management and other companies. Although the key analysis and solution components of informal and formal proposals are similar, there are a few noticeable differences. Table 8–1 lists parts of the informal proposal and the formal proposal.[6]

Table 8–1   Proposal Formats

INFORMAL	FORMAL
1. Introduction	1. Letter of transmittal
a. Problem	2. Title page
b. Solution	3. Executive Summary/Abstract
2. Analysis	4. Table of Contents
a. Background	5. Body
b. Causes	a. Statement of problem
c. Scope, significance, implications	b. Proposed solution
3. Detailed solution	c. Facilities/equipment
a. Work and management	d. Personnel
b. Drawbacks	e. Schedule
c. Benefits	f. Costs
4. Action stimulus	g. Advantages/disadvantages
	6. Supporting materials

Source: Roze, 1997.

STRATEGIC CONSIDERATIONS

As with all other communications undertaken by managers, reports should reflect careful strategic decisions. These decisions fall into a number of areas, many of which are subtle but important.

Format

The format of a report is one of the report writer's careful strategic decisions. As we discussed in the previous section, generally, the more significant the contents of the report, the more formal it is. Length also corresponds to formality, with longer reports having a formal appearance. Several other factors that determine format are discussed next.

Audience

A report's intended audience guides, at least partially, the format and degree of formality. A manager preparing a report recommending the purchase of one component over another might choose memo form for the company controller but a short report form (with a title page) if the same report is to go to the chief executive officer. Just as we might dress more formally for an interview with the CEO than we might for subordinates, our reports similarly get more or less dressed up to match their readers.

Effort

Another significant factor in determining the report format is the amount of time spent researching and preparing the report. Usually related is the actual size of the report, which often reflects the effort expended. The report that requires a couple of phone calls and a half hour for the writing calls for less dressing up than does one resulting from several weeks of careful planning, the administration and evaluation of testing instruments, and several days of writing. The extra effort merits more formality.

> **STOP AND THINK**
>
> 1. When a business report is transmitted as an e-mail, does it appear to have taken more or less effort than a hard copy memo?
>
> 2. Why do you think format indicates effort?

Significance

We also must consider the value of the findings the report shares. Some findings are more important than others. For example, a report on options for a new janitorial service might conceivably reflect as much effort as one recommending a new product line. However, the significance of the second calls for a dressier treatment than that of the former.

The Original Assignment

A report writer should use any clues given in the initial assignment. It might be unwise to prepare a formal report if the original assignment from your manager was to "shoot me an e-mail when you've found the answer." If on another assignment that same manager indicated a different report might be forwarded to top management, you might give it a more formal treatment.

Precedent

Precedent is also relevant to the format a report will assume. A new manager is advised to learn what format is traditional for certain types of assignments. Many global companies, such as ExxonMobil, Honeywell, and Accenture, specify guidelines. Precedent is especially relevant with periodic reports, which are expected to look like previous periodic reports.

Recently, some companies and government agencies have begun using graphics software such as Microsoft (MS) PowerPoint as a report format. Considered by some managers to be simpler and more user-friendly than word processing software such as MS Word, graphics software will produce "decks" or "flipbooks" that include more text, data tables, and illustrations than are seen on traditional presentation slides and that can stand alone. On the other hand, this report format is more concise than traditional narrative reports because of space limitations.

Karl Keller, a corporate communication consultant in Chicago, notes that PowerPoint decks "are often used to marshal business arguments, e.g., 'we should do X' rather than reporting business activities in a broader sense. These decks accompany face-to-face or distance meetings with screen sharing."[7] Ulrike Murfett, a business professor at Nanyang Technological University, agrees, adding that for strategy consulting projects, companies in Singapore invariably want PowerPoint decks rather than traditional word-processed reports as the key document deliverable to accompany a presentation. Best practices for PowerPoint report formats have yet to emerge, but they seem to fill the gap between sparse bulleted lists on presentation slides and long, formal, corporate reports.[8]

Arrangement of Points

Another strategic decision that report writers must make is the order of the information appearing in the report.

Direct Order

As the previous chapter showed, direct order puts the main point first, followed by the details. In routine messages conveying good news or neutral information, direct order is appropriate. Similarly, with short reports, when the reader is likely to agree with the writer's main point, direct order is often best.

Most readers receive reports neutrally, and since recommendations are needed for deciding on actions to take, the sooner a reader gets to them, the better. Direct order is especially appropriate when the reader trusts the writer's work. If the reader needs to check on any point, the specifics are in the text.

Indirect Order

Indirect order is often favored for long reports and proposals. The traditional inductive organizational pattern of introduction, body, and conclusion described in Chapter 7 is common for such reports. The indirect approach is unquestionably called for when a reader is likely to interpret the conclusions as bad news. Then, too, in analytic reports, proposals, or persuasive reports, when readers might disagree with the conclusions, the writer must lead the readers logically to the conclusions using indirect order.

Organization of the Body

Whether a writer uses direct or indirect order to arrange the ideas, the body of the report also needs organization. The body, the part that gives the reasons for the conclusions and recommendations, needs unifying elements to ensure that the material is in its clearest, most useful form and that the ideas are presented in a logical, easily followed sequence. When deciding how to organize the body, be sure that you include only the information that your reader(s) expect. Despite your experience with writing term papers in school, length is not a virtue of business reports. In fact, short business reports are more likely to be read than long ones. When deciding what to include in the body of your report, remember the advice of Elmore Leonard, the prolific, award-winning American crime novelist: "try to leave out the part that readers tend to skip."[9]

The organizational plan chosen is situational and depends on the problem under study, the nature of the information being reported, and the reader's needs. The most common organizational plans are by time, place, quantity, and criteria (or factors). The plan chosen should be the one that moves the reader smoothly from the body's beginning to its end through a series of clearly interrelated parts.[10]

Time

Time organization is obviously appropriate for chronologically sequenced material. Any report that narrates events uses this pattern. For example, a quarterly report might have main divisions for each of the three months covered. Chronological organization works to the advantage of the writer since she can work either forward or backward through the time period being detailed. Once the writer chooses this order, questions about what comes next are easily resolved.

Place

Organization by place is more complex than is organization by time. This pattern would be appropriate for an activity report dealing with simultaneous but separate events (for example, a monthly report on the activities of several branch offices of a company). It is also appropriate for descriptive reports. Using spatial organization in complex reports dictates some order in which to proceed. Regions of the United States, for example, could be covered in a clockwise fashion.

Quantity/Size

Organization by quantity or size is another option that is relevant when the data lend themselves to quantification. For example, a report discussing a city's household characteristics might be best organized by the number of individuals per household or by the incomes of the household heads. A writer discussing cities might organize by population ranges. And sales reports might give information about the best-selling product first.

Criteria or Factors

The final category, organization by criteria or factors, is a catchall. It is also the most useful since it is so broad. Here, the report's body is organized by the relevant factors that led to the conclusions. In an informational report, these factors are the categories into which the information falls. For example, a report discussing the characteristics of a sales market that is largely homogeneous might deal with the income, age, education, and tastes of the market.

In an evaluative report, the conclusions and recommendations are based on a set of criteria or reasons on which a decision is based. For example, a writer may prepare a personnel report recommending the selection of a job candidate. He might divide the report by the optimum characteristics of an employee filling the position. Thus, an office assistant might be evaluated in terms of keyboarding skills, communication skills, and competence in office procedures.

<table>
<tr><td>

STOP AND THINK

Recall the concepts of BIF and BILL that were described in Chapter 6 as ways to organize routine messages. When organizing a report by criteria or factors, should you begin with the most important criterion/factor (BIF) or should you work up to it (BILL)?

</td></tr>
</table>

Recommendation reports may also be organized by the alternative solutions available. Each major section of the proposal would describe an option in detail. For example, a report recommending the fleet purchase of a particular car might begin with an overview of criteria used, such as safety, comfort, financial considerations, and dependability. Then, each of three or four car models under consideration might be described. Finally, the features the reader needs to compare would be presented in one place. For example, the purchase prices would probably be presented on one page of the report. The report would conclude with a recommendation for the fleet purchase.

Headings

All business reports (not just formal ones) benefit from the use of headings. Headings indicate to the reader the relative degree of significance of the material that follows. Headings are also useful signposts to guide the reader through the report. They make the structure of the report explicit. And headings provide white space in reports, which contributes appreciably to their visual appeal, as mentioned in the preceding chapter. The following paragraphs offer guidelines for developing report headings.

Content Headings

Write headings with the reader in mind. They should be descriptive of the content to follow but relatively short. Generally, seven words (or fewer) are appropriate for first-level headings, and even fewer than seven are usually needed for lower-level headings. Although single words and phrases are typical content headings, occasionally a question can serve as a heading. This format works especially well when the report is a response to an inquiry or a Request for Proposal (RFP) that included questions.

The report writer can choose from a variety of heading systems. The heading system described next and shown in Figure 8–1 is suitable for most needs. Be aware, however, that when reports are transmitted electronically, the position of headings on a page or screen may change. If a writer is unsure, it may be wiser to left justify all headings, changing only the font size and other design elements to indicate levels.

First-Level Headings

The first-level heading is used for all major divisions of the report, including headings for some prefatory parts (executive summary, table of contents), the introduction, the major divisions of the body of the report, and the closing sections. To indicate its major importance, it may be centered, bold, larger font, or all uppercase. When reports are double-spaced, first-level headings will sometimes be triple-spaced from the text. The writer may choose any variation but must apply it consistently throughout the report.

Second-Level Headings

The second-level heading indicates material subordinate to the main divisions of the report. These headings are often left justified, bold, and in upper- and lowercase. The text begins one or two spaces below the heading. The sample report at the end of this chapter provides examples of first- and second-level headings.

Third-Level Headings

Generally, the third-level heading is as far as a report needs to be divided. The writer might indent the heading, bold it, and capitalize the initial letter of only the first word (unless proper nouns appear in the heading). Often, the writer will follow the heading by a period and continue the text on the same line after skipping two spaces.

Transitions

Use other transitional devices besides headings. In moving from one major section to another, a writer should summarize the previous section and preview the next to show the change. In moving from one subsection to another, a brief sentence should signal the shift and help the reader see the flow of ideas. A good rule for judging transitions is to see if the text reads well without the headings. If it does, then the reader is not likely to become lost or confused in working through the text.

Figure 8–1   Report Headings Style Sample

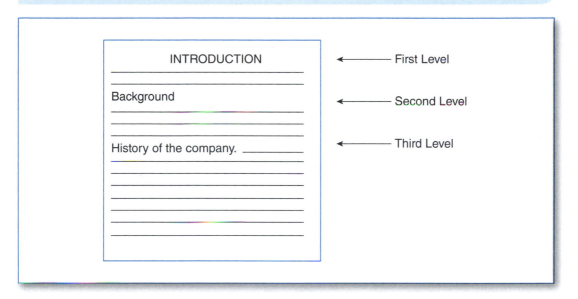

Now that we have discussed strategic decisions on format, arrangement of points, organization, headings, and transitions, we are ready to talk about the content of some of the more common types of business reports: memo reports, letter reports, and formal reports.

MEMO AND LETTER REPORTS

The first specific types of reports we examine are memo and letter reports. They fall toward the informal side of the formal-to-informal continuum for business reports. More and more often, short reports are delivered electronically, perhaps as e-mail attachments, rather than as paper documents. Whether hard copy or electronic, they should follow these guidelines.

Memo Reports

In addition to being the most informal type of report used within an organization, memos are efficient and suggest a no-nonsense approach. They invariably have some form of headings—*To, From, Subject,* and *Date*—at the top for efficient routing and a quick understanding of purpose. The comments made about *Subject* lines in the previous chapter apply here as well. In an indirectly ordered report, the *Subject* line should not give away the conclusions.

Introduction

The memo report begins with a brief introduction that usually tells the purpose of the report and who authorized it. For example, "This report, which you authorized on June 8, evaluates three copying machines and recommends the purchase of one." Often preferable, though, is something less formal: "Recently, you asked me to look into the purchase of a new copier."

It is also appropriate to indicate how the writer derived the information: "I called sales representatives from three manufacturers," or "I examined sales materials supplied by three companies." A statement of the scope, that is, how widely the research into the problem ranged, is appropriate as well, although it is often obvious.

Close to the beginning, a direct report indicates the conclusions and/or recommendations reached in the report. In the example on copiers, the writer using direct order might end the first paragraph with her choice of copier.

Body

Whether the overall report uses direct or indirect order, the body of a memo report details the findings that led the writer to the conclusions the report makes. For the sake of efficiency, headings often set off this material. Either centered or left justified, these headings guide the reader through the contents; he can tell at a glance what a given section discusses.

The list is another highly appropriate organizational tool in the memo report. The writer must introduce the list, but that introduction is often no more than a sentence. Lists help to cut down on prose, and their simplicity can improve reader comprehension and retention of the material. To maximize reader comprehension, lists should be constructed in parallel grammatical form. For example, in the report on copiers, the writer might state the following:

My evaluation of the copiers sought to determine four things about each unit:

- Use of energy
- Cost of operation
- Speed of operation
- Frequency of repairs

Writers must be careful not to let the memo degenerate into a mere catalog of lists. The report needs to be efficient without being an outline or series of phrases.

In a memo report, a manager may also choose to use visual aids (discussed later in this chapter) to help the reader identify key ideas and supporting material.

Close

The end of a memo report needs planning. If the report uses indirect order, the last paragraph will give the conclusions and recommendations reached. On the other hand, a report using direct order easily ends on the last point. The writer might wish to introduce the last paragraph with some transitional device that indicates the approaching end: "Finally, I evaluated the ease of operation of the copiers. I found . . ." Often this transition is enough to signal the end.

In the example of a memo report below, note the use of the direct strategy for organizing ideas. Also, note the use of design elements such as bullets and headings to make the message easy to read.

MEMORANDUM

To: Sanjay Gupta, Plant Superintendent

From: Max Holder, Manager

Date: June 20, 2015

Subject: Recommendation to Install Jetaire Hand Dryers

As you requested, this memo presents the results of my research about the relative cost effective-ness of installing hand dryers versus paper towel holders in the company restrooms. I recommend that we purchase Jetaire Hand Dryers.

BENEFITS

Wilson Manufacturing will gain three benefits by installing hand dryers.

- We will save $3,084 in three years, plus intangible costs.
- The restrooms will be more sanitary.
- The safety of our employees will be increased, since there will be less slipping on wet floors.

ANALYSIS

During the preceding three-year period, paper towels have cost us $3,168. The intangible costs are 50 percent of the three-year cost, which is $1,584 (see Table 1). The intangible costs come from issuing purchase orders, storing extra towels, hiring plumbers to fix clogged pipes, and the disposal of towels. In total, Wilson Manufacturing has spent $4,752 to support the use of paper towels.

By comparison, installing Jetaire Hand Dryers will cost just $1,668 over three years (see Table 2), saving the company an estimated $3,084.

Eliminating paper towels will have benefits beyond cost savings. For instance, the use of hand dryers will bring about a more sanitary environment. The toilets and sinks will not be as likely to overflow, thus reducing the need for repairs. This will make the workplace more enjoyable.

(Continued)

(Continued)

Table 1   Cost of Paper Towels

No. of Employees	200
Towels avg.	2.5
Daily visits	4
Cost per towel	0.002
Days per month	22
Monthly cost	$88
Three-year cost	$3,168
Intangible cost	$1,584
Total cost	$4,752

Table 2   Cost of Jetaire Hand Dryers

Three Jetaire units @$120 x four restrooms	$1,440
Installation cost	$84
Electricity cost for three years	$144
Total cost for Jetaire	$1,668

Another benefit is the reduction of safety hazards. Wet, slippery floors caused by clogged sinks and toilets could result in employee injuries. These will be eliminated when paper towels are no longer used.

ACTION ITEM

Haworth, Inc., should be hired to install three Jetaire Hand units in each of the four restrooms. The machines can be installed in one afternoon with no interruption to our operation.

Letter Reports

The letter report is similar to the memo report, but three essential differences exist: form, tone, and audience. The differences in form are products of necessity (the inside address, for example) and convention (the salutation and complimentary close). The inside address is necessary because the report is to be sent to someone outside the organization (as opposed to the memo, which is delivered within the organization).

A more subtle difference between the two is tone. Since the letter report goes to a reader outside the organization, it is a tool for building goodwill, and goodwill means increased business. Thus, the letter report stresses reader benefits more than the memo report and is likely to close with a goodwill statement that promises continued cooperation.

Organization

The letter report may use direct or indirect order, although most prefer indirect order because the reader's reaction might be difficult to gauge at a distance. When the findings are unquestionably positive, direct order is advisable. In these cases, a clear *Subject* line can orient the reader to the nature of the problem and solution addressed in the letter report.

Introduction

Like the memo report, the letter report needs a brief introduction. The opening acquaints the reader with the purpose. Often, the purpose and authorization (or reference to the request being granted) can appear in a single sentence. For example, "As you requested in your letter last week, here is a report on our experiences with Ace Maintenance Service." If appropriate, the scope of the report and the methodology used for developing the details can be included, although these may be clear from the discussion.

Body

The letter report has no set length, and it is not unheard of for such a report to reach eight to ten pages.

Headings are appropriate in a letter report, especially a long report, since they quickly guide the reader to whatever sections might be of special interest. Since managers write some letter reports in response to a series of questions submitted by the reader, the headings can reflect those questions. As with memo reports, bulleted lists and tables are appropriate for the letter report.

Close

If conclusions and recommendations are reserved for the end of the report, they precede the last short paragraph. The last paragraph of a letter report is a statement of goodwill. Readers appreciate the writer's personal involvement, and writers appreciate an opportunity to close on a positive note, procuring the likelihood of future business transactions.

In the example of a letter report below, note the use of the direct strategy for organizing ideas. Also, note the use of design elements such as bullets and headings to make the message easy to read.

LAMAR CONSOLIDATED HIGH SCHOOL

4604 Mustang Avenue

Rosenberg, TX 77471

Main Phone: (832) 223-3000

Main Fax: (832) 223-3001

November 3, 2015

Mr. Alphonse Garcia

207 Pine Ridge Road

Rosenberg, TX 77471

Dear Mr. Garcia:

What a great privilege it is to report on Jennifer's progress in Algebra I this year. I know Jennifer's success in Algebra is important to you and Jennifer. Evidence suggests that the support systems at home and class must work together to facilitate learning for high school students.

The table below summarizes Jennifer's scores on her weekly quizzes, unit exams, and homework.

Month	Quizzes (20 pts)	Exams (100 pts)	Homework (10 pts)
September	20	100	10
	18	90	10
	15		10
October	20	95	10
	17	100	10
	19	90	10
	20		10

As you can see, Jennifer is exceeding expectations across the board.

Finally, I would like to invite you to attend the annual Open House on Wednesday, November 15, so we can meet and discuss the rest of the semester. Here are the details:

Date: Wednesday, November 15, 2015

Time: 6:30 pm – 8:30 pm (come-and-go event)

Location: Lamar CHS cafeteria and classrooms

Additional information about the event can be found on the high school website at www .lchsisd.edu.

I am excited to partner with you this semester to help Jennifer learn and succeed in Algebra. Please contact me whenever you would like to discuss her work. I primarily rely on e-mail, but you can also phone me if you prefer. Conference Hours are Monday, Wednesday, and Friday between 3:30 and 4:30 pm, or by appointment. My phone number is (832) 223-3100. My email: mriggins@lchsisd.edu.

Sincerely,

Mark Riggins

Mark Riggins, MEd

Algebra and Mathematics Instructor

Source: Mark Riggins. Reprinted with permission.

The final type of report to be examined here is the formal report. Though we will review all the elements of long, formal reports, not every element will appear in every report. Remember that as reports get longer, they tend to pick up the trappings of formality.

ELEMENTS OF THE FORMAL REPORT

Though you may not often write long, formal reports, when the situation arises, you will want the report to look right. Formal reports are delivered as paper documents more often than in electronic form, whether sent to internal or external audiences. In the next sections, we will first discuss front matter, then review parts of the report proper, and finally describe back matter (see table 8–2).

Front Matter

These parts come before the report itself. They tend to be directly associated with report length and formality. The longer and more formal a report is, the more front matter it is likely to have. Each element appears on a separate page.

Table 8–2   Formal Report Elements

Front Matter	Report Proper	Back Matter
Title Page	Introduction	References
Transmittal Document	Body	Bibliography
Table of Contents	Summary	Appendixes
List of Illustrations	Conclusions	
Executive Summary	Recommendations	

Title Page

The title page is the first page for most formal reports. Generally, it consists of four main components: the title, the complete identifications of the reader and the writer, and the date. In constructing the report title, the writer should strive to make it a concise but complete description of the report's purpose and topic. Because of their charge of completeness, titles of business reports tend to be longer than titles of other literary works.

The complete identification of the reader and writer includes the person's name, position, organization, city, state, and (if needed) country. The identifying blocks of information are generally preceded by expressions such as "presented to" or "prepared for" and "prepared by." If the organization and/or location are the same for the reader and writer (internal reports), they may be omitted. These blocks of information should be spaced evenly down the page and laterally centered. See the sample report at the end of this chapter for a model title page.

Transmittal Document

The transmittal memo or letter is the next item found in most formal reports (although some writers actually clip it to the cover of the report). Internal reports get a transmittal memo; external reports get a transmittal letter. Generally, it replaces the conversation the writer would have with the reader if the report were being handed over in person.

The first paragraph serves three purposes. First, it announces the accompanying report with wording like "Here is the report . . ." It also briefly states the nature of the report and mentions authorization details. Note that all three purposes might be accomplished in one sentence, as in "Here is the report on cost-cutting options you requested in your memo of July 10."

The content of the transmittal's body may vary with the circumstances. Generally, it is viewed as an opportunity to motivate the reader to read, interpret, and use the report. Also, the writer might wish to acknowledge people who helped her do the research and compile the report. To keep the transmittal short, do not summarize the report here. That function is served by the executive summary.

Typically, the transmittal closes with a call to action ("After reading the report, please call me") and a goodwill gesture. It thanks the recipient for the assignment and looks forward to continued service. To some, the idea of thanking someone for giving them work might sound strange. Such skeptics should remember that report writing assignments present chances to showcase analytical abilities and communication skills—abilities and skills that might be carefully viewed and valued when promotional opportunities arise.

Table of Contents

The table of contents follows the transmittal document. Contemporary word processing software has a feature that allows automatic creation of the table of contents, following the order of headings and subheadings in the text. The real value of the table of contents is that it displays all the report sections at a glance and refers the reader to the page number of a section of particular interest.

If you must create the table of contents by hand, be sure the entries use wording identical to that in the text. Also, to connect an entry to its page number, use leader dots (made by alternating periods and spaces on the line, aligned for all the entries). The page numbers should have their right digits aligned.

List of Illustrations

The list of tables and figures is an optional feature appropriate to a report with five or more visual aids, such as a technical report. If needed, and if there is room, the list begins several spaces below the end of the table of contents. It is titled "List of Illustrations" and is set up like the table of contents. Most report writers divide the list into tables and figures. The table or figure number is followed by its title and is separated from its page number by leader dots.

Executive Summary

The next prefatory element found in formal reports is the executive summary. Also called the epitome, abstract, brief, digest, or synopsis, it provides a quick overview of the report.[11] Managers are often interested only in a report's highlights. They will use the executive summary as a replacement for the report. The challenge is to shrink the report down to its major facts, analyses, and conclusions, including everything that is key, while keeping it to about one-tenth the length of the report. The easiest way to accomplish this task is to first write the entire report; then, go through it and highlight the key statements, generalizations, and topic sentences. Typically, they appear at the beginning of each section and paragraph. Then, just transfer the key statements to a fresh file or page, in the same order that they appear in the report. After polishing, this list of the report's highlights turns into the executive summary. See the sample report at the end of this chapter for a model executive summary.

STOP AND THINK

1. Why is the executive summary so challenging to compose?

2. When composing a report's executive summary, to what extent should you apply the strategies you learned in Chapter 6 for writing concisely?

The Report Proper

The report proper begins with an introduction, presents all the information, and ends with the conclusions and/or recommendations. The following paragraphs detail the content of the various parts of the report proper.

Introduction: Required Elements

The first page of the body of the formal report contains the introduction, which should be identified as such with a first-level heading. The introduction contains a number of elements, some of which are required, and some of which are optional. No rule sets the order in which the elements may occur, although the order in which they are discussed in the paragraphs that follow is appropriate for most circumstances.

Every introduction should include the purpose of the report. Generally, the purpose statement indicates the problem addressed in the report.[12] You can state the purpose as simply as "The purpose of this report is to . . ." or "This report recommends a new procedure for . . ."

Another element necessary to most reports is the authorization. It can usually be stated quite simply, as in "This report, which you requested on December 10, is . . ." or "This report, which Mr. Bruce Ferrin authorized on March 5, shows why . . ." The authorization is valuable because it establishes a clear chain of responsibility. The authorization justifies the time, effort, and resources that went into the preparation of the report. The only time it is not needed is when the writer developed the report on her own.

A statement of methodology must be included in report introductions. Readers want to know how a writer found the data because knowing that may indicate the degree of authority the contents possess. If the material was previously published, it is called secondary research. But if the data were the result of primary research, the writer should describe the technique used (surveys, interviews, observations) in sufficient detail to allow the reader to judge the quality of the research.

The last necessary item, and almost always the last item in an introduction, is the plan of development in which the writer tells the reader how the body of the report is organized. This invaluable element of the introduction signals a major transition and sets the order of the report's ideas firmly in the reader's mind.

The plan of development is usually quite simply written: "This report first . . . then . . . and finally . . ." The report then must follow the precise order set out in the plan of development.

Introduction: Optional Elements

The introduction also might include other elements, depending on the reader's and writer's needs. For example, a statement of limitations details external factors that may have limited the range of exploration in developing the report. The most typical constraint is fiscal; report writers often work on limited budgets that prohibit extensive travel or detailed samplings of populations. Time is another common limitation. Deadlines often limit the depth in which you might research a problem.

Another optional element of the introduction is the scope. In preparing a scope statement, a writer might ask herself what the reader might reasonably expect in such a report. If any inconsistency exists between these expectations and the report content, the writer would delineate briefly those areas that are and are not covered. For example, in the scope statement for a report recommending a new plant site, the writer might note that the report covers only the top four sites and that architectural and engineering details are available elsewhere.

Definitions are another element required in some introductions. If several key terms used throughout the report are unfamiliar to the reader, they should be defined in the introduction. On the other hand, if only a few unfamiliar words are used a few times, they should be defined the first time they appear in the text. If numerous terms need defining, a glossary should be used.

Sometimes circumstances call for a brief statement about the background of the report problem. Some writers detail background in the introduction; others put it into the report. A short background statement fits better as part of the introduction than as a main section of the body.

Body

The body of the report follows the introduction. Since most proposals are set up using indirect order, the conclusions and recommendations appear at the very end of the report proper (but before any appendixes). If the report is informational or nonsensitive, it is written using direct order; those conclusions and recommendations will appear right after the introduction.

The information in the body of a formal report is usually set off using some sort of heading system, either that described earlier in this chapter or some other. Remember that a heading is not usually enough of a transition. If necessary, repeat the information in the heading as part of the transition into that section.

The body of the report should be clearly organized, using one or more of the bases of organization discussed earlier. It should also be coherent, allowing the reader to move smoothly from one part to another. Appropriate transitions will connect the major and minor parts of the report.

The report body should employ the right degree of objectivity. Generally, persuasive reports, such as proposals to potential clients, are not as coldly objective as informational and analytical reports. In all reports, however, writers need to distinguish between facts and inferences. Assumptions and inferences need to be recognized with words like "Assuming that . . ." and "The figures suggest that . . ." One assumption or inference treated as a fact could jeopardize the credibility of the entire report.

The report body should also use the correct time perspective. The time perspective deals with the tense used in presenting the report's findings and in making cross-references to other parts of the report. Present tense is suitable when the data are current, as in the case of a recent survey. The finding might be presented as follows: "Fully 68 percent of our employees *believe* that their benefits are adequate." Using this perspective, a writer would also use the present tense to cross-reference other parts of the report: "Table II, in the previous (or next) section, *presents* the responses to questions 4, 5, and 6 of the questionnaire."

When the data are not current, as in the case of secondary research referencing studies that are years old, the past tense is appropriate. For example, "In the Gifford study, 51 percent of the respondents *reported* dissatisfaction with their benefits." For consistency, the writer uses the past tense in referring to earlier parts of the report and the future tense in referring to parts of the report yet to come.

Summary, Conclusions, and/or Recommendations

The final elements in most formal reports are the summary, conclusions, and/or recommendations. An informational report ends with just a *summary* of the main points in the report body. An analytical report might end with a conclusion or with a conclusions and recommendations section. A proposal ends with a separate recommendations section.

The *conclusions* section does nothing more than list the results of the writer's analysis. If he were researching alternative sites for a new plant, he might conclude that site A is the least expensive and the most accessible, whereas site B is the largest, closest, and safest for the company's needs.

Recommendations move a step beyond. To prepare recommendations, the writer has to make a decision about the problem. Occasionally, the person authorizing the report may want conclusions but not recommendations. That is, she may want to know the results of the investigation, but she may want to reserve the decision making for herself.

The conclusions should not introduce any new material; the report body should support all conclusions. Of course, the recommendations will be new material, but they should arise from the conclusions. The evidence should not point in one direction while the conclusions point in the other.

The direct order formal report contains the conclusions and recommendations at the beginning of the report. A summary is an appropriate ending for this kind of report, or one might begin the final section with some kind of statement that makes it clear that it is the last section of the report.

Back Matter

Back matter is optional. Many formal reports are complete without attachments at the end. However, under certain circumstances, the writer may choose to add one or more of the parts described next.

References/Bibliography

If secondary research was used to compose the report, and if interested readers may want to trace back the information to its original sources, then a references list may be called for. Sometimes labeled "Works Cited," the references section lists just that. Further, the writer may add a bibliography of relevant sources that the reader may find useful. The difference between a References list and a Bibliography is that a Bibliography identifies all the secondary sources that a writer looked at when composing her report, while a References list identifies only the sources that the writer specifically "referred to" in the report. Thus, the References list for a research report may be shorter than or the same length as the Bibliography, but not longer than the Bibliography.

A standard bibliographic format should be followed for both lists—American Psychological Association (APA) style is the simplest and most popular for business research reports, but Modern Language Association (MLA) and Chicago styles are also used. Style guides for citations are readily available online, and a range of reference manager software tools, such as Zotero, offer the ability to store and export author, title, and publication fields, making it easy to format citations and References lists. The key for determining how much information to include in a citation is that the source must be recoverable.

Appendixes

Supplemental material should be added to formal reports as appendixes. Examples of such material are tables of financial data, graphs, work samples, pictures, interview transcriptions, survey results, and mock-ups. In short, if the writer feels that a reader may want to look at more information, but that information does not fit into the report proper because it is too lengthy or detailed or would disrupt the continuity, then this information should be presented in appendixes.

Appendix format conventions are as follows: Each table, chart, or other type of information should appear as a separate appendix, numbered and titled, on a separate page. Page numbering for the report proper should continue through the appendixes. If the report has a table of contents, the appendixes should be included in it.

The sample report at the end of this chapter provides a model of the parts discussed thus far. The last section of this chapter reviews the common types of visual aids found in business reports and guidelines for their most effective use.

VISUAL AIDS

Visual aids are a common, very effective means of clarifying trends and relationships that are not easily understood in verbal form. The great majority of the research done on visual aids shows that tables and graphics can boost the comprehension of material.[13]

Visual aids can appear in a report of any length or level of formality, but they are most likely to be used in formal reports. They can be incorporated into the report proper or attached as back matter. Visual aids take a number of forms including tables, line graphs, bar charts, pie charts, and pictographs. The choice a report writer makes depends on the nature of the material under discussion and on the audience.

Audience adaptation can best be explained by placing visuals on a continuum that ranges from dramatic to informational. In general, less sophisticated audiences and those not familiar with the workings of a business will appreciate dramatic visual aids. Thus, a pictograph might be effective in an annual report comparing a company's production figures for the past three years. A glass company might use small drawings of bottles to represent millions of units produced. While such a dramatic visual aid gives a clear idea of any significant rise or fall in production, it may not accurately portray smaller changes. The fractions of a bottle needed to represent fractions of a million are difficult to interpret precisely. The exact quantities or percentages can be added to the side to increase the informational impact.

On the other hand, a formal report submitted to upper-level management would use visual aids fitting the readers' need for precise data. For example, a comparison of several years of production figures broken down by products might appear in a table. A table, while providing large quantities of information, has very little dramatic impact. The reader has to analyze the data and even after that may see little that is dramatic.

Midway on the continuum between dramatic and informative visual aids is the line graph, which can emphatically show trends. Using this graphic aid, readers can easily determine what specific production rate, interest rate, or income the graph is charting. They simply read across to the scale representing the amount.

General Rules

Several general rules apply to all visual aids. By following them, report writers create visual aids that are clear and strategically suited to their readers.

Appropriateness

First, visual aids should add value to the section of the report in which they appear. The data they contain or symbolize should complement the text without duplicating it. The visual aid that merely repeats what the text has shown belongs in an appendix rather than in the report proper, which it merely clutters. Additionally, the type of visual aid chosen should be suited to the data being portrayed.

Reference and Placement

Second, when using visual aids, writers should always refer to them in the text. The best approach is to refer to the visual aid just before it appears. This reference can be as simple as "see Table 1" in parentheses. Keep the visual as close as possible to the relevant narrative. If the writer decides to put the visual into an appendix, the reference will be "see Appendix 3" or something similar.

Content

Third, the content of the visual aid needs to relate closely to the current discussion. Do not try to pack too many data into a single chart or graph. Some of the data may apply to later sections of the report and may be used more appropriately at two or more points in the report.

Related to the need for relevancy is the need for simplicity. Strive to keep visuals—especially bar graphs, pie charts, and line drawings—simple. The content should unambiguously reflect the discussion. The use of abbreviations and standard symbols is also advisable for simplifying complex visuals. While symbols are usually not appropriate in the text, the need for compactness in visual aids calls for such special references. A writer needs to make sure, however, that the reader understands the symbols and abbreviations used by including a legend.

Conventions

Several conventions apply to visual aids. For one, writers have traditionally distinguished between tables and figures in reports, with figures being considered all types of visual aids other than a table. A related convention has tables and figures being counted as two separate series in a report. Thus, a report containing three tables and four figures would label them as follows: Table 1, Figure 1, Table 2, Table 3, Figure 2, Figure 3, Figure 4.

A third convention calls for the titles of tables and figures to reflect the data included. In constructing the titles of visual aids, writers should keep two goals in mind: conciseness and completeness. In as few words as possible, a title should describe the information the visual conveys. Thus, a line graph comparing employees' level of job satisfaction to length of time on the job would be titled "Satisfaction by longevity."

The following paragraphs examine the visuals most commonly used in business reports: pie charts, bar charts, line graphs, and tables.

Pie Charts

Pie charts are the oldest type of visual aid. William Playfair, a Scottish businessman, created the first known pie chart in 1801 by using different colored slices of a circle to illustrate the relative proportion of landholdings among Asia, Europe, and Africa.[14] Pie charts are ubiquitous in modern business reports, probably because their shape is so visually appealing. Their division into wedges representing the proportions of a unit makes a dramatic impact on a reader, but only when the differences are great enough to visibly affect the sizes of the divisions. The wedges represent percentages, so the "pie" must add up to 100 percent. An example of an appropriate use for a pie chart in a business report is to illustrate the distribution of a budget or sources of income for a fiscal year. But pie charts will not show trends or groupings that represent less than the entire population of interest. When illustrating the relative performance of individual units, a bar chart is easier to read. Figure 8–2 illustrates a typical pie chart. The sample report at the end of this chapter also includes a pie chart.

Figure 8–2 Sample Pie Chart

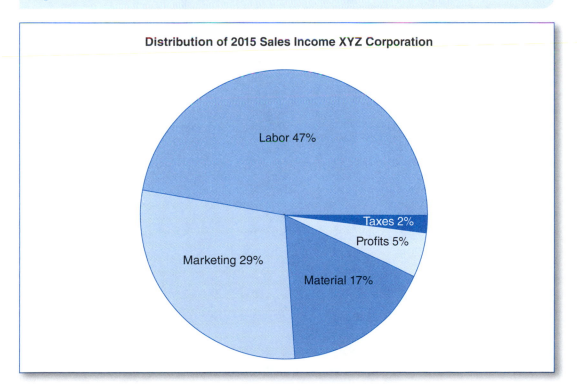

Distribution of 2015 Sales Income XYZ Corporation

Labor 47%

Taxes 2%

Profits 5%

Marketing 29%

Material 17%

Bar Charts

The pie chart is very useful for symbolizing parts of one whole, but it is not good for comparing one total and/or its components with another. With the naked eye, it is difficult to judge the relative size of two more circles and/or their wedges placed side by side. The bar chart is more suited to that need.

The bar chart, in its simplest form, is useful for comparing units at one point in time. The bar chart should be constructed with the bars positioned either horizontally or vertically (generally the latter). The axis from which the bars rise identifies the units, and the opposite measures quantity.

The more complex stacked bar chart can compare totals as well as components of totals. The stacked bar chart is one in which each bar (which represents a total) is subdivided into its component parts. This graph is handy for comparing totals and subparts of totals.

To show the composition of new car sales for a given year, a writer could draw one bar representing the total new car sales and then divide it, with each division representing

Figure 8–3   Sample Stacked Bar Chart

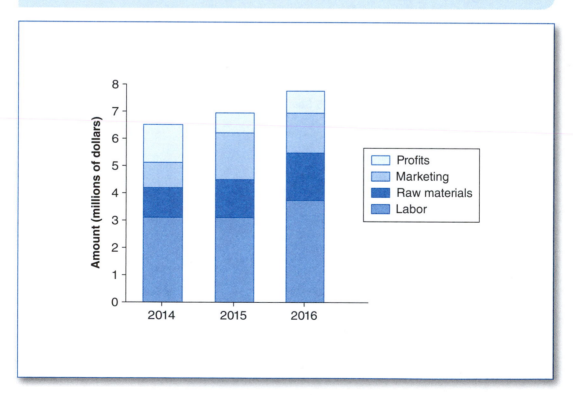

one company. Clearly, this visual aid is preferable to a pie chart for comparisons. The total differences would be easier to judge from a bar than from a circle, and components would be easier to compare as rectangles than as slices of pies. Figure 8–3 illustrates a typical stacked bar chart.

Line Graphs

The line graph represents a balance between informational and dramatic impact. It conveys change over time, including overall changes and specific dates and amounts. The line graph also allows the reader to compare changes of several factors. You can plot several lines (up to four) within a single graph, with each representing a different product or factor. Line graphs must represent information accurately. The scales chosen for a graph should be consistent. Graphs should not be manipulated to skew the facts. For example, a line graph showing yearly sales must not change the scale from years to months at a given point in order to de-emphasize a decline. (See Figure 8–4 for a typical multiple line graph.)

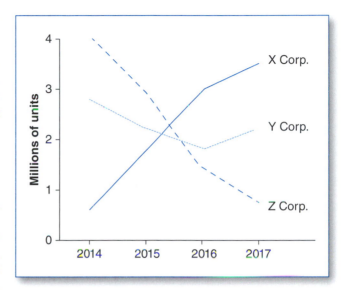

Figure 8–4   Sample Line Graph

Tables

Tables are very useful visual communication devices that arrange data in a concise manner to allow easy comparison of statistics. As mentioned earlier, they are informational and not as dramatic as other visual aids. They do not showcase trends or carry the credibility of graphs.[15] Nonetheless, they assist the reader in grasping complex statistical or factual data far more easily than if the material appeared in the narrative.

Tables range from informal word lists intended merely to aid comprehension, to complex formal reference tables. Tables are organized into columns and rows. Several rules apply to constructing a table:

- Identify each reference table with a title and number (and source notation, if appropriate).

- Use the left-hand vertical column, the stub, to list items detailed in the horizontal rows to the right. This row head defines its subject.

- Use the column headings (listed horizontally across the top) to indicate the material in each vertical column below them.

- Use rulings if necessary to set off column heads and stubs, but not so many that the table is cluttered.

- Use abbreviations and symbols where appropriate.

- Align figures on the decimal points; right align figures with no decimals.

- Keep the tables as simple and uncluttered as possible, leaving adequate white space.

Table 8–3 illustrates a typical table.

Table 8–3   Sample Table

	Year		
Product	**2014**	**2015**	**2016**
Heaters	632	716	805
Bread makers	231	367	592
Indoor grills	114	298	613

SUMMARY

Reports are among an organization's most important communications and help managers plan, organize, execute, evaluate, and improve an organization. They can address internal or external audiences. Managers write these reports because they have been assigned to do so or because they themselves see a need for one. In preparing to write a report, a writer must first define the problem to be addressed. Then, if the report is analytical, he must conduct research and determine a likely solution.

Reports can be classified according to their level of formality or according to their frequency. How formal or informal a report is depends on several strategic considerations: the audience, the effort expended on researching and writing the report, the report's value, the original assignment, and the company policy. Reports can also be classified as regular (occurring every so often) or onetime-only (under special circumstances). Examples of special reports include analysis reports, proposals, and evaluations.

The order of ideas chosen for a report is significant. Direct order is appropriate for good news or neutral information. It places the main conclusions and recommendations at the beginning of the report. Indirect order, best for reports delivering bad news and proposals, puts the main points last. The material within the body may be organized by time, place, quantity, and other factors.

Headings guide the reader through the report. The appearance and placement of the headings indicate the relative significance of the material they cover. Transitions such as internal summaries are another tool for broadcasting a report's structure.

The memo report is the most common informal report within an organization. The contents can be set off using headings, as necessary. Letter reports are similar but are intended for audiences outside the organization. They also usually attempt to build goodwill, a characteristic that is not as significant with memo reports.

The formal report, whether sent to internal or external audiences, typically consists of front matter, the report proper, and back matter. Front matter may include the title page, transmittal document, table of contents, list of illustrations, and executive summary. Usually, the longer and more formal the report, the more front matter it includes. The report proper includes the introduction, the major subdivisions that make up the report body, and the closing sections made up of summary, conclusions, and/or recommendations. Back matter contains supplemental information that does not readily fit into the report proper—usually a list of references and/or appendixes.

Visual aids may appear in the report proper or as appendixes. They exist on a continuum ranging from dramatic to informational. The choice of visual aids depends on the audience. The visual aids should be appropriate to the text and placed close to the first reference or as an attachment. Pie charts are useful for showing parts of a whole. Although largely dramatic, their informational impact can be enhanced. Bar charts are also dramatic, but they can clearly represent information as well. The stacked bar chart is particularly useful for making proportional comparisons between (or among) different units. The line graph shows change over time. It is both informational and dramatic, but it must be constructed with care to be accurate. Tables are not as dramatic as other visual aids, but they still make their content much easier to understand than the same information presented in narrative form.

Communication Audit Report

Prepared for
Jeff Walters, Executive Vice President

Prepared by
Kim Jacko, Senior Vice President

November 4, 2015

EXECUTIVE SUMMARY

During October 2015, I conducted a survey on communication effectiveness between the district managers and the regional managers of our company. The survey was designed to identify areas that are lacking and gather input on improvements. District managers throughout the state were invited to participate in the survey. Secondary data regarding effective communication were obtained from business articles and books.

My research revealed the following:

- E-mail is the communication method preferred by regional operations managers and regional sales managers.
- Meetings with both regional managers are harmed by tardiness, repetitive conversation, and lack of planning/agendas.

The frequency of face-to-face meetings between district managers and their regional managers is considered insufficient.

Recommendations for improvement are:

- Do not use e-mail as a substitute for face-to-face communication.
- Provide regional managers with periodic business communication training.
- Require formal agendas and time constraints to be set to enhance meeting productivity.
- Require more frequent face-to-face meetings.
- Make the regional managers accountable for correcting miscommunications.
- Develop standards for what must be communicated to both regional managers and what can be reported to one.
- Expect regional managers to report pertinent information to each other.

INTRODUCTION

The quality and consistency of communication of supervisors with their direct reports is vital to the success of any organization. In the case of our company, district managers must communicate with two supervisors and the two supervisors must routinely communicate with one another. Each of the supervisors has a different focus. Efficiency and clarity of communication often suffer in this environment.

You are very familiar with the difficulties our organizational structure poses in regard to communication. This report evaluates the current model and includes my recommendations to improve communication between regional operations and sales manager partners and their district manager direct reports.

My primary data were collected via an electronic survey of eighteen district managers statewide. I also incorporated my personal observations from my prior role as a regional manager and my current role supervising the regional operations managers. I used an Internet article and a book as secondary resources.

In the report you will find general information about the benefits and pitfalls of current communication practices, including e-mail usage, various meeting forms, phone calls, and text messages. Finally, you will note my recommendations for improvement to overall communication.

E-MAIL

Regional managers and district managers employ various types of communication vehicles, but e-mail is used most frequently. While this is an efficient way to communicate to multiple parties, it is not always the right choice.

From Regional Manager to District Manager

E-mail is overwhelmingly the mode of communication used between regional and district managers. When asked, it was the district managers' preferred method to receive information from their regional managers. Although the district managers do not have a dedicated work computer, they have access to Webmail and centralized district manager workstations. Many reported their Treo phone/multimedia equipment has been very useful.

Most messages are sent via e-mail in the interest of time and dual notification to individual district managers. Messages are easier to deliver to two busy people via e-mail. The "courtesy copy" to a regional partner is standard practice. Communicating with two busy people verbally by phone or in person is generally more complicated. However, the nonroutine or time-sensitive messages would often be better delivered face to face or by phone.

The district managers also receive information as regional groups from their regional managers. The nonroutine nature of some of these e-mails has the same complications as e-mails received individually. "When your message is sensitive or contains an emotional component, no communication channel is superior to being there" (Deep & Sussman, 1995, p. 70).

Providing the regional managers with periodic training on the importance of choosing the appropriate communication method would keep their perspective fresh and improve the quality of communication received by the district managers.

From District Manager to Regional Manager

The district managers' preference to receive communication by e-mail matches their preference to use e-mail to communicate upward. The same underlying reasons apply—time and dual notification.

District managers often use e-mail to clarify conflicting directives they receive. If one boss tells them something contradictory to the other, e-mail is an effective way to ask both simultaneously for a consistent answer. The responsibility of sorting out the conflict then rests on the regional manager team.

MEETINGS

Meetings can be an extremely effective way to communicate goals, disseminate information, and solve problems. The district managers attend various types of meetings involving their regional managers: conference calls, face to face with their region's team, and individual meetings with each boss or both bosses. These meetings are discussed below.

Conference Calls

Regional managers generally meet with their district manager groups on conference calls. Some of them meet weekly and some bimonthly. While these meetings are seen as necessary and generally productive, improvement is possible.

These meetings are reportedly plagued by tardiness, repetitive topics, and a lack of proper planning. This creates "wasted time and deflated energy for the participants, not to mention a culture of meeting-dread" (Walters, 2003). Therefore, corrective action should be taken. Primarily, setting an agenda and following it would alleviate most of these shortcomings. The agenda would establish a time frame, ensure relevant topics are covered, and encourage preparedness, if published in advance.

Regional Meetings

These meetings have some of the same challenges as the conference calls. Formalized agendas would have the greatest positive impact.

The frequency of these meetings is another area to be considered. Most district managers surveyed felt that they needed more face-to-face interaction with their direct superiors. The majority felt that monthly face-to-face meetings would be helpful. Instituting a monthly standard for all regional managers to follow would aid all of the regional teams.

Interpersonal Managerial Communication

District managers meet with one boss or with both depending on what is needed. Many district managers felt they would benefit from increased contact with regional management.

Any time there is communication with one regional manager without the other present, an additional burden is placed on the district manager to tell any issues discussed to the absent regional manager. The district managers need to be able to report issues to one manager without fear of conflict with the other regional manager. The regional managers should communicate with one another to reduce the bureaucracy their more hands-on direct reports shoulder now.

Figure Two-Boss Difficulty Rating by District Managers

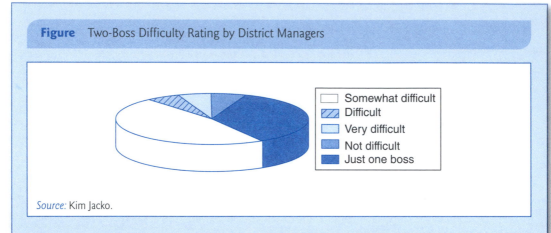

Legend:
- ☐ Somewhat difficult
- ▨ Difficult
- ☐ Very difficult
- ☐ Not difficult
- ☐ Just one boss

Source: Kim Jacko.

Additionally, standards of "who to tell what" could be instituted. If a district manager is meeting with his operations manager, there should be certain topics that are clearly her responsibility—for example, teller outages. The regional operations manager could then be responsible for notifying the regional sales manager, if necessary.

PHONE CALLS

Phone communication is typically used when there is a time-sensitive issue. Some regional managers call their district managers individually each day to stay connected. The phone is a vital communication link for regional teams who are all geographically divided.

One Regional Manager with One District Manager

The phone provides a quick answer to many questions. Most calls from district manager to regional manager are to report issues and get answers. Reporting issues involves two conversations under current guidelines, unless the district manager is able to get both regional managers on a conference call.

Instituting standards of "who to tell what," as mentioned with face-to-face meetings, would alleviate this reporting burden from the district managers. The added stress of having two bosses was viewed as somewhat to very difficult by over 50 percent of respondents, as shown in the figure.

Both Regional Manager Partners with One District Manager

While this communication is unencumbered by an extra communication to the missing party, it can be complicated by logistics. However, the speed and unity of three-party phone calls are helpful to the district manager.

TEXT MESSAGES

Text messages are used frequently to communicate quick information by both regional and district managers. The reliance on pages as a replacement for phone calls speeds the work flow. Text messages are often used when an immediate phone call response is needed or to indicate that someone was sent a high-priority e-mail. The new Treo phones have decreased text message use for full informational purposes due to a 120-character limitation on messages and more difficult keyboarding than prior pager hardware.

SUMMARY

To summarize, our organizational structure creates barriers to clear communication at the regional and district manager levels. While varying forms of communication used all have value, each has its own impediments. The main mode of communication between regional and district managers is e-mail, which is generally efficient, but has limitations when nonroutine information is included. Alternately, meetings that include the district and regional managers are handicapped by a lack of planning. The district managers want to increase the frequency of interpersonal communication. Phone calls are a good tool, but may not include all parties affected. This can lead to misunderstandings, just as other forms can, due to dual reporting responsibilities. Text messages are a useful supplemental form of communication.

RECOMMENDATIONS

The following recommendations are thoughtfully submitted to help our company eliminate obstacles that hamper the success of the regional and district managers.

- Do not use e-mail as a substitute for face-to-face communication.
- Provide regional managers with periodic business communication training.
- Require formal agendas and time constraints to be set to enhance meeting productivity.
- Require more frequent face-to-face meetings.
- Make the regional managers accountable for correcting miscommunications.
- Develop standards for what must be communicated to both regional managers and what can be reported to one.
- Expect regional managers to report pertinent information to each other.

REFERENCES

Deep, S., & Sussman, L. (1995). *Smart moves for people in charge.* Cambridge, MA: Basic Books.

Walters, J. (2003, January). Meetings 101: Was that a good meeting, or a bad one? *Ivy Sea, Inc.* Retrieved October 29, 2005, from http:/www.inc.com

Cases for Small-Group Discussion

CASE 8–1

Reports and Technology

Jesse Matthews sat in his office with a puzzled look on his face. He had received a Word file from Ellen Linares, a report that was to be presented to upper management in the morning. Ellen's e-mail message said, "The report is attached. Please let me know if everything is OK before I leave tonight." The message had been sent at 2:45 p.m. It was now 6:15 p.m., and Jesse was just getting around to looking at Ellen's attachment.

He opened the Word file. Title page: check. Table of Contents: check. Introduction: check. Table 1: uh-oh. Table 1 looked like a jumbled mess! Jesse clicked at various locations within the table, noticing that the formatting was haphazard and that the alignment was badly out of line. Table 2 looked worse. All of the pertinent information was there but all jumbled up in no apparent order. Jesse tried opening the file again, with the same results. The rest of the tables were in similar disarray.

Ellen had left work at 5:00 p.m. Jesse tried her home phone, with no luck. He didn't have her personal cell number. Jesse made a half-hearted attempt at reworking the tables using his word processor's table functions but only made things worse. He chastised himself for not looking at the report sooner. He was due to present it at 8:00 a.m. the next morning, and that was the exact time Ellen came in to work. There would simply be no time for her to try to revise it or to try to recover her originally intended format.

As software packages are updated, the way in which they process documents changes. Ellen had saved the file in an earlier format, although in the same software package, but her tables had slipped in transition. Without the original software version, and perhaps even the same computer on which it was produced, it was unlikely that the updated software could recover the orderly format Ellen originally created.

CASE QUESTIONS

1. What should Ellen have done in order to prevent this type of issue from arising?

2. Now that the problem is Jesse's, what do you suggest should be done?

CASE 8–2

Writing a Recommendation Report

You are a middle-level marketing manager in a large wholesale organization. This morning, your boss called you into her office and informed you that 126 cars in the company's sales fleet were ready for replacement. She asked you to do the research and write a report that would recommend a purchase to replace the cars about to be retired.

Pick four cars that are comparable—for example, the Ford Fusion, the Honda Accord, the Chevrolet Malibu, and the Toyota Camry. In selecting a particular type of car, you might want to make some assumptions about the products handled by your salespeople and whether they carry bulky samples. For the purposes of this report, we will assume you considered other similar cars but the four you chose are the top contenders.

Your next task is to identify the criteria to be used in selecting the car to be purchased. Remember that the quality of your research and report will hinge largely on how thoroughly you identify the relevant criteria to be weighed. Once you have identified the criteria to be used and all subfactors of those criteria, you are ready to begin your research. You will probably find *Consumer Reports* and websites such as cars.com to be invaluable sources of information, but do not overlook other less obvious sources such as dealerships.

After collecting and organizing your information, you will be ready to write your report. What format should that report take? Which strategic aspects ought to be considered in determining that format? If you choose to use a formal report format, which prefatory parts should you include? Which subsections should you include in the introduction? How should the body of the report be organized? What will the ending sections of the report proper contain?

CASE NOTE

This type of report should use a direct, formal format since it is being written for superiors and contains neutral information. Prefatory parts must include a transmittal memo reflecting the authorization of the senior management official who originally assigned the writer responsibility for this report. The introduction should include the research method used, as well as the purpose and scope of the report. The report should be organized to include all of the automobiles considered and tables that report the necessary statistics on each auto to the deciding committee. Conclusions should be presented that will lead management to the same outcome outlined in the writer's report, as specified in the recommendation section.

CASE 8–3

Writing an Informational Report

Develop a questionnaire containing at least ten statements about typical ethical dilemmas faced by businesspeople. Use "strongly agree—agree—undecided—disagree—strongly disagree" as response options. Possibilities might include "It is acceptable for an American businessperson in a foreign country to bribe a public official if that practice is accepted and expected in that country." Another possibility might be "It is acceptable to give a poorly performing employee a good reference to get rid of him or her."

At the end of the questionnaire, ask for some demographic information that might make the analyses of your findings more interesting. You might ask for gender, employment status, age, marital status, years of work experience, educational level, and so on.

Next, circulate the questionnaire randomly on campus. Try to get at least one hundred respondents. Remember that the larger your sample, the better your findings will be statistically. You might consider having a ballot-like box with you to ensure confidentiality.

After you have collected your data and analyzed your findings, you will be ready to put your information into a report to be presented to your instructor. What format will that report assume? What factors should you consider in determining that format? What parts will the report contain? Will you use the direct or indirect order? On what basis will the body of the report be organized?

An interesting twist on this report might be to circulate the questionnaire to businesspeople. If it were possible for you to circulate the questionnaire to people on campus *and* to businesspeople, you might then be able to compare the results overall.

CASE NOTE

If addressing a business executive in this report, your results should be presented both informally and indirectly, since the findings and conclusions may not be welcomed.

Student Study Site

Visit the Student Study Site at **study.sagepub.com/hynes6e** for web quizzes, video links, web resources, and cases studies.

Notes

1. Anita S. Bednar and Robert J. Olney, "Communication Needs of Recent Graduates," *Bulletin of the Association for Business Communication* 50, no. 4 (December 1987): pp. 22–23.
2. C. Gilbert Storms, "What Business School Graduates Say about the Writing They Do at Work: Implications for the Business Communications Course," *Bulletin of the Association for Business Communication* 46, no. 4 (December 1983): pp. 13–18.
3. Marie Flatley, "A Comparative Analysis of the Written Communication of Managers at Various Organizational Levels in the Private Business Sector," *Journal of Business Communication* 19, no. 3 (Summer 1982): pp. 35–50.
4. Patricia Dorazio, "Preparing Technical Proposals: Planning and Prewriting Considerations," *Bulletin of the Association for Business Communication* 55, no. 3 (September 1992): pp. 49–52.
5. Steven H. Gale and Mark Garrison, *Strategies for Managerial Writing* (Mason, OH: South-Western, 2006), p. 209.
6. Maris Roze, *Technical Communication: The Practical Craft* (Englewood Cliffs, NJ: Prentice Hall, 1997), pp. 107–111.
7. Karl Keller, Owner, Communication Partners, *Association for Business Communication Consulting SIG Blog*, November 7, 2013, www.businesscommunication.org.
8. David K. Farkas, "Toward a Better Understanding of PowerPoint Deck Design," *Information Design Journal + Document Design* 14, no. 2 (August 2006): pp. 162–171.
9. "Elmore Leonard: 1925–2013—Prolific Novelist Rewrote the Crime Thriller," *New York Times*, August 21, 2013, p. A2.
10. James Van Oosting, "The 'Well-Made' Report," *Bulletin of the Association for Business Communication* 45, no. 4 (December 1982): pp. 9–10.
11. Frank Weightman, "The Executive Summary: An Indispensable Management Tool," *Bulletin of the Association for Business Communication* 45, no. 4 (December 1982): pp. 3–5.
12. F. Stanford Wayne and Jolene D. Scriven, "Problem and Purpose Statements: Are They Synonymous Terms in Writing Business Reports?" *Bulletin of the Association for Business Communication* 54, no. 1 (March 1991): pp. 30–37.
13. Becky K. Peterson, "Tables and Graphs Improve Reader Performance and Reader Reaction," *Journal of Business Communication* 20, no. 2 (Spring 1983): pp. 47–56.
14. Ian Spence, "No Humble Pie: The Origins and Usage of a Statistical Chart," *Journal of Educational and Behavioral Statistics* 30, no. 4 (December 21, 2005): pp. 353–368. doi: 10.3102/10769986030004353.
15. Jeremiah J. Sullivan, "Financial Presentation Format and Managerial Decision Making: Tables versus Graphs," *Management Communication Quarterly* 2, no. 2 (November 1988): pp. 194–216.

PART IV

Strategies for Understanding Messages

CHAPTER 9

Managerial Listening

To listen is an effort, and just to hear is no merit. A duck hears also.

—Igor Stravinsky, Russian composer

During the past several decades, the essential role of listening in business and management has received increased attention. Over thirty-five studies reveal that listening is the form of communication that is

- most important for entry-level positions,
- most critical in distinguishing effective from ineffective subordinates,
- most critical for managerial competency.

Yet many of these studies report that listening skills are seriously lacking in subordinates and managers.[1]

Communication is more than just talking and waiting to talk. Communication is a two-way process, an exchange of information, ideas, and feelings that requires participants to receive as well as send messages. Further, the process on the receiving side is often more difficult and complicated than on the sending side of the exchange. Listening is more than just hearing, and the effective manager differentiates between the two. Hearing is mechanical, an automatic sort of thing often difficult to avoid. A horn blaring, heavy construction equipment groaning, children shouting in a playground—all these sounds, plus others, may be heard even though they are not listened to actively. Hearing usually requires little special physical or mental effort.

By contrast, listening results from a concentrated effort; it requires both physical and mental effort. Listening requires a special effort because physical and psychological factors work against the process. In this chapter, we review those physical and psychological barriers to listening and then analyze techniques to reduce these barriers. But first we examine why listening well is worth the effort.

BENEFITS OF LISTENING

A number of essential managerial skills involve listening. First, many of the data necessary for decision making come through listening to employees, and poor listeners miss important information. One company that requires its managers to spend significant time listening to employees is Zappos, the online retailer of shoes, clothing, and accessories. In his best seller, *Delivering Happiness*, former CEO Tony Hsieh wrote that he required his managers to spend 20 percent of their time away from their desks, informally interacting with their employees. The result, according to Hsieh, was a 20–100 percent increase in productivity that he attributed to the increased communication level.[2]

A second benefit is that listening makes a person more dependable. People who listen well follow directions better, make fewer errors, say foolish things less often, and generally become the kinds of people others will ask for advice or direction. Third, good listeners are more respected and liked by those they work with. Managers who listen complement those they listen to, in effect telling them they are worthy people.[3] This trait can lead to harmonious labor relations since employees generally trust and support managers who "listen them out" rather than merely "hear them out."[4]

Fourth, better listening enables a manager to be better informed overall. We learn about the world around us from listening, not talking. Fifth, good listening spares a person many embarrassments. In many situations, people may miss a name because of poor listening, or they may need to have critical information repeated because of daydreaming. Worse yet, a direct question may be unanswered because of inept listening. Such embarrassing situations can quickly label a manager as unconcerned or even apathetic.

Ultimately, the major reason for developing effective listening is to build relationships between people. All people need to be heard for their own emotional well-being and to create understanding among each other. Mutual understanding leads to trusting relationships, which are required in any work group.

Several successful organizations provide models for including listening in the list of key managerial skills. Harley-Davidson has survived and grown over the past one hundred years to be one of the world's leading motorcycle manufacturers. Jeffrey Bleustein, who served as CEO from 1997 to 2009, led the company to dominance in the industry. Under his leadership, Harley-Davidson increased its market capitalization by $13 billion. Bleustein attributes its success to respecting customers' wishes. "Other companies talk about customer loyalty, but we have a loyalty that goes beyond most businesses," he says. Further, Bleustein was known for listening to his employees. "He gets out and visits with his dealers and really promotes a strong team atmosphere in the company," according to one retailer.[5] Today, stakeholder engagement and customer loyalty continue to be values that drive the company.

Another corporation that understands the power of managerial listening is Procter and Gamble. A recent profile in the *Harvard Business Review* describes how the company has developed an elaborate system for surveying employees, customers, and other stakeholders to gain new ideas for improving products, processes, and services.[6]

Despite good intentions and recognition of the benefits, managers' listening success at work is affected by many factors, some of which are beyond their awareness. For instance, managerial listening can be limited simply by the fact that they have authority over their employees. Recent research indicates that the more powerful the listener, the more likely they are to judge or dismiss advice and ideas they hear.[7] Thus, managers might be listening from a concrete bunker of which they are not even conscious. On the other hand, there are a number of strategies that managers can adopt in an effort to improve their listening. This chapter takes closer looks at the most common barriers and offers strategies for overcoming them.

BARRIERS TO LISTENING

Communication does not occur in discrete units and the term *barrier* may remind us of something mechanical rather than an interactive, dynamic process such as listening. As a result, the term *listening barrier* may misrepresent listening somewhat; however, dynamic, interactive processes are easier to discuss when categorized and put in a list. Table 9–1 lists the listening barriers presented here.

One of the greatest barriers to listening arises from our own *physical limitations*. People speak approximately 25 percent as fast as they think. Thus, while most Americans speak at a rate of about 125 words per minute, they are able to think at least four times as fast. This barrier is known as the 25–75 problem.[8] As a result, instead of listening carefully, some people think about other things and devote only a fraction of their capacity to taking in what is said. They become impatient with the slow rate of the spoken word and begin to think about topics other than the words being spoken; consequently, our inability to speak more rapidly becomes a physical barrier in listening situations. The listening–speaking differential, or the 25–75 problem, is listed first because our wandering attention partially causes many of the other listening barriers.

A lack of *motivation* is another barrier to listening. Many people find maintaining the continuous motivation required for listening to be a challenge. Managers who should be listening may be daydreaming, making private plans, or even focusing on an emotional problem. During that 75 percent void, many things can overpower the 25 percent listening.

Researchers have long known that motivation or incentive is a prevalent problem in the listening process. Research completed almost thirty years ago demonstrated that people score better on listening achievement tests when they know in advance they are going to be tested than when they think they are just supposed to listen.[9] More recent research has also indicated that scores on listening tests rise as the incentive to listen increases.[10] Since listening is hard work, we can expect greater effort when the goal is known and listeners can observe a positive outcome of the effort. This is why the listening goal discussed later is so important.

Table 9–1   Barriers to Listening

1. Listening–speaking differential (25–75 problem)
2. Motivation
3. Willingness
4. Internal and external noise
5. Detouring
6. Debate
7. Time

A barrier related to motivation is lack of *willingness*. A manager may not *want* to listen. Before listening is even required, he may have lost any desire to listen. Since we have already discussed motivation as a barrier to listening, we must differentiate willingness from motivation. These concepts are closely related, but for this discussion, assume that a lack of willingness develops *before* listening even begins. This is why it may supersede all other barriers. If a person consciously or unconsciously decides not to listen, listening skills are of no advantage. Manny Steil, who does extensive listening training for companies such as Honeywell, often refers to the LAW of listening— Listening equals Ability plus Willingness.

Why would a manager lack the willingness to listen? Several reasons explain this attitude. First, most people would rather talk than listen; and even when they ask a question, they often interrupt the first sentence of the response.[11] Second, the listener may quickly stereotype the speaker as one who has little to contribute and is not worth listening to. Third, a listener may lack willingness because she may not want to receive negative information. For the speaker who bears bad tidings, what incentive is there to listen? Defensive behavior works against listening. Some managers consider the slightest attack on one of their opinions as an attack on them personally; consequently, they will rise to the defense. This defense often involves verbal attacks that preclude the possibility for listening.

Internal noise that cannot be ignored is another barrier. Our autonomic nervous system involuntarily pays attention to certain events such as a headache, sore feet, or an empty stomach. It is difficult to divide attention between these internal involuntary distractions and concentrated listening. *External, environmental noise* that may compete with the main topic of interest is also a barrier. It is hard to listen to a subordinate who speaks softly in a noisy foundry or to a phone conversation mixed with static on the phone line. In these situations, separating the speaker's voice from all the surrounding noise can be exhausting.

Another barrier may be termed *detouring*. The listener may become distracted by a phrase or concept and detour toward the distraction. This distraction then stimulates thought on another subtopic more interesting than the central point of the message; consequently, thoughts detour to the more interesting topics. Detouring is closely related to bias. For instance, a listener's negative bias toward a mannerism can distract from the content of the message. If a speaker places her hands over her mouth while speaking, or continually plays with a pencil, or looks away from the listener, such mannerisms can distract and get in the way of messages.

The *debate* represents a sixth type of barrier. A listener may suddenly find herself disagreeing with the speaker and begin to plan her rebuttal. As she plans the rebuttal, she blocks out the speaker and misses his message. For instance, a manager listening to complaints from another department might prepare a rebuttal as the other person explains the incident. As a result, the manager creates a defensive climate and misses the most important information.

Finally, *time,* an important factor in every manager's day, can also be a barrier to listening. "I just don't have time to listen to this" is a common reaction for managers. Time seems to drag when people have to listen to something in which they have no interest. When listening appears to take too much time, managers tend to stop listening. One way some terminate listening is by making a hasty conclusion. This time pressure may lead to the tendency to judge, evaluate, approve, or disapprove a person's statement too hastily. To achieve real communication, it is important to resist the temptation to form hasty conclusions.

The preceding review is only a summary of the many barriers to listening. All those personal factors mentioned in Chapter 2—knowledge, culture, status, attitudes, emotions, communication skills—can also create potential barriers to listening. Nevertheless, research indicates we can improve listening skills. When managers strategically analyze the critical components of communication and apply the techniques suggested in the following section, their listening skills and effectiveness as managers will improve.[12]

STOP AND THINK

1. Which of the listening barriers listed in Table 9–1 and described in this section can you relate to the most?

2. Under what circumstances do these listening barriers occur?

GENERAL TECHNIQUES FOR LISTENING

Let us first identify two different types of listening, so we can adapt techniques to the appropriate situation: active and interactive.

For the purposes of this discussion, active listening occurs in situations in which a manager has little or no opportunity to directly respond to the speaker. People in a large audience use active listening as do those listening to a recorded message or reviewing an audiovisual replay. People use interactive listening when they have the opportunity to interact verbally with the speaker by asking questions or summarizing. Interactive listening occurs when a manager is involved in a conversation with another individual or in a meeting with many people.

Our commitment to listening is often determined by the relevance, the importance, or the significance of the information involved. Listening basically has three levels of intensity—casual, factual, and empathic. Table 9–2 shows examples of listening occasions for each intensity level. *Casual* or marginal listening is used when the specific or technical information being discussed is not critical. Because no goal for specific information is established, a manager need not be as alert as in other situations. For example, casual listening occurs in social conversations or when listening to the radio. Although it is not as

Table 9–2   Examples of Listening Situations

	Active Situation	**Interactive Situation**
Casual	Radio program	Social conversation
Factual	Informative presentation	Conference
Empathic	Sermon	Counseling session

intense as many types of listening, it is nonetheless important. A manager can indicate social support by simply listening to an employee talk about a special event in her life. By listening, the manager is saying, "You are important as a person."[13]

A note of caution is important here. What one person considers casual another may consider critical information. The importance of the information is not inherent in the information itself. Therefore, in the same situation, different people could be listening with different intensities.

The next level of intensity, *factual* listening, is necessary when specific information needs to be obtained. Probably the most common type of listening in business meetings and conferences, factual listening is the level that most people probably think of when they consider the topic of listening. At this level, the listener should ask questions and receive feedback to ensure effective communication.

A manager uses the *empathic* level of listening when she wants to understand another person from that person's own internal frame of reference rather than from the manager's own frame of reference. The empathic listener tries to get inside the speaker's thoughts and feelings. The listener expresses empathy when she verbally and nonverbally communicates such messages as "I follow you," "I'm with you," or "I understand." The empathic level of listening is not easy to achieve because we naturally tend to advise, tell, agree, or disagree based on our own view. It is well worth the effort to become an empathic listener, however. A speaker who sees that a manager is really trying to understand his meaning will trust the manager and be more willing to talk and explore problems. Empathic listening can be such a powerful form of listening that, even when it is only partially attained, the mere attempt can be enough to open communication.

To summarize, when listening, a manager should first determine the level of listening she needs to achieve—casual, factual, or empathic. She can accomplish this by establishing a *listening goal*, a specific statement of the purpose for listening. In the give-and-take of most communications, the need to adjust one's listening goal arises as the interchange develops.

Adjusting the listening goal is not always easy. Wal-Mart, the biggest retailer in the world, considers listening to be a key skill for its managers. The founder, Sam Walton, is quoted on Wal-Mart's website as having said, "Listen to your associates. They're our best idea generators." To capture associates' ideas, suggestions, and concerns, Wal-Mart developed a number of programs. One requires every area to create a "Grass Roots" action plan to make good on associates' ideas. Another, a policy called "Open Door," permits anyone to bring complaints to officers at the highest level of the company. A third program, "Associates Out in Front," is described in company documents as a way for Wal-Mart to show workers "that we do appreciate you and that we have an ongoing commitment to listening to and addressing your concerns."[14] It requires every store manager to meet with ten rank-and-file employees every week.

STOP AND THINK

1. What are some examples of casual, factual, and empathic listening in your day?

2. Which level of listening is the most difficult?

3. Which level of listening is the most important? Why?

Given the cultural values of this corporation, consider the listening levels used by a typical regional manager. She visits a different Walmart store at least every week where she wanders around talking to customers, stock clerks, and store managers. One minute she may be listening to someone describe the weather in Salem, Oregon, and the next minute she may be discussing the drop in sales of bedding items. Soon after that she may be listening to a manager describe why he is so frustrated with his work. Within five minutes, each of the different types of listening intensities is required, so the regional manager must be quick to adjust.

Once a manager has established the level of listening, it is important to prepare physically and psychologically to listen. She should complete the following steps during the preparation stage.

1. Pick the best possible place. While it is not always possible to change the place, the manager should not overlook better facilities when available.

2. Pick the best possible time. As with place, it is not always possible to change the time. However, the astute manager must be careful not to eliminate more favorable opportunities.

3. Think about personal biases that may be present.

4. Review the listening objectives.

A brief review of these four steps shows why they are important in reducing the barriers to effective listening discussed earlier. First, selecting the best time and place helps one reduce internal and external noise. In addition, because time influences the psychological barriers of motivation, emotion, and willingness, the choice of time may significantly alter the outcome of the conversation.

Is it polite to tell another that you cannot listen at the moment? In a survey of more than two hundred managers, respondents indicated they would not be offended if someone asked them to wait before discussing something for fear that important information might be missed. Of course, if time cannot be changed, it is important that the parties be aware of the barriers present and make a special effort to concentrate on the listening process.

A manager's personal biases may also have a drastic effect on the outcome of the communication. A manager unaware of personal bias may become selective and hear only what he wants to hear. The person may deal only with preconceived notions and even debate with the speaker on points of disagreement. For example, a manager who believes that young adults are unreliable may disregard any information indicating that a particular young adult *is* reliable. To control this psychological barrier of bias, first be aware; then, recognize the burden it places on the speaker–listener relationship.

Emotional words or phrases can also trigger listener bias. Such phrases as "typical humorless accountant," "it really isn't my job," "we tried that before, and it didn't work," or "all engineers think alike" can lead to emotional responses. The danger in such phrases is that they cause a listener to attend (or not to attend) to different parts of a message. The listener should be aware of the possible emotional responses and not let them distract from the message.

Finally, it is important to review and be aware of the listening objective. Without the objective in mind, a manager may use casual listening when factual listening is required or factual listening when empathic listening would be more effective. The person who can state in one sentence the specific goal and the type of listening involved is well aware of the listening objective.

One typical situation when the speaker's and listener's objectives may be at odds is this: When a subordinate approaches a supervisor with a complaint, the supervisor may assume that the worker expects the boss to solve his problem, so the boss listens to determine the facts of the situation and identify alternative actions. If these possible solutions are resisted, and the employee responds with "yes, but" statements, then the manager should rethink the listening objective. It may be that the employee is only seeking attention, or "face time," with the boss.

Thus far, we have examined some general listening strategies. The manager who is physically and psychologically prepared to listen should use additional, more specific techniques to improve listening. Let us next look at techniques that are appropriate for active and interactive listening.

SPECIFIC TECHNIQUES FOR ACTIVE LISTENING

A person uses active listening in situations where direct response to the speaker is difficult or impossible. For example, a person who is sitting in a large audience or listening to a recording cannot interact with the speaker. If asking questions is not possible, a listener needs to have a clear and complete understanding of the message the first time. An active listener should implement the following techniques.

Identify the Main and Supporting Points

A message usually has one or two main points followed by supporting information (examples, figures, or descriptions). One good clue to main points is the nonverbal techniques the speaker uses when giving them; she might raise her voice, speak faster, repeat key words, or use gestures. Later, we will detail nonverbal aspects that can be invaluable when identifying the main and supporting points. In the following example of a president speaking at an annual meeting, note the emphasis on main and supporting points in a speech:

The main points in this example are the four new products, expansion of the Western division's sales force, and a stable home implement market; the remainder of the message is supporting information. Separation of main and supporting points helps the listeners retain the critical information.

The electronic division was pleased with the successful introduction of *four new products* (raised voice) in the last year. All four of these products sold at a better rate than projected. We were especially pleased with the temperature sensor that sold 14 percent above projections. This small sensor, which has many applications and is easy to install, should do as well or better next year.

Besides introducing four new products (pause), we expanded the Western division's sales force by adding sixteen high-quality salespeople. These salespeople were recruited from all over the United States, and we're confident of their ability to help us expand in the West. They all have a thorough understanding of the product and the changing nature of our industry.

No immediate changes are seen in the home implement division (lowered voice). It will be necessary to wait and see what happens with the entire housing industry. We're stable here since garage openers, intercom systems, and burglar protection devices are all holding their own. We developed a new burglar protection system that can be programmed by means of a digital device. This has been an interesting project to watch as it developed.

Organize the Message

Often, a speaker has some type of organizational pattern that a listener uses to understand the message. For instance, a speaker may organize the message by pros and cons, advantages and disadvantages, likes and dislikes, similarities and differences, chronological events, or functional duties. Just as it is easier to remember the basic structure of a chapter rather than every word in it, it is easier to recall the structure of a spoken message rather than all the specifics. A skilled listener will pay attention to the signs, markers, or transitions that speakers use to indicate structure. Numbering the points ("My second point is . . .") is one technique that speakers use, as described in Chapter 5. Another is the preview of points ("Today I'll discuss . . ."). A third strategy to listen for is the summary ("So today I talked about . . .").

Summarize the Message

Another active listening technique is the summary, which can take the form of a mental picture of the main points. The summary need not contain elaborate sentences and details; simple words or sentence fragments may suffice. Furthermore, summarization does not have to wait until the end of the message; it may be more efficient at major transition points. The president's speech, shown earlier, could be summarized in three phrases: (1) four new products in electronics, (2) sixteen new salespeople in the Western region, and (3) a stable home implement market.

The three techniques tested so far—differentiating between the main and supporting points, organizing, and summarizing—operate together for accurate listening. The effective use of a fourth technique assists in the development of the others.

Visualize the Message

A fourth strategy for active listening, putting the message into a picture, will help keep the listener's mind on the message. The beauty of this technique is that it allows a person to use some of that 75 percent of her mental capacity not required to keep up with the message. Consequently, a manager can commit more effort to listening, thus reducing the possibility of missing a major part of the message. Finally, retention of the message improves because a picture can now be associated with it. In the annual meeting described earlier, a manager might imagine the sixteen new sales personnel in the Western region as sixteen little people running from different points of a US wall map to California. Absurd as the device might seem, these sixteen little people running across a wall map will help the manager remember one of the main points of the message.

Related to visualization is mnemonics. One mnemonic device is the acronym, a combination of letters, each of which is the first letter of a group of words essential to the message. For instance, suppose a person is presenting his main objection to taking additional training in computer programming. The objection may stem from the cost, the individual's ability, and the time involved. The mnemonic CAT—cost, ability, time—can be used to record these main ideas whenever the speaker refers to them. Mnemonics have practical use in the business sector. At one popular restaurant in Houston, Greek salads are prepared at table side. The servers remember the order of ingredients by recalling this mnemonic: "Very Fast Leopards Die Old." It translates to, "First add the Vegetables to the bowl, then the Feta, Lemon juice, Dressing, and Olives." Mnemonics in general, and acronyms specifically, may be considered a type of visualization because it is easier to see and recall the acronym. Other types of memory games, such as word association and riddles, are also beneficial.

Personalize the Message

Effective listeners are those who search a message for information that has special meaning for the listener. A topic is naturally more interesting and easier to concentrate on if it personally relates to the listener. In fact, those who relate the message to personal experiences ensure that two key elements of listening—willingness and motivation—are present. The managers listening to the president in the previous example may also personalize the message by asking questions of themselves: "How will these four products affect my job?" "Will continued expansion of the electronic group affect me?" "Will those sixteen new salespeople increase my workload for the Western region?" "How will the stable market in the home implement group affect our division?" In answering these questions, the managers find how the message personally relates to them. Then their incentive to listen to the message increases.

Take Notes

All these techniques are strengthened when the listener takes notes. College students understand the importance of notes, but they may lose this good habit once they leave the classroom. A listener can easily make short notes to help organize, visualize, and personalize a message. Not only do notes provide a written record of the communication, but they can also provide valuable feedback that tells the listener just how well she is listening. If the notes are not well organized with main and supporting points, the listener probably has not mentally organized the message. If a quick review indicates no notes have been taken for some time, the listener may find that his attention has been wandering.

Notes also benefit a listener by keeping her physically involved. Listening is a predominantly mental activity; consequently, people who are accustomed to being physically active get restless or impatient when listening for long periods.

Of course, note taking can be a problem for people who overdo it. One can concentrate on the notes to the extent that major components of the message are missed. Instead, jot down just key words and phrases in outline form using abbreviations when possible.

A final thought on notes: The listener who takes notes indicates a sincere interest in both the message and the speaker. Seeing the note taking, the speaker will have a greater degree of confidence that note-taking listeners are paying attention to the message. The fact that it is important to demonstrate effective listening is discussed in more detail later.

STOP AND THINK

Imagine that you are listening to a disgruntled customer on the phone. What is the customer's likely reaction if you say, "I'm taking notes on this. Will you spell the person's name for me?"

Each of these techniques—identifying the main points, organizing, summarizing, visualizing, personalizing, and note taking—is useful in both active and interactive listening. However, the techniques are especially critical in situations where the ability to ask questions and observe nonverbal messages is limited. When questions are possible, the ideal is to ask questions of the speaker for clarity, in addition to the six techniques just discussed. The next section discusses situations in which it is easy to ask questions. We refer to this as interactive listening.

SPECIFIC TECHNIQUES FOR INTERACTIVE LISTENING

Table 9–3 summarizes techniques to use in active and interactive listening situations. When managers are engaged in two-way communication, they can improve their listening effectiveness by paraphrasing and asking questions.

Paraphrasing

Paraphrasing is commonly thought of as simply repeating what a speaker has *said*. However, a true paraphrase reflects what the listener thinks the speaker *intended to say*.

The listener uses different words to express the speaker's meaning, thereby checking understanding. Further, a paraphrase reflects the underlying attitudes or emotional tone of the message. While many people are reluctant to paraphrase for fear of sounding like a parrot, paraphrasing is an excellent listening technique for two reasons. When properly done, a paraphrase allows the listener to not only be sure she has received the message as the speaker intended but also strengthen the relationship between speaker and listener. When a listener paraphrases, she indicates effort, commitment, and good intentions, thereby increasing the likelihood that the speaker will respond in kind.

Table 9–3   Specific Techniques for Active and Interactive Listening

Active Situation	Interactive Situation
Identify main and supporting points	Paraphrase
Organize the message	Ask open and closed questions
Summarize the message	Ask primary and secondary questions
Visualize the message	Ask neutral and directed questions
Personalize the message	
Take notes	

Knowing the important benefits of paraphrasing, you might wonder why we all do not do it more frequently when listening. It may be because we are afraid it will sound foolish. Consider a time when a family member came home from work or school and you asked, "How was your day?" If the answer was something like, "I hate that place; I'm never going back!," and you decided to paraphrase, you would not say, "So you hate that place and you're not going back," because that response would probably trigger derision and a comment like, "That's what I just said!" Instead, as a good listener, you would say, "Sounds like you had a tough day." Remember that a paraphrase should reflect the meaning of the message you received, both verbally and nonverbally.

Questioning

The skillful use of questions adds immensely to a manager's ability to listen. This book recommends several areas when questioning techniques are appropriate: listening, interviewing, resolving conflict, and coaching. Questions are important because they provide the two-way process of communication that Chapter 2 discusses. Without the use of questions, feedback and mutual understanding are severely curbed. Thus, in the example just described in the previous section on paraphrasing, a good listener should follow the paraphrase, "Sounds like you had a tough day," with a question like, "What happened?"

In an interactive situation when the meaning of a message is either unclear or incomplete, a listener should ask questions. When key words, phrases, or concepts are vague or when inconsistencies or contradictions appear, questions help to develop clarity. Questions may also help a speaker clarify his thoughts. When questioned, the speaker may be forced to reanalyze his message to the listener's benefit.

A manager must strategically determine the most appropriate questions for different situations. Three types of questions are appropriate to this discussion: open–closed, primary–secondary, and neutral–directed. Question types are also described in Chapter 14 because they are critical in the context of interviewing.

Open–Closed Questions

The phrasing of an open-ended question gives the respondent a wide choice of possible answers. At the other end of the spectrum is the closed question, which calls for a narrow range of possible answers. Here is an illustration of this point. Suppose a frustrated subordinate describes to you a major problem with a new project. In her agitation, the employee jumps from one point to another while describing the problem. Naturally, this disorderly description makes it difficult to listen, so you ask questions for both clarity and completeness of information. The following list includes open and closed questions that you might ask the employee for clarification.

- What do you think are the major causes of the problem? (open)

- What more can you tell me about it? (open)

- Did you check the steam gauge? (closed)

- Where do you think we should go from here? (open)

- Would it be a good idea to wait until tomorrow? (closed)

While open questions ask for additional information, they also allow possible digression. Closed questions are more direct and help one to focus on the problems or facts. Closed questions also call for commitment ("Will you?"). Managers must use strategic analysis to determine the best type of question in each case.

STOP AND THINK

Imagine that you are attending a company function and trying to start a conversation with a coworker. You decide to ask a question. What is a good open question to get her to talk? HINT: "How are you?" doesn't count.

Primary–Secondary Questions

Two other options open to managers are primary and secondary questions. A primary question is the first question about a topic. A manager may choose to follow up with a secondary question designed to obtain more specific information after the primary question has been answered. A secondary question is not merely an additional question; it also seeks to get at a deeper level of information than the primary question. Such probes call for clarification or elaboration. The following dialogue shows the strategic use of primary and secondary questioning.

Manager:	Do you think you'll be able to have the analysis done by Wednesday? (primary)
Employee:	That shouldn't be any problem, if everything goes right for a change.
Manager:	What might go wrong? (secondary)
Employee:	The accounting information is hard to get sometimes.
Manager:	What specific part is hard to get? (secondary)

Notice that each secondary question seeks further information on the preceding answer.

Neutral–Directed Questions

The third classification involves neutral versus directed questions. While a neutral question seeks information without attempting to lead the speaker to answer in a certain way, the directed question leads the speaker to a response the inquirer desires. A directed question, or leading question, opens with such phrases as "Doesn't it seem logical that . . . ," or "Wouldn't you agree that . . . ," or "Surely you won't . . . , will you?" Directed questions may be used to obtain confirmation or clarification on one specific point, whereas the neutral question can obtain an unintended response.

In summary, a manager who uses paraphrases and appropriate questions adds clarity to communication because of the interactive process that develops. Interactive listening is clearly not a passive activity; rather, it requires the involvement of the manager through the use of questions and paraphrases. To help us see these two techniques in action, let us examine a hypothetical interview between the general manager (GM) of a manufacturing facility and her shop foreman. The topic is the delivery deadline for a customer order. The manager begins the interview by reviewing the contract and asking the foreman what has gone wrong. The foreman turns his chair toward the GM, leans in toward her, and makes eye contact. He begins his response by paraphrasing the question, making it much simpler to understand and demonstrating that he understood it. "So you are asking about the likelihood that we will deliver the order on time? The answer: No."

He further clarifies that delays in equipment repairs on the line, caused by severe weather, prevented necessary parts from arriving the previous week. This cascade of events culminated in extended downtime and a reduction in product volume.

The general manager, also maintaining eye contact, then summarizes the answer and proceeds to probe the foreman by asking if the equipment is now repaired and working. The foreman again paraphrases and provides details, explaining that the repairs have been completed and the shop is now up and running. The GM, maintaining eye contact as well, summarizes and ends by saying, "So what is the new delivery date?" Both participants in the interview demonstrate good listening skills, including paraphrases, open and closed questions and probes, and nonverbal cues.

LISTENING TO INFORMAL COMMUNICATION

So far, this discussion on listening has emphasized times in which a formal speaking–listening situation is established. But informal, casual listening can also be extremely important—what began as casual listening can quickly become factual or empathic listening. A manager should always be aware of the rumors that circulate on the grapevine. At times, these rumors can provide important information; at other times, it may be important to attempt to alter the content of the rumor; and at still others, it may be best to ignore the rumors. But managers must stay tuned in.

The term *grapevine* has an interesting history. It arose during the Civil War when intelligence telegraph lines were strung loosely from tree to tree in the manner of a grapevine. Because the messages from the line often were incorrect or confusing, any rumor was said to be from the grapevine.

What causes rumors in modern organizations? To answer this question, the following formula is helpful:

$$Rumors = Ambiguity \times Interest$$

Rumors are created when the available message is ambiguous. If all information were available and clear from the formal channels, no rumors would be created. When the message is ambiguous but interesting, rumors will result.

This relationship has an important implication for managerial communication. Management can determine what is interesting to employees by listening to the rumors. For instance, a vice president recently resigned from a computer company. But the rumors on the grapevine do not address the replacement; rather, a new relationship between two employees is the major topic. This would imply that the employees are relatively secure about the management team and that one replacement will probably not rock the boat. Compare this to a company where the president suddenly retired. All that was discussed whenever people gathered was the latest rumor about the replacement. Obviously, this matter was of great concern to the employees.

Research indicates that information transmitted via the grapevine in organizations is 70 to 90 percent accurate. However, some amount of distortion always exists.[15] This core of truth along with the degree of distortion is often what makes a message on the grapevine believable, interesting, and durable.

As information proceeds from person to person on the grapevine, it tends to undergo three kinds of change. The first is *leveling,* the dropping of details and the simplifying of context and qualifications. This process is especially prevalent when the rumor is extremely complex. It must be made rather simple to pass on to the next person. The second kind of change is *sharpening,* the preference for vivid and dramatic treatment of data. Employees work to make a story better and more entertaining as it is passed from one person to another. Third is *assimilating,* the tendency of people to adjust or modify rumors, to mold them to fit their personal needs. This makes the rumor more interesting to those on the grapevine.[16]

Effective managerial listening requires that managers critically assess informal communication to determine the extent to which leveling, sharpening, and assimilation have occurred. Inaccurate rumors can sometimes call for action. In one manufacturing plant, rumors maintained that a massive personnel layoff was about to occur because of the new machinery being installed. Management heard these incorrect rumors. Members of the management team met with employees to assure them no layoffs would occur. Listening to rumors helped prevent a loss of employee morale. As one manager once said, it is important to listen to "the talk on the street." Research shows that employees prefer to get their information from the formal channels, and they turn to informal channels when the formal have dried up because no one can work in a vacuum. Managers concerned about rampant rumors should remember the relationship between formal and informal channels.

LISTENING TO THE TOTAL ENVIRONMENT

This chapter primarily discusses listening to the spoken word. Chapter 10 discusses nonverbal communication. Managers must listen to spoken and nonverbal messages both separately and jointly in formal and informal settings. Strategic managerial communication requires listening to messages that are not always obvious. Figure 9–1 graphically demonstrates the three possible aspects of a message: formal to informal, verbal to nonverbal, and obvious to hidden. The three possibilities are displayed in a triangle with equal sides because all three aspects should be considered equally.

Figure 9–1   Three Dimensions of a Message

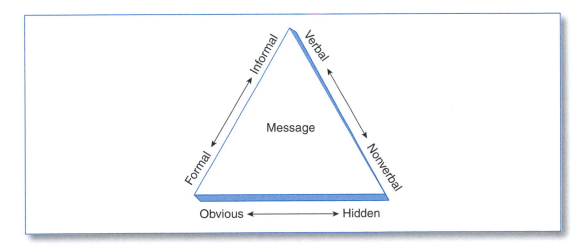

This implies it is necessary for managers to keep their eyes and ears open for all kinds of signals in their organization and its industry. When a person is aware of the signals of a forthcoming event, it is possible to take corrective action—but first the manager must listen to be aware. An online magazine, *Madame Noire*, recently featured an article called "The Fourth Quarter Curse? How to Tell If a Layoff Is Coming."[17] The article discusses signals of potential restructuring, such as employees who voluntarily quit but are not replaced, increased debt, layoffs at other companies in the industry, rumors, unannounced meetings, and departures of top executives. It is possible that most employees could know about pending layoffs long before they were formally announced.

Of course, restructuring is a drastic action. It is important that managers listen to and analyze many other events in the company that can affect their careers. For example, which departments seem to be getting the best budgets? Employees in these groups will probably have the greatest opportunities for advancement. Although it is not always possible to determine budget allocations, it is possible to watch for the results of greater allocations. The hiring of additional support staff, the purchasing of newer and better computer equipment, the acquisition of new office furniture, and more frequent traveling to professional conferences can each signal a favored department.

The point is that managerial listening goes beyond listening to the obvious words. It requires listening to nonverbal behaviors and the continuous signals that come from the environment. Recall our discussion of the strategic communication model in Chapter 2. The outer layer—culture and climate—is relevant here.

DEVELOPING A LISTENING CLIMATE

In addition to actually listening carefully, managers must also seem to be listening and establish a climate that demonstrates receptivity. Without this climate, the communication environment in an office can become like that in some homes:

Parent: Why don't you ever tell us what you are doing?

Child: I do, but you don't listen. You're always so busy.

Parent: We're never too busy to listen to you, but you just don't seem to want to tell us anything.

Are the parents too busy to listen, or do they just appear too busy? The same question may be asked of many managers. Is it possible that they appear too busy to listen? A manager may unintentionally establish a nonlistening climate by subtle behavior that says to the subordinate, "Why talk if nobody is listening?" You might recall that an organization's culture and climate were discussed in Chapter 2 and highlighted as the outer layer of the strategic communication model for developing a communication strategy.

While a manager is responsible for a tremendous amount of information and spends as much as 50 percent of the working day listening, one cannot listen if nobody is talking. Managers need to develop a listening climate to motivate people to open up. Consequently, managers should strive to eliminate listening habits that discourage communication. Table 9–4 lists 16 irritating listening habits.[18] A listener demonstrating these behaviors is not

Table 9–4   Irritating Listening Habits

1. He doesn't give me a chance to talk.
2. He never lets me complete more than a couple of sentences before interrupting.
3. He never looks at me while I'm talking.
4. He constantly fidgets with a pencil or a paper, studying it rather than listening to me.
5. He never smiles.
6. He always changes the subject with his questions and comments.
7. Whenever I make a suggestion, he throws cold water on it.
8. He's always jumping ahead of me to tell me what my next point is.
9. He puts words into my mouth that I did not mean.
10. Occasionally, he asks a question about what I've just told him.
11. When I'm talking, he finishes sentences for me.
12. When I have a good idea, he always says, "Yes, I've been thinking about that, too."
13. He overdoes nods of the head, yeahs, uh-huhs.
14. He tries to insert humorous remarks when I'm trying to be serious.
15. When I come in, he doesn't put down what he's doing and turn his attention completely to me.
16. He asks questions that demand agreement with him. For example, he makes a statement and then says, "Don't you think so?" or "Don't you agree?"

exhibiting a positive communication climate; consequently, the speaker may not believe he is being listened to. This list can serve as a personal checklist for managers to see if they demonstrate any of the irritating behaviors.

Two levels of the listening climate require attention. The first is the micro level, or the one-on-one, situation. The second level is the macro, or total, climate. First we will review the micro level.

The Micro Listening Climate

A research study asked employees to indicate which of the poor listening habits in Table 9–4 they found the most common.[19] Two items seemed to stand out:

When I'm talking, he finishes sentences for me.

When I come in, he doesn't put down what he is doing and turn his attention completely to me.

This finding is especially revealing. Clearly, the listener needs to give undivided attention to the speaker, who does not want to be rushed to complete the message. This fact relates to the 25–75 rule discussed earlier. The listener's mind moves so much more rapidly than the spoken word that the listener's impatience may show as she attempts to complete the speaker's sentence. Even though the listener is paying attention, this impatience to complete the speaker's communication may develop a negative listening climate. The same is true when the listener works on something else while attempting to listen. The speaker may soon get the feeling that the message being delivered is not very important.

Demonstrating a positive climate is most important when a manager is involved in empathic listening. As discussed earlier in this chapter, an empathic listener tries to understand the speaker's feelings. Most people have a very difficult time expressing their feelings, so an encouraging, supportive, receptive climate needs to be established. Managerial strategies include maintaining eye contact, leaning slightly toward the speaker, changing facial expression in relationship to the message, and taking notes. All of these behaviors demonstrate a positive listening climate.

For a valuable exercise, review the list of irritating listening habits and watch for them in your own behavior for a week. This form of personal feedback should provide insights for improving your micro listening climate.

The Macro Listening Climate

Managers must take responsibility for ensuring that those who work around them are free to exchange information in a timely and accurate manner.[20] They must develop a general atmosphere that promotes rather than hinders the opportunity to communicate. This macro level of listening is demonstrated by the manager's general demeanor and style. One basic approach is managing by wandering around. For example, when Ed Whitacre stepped in as CEO of General Motors in 2009, one of the first efforts was to make over GM's culture from an authoritarian, top-down environment to an open one. He preferred personal interaction to e-mail, making himself accessible to employees by using the people's elevators, bathrooms, and dining rooms. He regularly stopped by workstations to ask how they were helping to sell more cars, and employees grew to look forward to his visits.[21] When managers are physically available and not locked away behind closed office doors, they create an atmosphere that says "I am here to listen to you."

In his popular book *Thriving on Chaos,* Tom Peters presents a number of suggestions that create strong listening environments.[22] First, he suggests that opportunities to listen be built into managers' daily routines. This can be done by frequently visiting the cafeteria or break room. Unfortunately, many managers do not work these activities into their schedules because of time pressures and do not realize this is an integral and critical part of their jobs.

Another technique is to have informal meetings; "huddles" or spontaneous gatherings of a few people to discuss a problem indicate the manager wants and needs to listen to employees' ideas. Another technique is to keep official titles and symbols of authority to a minimum. People are more willing to talk when they do not feel inferior to another. In some contemporary organizations, job titles have disappeared not only from office doors but also from business cards. The implication is that everyone works together—communicates together—to get the job done.

The open-door policy expressed in more traditional companies can be either a positive or a negative macro listening climate. Managers often pride themselves on announcing an open-door policy. They tell their employees to stop by anytime—their "office door is always open." But managers become frustrated when employees do not come through the open door.

Why is the open-door policy not used? A negative listening environment probably exists. First, it may be necessary to make an appointment with an administrative assistant before the door is opened. Second, the office may be located far from employee work areas. Would it not be better to be easily and readily available? This would be a positive open-door climate. A supervisor in a large organization once remarked, "If they have to announce an open-door policy, it probably means that there really isn't one!"[23]

The importance of the macro listening climate was aptly demonstrated by Celeste, a first-line supervisor in a foundry. Her company was on the far south side of the Chicago suburbs. Celeste was probably one of the most respected supervisors. She gained respect by always being available to the employees. For instance, one Saturday the company rented a bus and arranged for employees to attend a Chicago White Sox baseball game. Celeste was one of the first to sign up. During the bus trip and at the game, she was part of the group even though she was the only supervisor to attend. This is probably one of the reasons her employees truly believed that Celeste always had an open door when it was time to discuss a problem. She developed a positive listening climate.

A number of elements influence employees' perceptions that managers are willing to listen.[24] Employees' work and personal backgrounds, the organizational culture, the employees' roles within the organization, and the little symbolic behaviors of the manager all affect the macro listening climate. Managers would do well to take a periodic audit of their personal listening behavior and their environment to ensure they have established a climate that says "Yes, I am willing to listen."

SUMMARY

Managers need to work on their listening skills. The major benefit is improved understanding between people. Many of the data necessary for good decisions come through listening. Listening makes a person more dependable. Good listeners are more respected and liked by coworkers. Better listening enables a manager to be better informed overall.

Managers must exert an active, concentrated effort to overcome listening barriers. One of the primary barriers is that people think about four times faster than they can speak; consequently, the listener's mind tends to wander. Motivation and willingness are highly related barriers. Willingness develops before listening even begins, whereas poor motivation is largely caused by the 25–75 problem. Other barriers to listening include internal distractions, detouring, debate, and time.

Two main types of listening are *active* and *interactive*. Active listening occurs when a manager has little opportunity to respond directly to the speaker. Interactive listening occurs when the manager can verbally interact with the speaker by asking questions or summarizing.

Listening has three levels of intensity: *casual, factual,* and *empathic.* The level to use is determined by the importance and complexity of the message and occasion. Once the manager has determined the type and intensity level of listening called for, the manager must prepare physically and psychologically to listen.

Techniques for active listening include identifying the main and supporting points, organizing, summarizing, visualizing, personalizing the message, and taking notes. Techniques for interactive listening include paraphrasing and asking open–closed, primary–secondary, and neutral–directed questions. When listening to informal communication, a manager should remember that information transmitted informally undergoes some distortion. Leveling, sharpening, and assimilating occur. A manager who is a good listener will listen to the total environment—both spoken and nonverbal messages are important.

Finally, a manager should work to develop a climate that demonstrates receptivity so that people are motivated to communicate. On a micro level, a manager should avoid poor listening habits, such as interrupting. On a macro level, a manager's general demeanor and style will indicate approachability.

Cases for Small-Group Discussion

CASE 9–1

Listening and Technology

Veronica Sharpe, marketing manager for Diamond Communications, an outdoor advertising company, arrived in the boardroom for her teleconference with Brad Jones, a potential client. She was extremely busy today and brought her smart tablet with her, checking e-mail along the way. She also brought her digital voice recorder so that she could record the conversation for reference later. She intentionally left the cameras off, opting to only use audio transmission. Brad called right on time, and they began to speak about Brad's plan for utilizing advertising space on the variety of electronic billboards along Interstate 45, a north-south route through Houston, Texas.

About two minutes into Brad's exposition of his plans, Veronica's smart tablet buzzed. It was an e-mail she had been waiting on for two hours, and time was of the essence—she had to reply quickly to settle a payment before the 4:00 p.m. deadline, 5:00 p.m. in the Eastern time zone from where the e-mail was being sent. She thought to herself, "I'm recording all this, so I can just review it later—I have to answer this e-mail now. Time to multitask."

About a minute later, in the middle of her e-mail response, she noticed a distinct pause in Brad's speech. "Veronica?" Brad asked. "Still there?"

"Oh, yes," Veronica answered, embarrassed. "Can you repeat that last thing?"

"I want to know if the plan is something that your firm can accomplish, or do I need to find another firm with electronic boards?" Brad asked.

QUESTIONS

1. What principles of effective listening was Veronica violating?

2. What do you think her best alternative is at this moment in time, given her lack of attention to Brad's proposal?

CASE 9–2

Holgate's Listening Problems

John Holgate, a section manager in a chemical plant, has several engineers reporting to him. As part of his job, Holgate attends meetings during any given day with some of his junior engineers, as well as with people outside his immediate group. Occasionally, people higher up in the company (the technical director or vice president, for example) attend these review meetings.

The engineers who work for Holgate believe he often misrepresents them, and they also think Holgate does not listen to what is being said. He often interrupts the speakers and completes the sentence for them. Since the engineers do not want to disagree with their boss openly, they do not contradict him in front of higher management.

Naturally, this habit results in confusion, wasted time and effort, and poor morale. When members of higher management return for their next review, they usually find that the work they requested has not been done. In fact, they occasionally find that unrequested tasks have been carried out. As they listen to Holgate's project status review, management has lately been wondering what is going on. This doubt reflects not just on Holgate but on his subordinates as well. The subordinates' morale and productivity have been slipping.

QUESTIONS

1. Why does Holgate complete the speaker's sentences?

2. How can Holgate improve his listening skills?

3. Assuming you are Holgate's subordinate, how could you point out this problem to him?

CASE 9–3

Pardon Me!

Bob Pierce, a gentleman of about fifty, is the president of ABC Construction Company. The company is considered the most progressive and innovative in highway, bridge, and dam construction in the area.

Pierce has served in different functional areas of the company, is fairly well educated, and is oriented toward engineering.

Before becoming ABC's vice president of field operations, Walter Horton was the chief engineer of a rival firm. He has a reputation for being a very good project manager and for knowing intimately the details of ABC field operations.

Pierce has just returned from sick leave. His bad cold is still slowing him down. It is now noon, and Pierce, who has finally caught up with the backlog of work, is preparing to go to lunch. Just then, Horton walks into his office. Horton has been trying to get in touch with Pierce the past few days for his decision about the construction plan for the new dam. Horton spreads his blueprints on the president's desk and starts his presentation.

After the presentation, the following conversation occurs.

Horton: Well, how do you feel about the plan?

Pierce (somewhat absently): Well, uh, pretty good . . .

Horton (a little too quickly): Is there anything I haven't made clear?

Pierce: Hum . . . no . . .

Horton: OK, good. Now I would like to present the plan to the board of directors and maybe . . .

Pierce: Board of directors? Wait a minute. You're moving pretty fast.

Horton: You agreed the plan's a good one, didn't you?

Pierce (not with it at all): Well, yes.

QUESTIONS

1. What are the physical and psychological listening barriers Pierce faced during the presentation?

2. What assumptions is Horton making about Pierce's ability to grasp the situation?

3. What could Pierce have done to prevent the situation?

4. What are Horton's shortcomings as a communicator that would complicate the situation for anyone listening to him?

CASE 9–4

Hearing but Not Listening

Cedar's Furniture and Appliance is a chain of five stores, two located in Youngstown, two in Akron, and one in Cleveland. Cedar's main office is in Akron.

Jane Pyle is the office manager at the main office. She supervises four word-processing operators. Three of Pyle's employees are efficient and thorough. She tells them what she wants done once, and it is done. However, the fourth employee, Harriet Enders, seems to get little done right. She finishes her daily work, but she frequently has to redo it, thus putting an extra burden on the other three operators. They have to make up the work Enders has no time for because she is redoing her original work. The other three employees are beginning to complain to Pyle about the problem.

Pyle does not want to terminate Enders because Pyle knows her subordinate can be a hard worker. When she does follow directions, Enders is the first of the four word-processing operators to finish. The office manager wonders why Enders does not understand directions, while the other three people always seem to. She is almost sure that, although Enders is hearing, she is not listening. Enders's problem is preventing the office work from running smoothly.

QUESTIONS

1. Write the dialogue Pyle might use to open the discussion with Enders about this problem.

2. What environmental factors might be responsible for Enders's difficulty in listening?

Exercise for Small Groups

This exercise offers practice in a disciplined approach to listening to others that provides focused support and clarity. It was developed by Dr. Mary Vielhaber at Eastern Michigan State University.

PREWORK INSTRUCTIONS

Please take some time to think about a communication problem that you face in your job. The problem can be either a unique, unusual communication problem or a reoccurring communication problem that you continue to face in spite of several efforts to resolve the problem.

Select a problem that you are willing to share with your colleagues. Avoid problems with complicated technical details. You can disguise names and other facts so that people involved in the problem are not identified.

Briefly write down the problem in one or two paragraphs. Describe the context and key facts of the problem so that when you read your description, others will be able to quickly understand what you are facing.

PROCESS

Divide into groups of three or four members. Each person either reads their description of their business problem or *briefly* explains the problem to the group. After all people in the group have presented their problem, select one problem for the group to focus on. Ask the person to read his or her written problem one more time to the group. Take a few minutes to jot down open-ended questions you can ask the person about the problem.

Note: The questions you ask should be designed to help the person think through their difficult situation. You should not be trying to "solve" their problem. Instead, you are asking questions to help the person think through the issues involved.

QUESTIONING PROCESS

Ask open-ended questions and probe for understanding the facts and the reasoning behind the person's assertions and conclusions. The presenter responds to the questions unless he or she does not have a response. In that case, the presenter may simply say, "I don't have an answer to that question." There should be no discussion among the group members or any statements hidden in the questions.

POST-QUESTIONING PROCESS

After approximately ten minutes, the group stops to discuss the process used. The presenter is invited to describe his or her experience answering questions. Did the questions lead to a new insight? Did the presenter feel that the group was listening? A second or third round may continue if time permits.

DISCUSSION QUESTIONS

1. What are the advantages of disciplined listening?

2. When can this technique be used in the workplace?

3. What are the barriers to disciplined listening?

Student Study Site

Visit the Student Study Site at **study.sagepub.com/hynes6e** for web quizzes, video links, web resources, and cases studies.

Notes

1. C. G. Coakley and A. D. Wolvin, "Listening Pedagogy and Andragogy," *Journal of the International Listening Association* 4 (1990): pp. 33–61.
2. Tony Hsieh, *Delivering Happiness: A Path to Profits, Passion, and Purpose* (New York: Business Plus, 2010).
3. Judi Brownell, "Perceptions of Effective Listeners: A Management Study," *Journal of Business Communication* 27, no. 4 (Fall 1990): pp. 401–415.
4. B. D. Sypher and T. E. Zorn, "Communication Related Abilities and Upward Mobility: A Longitudinal Investigation," *Human Communication Research* 12 (1986): pp. 420–431.
5. Margot Denney, "CEO Drives Home Message," *Bryan-College Station Eagle,* April 10, 2003, p. 1A.
6. James R. Stengel, Andrea L. Dixon, and Chris T. Allen, "Best Practice: Listening Begins at Home," *Harvard Business Review,* November 2003, pp. 106–116.
7. Kelly E. See, Elizabeth W. Morrison, Naomi B. Rothman, and Jack B. Soll, "The Detrimental Effects of Power on Confidence, Advice Taking, and Accuracy," *Organizational Behavior and Human Decision Processes Journal* 116, no. 2 (2011): pp. 272–285.
8. Philip V. Lewis, *Organizational Communication: The Essence of Effective Management,* 3rd ed. (New York: Wiley & Sons, 1987), p. 146.
9. Franklin H. Knower, D. Philips, and F. Koeppel, "Studies in Listening to Informative Speaking," *Journal of Social Psychology* 40 (1945): p. 82.

10. Larry R. Smeltzer and Kittie W. Watson, "Listening: An Empirical Comparison of Discussion Length and Level of Incentive," *Central States Speech Journal* 35, no. 3 (1984): pp. 166–171.

11. R. N. Bostrom, *Input! The Process of Listening* (Northbrook, IL: Waveland Press, 1988).

12. Larry R. Smeltzer and K. W. Watson, "A Test of Instructional Strategies for Listening Improvement in a Simulated Business Setting," *Journal of Business Communication* 22, no. 4 (Fall 1985): pp. 33–42.

13. Edward E. Lawler, *The Ultimate Advantage* (San Francisco: Jossey-Bass, 1992).

14. Michael Barbaro and Steven Greenhouse, "Wal-Mart Says Thank You to Workers," *The New York Times*, December 4, 2006, http://www.nytimes.com/2006/12/04/business/04walmart.html?_r = 0. See also Wal-Mart Corporation, "Working at Walmart: Our Culture—Beliefs and Behaviors," accessed August 19, 2014, http://careers.walmart.com/about-us/working-at-walmart/.

15. Hugh B. Vickery, "Tapping into the Employee Grapevine," *Association Management,* January 1984, pp. 59–64.

16. Lewis, *Organizational Communication,* pp. 46–48.

17. Tanvier Peart, "The Fourth Quarter Curse? How To Tell If a Layoff Is Coming," *Madame Noire*, November 24, 2013, http://madamenoire.com/325388/4th-quarter-curse-tell-layoff-coming/.

18. Eugene Raudsepp, "Is Anybody Listening," *Machine Design,* February 24, 1977, p. 7.

19. Larry R. Smeltzer and Kittie Watson, "Barriers to Listening Comparison between Business Students and Business Practitioners," *Communication Research Report* 1, no. 1 (December 1984): pp. 82–87.

20. E. H. Schein, *Organizational Culture and Leadership* (San Francisco: Jossey-Bass, 1985).

21. Jason Buch, "His Repair Job: Texas Executive Ed Whitacre Steered GM at a Critical Time," *Houston Chronicle*, August 22, 2010, p. D1.

22. T. Peters, *Thriving on Chaos* (New York: Alfred A. Knopf, 1988).

23. Charles E. Beck and Elizabeth A. Beck, "The Manager's Open Door and the Communication Climate," *Business Horizons,* January–February 1986, pp. 15–19.

24. Marilyn H. Lewis and N. L. Reinsch Jr., "Listening in Organizational Environments," *Journal of Business Communication* 25, no. 3 (Summer 1988): pp. 49–67; and J. Brownell, "Listening Environment: Critical Aspects of Organizational Communication" (working paper, Cornell University, Ithaca, NY, 1992).

CHAPTER 10

Nonverbal Communication

What you do speaks so loudly that I cannot hear what you say.

—Ralph Waldo Emerson, American essayist and poet

Understanding the importance of nonverbal communication is often difficult because it is such a natural part of any managerial interaction. To appreciate the contribution nonverbal communication makes to managerial communication, imagine yourself at a meeting with six others discussing an upcoming event—say, the opening of a new facility for your company. It is a meeting like any number you have attended before, yet it is radically different because you cannot see the others. Something keeps you from this. It could be a fabric veil, fog, wooden panels—you decide. Your location is also a puzzle. Is it the boardroom for the corporation, or is it a meeting room just anywhere? How important is this meeting in the whole scheme of things? Your environment provides no clues. In addition, you cannot really hear the others very well. All voices have been altered by the device used during investigatory reports on television. You can hear the words, but the voices have little or no character. The words are slowed down and slurred to some extent.

You are all seated in the same room, but because of the room's setup, you cannot see who is seated where—who is at the head of the table (perhaps you are), or who is at the sides, or even who is seated next to whom. While you and several others flew in to attend the meeting, you did not have a chance to shake hands before the meeting began. In fact, today you have not seen the others or what they are wearing. Are they dressed as well as you are, or are they dressed informally? The only communication possible during the meeting is what you can get from you and the six others talking.

Unfortunately, even that part of the communication process is a challenge. You verbally trip over each other as the meeting proceeds since you have no efficient way to signal whose turn it is to speak. In addition, because speakers must identify themselves before speaking, the interactions take longer than usual. Furthermore, you must keep these verbal identities in mind as you listen because you have no visual or tactile cues to go on. As the meeting progresses, whenever you contribute, you are unsure of all but the verbal reactions because you cannot see the shrugs, posture shifts, or expressions on the other faces.

The interaction is also lengthened by the need to evaluate each remark for intent. Did he mean that ironically? Was she being sarcastic? Was that last remark meant as a joke? The audio scrambler makes quick judgments on these fine points nearly impossible. And while you can hear the voices, which voice belongs to whom? Someone suggests that all the employees in the store dress up as clowns. You are just about to say "ridiculous" when you check yourself—be careful, maybe the boss said that.

You know the meeting is scheduled to last two hours, but because you had to surrender your watch at the door, you have no idea about the time, although it seems an eternity. You know the agenda for the meeting, but are you going to be able to cover all the items in the time allotted? Are you giving enough time to each item? Are you going to get out of the meeting and find that only half the time has elapsed? Whatever the case, you wish you were out of the meeting now.

THE IMPORTANCE OF NONVERBAL COMMUNICATION

Nonverbal factors are clearly a crucial element of managerial communication. Without nonverbal communication as a source of information, most of the richness and much of the meaning in messages would be lost. In many cases, conversations would be complicated by the need to repeat messages for clarity, and the time required would multiply enormously.

Nonverbal communication accompanies oral and, by logical extension, written messages, while consisting of the signals delivered through means other than verbal. In short, it includes *everything but the words*. Managers send, receive, and interpret nonverbal messages in the same way they send, receive, and interpret verbal ones. The same communication dynamics come into play as the sender intends (although often unconsciously) to send a message and chooses some medium through which to do so (a gesture, for example) that receivers perceive and interpret just as they do with verbal messages. Nonverbal communication may bear a clear meaning in itself, but often it serves as an adjunct to the spoken words, adding nuance in one place and clarity in another. At other times, this complex source of messages may even contradict the words being spoken.

> **STOP AND THINK**
>
> If a nonverbal message contradicts the verbal, such as when a speaker's voice shakes and her facial expression is anxious but she says, "I'm delighted to be here!" which do you believe?

Nonverbal communication is an important part of our daily managerial interactions.[1] While the extent of the nonverbal aspect varies from interaction to interaction, one set of oft-cited statistics shows that 55 percent of a message comes from the speaker's appearance, facial expression, and posture, while vocal aspects deliver 38 percent, and the actual words deliver only 7 percent.[2] Nonverbal communication is a rich and complex source of communication data, and this chapter provides an overview of the areas relevant to the managerial function. But first, three generalizations about nonverbal signals should be stressed here. While the first two apply to most other signals, it helps to keep them in mind when interpreting nonverbal communication.

First, with the exception of so-called emblems, nonverbal signals rarely have one set meaning. Rather, they usually add to the message's meaning, as shown in the following section of this chapter.

Second, nonverbal signals vary from culture to culture, and region to region, in their meaning. Nonverbal signals derive from experiences within the communication environment (cultural, regional, or social) and are generally dispersed throughout it.[3] It is not enough merely to translate the verbal language; the nonverbal must be expressed as well.[4] The Japanese, for example, usually present a noncontroversial demeanor and are excessively polite by North American standards. In negotiation, the accompanying nonverbals can create confusion across cultures.[5] In cross-cultural situations, in fact, while the verbal takes on greater importance, knowing and using basic nonverbal signals—for example, bowing in South Korea—can communicate respect.[6]

Third, when nonverbal signals contradict verbal ones, the nonverbals are usually the ones to trust. When verbal and nonverbal disagree, credibility can suffer.[7] Law enforcement agents, trial attorneys, and insurance investigators are professionals who extensively study nonverbal behavior in order to improve their interrogation skills. They know that nonverbal signals can provide valuable clues to the truth of a message.

More specifically, the law enforcement community provides a contemporary example of nonverbal behavior's importance. When attempting to identify terrorists and criminals in public places, such as airports and subways, officials are trained to "read" suspects' body language. The technique is called behavior detection and is rooted in the notion that people convey emotions, such as fear, in subconscious gestures, facial expressions, and speech patterns.[8] Since the September 11, 2001, attack on the United States, behavior detection has been adopted by police, the Transportation Security Administration, and other authorities at over forty airports, universities, and mass transit systems.

Telling people how to dress, talk, and even move is a far easier task than putting it all into play in one's life. While we can read about the importance of smiling behavior, for example, how much is too much? Women and men aspiring to be managers can view excellent models for nonverbal behavior on business-oriented TV programs. To get the maximum impact of the nonverbal elements in the conversations, with the exception of vocal style, watch these programs with the sound turned off. Not only do they show the kinds of gestures leaders make, but they generally reflect current appropriate dress as well.

THE FUNCTIONS OF NONVERBAL CUES

Nonverbal communication is a broader concept than many realize. It is far more than just gestures and eye contact. A simple definition already offered is that in managerial interactions, nonverbal communication is everything but the words. A more precise definition is that offered by Harrison, a leading expert, who said, it is "the exchange of information through nonlinguistic signs."[9] These nonlinguistic signs are like any kind of sign in communication in that they are something tangible, capable of bearing meaning, just as linguistic signs are. They differ in that they are nonverbal.

Even color, and how it is presented in the context of a message, can serve as a non-linguistic sign. Some studies have looked at the impact colors have on cognitive performance. Researchers at the University of British Columbia conducted tests with six hundred people to determine the effects of the colors blue and red. Red groups did better on tests of recall and attention to detail. Participants in the blue groups tested better with skills requiring imagination and creativity.[10] So if your team is tasked with brainstorming for a new product or service, you may want to have them meet in a room with blue walls.

Depending on the culture, color is a nonlinguistic sign of certain emotions. For instance, Western brides generally wear white, but Eastern brides wear red. In China, white is a sign of bereavement and loss, just as black is in the United States.

A study of emotional responses to cell phone ads demonstrates how color creates different emotions in different cultures. Thirty-two people from six cultures (Finland, Sweden, Taiwan, India, China, and the United States) were asked to interpret a Nokia ad's external characteristics. The predominant blue and white colors, recognized by the Finnish respondents as their country's flag colors, provoked a positive impression. Further, the Finns found the colors "reliable," "natural," "trustworthy," and "comfortable." By contrast, the Chinese and Taiwanese respondents said that white is a funeral color for them, creating a negative impression. The Swedes recognized that blue and white are "Finnish colors" and rejected them as "boring" and "cold." The respondents from India thought the colors warm and summery. The US respondents were inconsistent about whether the blue and white colors were warm or cold, summery or wintery. Interestingly, several Americans connected the blue and white colors to "unlimited freedom" and "innovation," which no informants from other cultures mentioned.[11] Unfortunately, nonverbal communication can result in frustratingly inexact interpretation. Scholars have carefully studied nonverbal communication but have only scratched the surface of the topic in many areas. If placed in the proper perspective, it can be a valuable source of cues in communication situations.

Burbinster identified six functions for nonverbal communication (see Table 10–1).[12]

Nonverbal signals that *complement* the verbal message repeat it. Typically, these signals accompany what is being said. For example, a technician explaining the varying gap widths in faulty components in a heating system might hold up her thumb and index finger and vary the gap between them as she discusses the problem. Or a supervisor welcoming a subordinate back after a lengthy illness might give him a warm handshake to stress how pleased he is at the other's return.

Those nonverbal signals that *accent* call our attention to a matter under discussion. A common example is a person pounding on a desk as she makes an important point. People

Table 10–1 Functions of Nonverbal Behavior
Complement
Accent
Contradict
Repeat
Regulate
Substitute

may also use vocalics, the nonverbal aspects of the voice itself, to highlight a point. Someone differentiating between one choice and another might say "I want *this* one and not *that*."

The nonverbal signals that *contradict* are less obvious. These are usually sent unintentionally by the subconscious to say nonverbally the opposite of what is being said verbally. Either subtly or obviously, nonverbal cues will often tell the careful observers the truth when the verbal cues do not. This complex area of nonverbal communication will be discussed later under the heading "Nonverbal Signs of Deception."

Repeating occurs when we have already sent a message using one form of communication and wish to emphasize the point being made. It differs from complementing in that it is not done simultaneously with the verbal comment. For example, a demonstration following a verbal description of a tool's use is a nonverbal repetition.

Regulating, the fifth purpose Burbinster suggests, is a subtle and important one. Regulating occurs during conversations to signal to our partner to "slow," "stop," and even "wait your turn" and let the other person know when we are ready to listen or to speak. Watch an ongoing conversation, and you will quickly spot a variety of these cues. A speaker who is not finished with his point but is being interrupted might speak louder or faster to keep his turn (thus using vocalics). Another might hold up her hand to say "not yet, let me finish." On the other hand, a speaker will usually look directly at the listener to indicate that the listener's turn is imminent.

Substituting is a less common nonverbal signal than the others. When we cannot send a message by verbal cues, we might choose to use nonverbal ones—especially emblems, which will be discussed in the next section on movement and gestures—to get the point across to our receiver. A supervisor visiting a loud factory might use the OK sign to signal an employee. This will likely be more effective than something shouted.

> **STOP AND THINK**
>
> Which of Burbinster's functions is exemplified by the following gestures:
>
> 1. A woman dropping her voice as she flirts with someone she is attracted to?
>
> 2. A man jiggling his leg as he is being interviewed for a job?
>
> 3. A grandmother putting her finger to her lips as her four-year-old grandson screams for candy?

From a theoretical perspective, nonverbal communication also serves another important function: communication redundancy. This concept refers to the phenomena built into any language system that combat the effects of noise. It simply means that much of the meaning of a message can be deduced from other elements in the message that have already appeared. The TV game show *Wheel of Fortune* is an example of redundancy in that not every word or letter must be on the game board before one can guess the correct phrase.

While part of a message delivers new information, much of it exists to ensure the points being made are understood. Far from being a negative phenomenon, communication redundancy is vitally important because it helps ensure that our message gets past the various barriers that environmental, organizational, or interpersonal elements erect. When a message is made more redundant, that is, when the information in it has been made more predictable to the receiver, the message has a greater chance of transferring the meaning the sender intends it to convey.

Every communication system is redundant. Verbal languages build in redundancy through a variety of means including grammar and syntax. Most of the functions addressed by nonverbal communication serve in some way as redundancy. Thus, as we discuss an issue with someone, we will use nonverbal signals to complement, accent, repeat, and even substitute to get a point across. This may be done without even thinking about it. Even when a nonverbal signal contradicts the verbal, additional nonverbal signals are likely to follow to underscore the contradiction.[13] Thus, a shake of the head denying a request is followed by a smile to indicate goodwill.

Some nonverbal behaviors are *innate,* others are *learned* from the community around us, and some are *mixed.* For instance, eye blinking patterns and blushing appear to be innate—universal, involuntary behaviors that occur in certain communication situations. Other cues such as the eyewink and the thumbs-up are learned, and they signal different meanings in different cultures. A third group of nonverbal behaviors (laugh, smile) is mixed in that they occur in every culture, but they can be controlled, and their meanings can change. In some Asian cultures, for example, a small laugh may occur naturally but may convey discomfort and submission rather than affiliation and pleasure.

This chapter now explores several key areas of nonverbal communication and suggests how managers can use them to their advantage. It also looks at how nonverbal indications of deception can be detected through careful observation.

MOVEMENT

Say "nonverbal communication" to most people, and they probably think of movement, which is technically kinesics. Nonverbal communication consists of far more than just one general category, but movement is the most studied of the categories. It includes gestures, posture, and stance as well as bodily movement.

As summarized in Table 10–2, gestures may include *emblems, illustrators, regulators, affect displays,* and *adapters.*[14] While people usually use gestures without thinking, a conscious awareness of them can help a manager communicate more efficiently. An understanding of, and training in, effective signals can open up the possibility of our strategic, conscious use of them. A leader in customer service, The Walt Disney Company, understands the power of nonverbals. The Disney Institute, the company's consulting division, teaches employees at all their theme parks to give directions by pointing with two fingers rather than one because it seems more polite. Similarly, if a teacher calls on a student by extending an open palm rather than pointing a finger at the student, it seems more respectful and welcoming.

Earlier, we noted that nonverbal signals usually suggest meaning; they do not give direct meaning. *Emblems* are an exception in that they actually stand for something else. The OK sign is one example; another is the time out—one palm held at a right angle to the other.

Table 10–2	Types of Gestures
Emblems	
Illustrators	
Regulators	
Affect Displays	
Adapters	

Illustrators complement verbal communication by providing an example of, or reinforcing, what is being said. When a person is trying to explain an item that is not present, what is more natural than drawing it in the air?

Regulators are gestures that both subtly and obviously control what a speaker says. They arise from a variety of sources, including the hands—for example, when one holds up the hand palm outward to keep another from interrupting. Turning the palm toward you and wiggling the fingers is a beckoning gesture in the United States. We also regulate to draw some speakers out and rein others in with gestures.

The *affect display* is more complex than most gestures and involves several parts of the body. For example, suppose you are talking to someone who has a scowl on his face as he sits up straight but is turned slightly away from you. His arms cross his chest, and you have little doubt this person does not like the idea under discussion. The affect display signals to another person what we are feeling and can show pleasure as well as anger, boredom as well as interest. Reading such nonverbal signals from others is rarely a problem. The challenge lies in controlling these within ourselves in some situations. We may not always want to show what we are feeling, so we must control these nonverbals, particularly if it could affect our current communication strategy.

The *adapter* may be the least appreciated source of kinesic messages; however, it can be quite important. In many situations, when one behavior might be inappropriate, the body will adapt by sending signals that would provide a solution, if one could only implement it. For example, the person wishing to leave, but unable to do so, might start to move his crossed leg in imitation of walking. Another person under stress may begin to twist the paper clip she is holding as a socially acceptable substitute for what she would like to do with the person she is reprimanding. That employee being reprimanded may wrap his arms around himself as a sort of substitute hug to provide the comfort he needs at that moment. A nervous speaker may rock to calm herself. Adapters often appear as a pattern of seemingly irrelevant nonverbal signals, but to the careful observer, their presence may suggest discomfort. Similarly, in stressful situations when projecting an image of self-control is crucial, be aware of the nonverbal signals you may be sending. Keeping a calm face while clenching your fists may reveal more than intended.

While gestures may be the most obvious example of meaningful movement, other kinesic behaviors contribute significantly to message meaning as well. Take posture, for example. Slumping, leaning, standing with weight on one leg, and rounding the shoulders all connote weakness and lack of confidence. By contrast, standing at military attention (head up, shoulders back, chest forward, and weight evenly distributed on both feet) connotes power, alertness, and confidence. Managers who have mastered the elements of good posture often are attended to even before they begin to speak.

Amy Cuddy, a Harvard Business School professor who specializes in nonverbal communication, delivered a TED talk in 2012 that explained how "faking" body language associated with dominance could actually improve a person's self-image. Since then, 16 million viewers have watched her talk on YouTube, putting it in the top 5 of all 1,600 TED talks. Dr. Cuddy argued that "power posing" with head erect and arms and legs out-stretched not only gives others the impression that one is worthy of belief and respect, but it actually helps the poser to also adopt those beliefs about himself. In short, she points out, "Fake it 'til you make it and then you will become it."[15]

Another example of kinesic communication is head movement. As mentioned in the previous chapter, a good listener often indicates that he is paying attention by nodding and/or tilting his head. On the other hand, a speaker who nods or tilts his head while talking may be interpreted as unsure of himself or even submissive.

Mimicry is a form of gesturing where two people mirror each other's movements. It is typically an unconscious and automatic behavior triggered by an abundance of mirroring neurons in the brain. Mimicry has been shown to positively influence the flow of conversation, as well as mutual liking. The back-and-forth exchange of smiles, head nods, arm crossing, and hand movements creates this social circuit that leaves two people feeling better and better about the other person. Studies have proven this to be true in salary negotiations and job interviews, where ample mimicking correlated to strong feelings of trust and likeability.[16] We also communicate meaning by the way we walk. When a speaker strides quickly to the platform, she seems energetic, bold, and in command of the situation. Her credibility is enhanced by this nonverbal element. However, if she walks around while speaking or perhaps sways, rocks, or shifts her weight from foot to foot repeatedly, her impression is diminished.

STOP AND THINK

The next time you are dining with friends or family, deliberately take a sip of water, or wipe your lips with your napkin, or lean away from the table. What happens next? Yes, within a minute everyone else at the table will mimic your nonverbal behavior.

To summarize, movement is a very important category of nonverbal communication. We pay attention to various parts of a communicator's body—head, trunk, arms, legs—as we watch and listen, drawing inferences from their movements. A list of common interpretations of kinesic cues appears in Table 10–3. But take note: As you will read in Chapter 11, our culture defines both verbal and nonverbal behavior, so keep in mind that the "meanings" of the kinesic cues in the table may change from culture to culture. For example, head nodding is a sign of affirmation in the United States, but it's a sign of disagreement in the South Slavic States, Iran, and Sri Lanka. Managers in any culture must attend to kinesics when they communicate so that their body language contributes to, rather than contradicts or detracts from, the intended meaning.

SPATIAL MESSAGES

Proxemics refers to the space around us and how we and others relate to it. Space and distance can reveal much and merit careful attention. Most people hearing "proxemics"

Table 10–3   Kinesic Cues

Body Segment	Movement	Interpretation
Head	Gazing	Attentive; honest
	Shifting, darting eyes	Uncertain; lying
	Eyebrows up	Challenging; open
	Smiling mouth	Enjoyment; pleasure
	Nodding	Listening; agreeing
	Tilting head	Interested
	Head down	Defensive
Trunk and shoulders	Leaning toward	Interested; rapport
	Leaning away	Lack of interest; skeptical
	Posture slouched	Low self-esteem
	Expanded chest	Confident
	Shrunken chest	Threatened
	Buttoning jacket	Formal; leaving
Hands and arms	Touching others	Powerful
	Touching self	Nervous; anxious
	Repetitive movements	Lying; unsure of self
	Hand over mouth while speaking	Want to escape
	Arms crossed	Bored; closed to ideas
	Fingers steepled	Confident
	Hands on hips	Challenging; arrogant
	Hands in pockets	Secretive
	Palms showing	Trusting
	Pointing	Authoritative; aggressive
	Clenched hands; wringing hands; picking cuticle	Need reassurance

think only of personal space, the personal "bubble" surrounding a person. That is a good place to start, but the concept encompasses far more than just that.

Spatial Zones

Edward Hall studied use of personal distances and determined that Americans have four arbitrarily established proxemic zones, described in Figure 10–1, in which we interact.[17] Strategic managers are aware of these zones and appreciate how they and others react when their spaces are invaded.

Our language suggests we all are aware of personal space to some degree. We talk about someone "keeping his distance," or we complain when we perceive others "invading our space," or say "They are crowding me on this issue" when in fact what they are doing has little to do with territory. When someone is pressing another on an issue, the other person may respond, "Give me breathing room," or less politely, "Keep out of my face."

In the United States, business people generally operate within four zones: intimate, personal, social, and public. In the discussion that follows, keep in mind that the figures are averages. They reflect the general culture, situational mandates, and the relationship between the parties. A number of factors enter into any interpersonal exchange. These can include personal appearance, culture, gender, and age. Thus, we may react differently to a tall person compared to a short person, and we may draw nearer to an attractive person than to another who is less attractive.[18]

As discussed in the next chapter, meanings for nonverbal behaviors differ from culture to culture. In the United States, the *intimate zone* ranges from physical contact to roughly 1.5 to 2 feet. It is reserved for those who are psychologically close. When others invade it, especially for more than a moment, a person usually feels uncomfortable and is likely to draw back or put up some sort of barrier, although often without consciously knowing why.

The *personal zone* extends from the edge of the intimate zone out to roughly 4 feet. Americans reserve it for close friends but permit others to enter it temporarily during introductions. Watch as two strangers come together for an introduction. As they shake hands, they will often stand with one leg forward and the other ready to back up. Then, when the greeting is over, both will usually retreat into the next zone. Cooperating on a task or simultaneously studying a document may bring people into their personal space, but they typically compensate by not making eye contact.

The next area is the *social zone*. It extends from about 4 feet to 12 feet and is the space in which we would like to conduct much of our daily business. Relationships between managers and their employees might begin in this area and continue for a time. They will often move into the personal zone once trust has developed, but this takes time.[19] In the US culture, the *public zone* extends beyond 12 feet and reflects the distance at which most would like to keep strangers. Little communication of a business nature takes place in this zone. Perhaps the only spoken communication that occurs is the public speech. We see the formal institutionalized reflection of this distance in the arrangement of public auditoriums

Figure 10–1 Spatial Zones

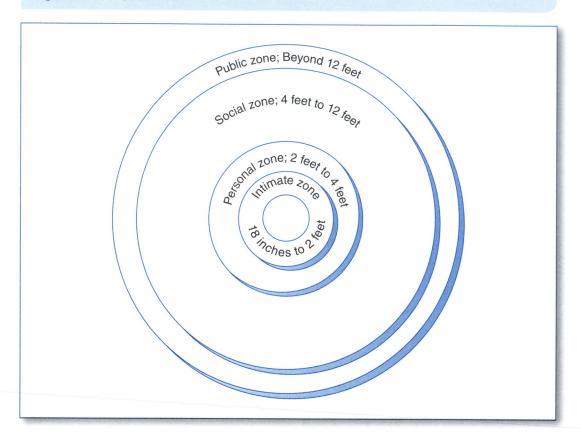

or even in the layout of many political rallies. Even if the latter is not too crowded, the audience will often keep its distance.

For managers, the value of understanding spatial zones is clear. An observant communicator can gauge the relative warmth that exists in a relationship by the distances individuals keep during interactions. As trust grows, distances generally diminish. Thus, allies sit next to each other in meetings. However, other factors determine spatial differences as well. Let us consider some of these.

Spatial Differences

As we have said, proxemic zones vary from culture to culture. For example, businesspeople in many South American and Arab countries typically interact with people at far closer ranges than do US businesspeople. Often, when people from the United States interact with individuals from these cultures, the varying proxemic zones expected by the groups create awkwardness until someone adapts to the needs of the others and either gives up some ground or extends the distance.

Distance preferences also vary by gender. Men tend to maintain larger personal space bubbles than do women. Women are more likely to allow men or other women to come closer than men, and women will be more tolerant of temporary violations of their own space.[20] Men take up more space with their bodies and their artifacts, a tendency that is often perceived as indicating power.

A recent study of 850 workers at midsize companies resulted in interesting gender differences regarding workspace preferences. Women voiced preferences for privacy, natural light, and the option to personalize their space. Men, on the other hand, spoke out strongly for just one environmental attribute: the ability to control the room temperature.[21]

STOP AND THINK

The next time you are in a meeting, look around the table at the amount of space each person takes up. Do you see any consistencies across gender? Age? Power?

Naturally, circumstances may artificially affect our use of zones. The classic example of this is the crowded elevator, where people allow others to invade personal and intimate zones. Here, though, people will try to adapt by avoiding eye contact or blocking—that is, by folding the arms across the chest or putting up their briefcases as a sort of shield. If someone accidentally touches another, apologies quickly follow.

When traditional zones need to be ignored for an extended period, people will stake out their territory. One way is to create even spacing between participants, as when seated around a meeting table with movable seats. In other situations, people will erect some sort of barrier to signal the limits of their own space. Watch at meetings around a conference table as people unconsciously arrange notebooks, jackets, coffee cups, and other business artifacts around the perimeters of their territory. They are signaling where the boundaries of their personal space lie in that crowded environment. Similarly, students in a class typically occupy the same seat throughout the term, claiming it as "their" space and piling their belongings around them.

Permanent, or "fixed," spaces such as cubicles or large desks often are perceived as barriers. It is rude to come behind the boss's desk or peek over the top of the cubicle. But semifixed spaces such as conference tables can connote cooperation and shared responsibility (see Figure 10–2), as the next section explains.

Strategic Use of Space

Managers should be aware that intruding into another's territory without an invitation can be an annoyance or even a threat, no matter what a person's rank. Recognizing the boundaries of both fixed and semifixed spaces communicates respect to the individual. Artifacts belonging to another individual should be regarded as personal. One should never rifle through a coworker's desk drawers for writing implements or sit on the edge of that person's desk.

Managers can use space to create an air of power and authority or an air of collegiality and respect. Everyone reads the environment for nonverbal clues. The amount of space allotted to another, the amount of privacy that space entails, and where in the building that space is located can speak volumes about organizational power. Generally, more is better than less, bigger is better than smaller, and especially in the United States, new is better than old. In addition, the closer people are to the organization's leaders, the more power they are perceived by others to enjoy.

On the other hand, managers who value open communication will work in proximity to their subordinates and coworkers, will minimize status-filled artifacts such as heavy furniture, and will discourage territoriality. Indeed, contemporary organizations require that all employees share their "space" as a symbol of cooperation and teamwork. When Michael Bloomberg was elected mayor of New York City, he rearranged New York City Hall to resemble a giant, open bullpen, eliminating private offices. This look resembled the trading area at Salomon Brothers, the investment firm where he had been a partner. Again, his aim was to free the flow of information. In 2014, when Bill de Blasio became mayor of New York City, he decided to keep his predecessor's open-air office arrangement, though he had criticized it during the campaign.

Office design can put the right people together. At WPP, a British marketing group (formerly Wire and Plastics Product), walls were removed and coffee areas created. Rather than assigning accountants and media people to separate floors, they work side by side in teams to ensure that they keep talking to each other.[22]

Some studies have noted differences in office space preferences among age groups. In one study, 40 percent of younger workers, commonly labeled Generation Y or Millennials (born between 1980 and 2000), preferred to work in open office plans; only 18 percent said

Figure 10–2   Fixed and Semifixed Space in the Same Office

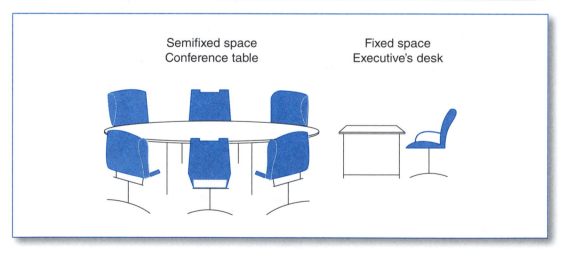

Semifixed space
Conference table

Fixed space
Executive's desk

they preferred cubicles with privacy panels. Older workers, on the other hand, said they worked best in private offices (45 percent); just 16 percent said they preferred collaborative spaces.[23]

PERSONAL APPEARANCE

The old saying "beauty is only skin deep" may not be true in the business world. Recent studies have identified a connection between wages and appearance. Daniel Hamermesh, a University of Texas economist who has studied the beauty benefit for twenty years, determined that above-average-looking men earn 17 percent more than below-average-looking men, and above-average-looking women earn 12 percent more than below-average-looking women. That translates into $230,000 more earnings over a lifetime, on average.[24]

Further, there appears to be significant agreement about what is considered attractive. For one thing, height is a factor. In the United States, the average adult male is 5 feet 9 inches tall, yet 30 percent of CEOs are at least 6 feet 2 inches. Another aspect of appearance that equates with success is a strong chin. Among forty-two CEOs from the top 50 *Fortune 500* companies, some 90 percent showed nonreceding-to-prominent chins, versus 40 percent of the US population. Apparently, we equate such jawlines with business success and confidence.[25]

Aspects of our appearance such as height, chin prominence, and physical beauty are not easily changed. One might argue that they should not be relevant factors for business success, anyway. Nevertheless, most business people try to maximize the positive impact of their appearance, and one relatively simple way to reach that goal is with our choice of clothing. What we wear says much about who we are, or at least who we want to be perceived as. Dress is an integral part of the first impression we form on meeting someone and is often the key to initial credibility.[26] Consequently, managers should pay close attention to what they wear in order to send the right message to others. This section will focus on general principles for effective dress since clothing styles are so changeable. One piece of advice is enduring, though. Be neither the first nor the last to adopt a fashion.

The key to dress is to fit in with the organization's culture, to show by your appearance that you have adopted the organization's values. Thus, financial institutions expect employees to look conservative, assuring customers and clients of their stability. Ad agency employees are often expected to dress more fashion forward, indicating their flair, creativity, and contemporary style. High-tech organizations de-emphasize a "corporate" appearance, to the extent that executives are dressed as casually as the lowest-level employee. Mark Zuckerberg, founder and CEO of Facebook, Inc., is one of the world's wealthiest and most influential business leaders and philanthropists. His typical casual style of dressing in a T-shirt, hooded sweatshirt, and jeans has become the norm for people in his industry. Why? Mr. Zuckerberg's style reflects his personal values, as stated on his own Facebook page: "openness, making things that help people connect and share what's important to them, . . . minimalism."

The occasion will also dictate personal appearance. While observing people at events such as weddings and funerals may lead one to conclude that our culture is moving toward more informality, in many business settings, casual dress is considered disrespectful. Job interviews, client visits, and sales presentations call for careful attention to appearance. Recruiters often draw conclusions about applicants based on the style and condition of their footwear and hair. Thus, when shopping for an "interview suit," applicants should also shop for dress shoes.

Managers must remember that everyday appearance also conveys important messages. Many contemporary organizations have developed a detailed dress code or employee uniform in recognition of the importance of personal appearance. According to a 2006 survey by the Society for Human Resource Management, six in ten employers allow a dress-down day at least once a week. But the number of employers allowing casual dress every day has plunged from 53 percent in 2002 to a new low of 38 percent.[27] The reason for the return to more dressy attire is, in part, because of the confusion generated by business casual standards. But mostly, managers have the impression that when employees dress casually, the quality of the work suffers.

Legal issues can arise from dress policies, too. Employers must be careful to enforce dress codes on all employees, not just one group (such as women) to avoid accusations of discrimination. In 2007 a Phoenix, Arizona, jury awarded $287,000 to a Somali employee who had worked at Alamo Rent A Car. The Equal Employment Opportunity Commission argued that the company engaged in religious discrimination for firing her when, as a practicing Muslim, she wore the hijab, a type of head scarf, during the holy month of Ramadan.[28] Employers whose dress codes require wearing certain apparel or refraining from wearing certain apparel need to show business justification for the requirements, reasonably accommodate their employees' religious beliefs, or ask the employees to seek an exemption from wearing religious garb while on duty.

STOP AND THINK

1. Look around your workplace. Is the old advice, "dress for the job you want, not the job you have," still true?

2. To what extent is appearance a relevant factor in hiring and promotion decisions in your organization?

Observers always assign meaning to details such as accessories, color, jewelry, and emblems worn on the jacket lapel or hat. A prominent example of the symbolic nature of clothing is IBM. In Lou Gerstner's book, *Who Says Elephants Can't Dance?,* the former CEO describes how he revitalized the failing corporation. One of his major efforts was culture change, and one of his methods was prescribing changes in employee dress. The famous "old" IBM look had been crisp white shirts, dark suits, and conservative ties. Originally, it had been adopted to match customer expectations. But by 1993, when Gerstner took over, it seemed anachronistic, stuffy, and emblematic of the company's demise. The "new" IBM look was more casual and contemporary. Again, Gerstner advises, "Dress according to the circumstances of your day and recognize who you will be with (customers, government leaders, or just your colleagues . . .)."[29]

In summary, no matter whether the organization's culture is formal or casual, no matter whether the occasion is special or ordinary, managers' appearance should reflect the expectations and values of their audience. By adhering to the principle of "fitting in," managers will enhance their credibility and improve their communication effectiveness.

VOICE

The final source of nonverbal signals this chapter will focus on is paralanguage, or vocal style. The spoken word contains more than linguistic cues. Nonverbal aspects of vocal delivery include the pitch, rate, volume, tone, onset, and duration of messages. These cues are among the least obvious to most listeners, with the likely exception of tone, yet they can be as important as, or even more important than, the actual words used.[30] The pitch of the speaker's voice, the onset of the message—that is, the time that it takes between the person's taking the turn and the message's beginning—and the length of the message send subtle cues.

The following is an example of the effect of onset. If we are asking someone about a serious issue and the person's responses come more quickly than expected, we might suspect he is not serious or has rehearsed the responses. Similarly, when someone takes far longer to answer a question than expected, we begin to wonder if all that is being said is true. And, as the discussion in the next section on nonverbal signs of deception shows, we even monitor pitch and can read meaning into changes of it.

Here is another example of how pitch affects the impression. Spoken English sentences follow certain pitch patterns, depending on their meaning. That is, declaratory sentences (statements) end with a dropped pitch, and interrogatory sentences (questions that ask for a yes or no response) end with a raised pitch. A common violation of these pitch patterns, known as "uptalk," occurs when speakers end their statements with a raised pitch, making them sound like questions. The listener, noticing the uptalk, often concludes that the speaker is unsure of the truth of their statements and is asking for validation. In a business meeting, when someone says, "Here's what I think the customer wants," with a raised pitch at the end, others may well conclude that the speaker in fact does not know what the customer wants.

The importance of vocal cues to managers is obvious in sending as well as receiving. It is important to monitor the signals being sent, particularly for tone, to ensure that the intended communication strategy is not being undermined by subtle nonverbal cues.

Speakers have a typical vocal style that distinguishes their voice from that of other speakers. The elements consist of a basic pitch, rate, pause pattern, and volume. Certain characteristics of voice are also regional in origin, such as articulation and pacing. The southern US drawl and the northeastern US clipped dialect are examples. In addition to these basic vocal characteristics, speakers can vary their pitch, rate, and volume to emphasize their meaning and to communicate emotion. Failure to vary these vocal characteristics results in what is commonly known as a monotonal vocal style. In the US business culture, a monotonal speaking style connotes lack of interest and even lack of authority. Managers may unintentionally undermine their message by the style in which it is delivered. Chapter 5 described good vocal style in more detail, but these criteria apply to everyday speaking as well as to formal presentations.

To summarize, in business, speaking in a clear, firm, low-pitched voice connotes confidence and results in more attentive listening. Nasal, shrill, quiet, breathy, or harsh voices are devalued. Excessive use of filled pauses ("uh," "well,") gives an impression of uncertainty. Managers must learn to use their vocal characteristics to maximize the message, rather than detract from it, just as they must use the preceding nonverbal categories.

APPLICATIONS OF NONVERBAL COMMUNICATION RESEARCH

Until recently, the impact of managers' nonverbal behavior was impossible to objectively measure. However, researchers at the Human Dynamics Group of the Massachusetts Institute of Technology (MIT) Media Lab have developed a range of small, wearable electronic devices that can easily and accurately gather data on tone of voice, proximity, and body language.[31] Their data about these nonverbal communication patterns can be applied to improving communication effectiveness in business settings.

Phone Sales and Service

In one case, the MIT researchers worked with a British call center outsourcing company, Vertex Data Science, to improve the effectiveness of call center operators. The MIT group used electronic sensors (or e-sensors) to measure the speech patterns of operators during calls with customers. The group did not measure the actual words used by the operators but focused on variations in tone and pitch as well as the amount of time that the operators spent talking versus listening to the callers. The researchers concluded that successful operators spend more time listening than talking and use strong fluctuations in their voice amplitude and pitch to suggest interest and responsiveness to the customers' needs. After only a few seconds of measuring these factors, the researchers were able to accurately predict the eventual success or failure of a call the majority of the time.[32]

Teams and Meetings

The results of the MIT studies have implications for team communication. As discussed in Chapter 4, *groupthink* is a common problem in teams. That is, individuals often conform to the perceived group consensus despite their personal reservations. E-sensors measuring nonverbal communication behaviors could potentially help prevent groupthink by raising awareness of nonverbal communication patterns of individual team members. For example, one or two individuals in the team might be overbearing while not realizing that their nonverbal behaviors discourage others from voicing their opinions. The MIT group believes that they could eventually use e-sensors to select team members with complementary nonverbal communication styles so that the team would be "optimized" for communication effectiveness. Further, they believe they can create "smart environments" by using e-sensors to identify negative nonverbal behaviors in real time, thereby allowing them to prevent communication breakdowns.

The MIT research results can also be applied to formal meetings. Managers may inadvertently sabotage meetings by using inappropriate nonverbal communication or sending incongruent verbal and nonverbal messages. E-sensors can determine whether a manager is using enough vocal variation or body movement to convey the importance of a message. E-sensors also can show the manager what behaviors are confusing the meeting participants, eventually leading to more effective and efficient meeting management.

Body language can affect the outcome of negotiations during meetings. In a separate study, the MIT group simulated face-to-face salary negotiations and was able to accurately predict the "winner" of the negotiation with 87 percent accuracy after only five minutes of measuring body movement patterns.

Informal Communication

Informal coworker conversations are a common method of spreading messages throughout a company, and nonverbal communication is a part of how these messages are interpreted. E-sensors developed by the MIT researchers have been used to monitor nonverbal communication in informal settings; the data on proximity, body language, and vocal style allow more accurate sharing of information, with more people being on the same page.

For example, Bob from the accounting department has a habit of standing very close to coworkers when he talks to them, making listeners uneasy. Data from wearable e-sensors that compare the proximity of individuals during their informal communication events would make Bob aware that he stands the closest to others during conversations and that his messages are also least likely to be conveyed effectively. Bob would then give listeners more space, allowing them to relax and concentrate on what he is trying to tell them.

External Communication

Customer service is another area where data about nonverbal communication patterns can be used to benefit the company. Vertex Data Science's use of electronic monitoring of their call center operators (described above) is one example. Sales teams and customer service personnel (e.g., hotel reservation clerks) could also receive valuable information from studies like the one conducted at Vertex. Again, the goal is to improve the level of service that customers receive, resulting in more business and an enhanced company reputation.

Nonverbal communication research can be applied to customer service in the tourism and hospitality industry. Following service failure, customers want their problems resolved as quickly as possible and, in doing so, they have certain expectations with respect to service providers' behavior. During this period of anxiety, customers are particularly vigilant about nonverbal cues in attempting to discern the service provider's intentions and attitudes. The display of inappropriate nonverbal behaviors, such as frowning, lack of eye contact, and closed body posture, is likely to create even more negative feelings.[33] The ability to objectively measure nonverbal communication with e-sensors and use that information to train customer service employees would greatly benefit the organization.

Another application of this type of research is with managers who operate in the global economy. As you will read in Chapter 11, acceptable nonverbal behavior varies from culture to culture and country to country. E-sensor data could be used to train business travelers in the most effective nonverbal communication patterns for the country and culture that they will be working in.

Finally, independent agencies (such as advertising firms) and/or individuals within a corporation who participate in business-to-business (B2B) relationships with other professionals could benefit from the use of e-sensors that measure nonverbal communication. These individuals regularly make formal presentations and give briefings to clients and other executives. E-sensor data would help them learn the most effective nonverbal communication patterns, such as conveying confidence, during presentations. Other applications include effectively using nonverbal communication to convey negative messages and strengthen client relationships.

NONVERBAL SIGNS OF DECEPTION

In many situations, managers must evaluate other employees to determine if the data they work with are accurate. While the data set out in a report can usually be tested objectively, information derived from interpersonal interactions such as disciplinary and preemployment screening interviews frequently offers little opportunity for immediate objective verification. Fortunately, some nonverbal signals can help managers assess the veracity of verbal statements. As we have seen, nonverbal signals usually complement verbal ones and serve as needed reinforcement to reduce the uncertainty in communication. However, they may also unintentionally contradict the verbal ones they accompany.

When contradictory nonverbal signals betray deception, they are called *leakage*. During deception, certain types of nonverbal signals often escape from the deceiver despite attempts at control. The subconscious apparently betrays the speaker through this nonverbal leakage. People also often unconsciously read and interpret these signals. Managers can learn to spot nonverbal signs of deception.

Several patterns of nonverbal behavior crop up during deception.[34] Since some sources of nonverbal signals can be controlled in deceptive situations better than others—for example, looking another in the eye while deceiving—we will focus on signals that are difficult to control consciously. These include movement, dress, personal space, and voice.

Remember that nonverbal behavior usually *suggests* meaning rather than having a one-to-one correlation with a specific word or concept. The meaning of nonverbal signs might vary, and a gesture might be motivated by something besides what is suggested here.

To detect possible nonverbal signs of deception, it is important to be in the right place. Often, interviewees are seated behind desks so significant cues go undetected. The face, always likely to be visible, can be a poor source of deception cues (although hand-to-face contacts are valuable cues). When possible, seat the other person in an open chair facing you. Nonverbal signs from the hands, trunk, legs, or feet then will be more evident.[35]

Baseline

Deception signs are behaviors that differ from normal nonverbal interactions, so you also need to know what behavior is normal for that individual. Researchers have found that when observers see an individual giving honest answers before the person is seen lying, the observers' ability to detect dishonesty increases significantly over situations with no behavioral baseline. You do not detect dishonesty by looking for the lie, according to psychologist Paul Ekman of the University of California–San Francisco, but by identifying the change in behavior that suggests a person is nervous when he/she should not be.[36]

The individual's baseline is also invaluable because one person might behave differently from others in identical circumstances. A baseline allows one to gauge if nervous behavior reflects the overall situation or is a reaction to the question being asked.

In the job interview, a baseline is relatively easy. During the preliminary chat, ask non-threatening questions. Begin with the résumé before moving into the unknown. Watch for nonverbal cues. An investigatory interrogation could use the same pattern. Small talk serves its traditional primary purpose of putting the other at ease and a secondary one of providing a behavioral baseline.

The following sections identify some typical signs of deception as summarized in Table 10–4.

Table 10–4   Nonverbal Signs of Deception
Unexpected movements and gestures
Manipulation of clothing
Increase of personal space
Vocal variations

Movement

Gestures and trunk movements, part of the broad category of kinesics, are probably the most valuable nonverbal signs of deception. Perhaps the most common deception-related gestures are the hand-to-face movements, and the most common of these is the mouth cover. More subtle is the single finger to the mouth, the moustache stroke, or the nose rub. Other gestures suggesting deception are nail biting and lip biting. Hiding the hands by putting them in pockets or pulling shirtsleeves down to the fingertips is a sign that the person is "hiding" something more than their hands.

Conversational gestures vary as well. Generally, when one is comfortable with honest responses, gestures are open and outward. During deception, people both limit their gestures and keep them closer to the body. And while smiling decreases and the frequency of gestures used to illustrate conversational points slows down in deception, the gestures suggesting deception increase. One of these is the hand shrug emblem. Researchers have found that deceptive speakers will *shrug their hands*—turning the palms up from palms down position—twice as frequently as in nondeceptive messages. This signal suggests a subconscious pleading for the listener to believe what is being said.

Some authorities also believe that an increase in leg and foot movements may indicate deception.[37] Foot tapping, leg rocking while the legs are crossed, and frequent shifts in leg posture are examples of this kind of activity. A rhythmic "walking" motion with one crossed leg has long been recognized as an intention gesture suggesting the person would like to walk away. But keep in mind the need to compare behavior with the baseline.

Signals of deception are not just confined to the body. They can involve dress, space, and voice.

Dress

With clothing, nonverbal leakage mainly shows up in the manipulation of dress, which may suggest a respondent feels threatened by a given question. An interviewee may suddenly close and button his or her coat or begin to tug nervously at a pants leg or skirt hem. This may betray a fear of having some deception uncovered. Other signals include straightening or tugging at the collar, smoothing the tie, picking at lint, or rubbing at a spot.

Personal Space

Proxemics, relating to the distance that one keeps from others as well as one's relation to the surrounding environment, may be a rich source of deception cues. An interviewee might shift the chair's position or might suddenly lean back on the chair's rear legs. Moving away from the interviewer may show a lack of cooperativeness or be a feeble attempt to put distance between the interviewee and interviewer by altering the environment. Often, when a person physically backs up, the other person comes closer. In formal conversations occurring while standing, the interviewee may lean back or step back during a deceptive response even while blocking by folding the arms across the chest.

An interviewee who has been relaxed may shift under pressure. For example, deception may leak out when the person suddenly crosses her arms and legs and leans back. The vulnerable forward posture is less comfortable when facing the fear of discovery. Conversely, an interviewee might "open up" during a response, suggesting openness and honesty. An interviewee may also try to erect "signal blunders" to hide behind. These may be such subtle activities as placing a purse or briefcase in the lap as a barrier.

Artifacts

One's personal possessions in the office and the physical environment of the office itself offer cues, and they can be manipulated to create the intended perception. Some people will meticulously decorate their offices in an attempt to manage the impressions of their visitors. Although many of these decorations can reflect honest identity claims, some can be strategic and even deceptive.[38] How many times have you been lured back to a car salesperson's office to find an overabundance of religious symbols? How about cute kiddie photos? They seem to say, "You can trust me. I'm a man of faith, and a family man, and I would never give you a raw deal." Excessively showcasing awards, plaques, and framed certificates on a "brag wall" is an all-too-common attempt at self-promotion. Personal effects in the office should be used as clues toward the bigger picture of who the real person is, but the impression they give off needs to be interpreted carefully.

Voice

Voice is another rich source of cues. Most relevant in detecting deception are the voice's pitch, tone, and volume, as well as the response's onset and duration. Authorities have long known that deceptive answers have a slower onset than honest ones.

In addition, deceptive answers are likely to be longer and less specific than honest ones. The deceiver may be attempting to fill in the gap with needless material. Some see length as an attempt to make a deceptive answer more elaborate and thus more convincing than the deceiver knows it is. The answer's length may also reflect the pauses and hesitations needed as the interviewee stumbles through the answer.

The final source of deception is pitch. Researchers have found that vocal pitch rises measurably in deceptive responses. While observers frequently could not say why they labeled such a response as deceptive, they knew it was, and research instruments could show the difference.[39]

In many interpersonal, managerial interactions, nonverbal elements are the source of most of the message. While not everything communicated nonverbally is done so consciously or intentionally, the unintentional signals may be as valid as the intentional ones and potentially more useful. Keep in mind, though, the suggestions about establishing a behavioral baseline for each person in specific situations. In addition, if deception is suspected, use that as an impetus for further investigation or at least caution, not as the final word.

SUMMARY

Everything but the words themselves may be considered the domain of nonverbal communication. Every managerial interaction has nonverbal elements that add to or qualify the interaction. It is difficult to put precise meanings to nonverbal signals, and they vary from culture to culture; however, when nonverbal signals contradict verbal ones, the non-verbal signals are usually the ones to trust.

Nonverbal cues have six functions: complementing, accenting, contradicting, repeating, regulating, and substituting. In addition, nonverbal cues add redundancy to the verbal message and increase the probability that the verbal message will be understood as intended by the sender.

The study of movement includes gestures, posture, head movement, and walk. Gestures may include emblems, illustrators, affect displays, regulators, and adapters. The space around us and how we and others relate to it are also important. Four zones are presented and discussed in this chapter, but care must be taken in interpreting them because zones may differ among cultures. Inappropriate use of space may make a manager appear rude, while an accurate analysis of space indicates much about the importance of power in an organization.

Personal appearance is another integral part of the impression we give and often the key to credibility. Consequently, managers should pay close attention to their clothing, accessories, makeup, hairstyle, and grooming to be sure their appearance fits the expectations of the organization's culture and customers.

Voice is the final source of nonverbal signals discussed in the chapter. Vocal delivery includes the pitch, tone, onset, and duration of messages.

The first step to detecting deception is to establish a baseline. Once this has been accomplished, movement, dress, space, and voice can each be used to evaluate the potential for deception in an interaction. But in all managerial communication situations, it is important to remember that no dictionary exists for the meaning of nonverbal cues.

Cases for Small-Group Discussion

CASE 10–1

Jumping to Conclusions

Julie D'Souza was a recent hire of Mantle Data, Inc. She was distressed as she walked toward the office of her supervisor. She had experienced some strange interactions with one of her male coworkers and felt compelled to say something about it.

Dana Kilpatrick, her supervisor, had an open-door policy. Julie knocked on her door and said, "Do you have a few minutes?"

"Sure, Julie. Come on in," said Dana. "What's on your mind?"

"I think one of my coworkers is hitting on me, or something. It's Rick—when I pass him in the hallway he says, 'Whoo!,' and he turns his head and looks at my backside. Oh, and the other day, he growled at me in the lounge. And he clicks his tongue . . ." Julie added.

"OK, that is strange," Dana agreed. "Have you told him it makes you uncomfortable?"

"Well, no, I was hoping you could give me some advice about how to handle this. I've never had a guy act like this toward me before," Julie said.

"Let me talk to the divisional manager," replied Dana. "He knows Rick, and I think he hired him years ago. I'll see what he says."

"OK, thank you," Julie said as she left the office.

About two hours later, Dana met with the divisional manager, Rob Watkins. Rob cleared things up rather succinctly; he explained that Rick had a very mild form of Asperger's syndrome, an autism spectrum disorder that is characterized by significant difficulties in social interaction and nonverbal communication, as well as restricted and repetitive patterns of behavior. Although Rick was categorized as high functioning (able to carry out typical requirements of living), he did retain some quirky behavioral traits, such as involuntary movements or sounds, and awkward social interactions. But Rick was also a very talented and efficient programmer and a valuable employee of the firm. Rob was certain that Rick was not hitting on Julie but that perhaps he did like her, and seeing her might trigger some behavior that may appear to be flirty, but it was more likely a by-product of the Asperger's.

QUESTIONS

1. Do nonverbal communication principles apply in this case?

2. The US federal laws governing physical or mental impairments would apply in this case, since a medical diagnosis was present. What should Rick's coworkers and managers know about his condition and how to interact with him?

3. What would you recommend to Julie if you were in Dana's position?

CASE 10–2

Facing a Series of Interviews

Hanna Jenson recently applied for a position that involves supervising the work activities of a large comprehensive insurance company. She has just received a letter notifying her to report for an interview for this position in four days. The letter indicates Jenson will be required to attend a series of interviews as follows:

9:00 a.m.	Rodney Custer, personnel manager
10:00 a.m.	Ahmad Syed, department chief
11:00 a.m.	Bobbie Kent, medical claims supervisor

If Jenson gets the job, she will receive a substantial raise in salary as well as her first opportunity to gain supervisory experience. Therefore, she wants the job very badly and is concerned about how to prepare for each of the interviews.

Although she has never worked in this particular department, Jenson has worked for the company for several years. She knows Custer and Syed on a casual basis, but she has never met Kent. Custer is thirty-eight years old, meticulous in dress, and obviously very proud of the managerial accomplishments he has made since he became personnel manager two years ago. Jenson's friends in the department believe Custer is sexist and tends to hire men in supervisory positions if possible.

Syed is an elderly, rotund gentleman who will be eligible for retirement in two years. He is somewhat unkempt in appearance, but his knowledge of policy and regulations has earned him the respect of managers throughout the company.

Jenson is especially concerned about the interview with Kent. If she gets the job, she will be working directly under Kent, yet she knows nothing about her.

QUESTIONS

1. What positive and negative suggestions would you give Jenson about her choice of dress for this interview?

2. What effective nonverbal signals would you suggest Jenson send during the interview, given the profiles of two of the individuals Jenson is to meet?

3. How could Jenson's strategy differ in each interview situation?

CASE 10–3

What Is Going on Here?

Art Margulis is the forty-five-year-old director of marketing research for a Fortune 500 consumer products company. He joined the firm nineteen years ago after he received his MBA with a marketing emphasis. Because of his technical expertise, management skills, and outgoing personality, he was made director of this fifty-person group four years ago. Six people report directly to him, but the management style is informal, so he frequently interacts with everyone in the department.

Two years ago, Margulis extensively recruited Maria Lopez, who had just completed her PhD in applied statistics. Margulis had a difficult time persuading her to join the company because she had many attractive offers. Although she was only thirty-four years old, she had outstanding experience in marketing research and a unique educational background. Lopez came in and quickly made a number of significant contributions to the department. As manager of statistical analysis, she reports directly to Margulis but has nobody reporting to her. Soon after joining the company, Lopez and her husband divorced. Many employees in the department believe her personal problems are why she has not been more sociable with other employees.

Lopez and Margulis have always gotten along well and often have lunch together to discuss various projects. They seem to have much in common as they both understand the advanced statistics used in the research. Recently, the conversations have turned more personal as Margulis went through a divorce and seems to be seeking more social support. In particular, he seems to miss his two teenage daughters and needs someone to talk to about it.

But Lopez sees a problem developing, and she recently talked to a human resource manager about it. She explained that she has a lot of respect for Margulis and enjoys visiting with him. But she notices a definite change in his behavior around her. The eye contact is more prolonged, and the personal physical space between them is reduced. Lopez feels uneasy about it and has tried to subtly change the trend. However, this only intensified what Lopez saw as pressure to spend more time with Margulis. Today, Margulis asked Lopez to have dinner with him so they could talk over a project. It seems they have not had time to cover the project during working hours.

QUESTIONS

Discuss this case in terms of nonverbal behavior and other topics presented in this chapter. What are the implications of this situation?

Student Study Site

Visit the Student Study Site at **study.sagepub.com/hynes6e** for web quizzes, video links, web resources, and cases studies.

Notes

1. Carol Lehman and Mark Lehman, "Effective Nonverbal Communication Techniques: Essential Element in the Promotional Strategies of Professional Service Firms," *Journal of Professional Services Marketing* 5, no. 1 (1989): p. 17.
2. Albert Mehrabian, "Communicating without Words," *Psychology Today,* September 1968, pp. 53–55.
3. Scott T. Fleishmann, *Employment Relations Today,* Summer 1991, pp. 161–162.
4. Roswitha Rothlach, "Anglo-German Misunderstandings in Language and Behavior," *Industrial and Commercial Training* 23, no. 3 (March 1991): pp. 15–16.
5. Om P. Kharbanda and Ernest A. Stallworthy, "Verbal and Non-verbal Communication," *Journal of Managerial Psychology* 6, no. 2 (April 1991): p. 49.
6. Larry H. Hynson Jr., "Doing Business with South Korea—Park II: Business Practices and Culture," *East Asian Executive Reports* 13 (September 15, 1991): p. 18.
7. Sandra G. Garside and Brian H. Kleiner, "Effective One-to-One Communication Skills," *Industrial and Commercial Training* 23, no. 7 (July 1991): p. 27.
8. Paul Ekman, *Emotions Revealed: Recognizing Faces and Feelings to Improve Communication and Emotional Life* (New York: Henry Holt, 2004).
9. R. P. Harrison, *Beyond Words: An Introduction to Nonverbal Communication* (Englewood Cliffs, NJ: Prentice Hall, 1974), p. 25.
10. Pam Belluck, "For a Creative Boost, Go Blue," *Houston Chronicle*, February 6, 2009.
11. Geraldine E. Hynes and Marius Janson, "Using Semiotic Analysis to Determine Effectiveness of Internet Marketing," *Proceedings of the 2007 Annual International Convention of the Association for Business Communication*, www.businesscommunication.org.
12. S. Burbinster, "Body Politics," *Associate & Management,* April 1987, pp. 55–57.
13. John L. Waltman, "Entropy and Business Communication," *Journal of Business Communication* 21, no. 1 (Winter 1984): pp. 63–80.
14. P. Ekman and W. Friesen, "The Repertoire of Nonverbal Behavior," *Semiotica* 1 (1969): pp. 49–98.
15. Amy Cuddy, "Your Body Language Shapes Who You Are," YouTube, October 1, 2012, http://www.youtube.com/watch?v = Ks-_Mh1QhMc.

16. Alex (Sandy) Pentland, *Honest Signals: How They Shape Our World* (Boston: MIT Press, 2008), pp. 10–40, 105.

17. Edward T. Hall, *The Hidden Dimension* (New York: Doubleday, 1966).

18. Loretta A. Malandro and Larry Barker, *Nonverbal Communication* (Reading, MA: Addison-Wesley, 1983), pp. 226–230.

19. Phillip L. Hunsaker, "Communicating Better: There's No Proxy for Proxemics," in *Reading in Business Communication,* ed. Richard C. Huseman (Hinsdale, IL: Dryden Press, 1981), p. 52.

20. Lynn Cohen, "Nonverbal (Mis)communication between Managerial Men and Women," *Business Horizons,* January–February 1983, p. 15.

21. Elizabeth Woyke, "Work Life: What Do Men Want? A Thermostat," *BusinessWeek*, May 29, 2006, p. 11.

22. "Press the Flesh, Not the Keyboard," *The Economist* 364, issue 8287 (August 24, 2002): p. 50.

23. Woyke, "Work Life."

24. Daniel Hamermesh, *Beauty Pays: Why Attractive People Are More Successful* (Princeton, NJ: Princeton University Press, 2011).

25. Kristie M. Engemann and Michael T. Owyang, "The Link between Wages and Appearance," *The Regional Economist*, April 2005, http://research.stlouisfed.org/publications/regional/05/04/appearance.pdf.

26. Lynn Pearl, "Opening the Door to Rapport," *Agri Marketing* 30, no. 2 (April 1992): p. 97.

27. Stephanie Armour, "Business Casual Causes Confusion," *USA Today*, July 16, 2007, accessed July 17, 2007, http://jobs.aol.com/article/a/business-casual-causes-confusion/20070716104409990002.

28. Ibid.

29. Louis V. Gerstner Jr., *Who Says Elephants Can't Dance? Inside IBM's Historic Turnaround* (New York: HarperCollins, 2002), p. 185.

30. Patricia Buhler, "Managing in the 90s: Are You Really Saying What You Mean?" *Supervision* 52, no. 9 (September 1991): p. 19.

31. Alex Pentland, *Honest Signals: How They Shape Our World* (Boston: MIT Press, 2008).

32. Mark Buchanan, "The Science of Subtle Signals," *Strategy + Business*, no. 48, August 29, 2007, www.strategy-business.com/press/article/07307?pg = all.

33. D. S. Sundaram and C. Webster, "The Role of Nonverbal Communication in Service Encounters," in S. Kusluvan, ed., *Managing Employee Attitudes and Behaviors in the Tourism and Hospitality Industries* (Hauppauge, NY: Nova Science, 2003), pp. 208–221.

34. Paul Ekman and Wallace V. Friesen, "Detecting Deception from the Body and Face," *Journal of Personality and Social Psychology* 29, no. 2 (1974): p. 295.

35. John L. Waltman, "Nonverbal Interrogation: Some Applications," *Journal of Police Science and Administration* 11, no. 2 (June 1983): p. 167.

36. Jeff Gammage, "Good Liars May Be Wired Differently," *Houston Chronicle,* January 29, 2006, p. 2D.

37. Charles J. McClintock and Raymond G. Hunt, "Nonverbal Indicators of Affect and Deception in Interview Situations," *Journal of Applied Psychology* 5, no. 3 (1975): p. 420.

38. Sam Gosling, *Snoop: What Your Stuff Says about You* (London: Profile Books, 2008), p. 13.

39. Paul Ekman, Wallace Friesen, and Klaus R. Scherer, "Body Movement and Voice Pitch in Deception Interaction," *Semiotica* 16, no. 11 (1976): p. 26.

CHAPTER 11

Intercultural Managerial Communication

The real death of America will come when everyone is alike.

—James T. Ellison, U.S. historian

Do you see yourself as a candidate for an overseas assignment? Depending on the company you work for, the extent of its overseas operations, and the rules and regulations of the host country, people at various levels may be offered assignments abroad. Some companies with limited operations overseas prefer to send some of their newest people to staff those sites. This point will be addressed in greater detail later in this chapter. But whether or not you plan to work for a multinational corporation, cultural sensitivity is an important quality for managerial success.

RATIONALE

There are at least three reasons you should become familiar with intercultural business communication practices.

First, we are truly a global economy. Looking at the past decade provides clear evidence of that fact. Until the most recent global recession began in 2008, the United States had witnessed tremendous growth in international trade for over three decades. Between 1990 and 2006, trade volumes grew by more than 6 percent a year. The total value of import/export trade in 2012 exceeded $3.82 trillion: over $2.27 trillion in imports and almost $1.54 trillion in exports.[1] But the world's economic machine went into reverse in 2008, and the World Trade Organization predicted correctly that volume of global merchandise trade would shrink by 9 percent in 2009. The immediate causes were a collapse in demand and a credit crunch. The speed with which international trade fell so uniformly around the world was due to *vertical specialization*, or global supply chains. That is, countries specialize not only in products but also in steps in the process of production. So, for instance, a tractor made in the United States may contain steel from India and be stamped and pressed in Mexico before being sold in China. Thus, changes in demand in one country affect the trade flows and economies of several countries.

On the other hand, this interdependence was also a key to revival. Once demand began to increase again, vertical specialization and the open system of trade brought more rapid world recovery.[2] By 2014, Ben Bernanke, the man at the helm of the US economy for the previous six years as chief of the Federal Reserve Bank, declared the financial system was in much better shape and the pace of job growth was encouraging. He attributed much of the recovery to the fact that foreign companies were investing in the United States, and he urged leaders to look "at the whole system" when crafting economic policy.[3]

Despite the recent global economic collapse, many countries continue to depend on international trade as an important contributor to their gross domestic product (GDP). The United States has steadily become more "open" over the last decade; that is, exports and imports have grown faster than GDP. In 2010, international trade accounted for over 12.7 percent of the United States' GDP.[4] But the United States is not the most globalized country, by far. For the past forty years, KOF Swiss Economic Institute annually has ranked 158 countries according to their degree of globalization, as measured by twenty-four economic, social, and political factors. Who is number one? Belgium.[5] In addition to high levels of trade in goods and services, Belgium experiences the most foreign investment. Furthermore, the country is profoundly affected by ideas, information, and people from abroad. Ireland, the Netherlands, Austria, and Singapore round out the top 5 most globalized countries. The globalization index for the United States has been continuously increasing since the 1970s. The United States ranked 34th in 2013, mostly due to economic activity rather than social and political globalization.

Another indicator of the extent to which businesses function in a global market is the recent redirection of international trade agreements. In the decades after World War II, trade deals focused on lowering tariffs. Today, the purpose of trade agreements is different. Nontariff barriers are more important, and negotiators work toward agreement on regulations. As Joseph Stiglitz, a professor of economics at Columbia University and a Nobel laureate, points out, multinational corporations argue that inconsistent regulations make it more costly to conduct international business, so "regulatory harmonization" is the goal.[6]

A second reason you should become familiar with best practices for intercultural business communication is that, even if you do not conduct business internationally, you may find yourself working for a firm owned by a company from another country. In the United States, for example, the direct investment of foreign-based companies grew from $9 billion in 1966 to more than $166 billion in 2012. The largest industry growth was in manufacturing, which accounted for almost half of the total investment outlays. Outlays were also sizable in transportation, utilities, mining, finance and insurance, real estate, and banking. Most outlays by foreign direct investors were to acquire existing US businesses rather than to establish new businesses in the

STOP AND THINK

1. What results of the global economic crisis have you noticed as a consumer?

2. What indications of global economic recovery have you noticed?

United States. The top investors in US businesses in 2012 were the Netherlands, France, the United Kingdom, Japan, and Canada.[7]

You may be surprised by the following examples of businesses you thought were American but are in fact owned by companies based in other countries: Texas-based Brinks Home Security and ADT Security Services are owned by Tyco International, a Swiss company. Dannon Co., the yogurt maker, is owned by Danone Group, a French company. Henkel, a German corporation, owns the Dial Corporation, makers of Dial soap, Renuzit air fresheners, and Purex. Great Britain's Diageo PLC owns Johnny Walker scotch, Bailey's Irish Cream liqueur, Ciroc, and Smirnoff vodka. A British company owns French's mustard. A Mexican company, Grupo Bimbo, owns Sara Lee, Entenmann's, and Mrs Baird's, all makers of bakery products. A major shopping mall in suburban St. Louis, Missouri, is owned by Paramount, a German real estate holding company. An Italian firm, Luxottica, owns LensCrafters, Pearle Vision, and Sunglass Hut. And Compass bank is a wholly owned subsidiary of a Spanish company, BBVA.

<table>
<tr><td>

STOP AND THINK

Can you find other examples of companies that you assumed were American but are actually owned by foreign-based companies?

</td></tr>
</table>

Continuing our examination of global business connections, we find many products that we think of as American that are manufactured by foreign companies. For instance, Dreyer's Grand Ice Cream, Purina Dog Chow, Nescafé instant coffee, and KitKat candy bars are among the 8,000 brands made by Nestlé, the world's biggest food company. Nestlé is based in Switzerland. On the other hand, products that we may think of as "foreign" may actually be domestic. Kraft Foods makes Grey Poupon mustard in the United States. Michelin tires are manufactured in South Carolina. And Evian water is distributed by Coca-Cola. Truly, we live in a global economy.

A third reason to learn about intercultural business communication is the increasing likelihood that you will work with, or for, someone who is not a native-born citizen. According to the US Census Bureau, 16.1 percent of the workforce was non-US native in 2012. New streams in the American labor pool include workers of Asian and Hispanic origin. Currently, there are 7.2 million workers in the United States from Asian countries (China, Japan, the Philippines, India, Vietnam, Korea, Indonesia, and Thailand). But the most rapidly growing ethnic or racial group is the Hispanic workforce. In 2013, over 20 million workers were of Hispanic origin. By 2016, the US Bureau of Labor Statistics predicts that the number will be almost 27 million, a 30 percent increase. By comparison, the rate of increase of white non-Hispanics in the workforce is predicted to be 1.4 percent.[8] As a result, US managers will be leading a noticeably different workforce in the years ahead.

Furthermore, employees often bring their culturally based behaviors to work. For instance, Muslims are required by their faith to pray five times a day. Most of the prayer times are flexible, but the sunset prayers must be said at dusk. Dell Inc. and Electrolux Home Products accommodate their Muslim workers in US plants with a "tag-out" policy that allows a few employees at a time to step away for prayers. As the workforce becomes ever more diverse, such cultural differences in behavior will have a major impact on the likelihood of successful business/worker interaction. Here is an example of the extent to which a commitment to cultural sensitivity has become ingrained in the business

STOP AND THINK

1. What are the benefits of a culturally diverse workforce?

2. What are the challenges?

environment. Legal Sea Foods, a chain of restaurants in the northeastern and southeastern United States, lists its corporate values on its paper place mats for customers to see. The company's first "pledge" is "to inspect and prepare the freshest, highest quality fish and shellfish." That is to be expected, right? The second pledge is "to assure you of a clean and comfortable environment." That is good but still unsurprising. Reading farther down the place mat, we find the third pledge: "to promote diversity and respect for all human differences." Clearly, cultural sensitivity is a priority at Legal Sea Foods.

In summary, whether or not you deliberately choose to conduct business internationally, you will need to be an interculturally sensitive communicator. Unfortunately, the quality of the training given to people headed for overseas assignments differs widely by company and by country. It has been estimated that 30 to 50 percent of American managers fail to perform adequately abroad because they have not been sufficiently prepared for adjusting to the foreign culture.[9] In a survey of emerging trends conducted by the Cendant Mobility relocation firm, 84 percent of companies said that they provide intercultural training to staff, but less than 50 percent of employees take advantage of that training.[10] Companies in Japan and Australia, on the other hand, are noted for the high quality of training their workers are given before being sent abroad.

This chapter will not cover everything anyone ever needed to know about being an intercultural managerial communicator in all parts of the world. That ambitious goal is the subject of thousands of books and articles in any library and could not possibly be condensed into one chapter. Our goal instead will be an introduction to the types of issues, concerns, and mores that managers need to study to become successful in intercultural business communication. Additionally, we will make a number of suggestions about what managers can do now and in the coming years to better prepare themselves to conduct global business.

WHAT IS CULTURE?

Before we review the many aspects of intercultural communication, we might want to get an idea of the meaning of the word *culture*. Though definitions of this term abound and vary widely in terms of their complexity, Gould defines it in a clear and straightforward manner.

> Culture is what we grow up in. Beginning in childhood, we learn the behaviors, habits, and attitudes that are acceptable to those around us. These are transmitted to us orally, nonverbally, and in writing. As time goes on, we gradually acquire the knowledge, beliefs, values, customs, and moral attitudes of the society in which we mature. A body of common understanding develops with which we feel comfortable. We know what to expect, and we know what is expected of us.[11]

Defined in such a way, culture includes the religious systems to which we are exposed, the educational system, the economic system, the political system, the recreational outlets, the mores governing dress and grooming, the standards of etiquette, the food and how it is prepared and served, the gift-giving customs, the morals, the legal system, the quality and quantity of communication among the people, the greeting practices, the rituals performed, the modes of travel available, as well as the many other aspects of people's lives that they come to take for granted.

Malcolm Gladwell explores the importance of culture in individual behaviors in his bestseller, *Outliers: The Story of Success*. He concludes that

> cultural legacies are powerful forces. They have deep roots and long lives. They persist, generation after generation, virtually intact, even as the economic and social and demographic conditions that spawned them have vanished, and they play such a role in directing attitudes and behavior that we cannot make sense of our world without them.[12]

Whether you like it or not, culture is all-encompassing and everlasting. When we recognize how pervasive a person's culture is and how much it can differ from country to country, we can then begin to appreciate more fully the difficult job facing a manager in an intercultural environment. The people in, or from, another country are quite comfortable with a culture that may seem strange to a US businessperson. Yet it is we who will have to make the adjustments and live with the uncertainty and the unusual occurrences and practices. If we want to succeed in this highly competitive global marketplace, we will have to learn to see and accept things as others see and accept them.

INTERCULTURAL MYTHS

Before we examine the various aspects of intercultural business communication, we need to dispel a few myths. The global village concept, end of history view, and universality myth are three theories worth examining.

The *global village concept* was introduced by Marshall McLuhan in his 1967 book, *The Medium Is the Message*, and promoted more recently by Tom Friedman in his book *The World Is Flat*. This concept proposes that advancements in communication and transportation technologies will ultimately shrink the world to a point where we will be one big, happy global village. Some believe the global village concept has been realized because we now know instantly of happenings in even the most remote parts of the world.[13]

Others believe we are nowhere near fruition of the global village concept. They contend that the great advancements in communication and transportation technologies have only created a greater proximity among the various peoples of the world and that proximity has only enhanced the perceived differences among those peoples.[14]

In conjunction with the latter view, it has been suggested that you, today's students, are responsible for whether or not we ever do see the fruition of the global village concept. To be successful in the global marketplace, you will need to adjust to other cultures, and you will need to gain and maintain the trust of your intercultural partners. In other words, you will need to bridge the cultural gap.[15] With each successful international business venture (successful for all parties involved), we move closer to the realization of the global village concept.

A second widely discussed theory is the *end of history view* advanced by Francis Fukuyama, a political economist at Stanford University. His assertion was that the end of the Cold War meant the end of the war of ideas. After the Berlin wall crumbled in 1989, he predicted that one relatively harmonious world would unite in liberal democracy. Somewhat modeled after the global village concept, Fukuyama's theory included the idea that significant global conflicts would be a thing of the past as we blend into one.[16] Unfortunately, this illusionary vision of world peace was quickly destroyed when former Soviet blocs struggled to adapt to Western culture and ideas.

The third myth of which we should be wary is the *universality myth.* This myth is often promoted by people who have spent a short time in a foreign country. Initially, they notice all the differences between their own culture and that of the host country. Then, they start to note all the similarities. They come away from the experience concluding that, under the skin, we are all alike: brothers and sisters in the common family of humanity. Promoters of this concept recommend the universal adoption of artificial languages, such as Esperanto, Unish, and Globish.

Milton Bennett, who describes six stages of intercultural sensitivity,[17] refers to this belief as *minimization.* He says that looking for similarities is a way to assuage our fears of difference and make us feel better about each other. A short visit does not provide people the deeper insight into a culture that would have revealed major differences in beliefs, values, and mores. To illustrate, we might look at some of the results of a survey conducted in a number of countries. One of the questions asked of the respondents was "Do you agree or disagree with the statement: 'Most people can be trusted'?" The levels of agreement are listed in the box below.

United States: 55%

United Kingdom: 49%

Mexico: 30%

West Germany: 19%

Italy: 1%

One could argue that language differences might have been responsible for some of the variation. But even if we allow for some margin of error, we would still have a significant variation in a very basic belief.

Another example of differences in basic beliefs was the 2004 incident in Minnesota when a Hmong deer hunter was convicted of killing five other hunters and wounding three more. The group of hunters had found him in a deer blind on private land, accused him of trespassing, and ordered him to leave. Instead, he opened fire. About 60,000 Hmong people live in the Minneapolis region. Refugees from Laos, the Hmong live by social organization founded on a clan system, and they do not understand the concept of private property. They hunt wherever they see fit. This tragic incident demonstrates that we truly are not all alike under the skin, brothers and sisters in the common family of humanity. We differ appreciably, and those differences must be recognized, understood, and accepted if we are to do business with one another.

SOME OF THE WAYS IN WHICH WE DIFFER

One of the most extensive studies of cultural differences was conducted by Geert Hofstede in a very large US-based multinational corporation. He collected more than 116,000 questionnaires from this corporation's employees in forty countries around the globe. A massive statistical analysis of his findings revealed six dimensions of national culture as shown in Table 11–1: power distance, uncertainty avoidance, individualism/collectivism, masculinity/femininity, high and low context, and monochronic/polychronic time.[18]

Power distance indicates the extent to which a society accepts the fact that power in institutions and organizations is distributed unequally. It is reflected in the values of both the more powerful and less powerful members of the society. The Philippines, Venezuela, Mexico, and the South Slavic States are countries with high power distances; and Denmark, New Zealand, Austria, the United States, and Israel are a few of the countries with low power distances.

A manager in a culture with high power distance is seen as having dramatically more power than a subordinate would have. This manager, who is usually addressed respectfully by title and surname, might favor a controlling strategy and behave like an autocrat. For instance, within the British Houses of Parliament, lawmakers can move to the head of the line at restaurants, restrooms, and elevators, whereas clerks, aides, and secretaries who work in Parliament must stand and wait. In a culture with a lower power distance, however, a manager is seen as having little more power than a subordinate, is often addressed by first name, takes her place in line, and manages by using an equalitarian communication strategy.

A dramatic example of how power distance affects business is provided by the airline industry. Between 1988 and 1998, Korean Air's plane crash ratio was at alarming heights—4.79 per million departures. That figure was seventeen times worse than the crash ratio for major US commercial airlines in that time period. Several investigations and studies were done to examine the cause of Korean Air's planes. Finally, it occurred to

Table 11–1   Hofstede's Dimensions of Cultural Differences

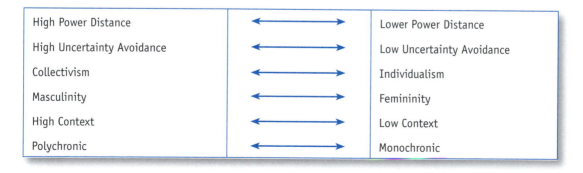

High Power Distance	⟷	Lower Power Distance
High Uncertainty Avoidance	⟷	Low Uncertainty Avoidance
Collectivism	⟷	Individualism
Masculinity	⟷	Femininity
High Context	⟷	Low Context
Polychronic	⟷	Monochronic

someone to apply Hofstede's power distance theory. What they discovered was fascinating. The first officers in the cockpit were paralyzed with fear to have to say anything that questioned the captain's ability. Afraid to speak up, they were trapped in subservient roles due to the high power distance ingrained in their culture. One Korean Air pilot revealed, "The captain is in charge and does what he wants, when he wants, when he likes, how he likes, and everyone else sits quietly and does nothing." Fortunately, by understanding the underlying importance of culture and how it relates to the airline industry, dramatic improvements were made. The Korean Air flight crews were retrained and have enjoyed a spotless safety record since 1999.[19]

Uncertainty avoidance relates to the degree to which a society feels threatened by uncertainty and by ambiguous situations. It tries to avoid these uncertainties and ambiguous situations by providing greater career stability, establishing and following formal rules, not allowing odd ideas and behaviors, and believing in absolute truths and the attainment of expertise. Greece, Germany, England, Portugal, Belgium, and Japan have strong uncertainty avoidance, while Singapore, Hong Kong, Denmark, the United States, and Sweden have weak uncertainty avoidance.

Belgium and Denmark are geographically close, and their people look similar. However, when it comes to uncertainty avoidance, the two nations are far apart because of different histories, politics, religions, literature, and other cultural factors. Recall that earlier in this chapter Belgium was identified as the most globalized of 158 countries. What do you think is the connection between that ranking and Belgians' avoidance of uncertainty, their respect for rules and plans, their insistence on following procedures regardless of circumstances? Uncertainty avoidance is probably a major dimension for most intercultural managers to contend with. Most likely, they will be expected to challenge the status quo and implement change, and uncertainty avoidance is a significant obstacle to change. Such managers ought to remember that using an equalitarian communication strategy to get people involved and highlighting the benefits of change can greatly help to reduce resistance.

On the *individualism/collectivism* dimension, *individualism* suggests a loosely knit social framework in which people are expected to take care of themselves and their immediate families only. *Collectivism,* on the other hand, is evidenced by a tight social framework in which people distinguish between in-groups and out-groups. They expect their in-group (relatives, clan, organization) to take care of them; and because of that, they believe they owe absolute loyalty to it. The United States, Australia, and Great Britain are the most highly individualistic countries on Hofstede's scale, while Guatemala, Pakistan, Colombia, Nigeria, Japan, and Venezuela are more collectivist countries.

The huge social-psychological gap between collectivist and individualist cultures can be illustrated linguistically. In Chinese, for instance, there is no word for *individualism*. The closest one can come is the word for *selfishness*. In Japanese, the word *I*—meaning the unconditional, generalized self—is not often used in conversation. Instead, Japanese has many words for *I*, depending on audience and context. This reflects the Eastern conviction that one is a different person when interacting with different groups.[20]

Managers from individualistic cultures and collectivist cultures conflict in many ways. In negotiations, for example, managers from collectivist cultures do not want to make decisions. They must first collaborate; consensus must be reached. But managers from individualistic cultures have difficulty collaborating, want to talk to a *decision maker*, and cannot understand why the other group must spend so much time in conference.

Masculinity/femininity, as a dimension, expresses the extent to which the dominant values in the society are "masculine." This masculinity, according to Hofstede, would include assertiveness, the acquisition of money and things, and not caring about the quality of life. These values are labeled masculine because, within nearly all societies, men scored higher in these values. Japan, Austria, Venezuela, and Mexico were among the most masculine societies. Feminine cultures, by contrast, value family, children, and quality of life. Denmark, Sweden, and Norway are considered feminine cultures.

Consider the following comparison. In the United States, men are judged at least partly on their ability to make a good salary. Frequently, this judgment precludes traditional US feminine values of caring for children. In Helsinki, Finland, however, a man may be called away from a meeting to tend to the baby in the child care center in the next building, and no one considers this a wrong priority. Despite the passage of the Family and Medical Leave Act in 1993, far fewer working men than women take the full time they are eligible for when dealing with family and medical problems in the United States.

STOP AND THINK

Think about a person you work with who comes from a different culture. How do Hofstede's dimensions of cultural differences help to explain some of the differences you have experienced when communicating with that person?

A fifth cultural difference an intercultural communicator needs to keep in mind is whether the culture is a high-context or low-context culture. These terms were first used by Edward T. Hall in 1977.[21] In a *high-context* culture, much information is either in the physical context or environment or internalized in the person. In such a culture, people look for meaning in what is not said—in the nonverbal communication or body language; in the silences, the facial expressions, and the gestures. Japan and Saudi Arabia are high-context countries, as are Chinese- and Spanish-speaking countries.

In a *low-context* culture, most information is expected to be in explicit codes, such as words. In such a culture, communicators emphasize sending and receiving accurate messages directly, usually by being highly articulate. Canada and the United States are low-context cultures. As one might suspect, negotiations between low-context and high-context cultures can be fraught with peril when the parties are not warned of the differences in approaches.[22] The value of contracts also varies widely between high- and low-context cultures. US business-to-business transactions rely on documents, not handshakes or personal relationships.

A recent study compared the About Us feature of Western and Eastern companies' websites. The results demonstrate how low-context and high-context cultural values can manifest in subtle but important ways. The researchers found that Western companies projected a strong image in the About Us page of their websites by directly stating their achievements, status, industry rank, and profits. By contrast, high-context Eastern companies used indirect methods to promote themselves, such as describing their heritage and history, relationships with high-status others, and links to the home country.[23]

The sixth dimension of cultural differences, according to Hofstede, is *monochronic versus polychronic* time. In a monochronic culture, such as Germany, the United States, and most Westernized nations, we talk about saving time, wasting time, making time, and spending time. We measure time by the clock, often in nanoseconds. In hyper-punctual countries like Japan, pedestrians walk fast and bank clocks are accurate. In Western businesses, we read quarterly returns and define *long-term* projections as those going out three to five years into the future. Time is linear.

In polychronic cultures, such as Spain, Latin American nations, and most Asian countries, time just *is*. These cultures trace their roots back thousands of years. Time is measured by events, not the clock. Thus, promptness diminishes in value, and being "late" is a sign of status. In Ecuador, for instance, politicians, military officers, and business people are less punctual than blue-collar workers. The story goes that when Ecuador's President Lucio Gutierrez realized that chronic lateness was costing his country $2.5 billion a year, he started a national campaign to promote the importance of clock time. But his spokesman arrived late at the television studio to make the announcement.[24] This example demonstrates how deep culture goes and how difficult it is to change.

In polychronic countries, "long-term" thinking is over generations and even centuries. The moment does not matter, by comparison. People in polychronic cultures are more patient, less interested in time management or measurement, and more willing to wait for their rewards than those in monochronic cultures. To them, time is flexible, unfolding naturally. And the fact that polychronic cultures typically are less economically successful than monochronic cultures is not a compelling reason for change.

STOP AND THINK

1. How does the concept of high- and low-context cultures explain an experience you have had at work when communicating with someone from another culture?

2. How does the concept of short-term and long-term orientation explain an experience you have had working with someone from another culture?

Given the globalization of today's marketplace and the increasing pace at which firms are becoming multinational, it has been suggested that organizations around the world will begin to look very much alike. One theory states that as the companies become more similar, the organizational culture might dominate or diminish the effects of the larger culture. Research thus far does not support the likelihood of these developments. Laurent found that employees of different nationalities working for a multinational firm maintained and even strengthened their cultural differences. German workers became more German, American workers became more American, and Swedish workers became more Swedish.[25] The implication is that we must accept, even value, our cultural differences for business success.

One way that multinationals are demonstrating cultural sensitivity is in their hiring practices. PepsiCo, for instance, named Indra Nooyi as the company's CEO in 2006. By 2013, she was ranked 10th in Forbes's list of the *World's 100 Most Powerful Women*. Nooyi was born in India. Since 2001, half of all new hires at Pepsi are either women or ethnic minorities. And managers earn their bonuses in part by how well they recruit and retain them. Six of its top twelve executives are women or minorities. Pepsi argues that a diverse leadership helps the company to better understand the disparate tastes of new consumers globally.[26]

Having explored some of the fundamental dimensions on which the people of the world differ and how profound the differences are, we now turn our attention to more practical matters. The next sections present approaches to success as intercultural communicators. More specifically, the rest of this chapter discusses dealing with language differences, being nonverbally sensitive, being a good intercultural communicator, and preparing for assignments or careers in international business.

SHOULD YOU LEARN THE LANGUAGE?

The first decision facing an international business traveler is whether to learn the language spoken in the country to be visited. People who have learned a second language will testify that it can be a long, involved, and tedious task. Furthermore, the difficulty level varies with the language to be learned. Some have many subtle nuances that non-natives have a hard time capturing. And the many dialects that exist within a country complicate the process even more. According to the US State Department, despite our immigrant roots, just 10 percent of US citizens can speak a second language. In contrast, more than half of the people in the European Union are bilingual, and 28 percent are trilingual.

Which languages are the most important to learn? According to the US Department of Education, Chinese, Arabic, Farsi, Korean, Japanese, Russian, Hindi, and Urdu are the languages most vital to this country's future, although less than 1 percent of American high school students are studying any of these. By contrast, in China, English is mandatory for students from third grade onward.[27]

For short stays in a country, perhaps just to set up a partnership or sign a contract, most people would agree that one need not learn the language. Since English is the recognized language of business throughout the world, the chances are good that the people one deals with will speak it. If they do not, one can always use an interpreter. Great care, however, should be exercised in selecting an interpreter, for they vary widely in ability and loyalty.

As the length of the stay increases, the need to learn and the wisdom of learning the language also increase. While occasional errors are inevitable and are often overlooked when tourists try to participate in conversations, the stakes increase with more formal and prolonged interactions, where the consequences of errors matter. Most authorities agree that an extended stay would justify the time and effort of learning the language of the land.

Literal translation errors can cause revenue loss in multinational companies. For example, in 2009, HSBC Bank had to launch a $10 million rebranding campaign to repair the damage done when its catchphrase Assume Nothing was mistranslated as Do Nothing in various countries. Accuracy is critical in many global business matters. Take intellectual property, for example. According to the World Intellectual Property Organization, the countries submitting the most patent filings through the Patent Cooperation Treaty are the United States, Japan, Germany, and China. The number of incorrect patent translations being reported is growing at an alarming rate. A recent study of 73 companies involved in patent translation showed that 81 percent have experienced problems with incorrect translation of patent applications that resulted in increased internal and external costs, reduced protection, and inadequate enforcement of patent laws.[28] The implications are that innovative companies seeking to do business abroad may experience delays, red tape, and unexpected limits to the scope of patent rights, all of which result in years of lost revenue.

Furthermore, familiarity with the local language enables familiarity with the culture, values, traditions, and business practices. A deeply held belief in Japan is captured by the simple term *kaizen*, which literally means "to change to become good." This concept has been widely adopted in US businesses that stress continuous quality improvement through reliance on team decision making and sophisticated, comprehensive communication networks. In addition, organizations following the kaizen philosophy value cleanliness and order. Walking through the workplace, one finds no litter on the floor and no tools out of place. Waste is minimized. As you can see, it takes many English words to describe this approach to business that is explained in Japanese by a single word.

To find other examples of how closely language is tied to the culture, we can examine some translation issues. Here is one: Over 47 million copies of a children's book, *Diary of a Wimpy Kid* by Jeff Kinney, are in print in the United States, and the book has been translated into thirty languages, including Spanish, Japanese, Greek, Hebrew, Thai, and German. But the German version is titled *I'm Surrounded by Idiots* because there is no German equivalent for *wimpy*. The closest German word is *ängstlich,* which translates into English as "uneasy, anxious." Doing a quick survey of words that reveal cultural values, we find more examples: In Arabic there is no word for *lie*. In Russian there is no term equivalent to the English word *privacy*. And in Chinese there is no equivalent to the individual *I*.

Machine translators, such as Google Translate, should not be relied upon because they do not account for many cultural factors, including slang usage, metaphors, and irony. Thus, the slogan for KFC, a chain of fast-food restaurants featuring chicken dishes, is "Finger lickin' good" in English, but in Chinese, this expression translates into "eat your fingers off." And Pepsi's slogan, "Pepsi brings you back to life," becomes "Pepsi will bring your ancestors back from the dead" in Taiwanese. Clearly, these literal translations are sure to hurt sales and damage the company's image. The more that managers understand about the culture, the more likely they are to be successful in that environment. Learning the local language leads to that end.

One advantage of learning the language and learning it well is avoidance of interpretational disasters that have visited companies in their advertising and product labeling. For

STOP AND THINK

Think of an example of a slang expression in your native language that does not easily translate.

1. Where does slang come from?

2. To what extent does the origin of slang explain why it is culture specific?

example, the Parker Pen Company unwittingly advertised in Latin America that its ink would prevent unwanted pregnancies. Similarly, Otis Engineering claimed on posters at a Russian trade show that its oil equipment would improve people's sex lives.

Here are a couple of other slogans and product names that backfired when translated into other languages. They are humorous to read about, but very costly to the companies. Pepsi's slogan, "Come alive with Pepsi," in German reads, "Come alive from the grave with Pepsi." Ford had a similar experience with a product's name—one truck model was called the Fiera—in Spanish it means "ugly old woman."

One last caution is advisable about language usage. Some people choose a middle-of-the-road approach and learn only specific statements that are common or are pertinent to a particular setting. Such people should remember that in some languages, particularly the Eastern languages, the same word can be used to mean many different things. The tone of the voice varies to indicate a specific meaning. Sometimes a little knowledge can be more damaging than no knowledge.

NONVERBAL SENSITIVITY

Whether or not traveling managers choose to learn the verbal language of the land, they should try to learn as much as they can about the nonverbal language common in that culture. Chapter 10 provided an overview of the range of nonverbal behaviors used in business settings to communicate meaning. Interpretations of greetings, dress, space, touch, posture, gestures, and rituals vary widely among cultures. Business deals have been lost over a seemingly harmless American signal that was interpreted as a grave insult in another part of the world.

Greetings

From the start of any business contact, one should be aware that the form of greeting used may vary from culture to culture. Though the handshake is a fairly standard greeting in most parts of the world, the pressure used may differ. The high-pressure grip, which in America is supposed to suggest warmth and confidence, may be too aggressive where a lighter grasp is traditional.

In Japan, the bow is still practiced by older businesspeople. Sometimes the bow and handshake will both be used to signal respect for both cultures. Note, too, the different levels of bowing, each with significant meanings. In other parts of the world, a traditional greeting may be a hug, a nose rub, a kiss, or the placing of the hands in a praying position.[29]

On the subject of greetings, note also that business cards are treated differently in different parts of the world. In Japan, they are carefully offered to the recipient with both hands with the information facing the receiver. Also, they are never put away hastily or scribbled on but studied at length and then arranged on the table during a business meeting. Finally, in any non-English-speaking country, printing the information on the reverse side of the business card in a second language is expected as a courteous practice.[30]

Dress

While the business suit is considered acceptable attire for a business meeting in most parts of the world, it may or may not be acceptable for an evening of entertainment. For men in tropical climates, a guayabera, or loose cotton shirt, worn over a pair of slacks is considered appropriate at even formal occasions. And in sunny Australia, business men may often wear dress shirts and ties with shorts and knee socks to the office.

On the subject of dress, we should exercise caution even when we are not in business meetings or at official social functions. Standards of travel and entertainment dressing are much more conservative in some parts of the world than they are in the United States. Bare legs, arms, shoulders, or heads on the street or in holy buildings are considered offensive in many Arab and Eastern countries.

Space, Touch, and Posture

The space maintained, touching practiced, and postures assumed in business and social encounters vary appreciably across the globe. Americans are said to have a spatial bubble of up to 4 feet into which strangers should not encroach. In Arab countries and Latin America, people speak almost face to face and nose to nose. It has been said that an Arab wants to be close enough to smell your breath and body odor when he communicates with you. In the United States, we avoid smelling each other at all costs.

In some countries—Iran, Palestine, China, and Indonesia, for example—it is considered acceptable for two men to walk down the street holding hands as a sign of close friendship. However, in many of these same countries, it is not acceptable for a man and a woman to walk down the street hand in hand. This immodest public display of affection is frowned upon.

Also on the subject of touching, managers should exercise some care about what is touched. In Thailand, the head is considered sacred. It should never be touched, and objects should never be passed above it. In Tonga, touching someone's head could get you the death penalty. Finally, in Muslim countries, it is considered insulting to show the sole of your shoe to someone else. Businesspeople are cautioned never to cross their legs with one ankle on the other knee and never to lean back in an office chair with the feet on the desk.

Gestures

In Bulgaria, Macedonia, Albania, Iran, and Sri Lanka, nodding the head up and down means "no." In Italy, Greece, and some African countries, the gesture Americans use for come here means "good-bye." The thumbs-up gesture means "everything is good" in the United States, but to Australians it is an obscenity. The V-for-victory sign means something entirely different when reversed, with the palm facing the signer. In Britain, it then becomes an insult. In Ethiopia, pointing and the one-finger come-here gesture are used only with children and dogs.

As demonstrated by the preceding illustrations, the gestures we use in international encounters can be fairly dangerous. A friendly or innocuous gesture can turn out to be a vivid and/or profane insult. Something that very clearly means one thing in one country may mean the opposite in another country. To increase our level of success in the increasingly competitive global marketplace, we are going to have to become interculturally sensitive.

Food

Perhaps we become most aware of cultural diversity when we discuss food—what foods are used to celebrate special occasions, how the food is eaten, or even what is considered edible. Any traveler has tales of "exotic" meals, accompanied by value judgments.

Host nationals will want visitors to experience the culinary delights that bring so much pleasure to their taste buds, their national dining treasures. It is hard for them to imagine or understand that these same treats might bring forth horror and revulsion in someone not experienced with them.

Thus, as the special guest at a banquet one might be called on to try sheep's eyes in Saudi Arabia or Kazakhstan, shark's fin soup in China, a roasted gorilla hand in one part of Africa, or a live fish brought to the table and carved in Japan. While US businesspeople may be reluctant to try such dishes, it would be supremely rude to refuse.

On the other hand, visitors to the United States are often critical of our daily consumption of processed foods and snacks, such as popcorn and Jell-O. Corn is animal food in most parts of the world. Further, Americans' tendency to nibble throughout the day rather than sit through long meals is considered uncouth. Italians and Japanese, for instance, do not eat on the street or while standing.

The importance of sharing food when building intercultural relationships is exemplified by this Pakistani proverb: On the first cup of tea, you're a stranger. On the second, a guest. By the third cup, you're family.

Gifts

The Foreign Corrupt Practices Act (FCPA) of 1977 specifies that bribing someone during the conduct of business is illegal. A violator's company may be fined up to $2 million, and the participants in the bribe individually may be fined up to $100,000 each and jailed for up to five years. Despite these stiff penalties, multinational corporations continue to take risks. US federal prosecutors issued indictments in April 2003 against two executives representing ExxonMobil. They were accused of bribing officials in Kazakhstan in exchange for oil contracts in the mid-1990s. Payments allegedly included $20.5 million deposited in Swiss bank accounts of senior officers of the Republic of Kazakhstan, a new Gulfstream jet aircraft for the president, funds for tennis courts at his home, and four trucks with satellite dishes to be used by his daughter's television network. The indictments also cited speedboats, jewelry, fur coats, and snowmobiles. ExxonMobil denied knowledge that any improper payments were made.

Another dramatic example of international bribery involves KBR, an engineering and construction services company based in Houston, Texas. KBR was a subsidiary of the Halliburton Company until 2007. KBR was accused of steering more than $180 million worth of bribes to Nigerian government officials to win contracts valued at more than $6 billion between 1995 and 2004. In February 2009, KBR pleaded guilty in the case and agreed to pay $402 million in fines. In addition, a court-appointed monitor was assigned to oversee KBR's international transactions for three years, at a cost to the company of $3–$5 million per year. Its former parent, Halliburton Company, agreed to pay most of the fine, along with an additional $177 million to settle civil complaints from the Securities and

Exchange Commission. KBR admitted authorizing the bribes for contracts to build liquefied natural gas facilities on Bonny Island, Nigeria.[31]

More recently, allegations arose that Wal-Mart paid over $24 million in bribes to "gestores" or business "facilitators" as well as directly to local governments in Mexico, attempting to win construction permits. Over 20 percent of Wal-Mart's stores are in Mexico. While Mexico has laws against bribery, in reality they are not routinely enforced, and there is no nationwide anticorruption policy. On April 22, 2012, the *New York Times* printed a story about the investigation of Wal-Mart's violation of the FCPA. News of the scandal triggered no outrage in Mexico, but the following day Wal-Mart stock dropped 4.7 percent.

Why would American corporations risk defying the FCPA? Anti-bribery laws are sometimes a source of competitive disadvantage when a company is trying to do business in a culture where gifts, fees, commissions, and "facilitation payments" to officials are normal practice and where other countries competing for lucrative contracts do not have anti-bribery restrictions.[32]

Gift-giving practices vary widely throughout the world. Common and expected in some countries, it is frowned upon in others. For example, while gift giving is important in Japan, it is generally considered inappropriate in Germany, Belgium, or the United Kingdom.[33] Tipping for good service, a common practice in the United States, is not expected in China, Denmark, Italy, and France.

Even where it is practiced, the nature and the value of the gifts may differ greatly. Though flowers are often safe if one is invited to dinner in someone's home, chrysanthemums should be avoided in many European countries because of their funereal association. In Japan, white flowers carry the same message, as do purple ones in Brazil and Mexico.[34]

Remember, too, that numbers and shapes might have some significance. The number four is associated with bad luck in Japan and China, as is seven in Kenya—though seven is seen as lucky in the Czech Republic. The triangle is considered a negative shape in Hong Kong, Korea, and Taiwan.[35]

Finally, investigate the interpretation of gifts bearing the company logo. While some people may interpret such gifts as a symbol of the business relationship being established or maintained, some might think the giver was simply too cheap to buy a gift on his or her own.

While not intended to be complete, the preceding discussion was designed to illustrate the very precarious world of the intercultural communicator. The dangers of nonverbal slippage are there whether or not a person chooses to learn the verbal language. In the end, the success of multinational firms will depend on how much effort their people expend toward being interculturally sensitive and thus sidestepping those dangers.

WHAT IS A GOOD INTERCULTURAL COMMUNICATOR?

While not a comprehensive profile, the following description portrays some of the most important qualities and characteristics of a good intercultural communicator. You are a good intercultural communicator if you avoid the pitfalls described earlier and if you maintain harmonious relations with your intercultural partners.

First and foremost, you are a good intercultural communicator if you avoid *ethnocentrism*. As mentioned previously, Bennett designed a six-stage developmental model of cultural sensitivity (see Table 11–2). His model identifies three stages of ethnocentrism: *denial, defense,* and *minimization.* An ethnocentric person may acknowledge the existence of cultural differences but sees his or her country as the best in the world and looks down on others as inferior because they are different. For whatever reasons, the ethnocentric person builds resentment rather than good relationships.

On the other hand, Bennett identified three stages of ethno-relativism: *acceptance, adaptation,* and *integration.* An ethno-relativistic manager recognizes and respects cultural differences and finds ways to make the workplace amenable to all.[36]

Second, you are a good intercultural communicator if you are *nondefensive* about your homeland. For example, when someone from another country criticizes the United States for problems such as the high divorce rate, drug abuse, gang warfare, child abuse, teen pregnancies, AIDS, racial discrimination, and corrupt politicians, Americans should not defensively deny their validity. While you may not be able to explain fully how these problems came to be, a straightforward discussion of the problems and what things are being done about them would be appropriate.

Third, you are a good intercultural communicator if you are *curious* about other parts of the world and *brave.* You must have a genuine interest in the people and the places that exist outside your national boundaries. Intercultural managers realize that the comforts of home are not always available throughout the world and are willing to try new foods and lifestyle behaviors before condemning them out of hand.

Fourth, you are a good intercultural communicator if you are *empathic, understanding,* and *nonjudgmental.* You are able to see the world through the eyes of your intercultural partners with some degree of objectivity. You understand that the initially strange behaviors and mores of others have locally very justifiable, long-standing reasons. You do not try to push your culture's ways on people for whom these ways may not work.

Fifth, you are a good intercultural communicator if you are *patient.* You learn to live with ambiguity; you come to expect the unexpected. Meetings will not always go as planned. Businesses will not always be open during the hours posted. Conveniences will not always be readily available. Though many of your coping behaviors will involve riding out the unexpected, you will also sometimes use your industriousness to come up with alternatives to

Table 11–2   Bennett's Stages of Intercultural Sensitivity

Ethnocentrism	Ethno-relativism
1. **Denial**—no perception of differences	4. **Acceptance**—recognize and explore differences
2. **Defense**—hostility against other cultures	5. **Adaptation**—ability to empathize
3. **Minimization**—differences are superficial	6. **Integration**—recognize and embrace differences

what was expected. If one mode of transportation proves too unpredictable, you simply look for another. If one means of communication fails, you just find another.

Finally, you are a good intercultural communicator if you are *genuinely personable* to the people of the other country with whom you are dealing. A good intercultural communicator truly likes and respects those people. It cannot be faked.

DEVELOPING INTERCULTURALLY SENSITIVE MANAGERS

Ambitious managers in multinational corporations should expect to work abroad sometime during their careers. A recent study by the Columbia University School of Business reported that successful executives must have multienvironment and multicountry experience to become a CEO in the 21st century.[37] In today's digital business world, why do managers and executives need to travel abroad in order to become fully informed citizens? Is not everything available on the Internet? Probably not. The best way to get to know people who are different from ourselves, to understand and appreciate customs and beliefs that are unfamiliar, is to immerse ourselves in that new environment. Mark Twain observed over a century ago, "Travel is fatal to prejudice, bigotry, and narrow-mindedness."

In 2002, an estimated 3 to 5 million businesspeople were working as expatriates, and it is predicted that the size of the international workforce will increase with increasing cooperation among nations.[38] IBM, a major corporation, has two-thirds of its workers abroad, both foreign nationals and American citizens. CEO Samuel Palmisano wrote in the 2007 annual report that IBM is a "globally integrated enterprise . . . which locates its operations and functions anywhere in the world based on the right cost, the right skills, and the right business environment."[39] Corporations primarily send their best employees on international assignments to grow new markets, maintain existing operations, or develop high-potential employees who can both contribute to the company strategy and craft a global view of the corporation's business.[40] Further, a survey of human resource professionals at three hundred "Fortune 1000" companies revealed that half of the responding companies selected their best employees for international assignments.[41]

Lant Pritchett, an economist at the World Bank and the author of *Let Their People Come*, argues that the global pressure for employment movement across national borders will continue to rise. Cheap communication technologies make relocation easier psychologically, too, since it is less stressful to move when one can stay in touch with home base.[42]

You can do several things to prepare for a successful foreign assignment. As specified earlier, you may want to learn another language. You should explore training and educational opportunities in multicultural communication at your organization, in your community, and at nearby universities. On the social side, you might look into hosting an international student. This experience will not only help the student become acculturated in the United States; it will also provide you with insight into the student's culture. Finally, stay abreast of business, political, and economic developments throughout the world. Read newspapers with an international focus, such as the *Christian Science Monitor* or the *Financial Times*. In our increasingly global marketplace, your cross-cultural expertise will bring competitive advantage.

In the meantime, what can one do at home? Managers denied an overseas experience can still develop intercultural sensitivity. After all, managing diversity successfully brings high value to all contemporary organizations, not just multinational organizations. Michael Morris, a business professor at Columbia University, recognizes the common pitfalls managers face when trying to treat all employees fairly and respectfully. At one extreme, a manager may take the universalist approach, treating all employees the same. At the other extreme, a manager may take the particularist approach, adjusting the treatment according to the worker's culture. Both behaviors can have a negative effect on employees' perception of justice. "If justice issues are not well-managed in a diverse workplace, detrimental consequences ranging from poor morale and turnover to intergroup rivalry and balkanization may result."[43]

Morris offers ten ways managers can create a more level playing field:

1. Rely on multiethnic strategies, not just on good intentions. For instance, a manager might implement a mentoring program to ensure that all employees develop important relationships.

2. Provide every employee constructive feedback so she/he may learn and grow.

3. Work to ensure that all cultural groups have access to opportunities.

4. Work to ensure that all cultural groups perceive that they are treated fairly.

5. Provide cultural competence training to supervisors who conduct performance reviews.

6. Monitor cultural boundaries to avoid engendering intergroup competition.

7. Manage misunderstandings by making staff aware that cultural differences may be the root cause of clashes rather than personality differences.

8. Be sensitive to obstacles facing members of certain cultural groups and be flexible about performance evaluations to even the playing field.

9. Call on those with cultural expertise just as managers would call on those with technical expertise for an IT problem.

10. Include all employees and all cultures in diversity discussions.

Women, non-native Americans, and people of color represented approximately 70 percent of new entrants to the US workforce in 2008. Therefore, cultural competence has taken on greater significance, both in recruitment and retention of multicultural workers and in reaching the multicultural consumer market. Managing diversity is every manager's challenge.

SUMMARY

Given the changes occurring in the world marketplace and the increasingly competitive nature of markets both at home and abroad, firms must become more active internationally to survive and prosper. These trends and developments all suggest that today's students have a noteworthy chance of becoming tomorrow's international businesspeople. To be successful international businesspeople, they will have to be successful intercultural communicators.

A person's culture is pervasive, a body of common understanding with which he or she feels comfortable. But cultures differ appreciably, and those differences must be understood and accepted if cross-cultural business ventures are to succeed. The world has not yet become one big global village, and people are not all alike under the skin. In fact, the opposite is true—as we become globalized, we hold onto aspects of our cultural uniqueness. International businesspeople must still work to bridge the cultural gaps that exist among the peoples of the world.

For short business trips to another country, it is probably not necessary to learn the language of that country. For longer stays, it might be a good idea to do so. Learning the language frees the businessperson from having to rely on interpreters. It also lessens the chances of encountering the interpretational disasters some companies have experienced in their advertising and product labeling. Most importantly, it offers insights into the local culture.

Regardless of whether or not the language of the land is learned, international businesspeople need to be as nonverbally sensitive as they can. They need to be aware of greeting rituals and standards of dress. They should be aware that space, touch, gestures, and posture are dealt with differently in some cultures. They need to accept patiently others' interpretations of time, to be open to culinary adventures, and to be familiar with gift-giving rituals.

A good intercultural communicator is not ethnocentric, is nondefensive about his or her homeland in the face of questions about its problems, is curious about other people and brave with regard to the conditions he or she might have to confront, is empathic and understanding and nonjudgmental of intercultural partners, is patient in living with ambiguity and expecting the unexpected, and is genuinely personable to the people of the culture with whom he or she is dealing.

Finally, managers who accept the possibility of an international assignment or career should seize whatever opportunities are available to prepare themselves. They might consider learning the local language. They should investigate the social and academic programs available. Additionally, they need to stay abreast of business, economic, and political developments throughout the world and the opportunities that arise from them. Managers who are denied an international experience can still develop cultural sensitivity. By doing so, they ensure that their employees perceive the workplace to be just, respectful of differences, and fair.

Cases for Small-Group Discussion

CASE 11–1

Intercultural Business Communication and Technology

Bryan Kilter opened the e-mail from his Chinese supplier. It seemed to be a request to alter some of the garment patterns currently in Kilter Fashions standard inventory items. Bryan was beginning to become overwhelmed with his relationship with the Chinese garment manufacturer. He did not speak Chinese, and the supplier did not speak English, so they both depended on software translation when they exchanged messages. This particular e-mail read, "Sweetheart Bryan, The dress have cheap wide contraction joints in the seams, if you get the goods to wear inappropriate, you can own in a local sewing shop click on it. The Costs need to accept yourself, Hope you can understanding us. Approve changes please don't correspond by click here."

Bryan scratched his head in bewilderment.

The e-mail had just come in, so Bryan quickly typed a reply: "Hello, Chin Lee. Are you saying that the new design will have an elastic panel in the sides, so that it will be easier to fit without alterations? I think I understand that the dress will cost $.70 more now. Please let me know if I understand you correctly. Thanks."

Bryan went back to work on the end-of-month inventory. Before five minutes had gone by, he received a reply from Chin Lee: "Sweetheart Bryan, The seams wear inappropriate for contraction joints, why not question your meaning. Your own construction technician able to do construct. OK?"

Bryan scratched his head in bewilderment.

QUESTIONS

1. What challenges in conducting business across cultural divides does this case demonstrate?

2. What, specifically, would you suggest to Bryan as the next step?

CASE 11–2

Preparing for Sonora

You are a human resources training specialist working for a large automaker. Your company will soon complete construction of a plant in Sonora, Mexico. This plant will specialize in the production of your very popular subcompact, the Chaperone.

Initially, all the new plant's management will be transferred from various locations in the United States. Later, supervisors will be promoted from the ranks of the Mexican nationals hired to work on the production line. It is hoped that many of these supervisors will eventually rise to the ranks of at least middle management.

The company now faces a twofold problem, however. First, it needs to identify the criteria used to select the managers who are going to be transferred from the United States to the Sonora plant. Second, it needs to train them to function in a different culture.

Because you earned an international business certificate along with your degree in human resources management, your boss has decided that this job is right for you. She believes this to be true even though your familiarity with Mexico is limited to two coastal vacations there three and four years ago.

She wants a three-page proposal, in memo form, on her desk in two days. The first page should cover the criteria to be used in selecting the managers to be sent to Sonora. She notes that you need not bother with their technical expertise. Others will screen the candidates on that basis. You should instead focus on the qualifications they should have to be good intercultural managers and communicators and how the company should assess those qualifications.

The remaining two pages of the memo should outline the training program through which the transferees would go. This program will have to cover, at a minimum, language training, the larger cultural variations, nonverbal sensitivity, managerial philosophies, and organizational cultures in the two countries.

PROJECT

As a team, write a memo that will establish the foundation for success in this international venture. Your selection criteria should single out the candidates with the greatest potential for success. Your training program should then ensure the likelihood that they will achieve that success.

CASE 11-3

Tsunami Relief

A $245 million stretch of blacktop intended to be the signature goodwill gesture from the American people to the Indonesian survivors of the 2004 tsunami instead became a parable of the problems of Aceh Provinces recovery.

Construction of the 150-mile road along the devastated coast never started, stalled by a host of obstacles like acquiring rights of way through residential and farmland and, particularly, through several hundred graves of mystical and religious significance.

Though some villagers welcomed the idea, some had reservations about a US-style thoroughfare with a wide shoulder on either side that would replace the existing ribbon of mostly churned dirt and mud. Villagers said they feared speeding traffic—they threw rocks at fast-traveling cars of foreign aid workers—and wanted to be able to sell snacks and tea from stalls snug by the roadside, as they had always done.

A demonstration outside the main Indonesian reconstruction agency turned violent when protesters complained that they still lacked basic services and demanded more financing for education.

The patience of US officials wore thin, too. They complained that the government had been too slow in buying up the land and resolving the issue of graves. Finally, the Americans had become so disconcerted about delays that they had tried to pry more action from the Indonesians by suggesting that the money for the road would be diverted to the reconstruction efforts in Lebanon.

"It was threatened they would take the money away," said Kuntoro Mangkusubroto, the director of the Indonesian rehabilitation and reconstruction agency in Aceh. "That's standard."

The Indonesians said the Americans were imposing First World standards of efficiency on a poor region that was pounded by civil war and then swamped by the tsunami, which killed more than 100,000. Records of land titles were washed away, and questions of inheritance among devastated families take a while to decide what they say.

The idea for the road evolved soon after the tsunami when the Bush administration wanted to show that the United States cared about Indonesia, the world's most populous Muslim country, in its moment of need.

It was decided early on to finance one substantial project rather than a number of smaller ones. At first, rebuilding a significant portion of the provincial capital, Banda Aceh, into a kind of "signature city" was discussed. Instead, a well-engineered road from the capital to Meulaboh, the southernmost coastal town, which was nearly completely wiped out, was considered a more fruitful project that played to the American strength of fast and modern construction. The new road would connect the poor fishing communities of the wasted west coast of Aceh to the outside world.

QUESTIONS

1. Identify the cultural values that are clashing in this case.

2. Which dimensions of cultural differences in Hofstede's model are relevant to this case?

Exercise for Small Groups

In groups, share stories about your experiences with cultural differences regarding each of the nonverbal elements listed below. In particular, talk about a time when you misinterpreted the nonverbal signals and what happened as a result. Select the best story in your group and be prepared to share it with the rest of the class.

- Facial expression and eye contact
- Body movements and gestures
- Clothing and personal appearance
- Distance and personal space
- Physical environment
- Time

Student Study Site

Visit the Student Study Site at **study.sagepub.com/hynes6e** for web quizzes, video links, web resources, and cases studies.

Notes

1. US Department of Commerce, International Trade Administration, "Top U.S. Trade Partners," accessed March 6, 2014, http://www.trade.gov/mas/ian/build/groups/public/@tg_ian/documents/webcontent/tg_ian_003364.pdf.

2. "Globalisation and Trade: The Nuts and Bolts Come Apart," *The Economist*, March 28, 2009, pp. 79–81.

3. Collin Eaton, "Bernanke Recalls Darkness and First Light of Recovery," *Houston Chronicle*, March 8, 2014, p. D1.

4. US Bureau of Economic Analysis, accessed March 6, 2014, www.bea.gov.

5. KOF Swiss Economic Institute, "KOF Index of Globalisation 2013," accessed March 6, 2014, http://globalization.kof.ethz.ch/media/filer_public/2013/03/25/press_release_2013_en.pdf.

6. Joseph E. Stiglitz, "On the Wrong Side of Globalization," *The New York Times*, March 16, 2014, www.nytimes.com/opinionator.

7. Organization for International Investment, "Foreign Direct Investment in the United States—2013 Report," accessed March 6, 2014, https://www.ofii.org/sites/default/files/FDIUS_2013_Report.pdf.

8. Charlotte Huff, "Powering up a Hispanic Workforce," *Workforce Management*, May 18, 2009, pp. 25–26.

9. C. Glenn Pearce, Ross Figgins, and Steven Golen, *Business Communication Principles and Applications,* 2nd ed. (New York: Wiley & Sons, 1988), p. 626.

10. Deedee Doke, "Perfect Strangers: Cultural and Linguistic Differences between U.S. and U.K. Workers Necessitate Training for Expatriates," *HR Magazine* 49, no. 12 (December 2004), accessed October 10, 2005, from OCLC FirstSearch Database.

11. John W. Gould as quoted in Norman B. Sigband and Arthur H. Bell, *Communication for Management and Business*, 4th ed. (Glenview, IL: Scott Foresman, 1986), pp. 69–70.

12. Malcolm Gladwell, *Outliers: The Story of Success* (New York: Little, Brown, 2008), p. 175.

13. Dale Level and William Galle, *Managerial Communication* (Plano, TX: Business Publications, 1988), p. 379.

14. Sigband and Bell, *Communicating for Management and Business,* p. 67.

15. Ibid.

16. Francis Fukuyama, *The End of History and the Last Man* (New York: Free Press, 1992).

17. Milton J. Bennett, "A Developmental Approach to Training for Intercultural Sensitivity," *International Journal of Intercultural Relations* 10 (1986): pp. 179–196.

18. Geert Hofstede, "Motivation, Leadership and Organization: Do American Theories Apply Abroad?" *Organizational Dynamics,* Summer 1980, pp. 42–63.

19. Gladwell, *Outliers,* pp. 177–223.

20. Richard E. Nisbett, *The Geography of Thought: How Asians and Westerners Think Differently . . . and Why* (New York: Free Press, 2003), pp. 51–56.

21. Edward T. Hall, *Beyond Culture* (Garden City, NY: Anchor Press/Doubleday, 1977).

22. Phillip Harris and Robert T. Moran, *Managing Cultural Differences,* 5th ed. (Houston, TX: Gulf, 2000), p. 36.

23. Yong-Kang Wei, "Projecting Ethos through 'About Us': A Comparative Study of American and Chinese Corporations' Websites" (unpublished paper presented at First Annual General Business Conference, Sam Houston State University, Huntsville, Texas, USA, April 18, 2009).

24. James Surowiecki, "The Financial Page: Punctuality Pays," *The New Yorker*, April 5, 2004, p. 31.

25. A. Laurent, "The Cultural Diversity of Western Conceptions of Management," *International Studies of Management and Organization* 13, nos. 1–2 (Spring–Summer 1983): pp. 75–96.

26. Jia Lynn Yang, "On the Radar: Pepsi's Diversity Push Pays Off," *Fortune*, September 4, 2006, p. 32.

27. Simon Winchester, "How American Can Maintain Its Edge," *Parade*, December 21, 2008, p. 8.

28. Lyle Ball and Tyler Young, "Translation Pitfalls Mirror the Asian IP Boom," October 2013, www.intellectualpropertymagazine.com.

29. M. Katherine Glover, "Do's and Taboos: Cultural Aspects of International Business," *Business America,* August 13, 1990, p. 4.

30. Ibid.

31. Tom Fowler, "KBR Pleads Guilty in Bribery Case," *Houston Chronicle*, February 12, 2009, pp. D1, D4. See also, "Two Charged in KBR Case in Nigeria," *Houston Chronicle,* March 4, 2009, p. B1.

32. "Bribery Has Long Been Used to Land International Contracts," *Alexander's Gas & Oil Connections*, May 8, 2003, accessed August 21, 2014, http://www.gasandoil.com/news/2003/06/fex32399.

33. Glover, "Do's and Taboos," p. 4.

34. Ibid.

35. Ibid., p. 2.

36. Bennett, "A Developmental Approach to Training for Intercultural Sensitivity," pp. 184–186.

37. Rosalie L. Tung, "Attitudes and Experience of Expatriates on International Assignments" (paper presented at Pacific Region Forum on Business and Management Communication, Simon Fraser University, Vancouver, Canada, January 22, 1998), http://www.cic.sfu.ca/forum/TungMarch181998.html.

38. "New Study: Facing Increased Uncertainty and Volatility on World Stage, Employees on International Assignment Often Feel Left on Their Own," *News Aktuell-DPA Firmengruppe,* May 15, 2002.

39. See "Chairman's letter," *2007 IBM Annual Report*, p. 1, para. 6, accessed August 21, 2013, https://www.ibm.com/annualreport/2007/ch_1.shtml.

40. C. Brooklyn Derr and Gary R. Oddou, "Are U.S. Multinationals Adequately Preparing Future American Leaders for Global Competition?" *International Journal of Human Resource Management,* no. 2 (February 1991): pp. 227–245.

41. "KPMG Survey: Majority of Companies Select Top Employees for Overseas Assignments, However Fail to Successfully Repatriate," *PR Newswire Association, Inc.,* October 25, 2000.

42. Michael Mandel, "Globalization vs. Immigration Reform: Can We Have Free Flow of Goods and Capital without Free Flow of Labor?" *BusinessWeek*, June 4, 2007, p. 40.

43. Michael Morris and Kwok Leung, "Justice for All? Progress in Research on Cultural Variation in the Psychology of Distributive and Procedural Justice," *Applied Psychology: An International Review* 49, no. 1 (2000): pp. 100–132.

PART V

Interpersonal Communication Strategies

CHAPTER 12

Conflict Management

Difficulties are meant to rouse, not discourage. The human spirit is to grow strong by conflict.

—William Ellery Channing, US abolitionist and Unitarian clergyman

The world seems to be full of conflict. Continuing tensions in the Middle East, the Pacific Rim, and Africa make the likelihood of global peace remote. Conflict is also pervasive at the corporate level as demonstrated by the frequency of mergers, acquisitions, and unfriendly takeovers.

Within companies, tensions can also run high. Workplace violence is the number one cause of death for women, and the number two cause for men, on the job. And the incidence of workplace violence is increasing at an alarming rate.[1] Managers must protect workers from violence by developing intervention efforts, including training in conflict resolution.

According to a survey of American Management Association executives, managers are likely to spend about 20 percent of their time dealing with conflict.[2] Conflict may occur as a simple disagreement over the meaning of a work procedure, or it may be an argument over priorities and involve deciding which of two projects should draw from the limited funds available for project development. Or it might bring into focus a long-standing irritation that could result in a work stoppage.

Managers were asked to describe the type of conflicts in which they became involved. One manager described a situation in which four computer programmers wanted to go to a training seminar, but funds were available for only one. Another manager described how both she and a colleague wanted to take their vacations at the same time. Their manager said they could not do that and told them to work out the schedule between them. In both these situations, conflicts had to be resolved.

Organizational conflict is a natural part of the traditional organizational structure because a built-in opposition between units often exists. Increases in conflict correlate positively with such factors as increases in an organization's levels of hierarchy, standardization of jobs, and increases in the number of workers.[3] In fact, organizational conflict is so pervasive that over seventy-five university-affiliated centers, institutes, associations, and consortiums are dedicated to research on this subject. One such organization, the Association for Conflict Resolution (ACR), has over six thousand members: mediators, arbitrators, facilitators, educators, and others involved in the field of conflict resolution and collaborative decision making. The ACR has chapters in twenty states of the United States.

An increasing number of companies are also creating programs that help employees resolve their problems quickly and without external intervention. The policies are integrated into the corporate culture and use a variety of approaches, including hot lines, peer review panels, mediation, and arbitration, to resolve conflicts. Current research indicates that about 10 percent of American employers have implemented such internal systems.[4]

BENEFITS OF CONFLICT

Conflict generally has a negative connotation; however, conflict is a positive occurrence if managed properly. Conflict requires managers to analyze their goals, it creates dialogue among employees, and it fosters creative solutions. Without conflict, employees and organizations would stagnate.

Generational conflict in the workplace is one example of how conflict can have positive effects. For the first time in US history, four generations are working together. Possibilities for conflict run high due to differences in work style and philosophy. Older workers view "work" as a place—a location you go to at a specified time, such as 9 a.m. to 5 p.m. Younger workers tend to view work as something you do—anywhere, anytime. They grew up in a digital world where information is always available. So it is easy for Boomers to conclude that Millennials who arrive at 9:30 are working less hard than they, who arrived at 8:30, not realizing that the younger generation may have already put in time at their home computers or smartphones while still in pajamas. To Millennials, the extent of scheduling that goes on in most workplaces is stultifying. Learning that much of today's work can be done asynchronously, Boomers benefit from their younger colleagues' preferences for maximum efficiency.[5]

Conflict also may foster creativity. Conflict helps to overcome individual psychological distortions and biases by forcing people out of their traditional modes of thinking. In this way, conflict promotes the unstructured thinking that some see as required for developing good, novel alternatives to difficult problems.[6]

In addition, studies show a higher decision quality when there is open opposition and resistance by subordinates than when the resistance of subordinates is weak or even passive. In one study, high-quality decisions occurred in 45.8 percent of the situations with strong subordinate resistance but in only 18.8 percent of the situations where the resistance was weak or nonexistent.[7]

STOP AND THINK

1. To what extent do age differences among employees at your workplace cause conflicts?

2. How can these differences be beneficial to productivity?

Thus, managers who pride themselves in running a smooth ship may not be as effective as they think. The smooth ship may reflect suppressed conflict that could have potential benefit if allowed free play. In fact, the conflict might not be as harmful as its suppression.

What causes conflict? When is it functional and when is it not? What methods can be used to resolve conflict? Is any one method best? The following discussion answers these questions, but first we review the relationship between communication and conflict.

THE RELATIONSHIP BETWEEN COMMUNICATION AND CONFLICT

As is true with many other terms, *conflict* has both a colloquial meaning and a long list of specific definitions. However, a quick review of these definitions will help to describe the nature of conflict. Katz and Kahn state that two systems—which could include persons, groups, organizations, or nations—are in conflict when they interact directly in such a way that the actions of one tend to prevent or compel some outcome against the resistance of the other.[8] Another author states that conflict characterizes a situation in which the conditions, practices, or goals of individuals are inherently incompatible.[9] A third definition presents conflict as a struggle over values or claims to scarce resources, power, or status. In this struggle, opponents aim to neutralize, injure, or eliminate their rivals.[10]

These three definitions help define the nature of conflict and indicate the role of communication in conflict. The first definition uses the word *interact,* implying a communication interaction of some kind. The second definition uses the phrase *inherently incompatible,* and the third definition includes *a struggle over values.* Communication is the method by which managers determine if something is inherently incompatible, and the struggle over values is carried out through communication behaviors. Thus, the ability to communicate effectively may eliminate conflict immediately; however, ineffective communication may cause a situation to appear inherently incompatible; thus, a struggle over values may ensue. The conclusion is that communicative behavior may cause, as well as resolve, conflict.

Let us examine the specific characteristics of conflict and the corresponding implications for communication. The following are four axioms that are particularly relevant to communication.[11] These axioms are reviewed to demonstrate how effective communication can make conflict a constructive, positive process.

1. *Conflict involves at least two parties.* Because conflict involves at least two parties, communication is an integral component. Conflict can be generated or resolved only through communication. Consequently, managers must understand the types of communication interactions that can cause conflict and the communication patterns that are most functional after conflict has developed. In fact, a good communicator can bring conflict to the surface and make it a productive process.

2. *Conflict develops from perceived mutually exclusive goals.* Mutually exclusive goals may exist as a result of objective facts or an individual's values and perceptions. However,

the key factor is that the parties involved perceive the objectives as mutually exclusive; frequently, through communication, the involved parties see that the goal actually is not mutually exclusive. But only through communication can the parties in conflict determine the existence of a superordinate goal that may meet both parties' goals. Again, the positive nature of conflict is evident because without conflict the parties may not know about the superordinate goal.

3. *Conflict involves parties who may have different values or perceptions.* To illustrate how conflictive parties may have different value systems, consider how a first-level supervisor who was once a member of a trade union would have values much different from those of a young engineer who has been out of college only two years. This value difference may result in a potential conflict when the two employees consider implementing a computerized production control system. The supervisor could perceive the computerized system as too difficult to learn and as a threat to employees' job security. However, the young engineer might perceive it solely as an engineering challenge. In this case, values affect perception.

The selective attention principle says that we tend to perceive what is important and pleasing to us and avoid what is not. The following example shows how differences in perception led to a major conflict.[12] A textile mill allowed a conflict to develop that resulted in a big labor turnover. The mill had informed employees when they were hired that it gave automatic raises each year and merit raises for deserving employees after nine and eighteen months. The employees, however, understood this to mean they would receive an automatic raise at *all three* of these periods—nine, twelve, and eighteen months. When they did not obtain their raises, many of them quit because they thought the employer had not maintained the original promise to grant wage increases. In this case, the differences between employee and employer perception led to conflicting views.

When conflicting parties have different values or perceptions, communication is important in two ways. First, exposure and communication between two individuals will likely result in the individuals eventually sharing values and becoming friendlier toward each other.[13] Second, as more accurate communication develops between two managers, the perceptual differences will subside; hence, the probability of conflict will be reduced.

Chapter 1 indicated that cultural diversity is increasing in organizations. This diversity will create conflict, but it will be exciting and productive because diverse viewpoints, when managed appropriately, will result in more creative outcomes.

4. *Conflict terminates only when each side is satisfied that it has won or lost.* Win–lose situations seem to dominate our culture—for instance, law courts use the adversary system and political parties strive to win elections. Competition to win in sports is so keen that fights among spectators are not uncommon. The pervasive win–lose attitude in our culture has made it difficult to imagine that both parties may "win" in any situation labeled a conflict. This problem recalls the first axiom, which states that conflict develops from mutually exclusive goals. However, accurate communication may reveal that a win or a loss is not the only alternative.

SOURCES OF CONFLICT

When managers perceive conflict in the workplace, they may assume it is due to incompatible personalities. "Why can't everyone just get along with each other?" they plead. But managers need to understand that the sources of conflict are often deeper than individual personality. Then they will be better able to select the appropriate communication strategy. The underlying causes or sources of conflict situations often are built into the organization's hierarchy and ways of doing business.

The lines of authority in an organization can encourage conflict. For example, the lending and the savings departments are interdependent in all banks. The lending department cannot lend funds until the savings department has collected funds. By the same token, the savings department would be hard pressed if the lending department had no customers. These two areas have common goals within the bank (profit and continued operation of the bank), but their interdependence can lead to conflict over their respective authority. While the savings department would like to give high interest rates to please its customers, the lending department wants to provide low interest rates to please its customers. When the interdependence of these departments becomes a central issue, conflict will arise over whose authority takes precedence or whose responsibility for the bank's profit goal is more relevant.

STOP AND THINK

1. In your work experience, which departments were in conflict the most often?

2. How could these conflicts be resolved?

The distribution of the limited resources available in an organization is another source of conflict. If resources were unlimited, few conflicts would arise, but this condition seldom exists. When resources are limited, and more than one person or group wants a share, conflict develops. The most obvious conflict occurs during the annual budget review. With funds traditionally limited, it is necessary to decide which department will get what amount. Since each department manager's goal appears most important from her own perspective, the funds allocated to one department may appear to be funds taken from another. The interdependency of the various departments vying for budget allocations thus can become a major source of conflict.

Diverse goals are a third source of organizational conflict. For instance, clashes may occur between quality assurance managers and production managers in a manufacturing environment. The goal of the quality people is zero defects, while the goal of production is filling the customer's order on time. Conflicting goals and roles can also explain why a company's salespeople routinely ignore the accounting staff's requests for expense forms and receipts or why a shift foreman refuses to let his workers attend an employee development session offered by Human Resources. To alleviate such traditional conflicts between functional units, senior executives should remind their managers of the overarching goals, mission, and vision.

Conflict and Perception

The relationship between conflict and perception has already been briefly discussed. Perceived conflict is present when the parties recognize the conditions or when the parties misunderstand one another's true position.

Clearly, failure to identify potentially conflictive situations may prevent conflicts from developing immediately. More often, though, the inaccurate or illogical perception of a situation causes unnecessary conflict. An example of inaccurate perception is the case of manager praise. A recent poll by Maritz Incentives found wide-ranging opinions on appreciation in the workplace: 55 percent of employees said their bosses never or rarely thank them for their efforts. On the other hand, only 6 percent of supervisors said they never praise their subordinates; 34 percent said they praise their direct reports daily, and 45 percent said they do so weekly or monthly.[14] It is easy to see how this discrepancy of perceptions can lead to conflict.

The grid in Figure 12–1 shows why inaccurate perceptions create conflict in the managerial process. Assume two managers are discussing an issue. Two possibilities exist for each manager: each correctly perceives the existence of a potential conflict or incorrectly perceives it. This results in the four possibilities diagrammed. The grid shows that an accurate mutual perception could possibly exist in only one of four occurrences. Of course, this is not always the case, but numerous conflicts not warranted by the actual situation may develop.

Further, two managers may be aware of serious disagreement over a policy, but it may not create any anxiety or affect their feelings toward one another. Competition for budget allocations, for example, do not need to be personalized.

Personally felt conflict may find expression in fear, threat, mistrust, and hostility. Consider the bank teller who called in a bomb threat on the day he was fired, so he could meet his former coworkers for drinks. No one knows the financial costs of such workplace revenge behaviors, but everyone agrees that a lack of communication causes most employee sabotage. "Getting back is the way of communicating when you can't, or when you're afraid to speak up for yourself," explains William Lundin, a workplace relations specialist.[15] According to one Phoenix management consultant, about 30 percent of workers

Figure 12–1   Accuracy of Perceptions and Conflict

		Manager 2	
		Accurate	Inaccurate
Manager 1	Accurate	Accurate mutual perception	Inaccurate mutual perception
	Inaccurate	Inaccurate mutual perception	Inaccurate mutual perception

try to "get back at the boss" on a regular basis. Incidents of workplace violence continue to increase. Based on Labor Department statistics, across the United States each week, more than ten employees are slain at work.[16] And just as we prepare for natural disasters, we need to prepare for workplace violence.

What can managers do to prevent violence and acts of hostility? It is important to maintain a communication program that allows employees (1) to understand how their performance level is being evaluated, (2) to know the consequences of changing (and not changing) their behavior, (3) to discuss their problems, (4) to explore options for solutions, and (5) to defuse anger. The venting of hostility can be therapeutic rather than detrimental, if managed properly. Group discussions can act as a safety valve for this hostility, as can periodic meetings between supervisors and subordinates. Effective managers do not become defensive even when they are the focus of the hostile communication. Nondefensive communication is the key to managing personally felt conflict.

The observable behavior of the manager, based on conditions, perceptions, and feelings, may be seen as either conflict or an attempt to establish mutual goals. The most obvious manifestations of conflict are open aggression or violence at one end of a continuum and integrative problem solving at the other end, as depicted in Figure 12–2. A continuum is used because generally neither totally open aggression nor completely satisfactory problem solving is manifest. However, the goal is to move as close as possible to integrative problem solving. As the remainder of this discussion shows, managers have numerous ways to manage conflict along this continuum as they attempt to resolve it.

Figure 12–2　Ways to Manifest Conflict

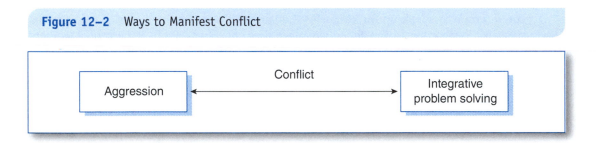

STRATEGIES IN CONFLICT RESOLUTION

Now that we have looked at the relationship of conflict to managerial communication, discussed constructive conflict, and reviewed the sources of conflict, we can identify strategies for conflict resolution. Managerial communication strategies for managing conflict could be put into many categories. For our discussion, we use the system presented in Figure 12–3. This figure demonstrates that during a conflict, managers may emphasize interpersonal relations, task production, or a combination thereof. Five possible strategies are presented: avoiding, accommodating, forcing, compromising, and problem solving.[17]

Figure 12–3   Strategies for Managing Conflict

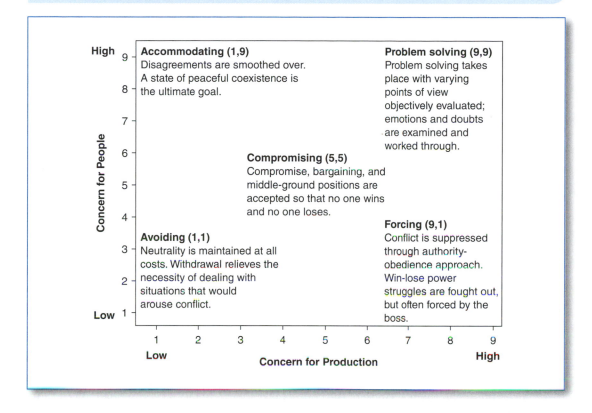

While reviewing these strategies, the contingency approach to managerial communication should be kept in mind. Various conflict situations require different strategies, so effective communication requires that managers match the strategy to the situation.

Avoiding

The avoidance or withdrawal strategy combines a low concern for production with a low concern for people. The person using this style sees conflict as a hopeless, useless experience. Rather than undergo the tension and frustration of conflict, managers using the avoidance or withdrawal style simply remove themselves from conflict situations. This avoidance may be physical or psychological. The person using this strategy will avoid disagreement and tension, will not openly take sides in a disagreement among others, and will feel little commitment to any decisions reached. This conflict management style is the second most popular among US managers.[18]

Avoidance need not be dramatic. Many managers avoid by ignoring a comment or quickly changing the subject when conversation begins to threaten. Another way to avoid is to place the responsibility for an issue on a higher manager. A third way to withdraw is to use a simple response of "I'm looking into the matter," with the hope that the other party will forget the issue.

This strategy is frequently used in large bureaucracies that have an overabundance of policies. Rather than attempt to resolve the conflict, managers simply blame it on *policy*. Managers who lack self-confidence in their communication abilities may hope the problem just disappears. However, this usually does not work. In fact, withdrawal from conflict has been negatively correlated with constructive conflict resolution. Withdrawal has been further negatively correlated with knowledge of the supervisor's feelings and attitudes; open, upward communication; helpfulness of the supervisor; and adequacy of the planning relationship. Thus, managers who avoid conflict do not operate effectively in these critical managerial areas.[19]

Accommodating

In accommodating, the second type of conflict resolution, managers try to deal with conflict by making everyone happy. When using this approach, the manager emphasizes maintaining relationships with fellow employees and de-emphasizes achieving productive goals. Since the manager wants others' acceptance, he will give in to others' desires in areas that conflict with his own. Managers using this style believe confrontation is destructive.

Typical attempts to accommodate may include such things as calling for a coffee break at a tense moment, breaking tension with humor, changing the topic, or engaging in some ritual show of togetherness such as an office birthday party. Since these efforts are likely to reduce felt conflict, they are more beneficial than simple avoidance. This reduction of felt conflict will probably have short-range effects and may even have some long-range benefit. However, just because someone does not experience a hostile or negative feeling does not mean the real cause of the conflict is resolved. In fact, accommodating is a camouflage approach that can break down at any time and create barriers to progress. Thus, research has found that it is used more in low- or medium-performance organizations than in high-performance organizations. In addition, accommodating correlates negatively with open, upward communication and with participation in goal setting.

Forcing

Forcing, the third conflict management strategy, is used by the manager who attempts to meet production goals at all costs, without concern for the needs or acceptance of others. For such a manager, losing is destructive because it is viewed as reduced status, weakness, and the loss of self-image. Winning must be achieved at any cost and gives this manager a sense of excitement and achievement. Not surprisingly, it is the number one conflict resolution strategy used by managers.[20]

A situation characterized by the forcing strategy will probably cause later conflicts. The language managers use to describe conflict situations in their organizations often reflects the negative effect this style may have: opposition, battle, fight, conquest, head-to-head, coercion, and smash. Such language and imagery can result in long-lasting, emotional wounds.[21]

While force can resolve immediate disputes, the long-term effects will probably include a loss of productivity. Forcing in conflict situations negatively correlates with such factors as adequacy of planning, helpfulness of the supervision, and participation in goal setting. The major difficulty of a forcing strategy is that employees are reluctant to plan or carry out plans when they perceive that the ultimate resolution of the conflict will put them on the losing side of a win–lose position.

Interestingly, while little doubt exists that forcing has limited use, managers consider forcing to be their favorite backup strategy for dealing with conflict.[22] Immediate compliance is misperceived as a long-term solution in these cases.

Compromising

Compromise, the fourth strategy for conflict resolution, assumes that half a loaf is better than none. This approach falls somewhere between forcing and accommodating. Since compromise provides some gain for both sides rather than a unilateral victory, many participants judge this approach as better than the other strategies just discussed.

Compromise is used when one of two conditions exists: (1) neither party involved believes he or she has the power to "force" the issue on the other party, or (2) one or both of the parties believe winning may not be worth the cost in money, time, or energy. Compromise is often highly related to negotiating, which is the topic of the next chapter; however, several important points are pertinent here. First, compromise may lead to both parties' perceiving themselves as winners, but they may also both feel like losers. A negative overtone may develop in the working relationship between the employees involved, and any sense of trust may break down. While both parties involved probably entered the negotiations with a cooperative attitude, a sense of competition may be the result of compromise.

A second concern with compromise is that the party with the most information has the better position. This power of information may restrict open communication among employees. This situation in turn often results in a lopsided compromise. A third factor is the principle of the least interested party: The party that has the least interest in the outcome is in the more powerful position in the negotiations. As a result, an employee who has little concern about the welfare of the company may have an inordinate amount of influence in a compromise.

PROBLEM SOLVING: THE WIN–WIN STRATEGY

Thus far, it may seem that no totally acceptable, productive strategy exists to manage conflict. Everything has been discussed in terms of loss. Fortunately, this is not the case. Problem solving, the fifth strategy to be discussed, is a win–win strategy for conflict. This complex and highly effective style requires skillful, strategic managerial communication, but it reaps a big dividend; thus, the remainder of our discussion centers on this strategy. Let us first describe the win–win strategy and then examine specific techniques for implementation.

Description of the Strategy

The key to this strategy is that it follows a mutual problem-solving approach rather than a combative one. In contrast to managers who use a forcing or compromising strategy, managers engaged in this type of problem solving assume a high-quality, mutually acceptable solution is possible. The parties direct their energies toward defeating the problem and not each other.

The following example presents a clear description of the problem-solving approach to conflict resolution. It details a meeting in Wisconsin that set out to explore possible prison reforms.

Nine of the state's top prison officials met to design an ideal correctional institution. In the course of the discussion, one group member proposed that uniforms traditionally worn by prison guards be eliminated. The group then began a lengthy argument about whether or not uniforms should be worn. One group member suggested that the issue be resolved democratically by vote. As a result, six people voted against uniforms and three voted in favor of them. The winning members looked pleased, while the losing members either got angry or withdrew from further discussion.

A group consultant present at the time suggested that the members take another look at the situation. Then he asked those in favor of uniforms what they hoped to accomplish (establishing goals). Those officials stated that part of the rehabilitative process in correctional institutions is that of teaching people to deal constructively with authority, and they saw uniforms as a means for achieving the goal. When asked why they opposed uniforms (analyzing the problem), the other group members said that uniforms created such a stigma that guards had an additional difficulty laying to rest the stereotypes held by inmates before they could deal with them on a one-to-one basis. The group consultant then asked the group what ways might be appropriate to meet the combined goals, namely, teaching people to deal with authority and avoiding the difficulty of stereotypes held about traditional uniforms (generating solutions). While working on the problem, the group identified ten possible solutions, including prison personnel using name tags, color-coded casual dress, or uniforms for guard supervisors but not for guards in constant contact with prisoners. After discussing the various alternatives, the group decided upon the third solution (selecting the best solution).

In its first discussion, the group engaged in clear conflict that was only partially resolved by vote. In the discussion led by the consultant, the group turned to problem solving, eventually reaching consensus and a win–win solution.[23]

Beliefs Necessary to Implement the Strategy

We are suggesting that the problem-solving strategy is the most desirable; however, a manager wanting to effectively use this approach must hold a series of beliefs.

Belief 1: Cooperation Is Better Than Competition

The manager must first believe cooperation is better than competition. American management seems to be based on competition, so it is difficult to envision cooperation as a viable possibility at times.[24] This competition may develop out of Darwin's concept of survival of the fittest: A manager who has a self-image of weakness may fear extinction. Lacking confidence, this person feels a sense of competitiveness with others in the company.

Competition also has an important role in stimulating employees to achieve more. However, as technology becomes more complex and employees more specialized, interdependence is required. Few tasks can be completed without the cooperation of many employees. The group as a whole becomes greater than the sum of all the individuals, so cooperation is required. This is not to say that differences of opinion should be prevented.

Different opinions can lead to new insights and creativity as long as the opinions do not disrupt the group process. A manager must enter the conflict situation believing others' opinions are beneficial. He must be willing to listen. The emphasis on teamwork in today's work environment makes cooperation mandatory.

STOP AND THINK

1. In today's team-based work environment, why do employees continue to be evaluated on the basis of their individual achievements?

2. What would be the effect of rewarding employees on the basis of their team's achievements?

Belief 2: Parties Can Be Trusted

The second belief is that the other parties involved in the conflict can be trusted. Managers who are trusting will not conceal or distort relevant information, nor will they fear stating facts, ideas, conclusions, and feelings that would make them vulnerable.

A researcher compared problem-solving groups. Half the groups were directed to trust other people, to express their views openly, to share information freely, and to aim at a high level of mutual confidence. The other groups were directed to behave in opposite ways. The researchers found that problem-solving groups with high trust will

- exchange relevant ideas and feelings more openly,
- develop greater clarification of goals and problems,
- search more extensively for alternative courses of action,
- have greater influence on solutions,
- be more satisfied with their problem-solving efforts,
- have greater motivation to implement conclusions,
- see themselves as closer and more of a team,
- have less desire to leave their group to join another.[25]

Trusting behavior causes reciprocity. Trusting cues will likely evoke trusting behavior from others. Conversely, when a manager does not trust others, the cues to mistrust will evoke mistrustful behavior on the other's part. So it is best to assume a person can be trusted and to change that view only with evidence to the contrary.

Belief 3: Status Differences Can Be Minimized

The third belief that managers must possess is that status differences between parties can be minimized in a conflict situation. Differences in power or status that separate two individuals into we–they orientation inhibit conflict resolution. A manager who is in a higher power position may yield to the temptation to use the power inherent in the position as the rationale for forcing the solution. If that happens, the participants, rather than confronting the problem and treating each other as equals, will regress into a win–lose style, and the result is much less productive. Managers who do not rely on status will spend time listening to everyone involved. The section in Chapter 9 on developing a listening climate provides ideas for managers who want to minimize their perceived power and encourage communication both upward and laterally.

Belief 4: Mutually Acceptable Solutions Can Be Found

The final belief managers must hold is that a mutually acceptable and desirable solution exists and can be found. Unless both parties believe this is possible, a win–lose strategy will result. Conflict resolution can be extremely frustrating and time consuming unless both parties remain optimistic about finding a mutually acceptable answer. This is not to say that both parties are meeting the same goal. Rather, both parties can reach their different goals in an acceptable manner.

Each of these four beliefs—cooperation, trust, equal status, and mutually acceptable goals—is important. A manager must believe in these concepts to implement an effective win–win conflict resolution strategy. But belief in these concepts is not enough; managers must also use the appropriate communication skills in a strategic manner. The next part of this discussion describes these skills and the appropriate method for implementing them.

Implementing the Strategy

Specific steps should be followed to achieve the problem-solving strategy. However, before these steps are reviewed, key communication principles must be identified.

1. Use neutral rather than emotional terms. "I still tend to prefer my approach" is better than "Your idea is not functional."

2. Avoid absolute statements that leave no room for modification. "I think this is the way . . ." is better than "This is the *only* way."

3. Ask open-ended questions.

4. Avoid leading questions. This rule is especially important where status differences are present.

5. Repeat key phrases to make sure all parties are communicating on the same wavelength.

6. Use terms that all parties clearly understand.

7. Allow the other person to complete statements. Do not interrupt.

8. Use effective listening skills, especially paraphrasing, to ensure the other person's ideas are fully understood.

9. Be aware of the importance of physical arrangements. For instance, sitting in front of a big desk may cause a person to feel defensive.

When managers use the communication principles just presented as they follow the sequence given next, they should be able to resolve conflicts successfully.

The first step in implementing the problem-solving strategy is to maximize environmental conditions, as summarized in Table 12–1 and discussed below:

- *Review and adjust conflict conditions.* Earlier, we identified sources of conflict inherent in the organization, including goals and resources. When a manager can identify these conditions, it is sometimes possible to adjust them to promote cooperation.

- *Review and adjust perceptions.* Managers should adjust and correct their perceptions through reality testing. "Am I viewing the situation or the behavior as it actually exists?" Perceptions become more accurate as an individual learns more facts about the condition and has resulting impressions confirmed by others' perceptions.

- *Review and adjust attitudes.* Since an optimal outcome depends on trust, mutuality, and cooperation, little success will result if the parties are distrustful, hostile, and competitive. Accordingly, one should identify the attitudes and feelings of the parties engaged in the conflict as far as possible. Often, the best strategy is to start with the easily solved problems. Once the easier problems are solved, a more positive attitude develops for the more complex conflict situation. The trust that results may make cooperative communication easier.

Once environmental conditions and perceptions have been identified and perhaps adjusted, you are ready to begin the actual problem-solving strategy. John Dewey, an American educator who lived and wrote in the early part of the 20th century, first articulated this process in one of his books, *How We Think*. Over one hundred years later, this rational problem-solving process is still frequently and

Table 12–1 Maximizing Environmental Conditions

Review and adjust conflict conditions.
Review and adjust perceptions.
Review and adjust attitudes.

successfully used in contemporary businesses. The reason for the popularity of this process is that it really does conform to human thought; it is "how we think." In Chapter 4, you learned Dewey's problem-solving process and how to apply it in meetings and team projects. Let us now review the five steps in the problem-solving process (summarized in Table 12–2) and see how it applies to conflict resolution.

1. *Define the problem.* A statement of the problem in a conflict situation is usually much more difficult than it seems. People tend to discuss solutions before they clearly define the problem. Because of this, our inclination is to state the problem as a solution rather than as a goal. This results in ambiguous communication, and it is common for the parties to focus on the solutions without having a clear definition of the problem. The outcome may be increased conflict. Second, managers must state the goals in the form of group goals rather than individual priorities. Third, the problem definition must be specific. One helpful strategy is to clearly write out the problem statement so everyone can see it and agree on it. Alternatively, the group can agree on a problem stated in a question format.

2. *Analyze the problem.* Again, managers tend to want to skip this step. After all, they may argue, they live with the problem. What is the point of spending more time wallowing in it? Dewey's answer is that by exploring the depths of the problem, by looking at its history, causes, effects, and extent, one can later come up with a solution that addresses more than symptoms and that is more than a bandage. It will address the root cause of the problem, thus improving its chances of being successful.

3. *Brainstorm alternatives.* All parties should offer potential solutions. One idea may stimulate other ideas. The more employees communicate in an open, trusting environment, the greater the potential for generating effective solutions. Trust, of course, evaporates when an idea is criticized during a brainstorming session. As soon as someone says, "That's a terrible idea. It'll never work," who would be willing to take the risk of offering another idea? Managers must ensure that premature judging of solutions is avoided during this step.

4. *Develop criteria for a good solution.* These criteria, or standards, may already be in place and available. Other times, the organization's executives will specify to the problem-solving managers what a good solution must look like. Occasionally, the managers are expected to develop their own criteria. Common criteria for an optimal solution include the following: it must be cost-effective, it must be easily or quickly implemented, it must use only resources that are currently available, it must be legal, and it must be consistent with the organization's mission or values.

5. *Evaluate the brainstormed alternatives using the independently developed criteria for a good solution.* This is really the easiest step. By this time, attention to the problem is unified, and an open communication environment has been achieved with active participation by all the parties involved. The best solution appears automatically as the brainstormed alternative that matches your list of criteria.

CONFLICT AND MANAGEMENT SUCCESS

The basic nature of organizational dynamics creates conflict.[26] As discussed earlier in this chapter, lines of authority, especially the supervisor-subordinate relationship, often engender conflict. A typical example is when the supervisor provides corrective feedback and the subordinate interprets it as aggressive, threatening, disrespectful, or offensive. Such negative emotions can escalate conflict and even prompt retaliation.[27] As a consequence, the supervisor-subordinate relationship suffers, and employee morale and productivity decline. To minimize the damage triggered by poorly communicated feedback, managers must understand and learn to manage conflict.

Table 12–2	Dewey's Problem-Solving Process
1. Define the problem.	
2. Analyze the problem.	
3. Brainstorm alternatives.	
4. Develop criteria for a good solution.	
5. Evaluate the brainstormed alternatives using the independently developed criteria for a good solution.	

6. Decision

This chapter proposes that communication is at the foundation of conflict management. Since conflict is a pervasive, vital, but often troublesome aspect of organizational life, effective conflict management has become a major focus for business and industry training programs.[28] Recent studies indicate that employee training that develops social and emotional competency (popularly known as emotional intelligence or EI) is a better predictor of professional success than cognitive intelligence or specialized knowledge.[29] Daniel Goleman's landmark book about EI listed six noncognitive competencies that help people cope with workplace pressures and the resulting conflict. These competencies are generally accepted as the starting point for employee training in emotion management.

- Become self-aware in managing emotions and controlling impulses
- Set goals and perform well
- Be motivated and creative
- Empathize with others
- Handle relationships effectively
- Develop appropriate social skills[30]

Mastery of these competencies greatly affects the way employees interact with their coworkers, subordinates, and managers. Clearly, whether one is a college student anticipating a career in management or a practicing manager with years of experience, it is necessary to continually hone constructive communication strategies for conflict management.

SUMMARY

Managers are likely to spend at least 20 percent of their time dealing with some kind of conflict, so it is important to understand the causes of conflict and productive methods for resolution. Because miscommunication is an integral element behind conflict, effective managerial communication is one key to resolution.

Conflict can be constructive as well as destructive. The nature of the word *conflict* implies opposing positions with negative results; however, when properly managed, conflict may be a positive force. An important managerial role is to be able to identify the difference between destructive and constructive conflict.

Managers can use one of five strategies to resolve conflict: avoiding, accommodating, forcing, compromising, or problem solving. The first four strategies are termed win–lose or lose–lose because one or both parties in the conflict will lose. However, the fifth strategy is termed a win–win approach because both parties in the conflict are potential winners; consequently, the effective manager should strive for the win–win style.

The problem-solving strategy can be achieved when the manager believes in cooperation, trusts the other party, minimizes status differences, and believes a mutually acceptable and desirable solution is available. These beliefs are a prerequisite to success, but satisfactory results cannot be obtained unless sound communication principles are used to put the beliefs into action. A sequence of steps should be followed when implementing the win–win strategy: review and adjust conflict conditions, perceptions, and attitudes; develop a problem definition; analyze the problem; brainstorm alternatives; evaluate alternatives according to criteria; and develop the best solution.

When a manager uses strategic communication skills, believes in the win–win approach to conflict resolution, and follows the correct sequence of activities, a constructive approach to conflict resolution can result.

Cases for Small-Group Discussion

CASE 12–1

Conflict and Technology

Janna White sat in her office, perplexed. Two days previously, she had been given responsibility to lead a team on a project that would have a significant impact on the investment decision under consideration at PlexiWarm Corporation. The decision involved an expansion of the firm's product lines to include high-density spray foam insulation (the firm currently produces rigid foam insulation panels). Janna had scheduled the first team meeting for this afternoon and was looking forward to working on such a significant project. She had just opened her e-mail to find a stream of confusing communications from two team members. Apparently, the two had been exchanging e-mail and text messages in such rapid succession that the replies had become very disjointed. The final messages had come about an hour earlier; both parties had basically concluded that they simply could not work together because of the poor communication of the other person!

Janna had the record only of the e-mail messages—the text messages had been sent between each person's individual cell phones. Without a complete record of the communication, Janna did not have a clue about how to try to resolve the conflict. She e-mailed each person, asking whether they had kept a record of the "text thread." She quickly got responses that neither had kept the stream of messages and that each now refused to work with the other.

QUESTIONS

1. What could Janna have done in advance to try to prevent the conflict?

2. Now that the conflict has occurred, and since this significant project still must be carried out, how should Janna manage the conflict?

3. Looking ahead, what is the likely effect of the conflict on team productivity?

CASE 12–2

Conflict over Job Duties

Linda Sims is the manager of the accounting department and Jose Martinez is the manager of the sales department for a production company. This is a fast-growing firm, and the staff of the accounting department (eleven employees) is often overwhelmed with work.

Since the accounting department is located immediately next to the credit department, Ruth Rankin, the administrative assistant in credit, sometimes works on journal entries assigned to her by Sims.

The company has experienced especially rapid growth over the past six months, which has caused everyone to be busier than usual. With the increase in sales volume, the credit office is under pressure to process applications more quickly, and Rankin is available to help Sims out with accounting overflow less often.

Sims complains to Martinez that she needs Rankin to work in accounting more than he needs her in credit. Martinez's response is, "If I can't move the credit applications through the pipeline in a timely manner, soon there'll be no need for an accounting department, because this company will be out of business."

QUESTIONS

1. What is the cause of this conflict?

2. Write a problem statement for this situation.

3. If you were Sims, how would you approach Martinez in this situation?

4. What style did Sims initially use?

5. What could Sims do to gain Martinez's cooperation rather than make him defensive?

CASE 12–3

Conflict among Team Members

Rod Edwards, the advertising manager for Waterlite Advertising and Associates, has two assistants. One is Gina Reese, an account executive who gets clients for the company. Edwards's second assistant is Mina Patel, a copywriter. She does the actual writing and designing of the ads for the clients.

Reese and Patel usually have a close working relationship because they work as a team on all clients' accounts. Reese gets the clients and discusses their needs with them. Afterward, she tells Patel about the conversation and the clients' needs, so Patel can design the right ad. Once Patel finishes the ad, Reese presents it to the client. If the ad is a success, it is usually Reese who gets the praise and recognition because she is the one who interfaces with the client.

In the past, Patel was not bothered by the recognition Reese got because she always knew she was the one who designed the ad. But the last ad Patel designed brought in a $1 million contract to the firm. Edwards immediately gave Reese a raise for bringing in the client but did not give Patel any recognition.

Naturally, this caused friction between Reese and Patel, and their relationship began to deteriorate. Four days after Reese got the raise, their conflict reached a climax. Reese borrowed Patel's stapler (a trivial occurrence) and forgot to return it. Patel caused a scene and refused to talk to Reese for the next few days.

The problem was brought to Edwards's attention because his department's productivity was declining. For the ads to be developed, the assistants had to work as a team.

Edwards called both employees into his office and immediately started lecturing them. He insisted they get along and begin working on the next ad. He told them he expected an ad finished by noon the following day. Reese and Patel walked out of Edwards's office without resolving the problem. They did get some work done the next day, but their close relationship was never resumed.

QUESTIONS

1. What kind of conflict resolution strategy did Edwards use? What kind should he have used?

2. This is an example of destructive conflict. Could it develop as a constructive situation?

3. What steps should Edwards have followed to develop a win–win strategy?

Exercise for Small Groups

Conflict Resolution Survey

For each of the thirty statements listed below, indicate how frequently you typically behave as described when you come into conflict with another person. (Rather than responding to these statements generally, you may wish to relate the statements to a particular person or setting familiar to you.) Use the following scale.

2–Most of the time.

1–Some of the time.

0–Rarely.

_____ (1)   1. I ask for help in resolving the conflict from someone outside our relationship.

_____ (1)   2. I try to stress those things on which we both agree rather than focus on our disagreement.

_____ (2)   3. I suggest we search for a compromise solution acceptable to both of us.

_____ (2)   4. I attempt to bring out all the concerns of the other person.

_____ (1)   5. I am firm in pursuing my goals.

_____ (1)   6. I strive to preserve our relationship.

_____   7. I seek to split the difference in our positions where possible.

_____   8. I work toward a solution that meets *both* our needs.

_____   9. I avoid the discussion of emotionally charged issues.

_____   10. I try to impose my solution on the other person.

_____   11. I emphasize whatever similarity I see in our positions.

_____   12. I try to postpone any discussion until I have had time to think it over.

_____   13. I propose a middle ground to the other person.

_____   14. I use whatever power I have to get my wishes.

_____   15. I attempt to get all our points immediately out in the open.

_____   16. I give up one point in order to gain another.

_____   17. I encourage the other person to offer a full explanation of her or his ideas to me.

_____   18. I try to get the other person to see things my way.

_____   19. I treat the other person as considerately as possible.

_____   20. I suggest we think our concerns over individually before we meet in the hope that the anger will cool down.

_____   21. I press to get my points made.

_____   22. I support a direct and frank discussion of the problem.

_____   23. I try to find a fair combination of gains and losses for both of us.

_____   24. I try not to allow the other person's feelings to become hurt.

_____   25. I avoid taking positions that would create controversy.

_____   26. I suggest we each give in on some of our needs to find a solution we can both live with.

_____ 27. I listen carefully in order to understand the other person as well as possible.

_____ 28. I soothe the other person's feelings if emotions are running high.

_____ 29. I assert my position strongly.

_____ 30. I shrink from expressions of hostility.

SCORING THE CONFLICT RESOLUTION SURVEY

Fill in the blanks below with the same scale scores you entered on the survey. Then total your scores for each conflict resolution approach. Note that the blanks to be filled in do not always appear in the same order as the items on the survey.

Scale Score	Item No.	Scale Score	Item No.	Scale Score	Item No.	Scale Score	Item No.	Scale Score	Item No.
1	1	1	2	1	5	2	3	2	4
2	9	1	6	0	10	2	7	2	8
2	12	1	11	0	14	1	13	2	15
2	20	2	19	1	18	0	16	2	17
0	25	2	24	1	21	2	23	2	22
2	30	1	28	1	29	1	26	2	27
9		8		4		8		12	
Avoiding		Accommodating		Forcing		Bargaining		Problem Solving	

This is your conflict resolution profile. Note that your score for each approach can range from a low of 0 to a high of 12. The approach with the highest score is your preferred approach to conflict. The second highest is the one you tend to use under pressure.

WHEN TO CHOOSE EACH CONFLICT RESOLUTION APPROACH

Conflict Resolution Approach	Context of Conflict
Avoiding works best when	• There's little chance you'll get your way • The potential damage of addressing the conflict outweighs the benefits of resolution • People need a chance to cool down • Others are in a better position to resolve the conflict • The problem will go away by itself

Conflict Resolution Approach	Context of Conflict
Accommodating works best when	• Preserving harmony is important • Personal antagonism is the major source of conflict • The issue itself is unsolvable • You care more about the other person than getting your way
Forcing works best when	• Quick, decisive action is needed • A rule has to be enforced • You know you're right • You must protect yourself
Bargaining works best when	• Two opponents are equal in power • Temporary settlements on complex issues are needed • Opponents do not share goals • Forcing or problem solving won't work
Problem solving works best when	• Both sets of concerns are too important to be compromised • It is important to work through hard feelings • Commitment to the resolution is important • A permanent solution is desired

Student Study Site

Visit the Student Study Site at **study.sagepub.com/hynes6e** for web quizzes, video links, web resources, and cases studies.

Notes

1. National Institute for Occupational Safety and Health, Centers for Disease Control and Prevention, US Department of Health and Human Services, "Homicide Alert," no. 94–101, accessed December 22, 2003, http://www.cdc.gov/niosh/94–101.html.
2. Warren H. Schmidt, "Conflict: A Powerful Process for (Good or Bad) Change," *Management Review* 63, no. 12 (December 1974): p. 5.
3. Ronald Corwin, "Patterns of Organizational Conflict," *Administrative Science Quarterly* 14, no. 3 (December 1969): pp. 507–520.
4. Association for Conflict Resolution, "Frequently Asked Questions," accessed June 2, 2009, http://www.acrnet.org/about/CR-FAQ.htm.
5. Tammy Erickson, "The Four Biggest Reasons for Generational Conflict in Teams," *HBR Blog Network* (blog), *Harvard Business Publishing—for Managers*, February 16, 2009, accessed March 24, 2009, http://blogs.harvardbusiness.org/erickson/2009/.
6. L. Putnam and S. Wilson, "Argumentation and Bargaining Strategies as Discriminators of Integrative and Distributive Outcomes," in *Managing Conflict: An Interdisciplinary Approach,* ed. A. Rahim (New York: Praeger, 1988).

7. L. R. Hoffman, E. Harburg, and N. R. F. Meier, "Differences and Disagreements as Factors in Creative Problem-Solving," *Journal of Abnormal and Social Psychology* 64, no. 2 (1962): pp. 206–224.

8. Daniel Katz and Robert L. Kahn, *The Social Psychology of Organizations,* 2nd ed. (New York: Wiley & Sons, 1978), p. 613.

9. Clagett G. Smith, "A Comparative Analysis of Some Conditions and Consequences of Intra-Organizational Conflict," *Administrative Science Quarterly* 10, no. 3 (1965–1966): pp. 504–529.

10. K. W. Thomas, "Conflict," in *Organizational Behavior*, ed. S. Kerr (Columbus, OH: Grid, 1979), pp. 151–181.

11. Charles E. Watkins, "An Analytical Model of Conflict: How Differences in Perception Cause Differences of Opinion," *Supervisory Management* 41, no. 3 (March 1974): pp. 1–5; and J. L. Hocker and W. W. Wilmot, *Interpersonal Conflict,* 2nd ed. (Dubuque, IA: Wm C. Brown, 1985).

12. Lewis Benton, "The Many Faces of Conflict: How Differences in Perception Cause Differences of Opinion," *Supervisory Management* 15, no. 3 (March 1970): pp. 7–12.

13. Robert Zajonc, "Attitudinal Effects of Mere Exposure," *Journal of Personality and Social Psychology Monograph Supplement* 9, no. 2 (June 1968), pp. 1–27.

14. "Does the Boss Say Thanks?" *St. Louis Post-Dispatch,* September 19, 2003, p. C9.

15. Carol Vinzant, "On the Job: Messing with the Boss's Head," *Fortune,* May 1, 2000, p. 329.

16. L. M. Sixel, "Preparing for Violence," *Houston Chronicle*, April 19, 2007, p. D1.

17. This diagram is based on the works of R. R. Blake and J. S. Mouton, "The Fifth Achievement," *Journal of Applied Behavioral Science* 6, no. 4 (1970): pp. 413–426; J. Hall, *How to Interpret Your Scores from the Conflict Management Survey* (Conroe, TX: Teleometrics, 1986); R. W. Thomas, "Conflict and Negotiation Processes in Organizations," in *The Handbook of Industrial and Organizational Psychology,* 2nd ed., ed. M. D. Dunnette and L. Hough (Palo Alto, CA: Consulting Psychologists Press, 1992), pp. 651–718; and K. W. Thomas and R. H. Kilman, *The Thomas-Kilman Conflict Mode Instrument* (Tuxedo, NY: Xicom, 1974).

18. E. Phillips and R. Cheston, "Conflict Resolution: What Works?" *California Management Review* 21, no. 4 (Summer 1979): p. 76.

19. W. A. Donohue, M. E. Diez, and R. B. Stahl, "New Directions in Negotiations Research," in *Communication Yearbook 7*, ed. R. N. Bostrom (Beverly Hills, CA: Sage, 1983), pp. 249–279.

20. Phillips and Cheston, "Conflict Resolution: What Works?" p. 76.

21. Gareth Morgan, *Images of Organization* (Newbury Park, CA: Sage, 1986).

22. Jay W. Lorsch and Paul R. Lawrence, eds., *Studies in Organizational Design* (Homewood, IL: Irwin-Dorsey, 1970), p. 1.

23. Alan C. Filey, *Interpersonal Conflict Resolution* (Glenview, IL: Scott Foresman, 1975), p. 33.

24. N. J. Adler, *International Dimensions of Organizational Behavior* (Boston: Kent, 1986).

25. D. E. Zand, "Trust and Managerial Problem Solving," *Administrative Science Quarterly* 17, no. 1 (1972): pp. 229–239.

26. Daniel Robey, *Designing Organizations* (Homewood, IL: Richard D. Irwin, 1986), pp. 176–201.

27. Tab W. Cooper and Lucia Stretcher Sigmar, "Constructive Supervisory Confrontation: What Employees Want," *International Journal of Management & Information Systems* 16, no. 3 (2012): pp. 255–264.

28. Linda L. Putnam, "Communication and Interpersonal Conflict," *Management Communication Quarterly* 1, no. 3 (February 1988): pp. 293–301.

29. Lucia Stretcher Sigmar, Geraldine E. Hynes, and Kathy L. Hill, "Strategies for Teaching Social and Emotional Intelligence in Business Communication," *Business Communication Quarterly* 75, no. 3 (2012): pp. 301–317.

30. Daniel Goleman, *Emotional Intelligence* (New York: Bantam, 1995).

CHAPTER 13

Managerial Negotiation

We cannot negotiate with those who say, "What's mine is mine and what's yours is negotiable."

—John F. Kennedy, thirty-fifth US president

Negotiation is an integral aspect of management. Successful managers negotiate for increased budget allocations, better purchasing prices, and higher salaries for themselves and their subordinates, increased time to finish important assignments, more favorable annual objectives, or even better salary offers when starting with a new company. Many managers, however, shy away from negotiation. They do not feel comfortable doing it because either they have not succeeded in previous negotiations or they have not learned the process of dynamic negotiation. Most knowledge about negotiation, unfortunately, comes from limited personal experience.

Managers should take advantage of situations in their personal life that give them the opportunity to negotiate. Managers can learn from those experiences and improve their negotiating ability, which can then transfer to their management position. Personal experiences can range from buying a car or selling items in a garage sale to negotiating chores and compensation with children. By thus building one's skills, managers will avoid ineffective negotiations in the workplace, which can reduce organizational productivity, demoralize those involved, and generate hostile feelings among other parties.[1]

Furthermore, recent research shows gender differences in the use of negotiation. In general, men initiate negotiation four times more often than women do. This tendency has important consequences in business, particularly concerning pay, promotion, and recognition. Linda Babcock and Sara Laschever report in their book, *Women Don't Ask,* that only 7 percent of female MBAs graduating from Carnegie Mellon University negotiated for a higher salary than the one initially offered by a potential employer, while 57 percent of male MBAs did. On average, those who negotiated raised the initial offer by $4,053. The starting salaries for males were more than 7 percent higher than those for females, overall.[2] Babcock and Laschever believe that a different negotiating style explains most of the gap in women's starting pay.

This gap explains a large part of the persistent pay differential between men and women throughout their careers. A recent study by the US Government Accountability Office found that women still make 81 cents for every dollar a man makes in a similar job, despite the fact that women make up 50 percent of the workforce, 51.4 percent of managerial and professional jobs, and 43 percent of MBAs. Controlling for a number of variables like tenure, age, company size, and market capitalization, a 2012 study of chief financial officers (CFOs) working in three thousand US companies found that gender is a strong predictor of CFO compensation; men earn 16 percent more than women on average.[3] Learning how to negotiate may eventually have an impact on this disparity.

NEGOTIATION AND NETWORKING

Networking skills are relevant to managerial negotiation skills. Since negotiating is a process, not an event or a one-shot deal in most business situations, it is important to maintain relationships while negotiating. Negotiating strategically means thinking long term, building our networks. It means balancing relationships and results, cooperation and competition. It also means using our networks to help us negotiate successfully.

Again, research has identified gender differences in the ways managers use their networks during negotiations. When asking for a pay raise or promotion, women are more likely to rely on their job performance alone. Conversely, men are predisposed to ask for a raise when they feel it is warranted by comparison to others' performance. Men use their networking abilities and relationships as leverage for their personal goals. Women tend to be less outcome oriented and more concerned with preserving goodwill. Often, women are also inclined to wait for someone else to sing their praises. All of these tendencies can be a detriment at the negotiation table.[4]

> ### STOP AND THINK
>
> What are some of the cultural values that might explain these gender differences in the way men and women network?

Networking is a skill. And like all skills, practice and preparation make perfect. When combined with merit, networking can be a valuable tool in influencing job searches, negotiations, and interviews. Building and using business relationships effectively can have a significant impact on your success. People enjoy mentoring people they like and then claiming credit for their mentee's career success.

When negotiating, a manager has to strike a balance between what is good for a business relationship and what is good for the manager and her organization. It is also important in a management position to network with other managers, so you can ensure you are on par with industry and company standards when negotiating.

NEGOTIATION AND CONFLICT

Before discussing the dynamic process of negotiation, we should first specify exactly what the term means. Chapter 12 dealt with conflict resolution in terms of win–lose, lose–lose, and win–win strategies. That discussion urged that a win–win solution to conflict is best, and it reviewed the beliefs necessary to implement this approach successfully. However, such an outcome is not always appropriate. When one or both parties see a situation as that in which one party will lose or gain something in exchange for the other party's loss or gain, a negotiation strategy is best. In this situation, one party cannot easily determine the needs or desired outcome of the other party, and one of the parties may not fully trust the other.

Win–lose situations occur every day in a manager's life. When managers consider the term *negotiation,* they may often think of special, formal situations such as collective bargaining between labor and management or a sports agent negotiating for an athlete. These examples are generally termed third-party negotiations. Research indicates managers are more frequently becoming involved in third-party negotiations.[5] However, this discussion emphasizes the type of everyday negotiation situations any manager may face, such as obtaining additional office space for an employee, winning a budget increase, or securing additional support from another department. Effective managers win more than they lose.

Every negotiator has two universal concerns. The parties must balance their concern for the outcome of the negotiation with the relationship needs between the parties.[6] However, the degree of these concerns varies from one situation to another. In some situations, winning is all that matters, but in other situations, the value of the relationship may outweigh the need to win. In between these opposite extremes is the risk of obtaining a winning outcome while damaging the relationship, which affects the losing party's willingness to fulfill the agreement. A manager may need to work with this party in the future, and if the relationship is damaged, future transactions could be controversial. For example, when a subordinate requests a salary increase, the manager must weigh the need to manage the budget at the lowest cost with the need to maintain a positive relationship with the subordinate. If the subordinate's work performance is highly valued, the manager may want to make concessions to ensure continued good work.

A manager's approach to the negotiation process may be served by referring to the negotiation styles that balance these universal concerns, as demonstrated in Chapter 12 (Figure 12–3) where a manager's concern for production is balanced against the concern for people. Knowing the appropriate negotiation strategy can help a manager reach success.

> **STOP AND THINK**
>
> 1. What are some of the key differences between negotiating to reach a compromise and negotiating to reach a consensus?
>
> 2. What are some of the key similarities?
>
> 3. Which type of negotiation strategy—compromise or consensus—works best for most manager/subordinate interactions?

A STRATEGIC MODEL FOR NEGOTIATIONS

The best way to approach the negotiation process is through the strategic analysis of managerial communication illustrated in Chapter 2.

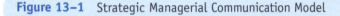

Figure 13–1   Strategic Managerial Communication Model

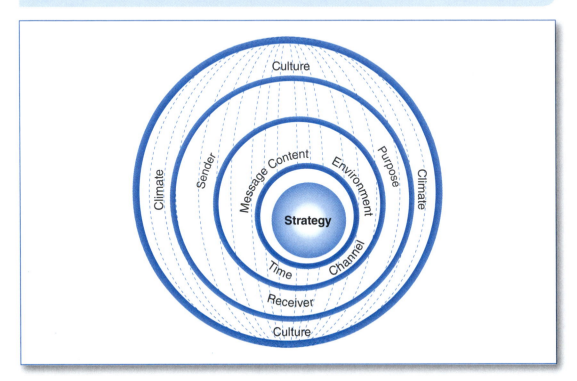

The basic model of strategic managerial communication presented in Chapter 2 is shown here in Figure 13–1. To use the onion analogy from Chapter 2, we must consider the factors in each layer of the model in order to arrive at a strategy (the core). Discussion first focuses on the culture and climate (layer 1).

Next, the sender (manager), the purpose or goal of the negotiations, and the receiver's (the adversary's) style are explored (layer 2). To develop a negotiation strategy systematically, one must also analyze style. One must analyze the time, environment, channel, and content of the message. These are the third layer of the strategic communication model. Although the following discussion treats these items independently, managers must consider all the layers simultaneously when developing a negotiation strategy (the core of the model) because they all affect each other. This chapter concludes with a description of six negotiation strategies at the core (or fourth layer) of our strategic communication model.

LAYER 1: CULTURE AND CLIMATE

As mentioned in many places in this book, culture is a primary concern in any communication situation. "First seek to understand, then to be understood" is Stephen Covey's fifth habit given in the *Seven Habits of Highly Effective People*.[7] Managers must review and analyze the situation that initiates the need to negotiate and the culture/climate that surrounds each negotiation scenario. Then, the manager can begin to identify alternative ways to resolve the need for the negotiation process. True understanding requires both talking and listening. The manager does not have to agree with the other party, but he does need to understand the other party's position. In addition, the manager can show empathy without feeling sympathy and evaluate the difference between fact and emotion that may derive from the nature of the culture or climate.

Both national and organizational culture must be considered when negotiating. Some cultures support an assertive, almost demanding, negotiation style, whereas in other cultures a more passive approach is expected. A culture may encourage long negotiation sessions that require patience, whereas others support quick resolution. Some cultures encourage initial offers close to an expected settlement, while in other cultures, the initial offer is nowhere near an expected outcome. In some cultures, it is important to develop a personal relationship before negotiating, but in others, only a superficial knowledge of the other persons involved is required. Managers must be thoroughly aware of the other party's national culture to negotiate successfully.

Organizational culture largely determines who has the power within an organization and the extent to which a person can make decisions. There is no reason to negotiate with someone if that person cannot make decisions, and this is often the case where power is centralized. Also, in bureaucratic organizations, numerous policies and procedures may preclude flexibility, so there is little that can be negotiated. But most organizations are not so highly centralized and bureaucratic that negotiation is of no value. The manager's challenge is to determine what can be negotiated and with whom. This challenge is a result of the organizational culture and climate as well as the political structure within the organization.

LAYER 2: SENDER, RECEIVER, AND PURPOSE

We next examine elements in the second layer of the strategic communication model (Figure 13–1)—the negotiator's personal style and purpose. Just as some people are outgoing and talkative and others are withdrawn and quiet, some managers enter a negotiation with confidence and a positive attitude, whereas others see defeat from the outset, believing they do not have a chance. Before negotiators can succeed, they must believe in themselves. E. H. Harriman, one of the US's leading railroad pioneers and a man bubbling with self-confidence, once remarked to a young financier, "Let me be one of 15 men around a table, and I will have my way."[8] A manager can gain confidence by becoming aware of the negotiation process and properly preparing for the interaction. In addition, practice in negotiation, if done properly, leads to greater confidence because of the positive results.

A manager creates power in negotiations when confident. Being confident, however, is not enough; during negotiations, you must also act and look confident. To begin, do not look as if you are expecting a long fight. One of the poorest practices is to remove your jacket, roll up your shirtsleeves, pour a cup of coffee, or otherwise appear to be settling in for an extended session. In addition, take care not to project a tired, listless image. An adversary's hope and confidence increase dramatically when an opponent looks tired.

In negotiation, appearance is an important source of communication; during much of the discussion, negotiators watch one another closely. You can promote success with a neat appearance that suggests you are well organized and a person that cannot easily be exploited. We dealt with nonverbal messages in Chapter 10 and will do so again later in this chapter, but remember that nervous habits, such as tapping a finger on the desk or playing with a pencil, can project a nervous, vulnerable image.

Although the negotiation process may be conducted by phone—so the nervousness would not show—this medium has some disadvantages. Negotiating by phone restricts the manager's ability to read body language. Phone communication can result in the message being misunderstood or appearing last minute in nature. Negotiation by phone may take the receiver by surprise as she may have not prepared for the conversation, and the resulting negotiation may become more competitive.

Some tension is always part of the negotiation process. This tension generally results from two separate unknowns inherent in any negotiation. The first is whether or not a deal can be struck. A second unknown is how long the negotiations will take. Simply knowing that it is natural to feel these tensions and being aware of their source helps to lessen them considerably.

Purpose

The purpose of the negotiation process is simple: to maximize your advantage. Initially, that purpose is one of the most critical elements to consider when developing a negotiation strategy. The purpose of the negotiation may translate to "know what you want" or, more appropriately, "know what is reasonable to expect." Obviously, wants and expectations are vastly different, but unless you have clearly differentiated between the two, confusion and failure can result.

Negotiation is useless in certain situations. Consider, for example, a production manager who has successfully negotiated personal salary increases in the past. Unfortunately, poor market conditions have affected the company, and nobody is receiving a salary increase. If the manager tries to negotiate now, he or she will not only fail to get an increase but also might create resentment because demands are made during hard times.

If the time is ripe and the other party is committed to the negotiation, then the manager can establish the negotiation goal. The following discussion presents three strategies: determining the maximum supportable outcome (MSO), the least acceptable outcome (LAO), and the best alternative (BATNA).

Defining the Maximum Supportable and Least Acceptable Outcomes

The maximum supportable outcome is the absolute most one can ask for in the opening position within reason. A negotiation can be quickly terminated if the MSO is beyond reason.

The LAO is the least acceptable result you will accept from the negotiation. If the outcome of the negotiation is anything less than your least acceptable outcome, it would be better to terminate the negotiation. Planning is important so the LAO is established before the negotiation.

Of course, both the LAO and MSO also reflect primary, secondary, short-term, and long-term considerations. An outcome frequently is complex and includes more than one aspect.

Since the least acceptable outcome and the maximum supportable outcome are the guide-posts for negotiation, their terms must be clear before you enter any negotiation. And it is a critical error (and possibly the most common) for a person to modify either of these two points after the negotiation has begun. Doing so suggests your adversary is influencing you unduly.

You should keep in mind throughout our discussion of LAO and MSO that the terms are reversed for your adversary in the negotiation. Consider the example of a sales manager for a clothing distributor who is negotiating the price of one hundred new suits with the purchasing manager of a clothing store. Table 13–1 demonstrates how the two see the terms differently.

It is important to keep this *reversal of terms* in mind when studying the following material. One outcome may be desirable to one person, but undesirable to another. In negotiation, as with other aspects of communication, individual perception and frame of reference are important to remember.

Table 13–1 Reversed Terms

Sales Manager		Purchasing Manager
Maximum supportable outcome (MSO)	$15,000	Least acceptable outcome (LAO)
Least acceptable outcome (LAO)	$11,500	Maximum supportable outcome (MSO)

Finding the LAO and MSO

Because the guidelines provided by the least acceptable outcome and the maximum sup-portable outcome are so critical, give careful thought to finding these outcomes. The LAO is probably easiest to establish. This is the point below which nothing could be accepted because of the potential loss. In effect, when a negotiator commits to this point, loss is unlikely.

The LAO is both objective and subjective, a combination of the facts surrounding the situation and the value placed on them. Because it is subjective, no magical formula deter-mines the LAO. Thus, make every effort to separate what is acceptable from what is wanted.

In determining exactly what your LAO is, it is worthwhile to develop some kind of deci-sion worksheet to ensure a systematic and objective process. Table 13–2 presents an example for determining the LAO of a job offer.

Any format that helps you to think through the process is of value. Of course, we would all prefer to be at the other extreme of the range, the MSO. The MSO is the furthest point from the LAO that the negotiator can reasonably justify.

That area between the MSO and the LAO is the settlement range.[9] Both parties in the negotiation will have a conscious (or unconscious) settlement range. To help achieve suc-cess, the negotiator must be able to justify the MSO convincingly. Otherwise, the MSO may

Table 13-2   Establishing the Least Acceptable Outcome

Item	Relative Importance	LAO
Salary	4	$68,000
Location	3	Within 500 miles of hometown and near a lake
Company size	1	Member of Fortune 500
Job duties	5	At least 20% of the job involving use of computers and computer skills
Social climate	2	Several young unmarried people (like me) in the department

be set at a point that is beyond the opponent's LAO. Even though the negotiator might be willing to settle for much less, this possibility may be obviated because the opponent will see no reason to continue the discussion. But the reciprocal of this is also true; the maximum should not be too low, because once the MSO is out, one cannot readjust it. Negotiation will surely cease at that point.

The establishment of the MSO reflects the one-trip-to-the-well principle. You get to state your opening position only once, and it is vital to make the most of it. It is almost impossible to reverse directions and ask for more when, after looking more closely at the situation, you belatedly realize your MSO was set too low.

But what is maximum? It is whatever one can support, and this justification may require some creativity. In developing the maximum supportable outcome, look for unique attributes to include. Do not become so fixed on one or two items that you never consider other possible combinations. Consider a marketing manager who is negotiating with the vice president for an additional employee position in the marketing department. The additional position may not be as big an obstacle to overcome as the salary requested for the position. How can the manager justify a salary of $80,000 for the position? It may be possible to divert attention to something positive like increased sales to distract the vice president from the salary. Do not hesitate to make a reference list that outlines the benefits to upper management of agreeing to the salary request as well as an undisclosed list of possible responses that could negatively affect your negotiating position. By establishing such lists, you can prepare possible responses to overcome criticism regarding the salary request.

Defining BATNA

So far, we have seen that to achieve your negotiation's purpose, you must determine your LAO and MSO. But sometimes negotiating with a bottom line is less effective and beneficial than developing a solid BATNA, or best alternative to a negotiated agreement. BATNA was the brainchild of Roger Fisher and Bill Ury of Harvard Law School, first described in their series of books on principled negotiation that started with *Getting to Yes*.[10] The basic idea is that each party in a negotiation needs to identify what, if any, options are available if there is a stalemate. If there is no alternative, you will walk away from the table empty handed. You should decide on your BATNA prior to the start of negotiations.

An example is an offer from a dealer to buy your car for $10,000. You decide to advertise your car in the newspaper classifieds for $12,000 (the MSO). Your BATNA is now $10,000, since you know you can fall back on that dealer's offer if no individual sale is successful. But wait. Other offers that you might consider include selling your car to your little sister for $7,500. This might or might not be a better alternative than the dealer's offer, because of your relationship value. Thus, finding BATNA requires weighing a broad range of factors.

BATNAs prevent you from accepting terms that are too unfavorable and from rejecting terms that you should accept. If the proposed solution is better than your BATNA, then it is your MSO, and you should take it. If the agreement is not better than your BATNA, then you should reopen negotiations. But your BATNA is not the same as your LAO, the minimum acceptable offer. Instead, it is where you will go if you do not get even the least acceptable offer. When the parties have similar BATNAs, then the negotiation is ripe for agreement. Much time and money can be saved by "settling" for a BATNA rather than continuing a dispute. In the United States, about 90 percent of lawsuits settle out of court because the lawyers understand the strength of each side's case and how likely each is to prevail in court. Thus, when negotiations threaten to break down, parties should reveal their BATNAs to see if they are similar.

LAYER 3: TIME, ENVIRONMENT, CONTENT, AND CHANNEL

After examining the factors in the first two layers of our strategic communication model (Figure 13–1), we come to the third layer, which has four new and more specific strategic considerations. The first one we shall describe is time.

Time

Time is a vital component of strategy.[11] Two issues should be addressed when considering time factors: (1) when to negotiate and (2) how to best use the time within the negotiation. The answer to the second question also provides insights for the best time to make an offer or counteroffer. First, let us look at when to negotiate.

To optimize energy and prevent major setbacks, try to conduct a negotiating session when you feel healthy and rested. Many individual idiosyncrasies exist, but the consensus seems to be that most people are at peak efficiency about 11 a.m.[12]

Although the ideal is to select the best time to negotiate, it is not always practical. Thus, the savvy negotiator is always fully prepared and never loses an opportunity to negotiate. A quick meeting in the cafeteria, a chance encounter in the elevator, or an apparently spontaneous telephone call can represent opportunities for negotiation. To quote John Ilich, author of several best sellers on power negotiation, including *The Complete Idiot's Guide to Winning through Negotiation,* "Never lose an opportunity to negotiate, but never negotiate until you are certain it's an opportunity."[13]

In any negotiation, the main question to ask is, "When do I have the most power and when is my adversary the weakest?" Naturally, the answer changes. Assume a manager wanted to adopt a flextime policy for her staff. The best time to negotiate this with upper management is probably just after some major accomplishment or even when another department has changed its work schedule. Strategic timing can add significantly to a person's power in negotiation.

A second question is how to best use time within the negotiation. Generally, one expects most significant concession behavior and settlement action to occur close to the deadline.[14] An approaching deadline puts pressure on the parties to state their true positions and thus does much to squeeze any elements of bluff out of the latter steps of negotiation. A number of major studies verify the power of time limits on the negotiation.[15]

Because of the significance of deadlines, note the following guidelines.

1. *Do not reveal the true deadline.* When an adversary knows the other person's deadlines, negotiations stall until the deadline acts as a pressure for concession. When a person has an extremely tight deadline, she may be wise to extend the deadline rather than to enter the negotiations at a disadvantage.

2. *Be patient.* This may also be referred to as forbearance.[16] Negotiators should take time to answer questions, provide information, and make decisions. This includes keeping defensive reactions under control as well as avoiding the tendency to take an offensive posture when being verbally attacked. The time provided through patience allows the opportunity to organize, understand issues, test the opponent's strengths and weaknesses, and weigh risks. Also, it creates a sense of pressure in the opponent, especially when the deadline approaches.

3. *Use the clock.* Because most Americans are so conscious of time, seek concessions or even provide minor concessions toward the end of a time period. Thus, you might elicit action on the part of the opponent immediately before lunch or dinner because people like to have a sense of accomplishment when taking a break. And a flurry of action can be used to the negotiator's advantage if taken at the right time.

Environment

In addition to time and timing, the physical environment is strategically important. This section explores two aspects of the physical environment: site and physical arrangement.

Site selection is often important because it bears directly on the amount of control each party may exercise over the physical arrangements at that site as well as the psychological climate in which the exchange occurs. In negotiations conducted in one's home territory, the host has a legitimate right to assume responsibility for arranging the physical space. This is similar to the home-field advantage in sports; the home team is more likely to come out the winner in both situations.

What is the best way to arrange a conference room or office for negotiations? First, prevent distractions such as phone calls. These can be costly if they occur at an awkward time in the negotiation. Second, avoid sitting in a position that suggests subordination or even equality. If in a conference room, sit at the head of the table. If in your office, sit behind the desk. Also, have appropriate equipment such as flip charts, computers, or writing tables ready. Having these items ready underscores the sincerity of your position. On the other hand, if the importance of the relationship of the negotiating parties is primary, this power arrangement may be less important. Sitting at a round table and showing mutual respect may provide the manager with more power because the manager has chosen an environment that indicates compassion for the other. This strategy may actually elicit more concessions based on the trust established between the two parties.

Observing the physical arrangements of a room and physical position that an opponent takes in a negotiation provides valuable information. Figure 13–2 illustrates several possibilities. For example, a researcher conducted observation and questionnaire studies of seating preferences in several social contexts and found that Americans engaging in casual conversation normally prefer to sit at right angles to each other (if seated at square or rectangular tables) or beside one another when seated at circular tables. He also found that side-by-side seating occurred in cooperative relationships. However, face-to-face seating was the most preferred configuration in competitive relationships, with a moderately wide space separating the parties. He also noted less conversation when people were seated far apart than when they were side by side or opposite one another.[17]

Figure 13–2 Seating Arrangements

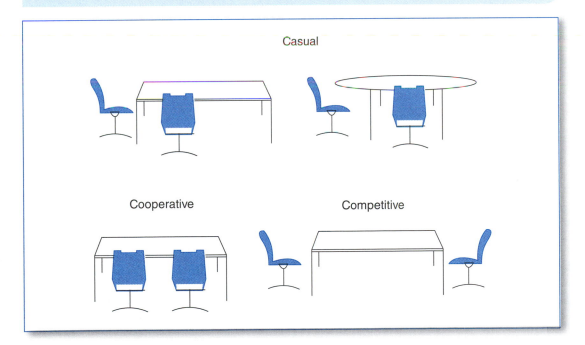

Casual

Cooperative

Competitive

Other nonverbal elements come into play in negotiations. For example, one can use distance to gain power. Famous anthropologist and author Ray Birdwhistell found that when two parties are in competitive situations, they find proximity threatening.[18] Consequently, if a manager wants to create stress in an opponent, he might move closer physically. Eye contact can also be a strong tool in negotiation. Research indicates people avoid direct visual contact in competitive encounters because it is stressful.[19] They find it intimidating, dominating, or overly revealing of motives they wish to keep hidden when engaged in competitive relationships.[20] In this same regard, other researchers have found that people have greater difficulty telling a convincing lie when they are being watched closely than when not.[21]

If you cannot use home ground for negotiation, try for neutral territory. Thus, in a negotiation with a high-level manager, it might be inappropriate to ask her to come to a lower-level manager's office. However, one could suggest that both parties meet in a conference room to avoid interruptions by saying, "I know you're busy and get a lot of interruptions. How about meeting in the conference room so we can get away for a few minutes?" Or a meeting at lunch might be an easy way to neutralize a situation. The adversary may be comfortable at lunch, and it may be possible to offset any status advantage.

When you have no alternative to meeting in the adversary's office, you do not need to assume a subordinate role immediately. Typically, the adversary is at a desk and you are in a side chair or, worse, in a low-slung occasional chair; you can quickly offset the disadvantage merely by standing up and moving around while speaking. With this little nonverbal technique, it is now possible to look down on the adversary.

Message Content

Sender, receiver, purpose, time, and environment all help to set the stage for what is really the essence of the negotiation: the message itself. Negotiation revolves around the amount of information that each party decides to relate (or not to relate) about true motives and preferences. Negotiators base such a decision not only on their own standards but also equally on their opponents' behavior, openness, and honesty before and during the exchange.

Although nonverbal messages are important, the spoken word is the predominant form of communication in negotiation. The major types of verbal messages appropriate for discussion here are making concessions and responding to and presenting questions. But first, we will consider the opening messages.

Opening Messages

Should the negotiations begin with an immediate discussion of key issues, or is it best to begin with a friendly, neutral conversation? The answer depends on the total time allowed for the negotiations, the type of previous relationship with the parties involved, and whether the general atmosphere is friendly or hostile.

In the United States, the accepted practice is to begin with a general conversation on neutral topics. But the conversation moves rather quickly toward the issues. The same pattern is true with many western Europeans; however, in Mexico, the Arab world, and most Asian countries, the initial, neutral conversations are generally much longer.

Concessions

We have mentioned that it is important to establish the LAO and MSO before negotiating. But it is not advisable to state these early in the negotiation. Rather, it is best to determine the other person's LAO. You then begin to move away from your MSO toward your LAO and toward the other person's MSO. This is generally accomplished through a series of concessions.

When and how to make concessions is determined by information obtained from questions—our next topic. However, principles of the equality rule can serve as a guideline for making concessions. The first equality principle suggests negotiators generally expect one another to make an equal *number* of concessions from their initial starting point. The second principle is that of an equal sacrifice. By this rule, "equality" is judged by *how much* an individual concedes relative to his aspirations—in other words, who makes the bigger sacrifice.

Imagine a situation in which two managers are negotiating a reorganization among several departments. A third manager has left and has not been replaced; consequently, the duties of her department will be assigned to the two remaining departments. During this negotiation, the two managers must perceive that each has made an equal *number* of concessions as well as an equal *amount*. But numbers and amounts are difficult to quantify when negotiating such items as job duties, reporting relationships, and budgets. Consequently, the manner in which these concessions are made is important. An effective negotiator uses positive language to ensure concessions appear frequent and large.

> ### STOP AND THINK
>
> 1. When you begin moving from your MSO (maximum supportive outcome) toward your LAO (least acceptable outcome), should you make relatively small concessions or big concessions? Why?
>
> 2. Later in the negotiations, should your concessions become bigger or smaller?

Questions

Making concessions is closely related to asking and responding to questions. Dorothy Leads discusses the power of questions in her book *Smart Questions*.[22] Leads points out that individuals pay more attention to a question than to a statement, because they know that they will be expected to respond to a question. When they hear a statement, on the other hand, they may not be expected to respond at all. While closed questions can be appropriate at times, open-ended questions often gather more valuable information that can be used in the negotiation process. It is through these questions that an effective negotiator determines when and how much of a concession to offer.

A negotiator may unintentionally strike an emotional chord with a question and arouse antagonism; consequently, it may be necessary to prepare the ground before asking questions. One way to accomplish this is by explaining the reason or reasons for asking a question if the potential exists for embarrassment.

Questions serve five purposes:

1. *To arouse attention:* "When did that change?" or "Did you know about . . . ?"

2. *To obtain information:* "What is the difference between the two items?" or "What's the value of that point?"

3. *To clarify:* "I still am confused about your motive here. What else is key to you?" or "What are the terms we've settled on so far?"

4. *To stimulate thinking:* "Could you give me your reaction to the second item?" or "What are some other alternatives?"

5. *To bring to a conclusion or summary:* "Will you summarize your proposal?" or "Are we ready to act?" or "Have we got a deal?"

While it is usually a good idea to prepare several questions, some people get so involved in asking questions that they stop listening. Also, few people can think of all the right questions during the actual negotiation. Preparation will help to overcome both possibilities.

If you want a particular answer, ask a *leading question.* A leading question directs the person who is answering from statement to statement until the logic of the questioner's argument is made. Here is a series of leading questions:

Is research included in your cost? Where? How is it prorated between jobs? Exactly why do you include it in our charges when you just said that this job requires no research?

In this example, the questioner may or may not know the answers, but she led her opponents to a planned conclusion.

When no need exists to lead the opponent in a particular direction, use *open-ended questions*—questions that usually begin with how, why, or what. For example, "How would you recommend we close the gap?" "Why is plan A preferable to plan B?" "What is the proposal?" Open questions invite people to express their thinking freely. These are the types of questions that Dorothy Leads refers to as *smart questions.*

Another type of question, the *rhetorical question,* is one that is asked not to get an answer, but for effect. Rather than seeking an answer, this type of question attempts to draw attention to a particular item. Examples of rhetorical questions include "What do you think the vice president would say to something like that?" or "Do you really want us to believe that?"

In general, avoid *bipolar, either-or,* or *shotgun* questions. Such a question as "Would you prefer a corner office with a computer, or would you rather have a larger desk and no extra chair?" needs to be divided into two questions. As the question is presently stated, confusion will result, or the opponent may even ask for both. Similarly, forced-choice questions will make your opponent feel cornered and may end the negotiations. Also, a wise negotiator avoids a rapid-fire questioning approach. An opponent needs time to respond, and the questioner needs to listen to the responses.

A final effective use of questions is to get negotiations back on track when an opponent has created a roadblock. Stuart Diamond, a professor at Wharton School of Business and a prominent expert in negotiation, emphasizes the importance of questions to pursue the goal. For instance, when an opponent states, "I can't possibly do that for you at this time," a closely listening negotiator might respond with, "When can you do it?" or "Who else can?"[23] By responding with questions, the negotiator continues the process.

Table 13-3 Questions to Ask When Negotiating

Question Type	Purpose
Closed	Arouses attention
	Gets commitment
	Clarifies
	Redirects
Open	Obtains information
	Stimulates thinking
Leading	Directs the answer
Rhetorical	Draws attention
	Creates an effect

To summarize, keep the purpose of your question in mind, listen for the right time, and then phrase the question to meet the prevailing needs. Table 13-3 summarizes various question types and their purposes in negotiations.

Answering Questions

Negotiation is a game of asking and answering questions. The preparation and mental alertness required to ask purposeful questions are just as essential for answering them. Perhaps the most important preparation is to brainstorm and write down in advance questions most likely to arise. Ask an associate to act as devil's advocate and raise a host of hard questions before negotiation. The more a person prepares possible answers, the better those answers will be.

Keep two universal guidelines in mind when answering questions: (1) never answer until the question is fully understood, and (2) take time to think through your answer. Besides applying these two guidelines, you can exercise two options in answering. First, you may answer the question accurately and completely. However, since such directness is not always advisable in many negotiations, the second option is to not be totally open when answering.[24] For instance, when negotiating for the salary to go with a new job, it is not wise to directly answer the question, "What is the salary you are looking for?" It is probably best to respond with a comment like "What do you generally pay for this type of job?" If your MSO and BATNA are below the other party's lower limits, you will not have revealed your limits too soon.

When you do not wish to give an answer, several alternatives are available. First, you may choose to answer only part of the question. For instance, a question may be, "What is required to have this project completed by May 1?" You respond by listing all that is required to have the job done without relating to the date. By receiving complete and detailed information, the interrogator thinks the question has been answered. Meanwhile, you can stay away from potentially damaging information.

Another possibility is to ask for clarification even when the question is fairly clear. Often when people are clarifying a question, they intentionally or unintentionally change the question substantially or provide additional insight into the type of answer sought. Also, the time it takes to restate the question provides additional maneuvering time for you to consider possible answers. A variation is to ask for clarification for part of the question, thus diverting attention away from the remainder of the question—as a result, you may end up having to answer only part of the question.

A third possibility is to answer a different question. In such a ploy, the question being answered is so similar to the one asked that the interrogator actually considers the answer satisfactory. For instance, when asked which budget item would be the best to drop from next year's request, you might answer that inflation is affecting all areas of the budget and then provide a specific example of inflation effects. This, in turn, could be followed by the next alternative: answering the question with a question—for example, "Where do you think inflation has had the greatest impact on the entire company?" This tactic may or may not divert attention away from the initial question but is often better than giving a direct answer.

A fourth alternative is to answer a negative question with a positive response. When negotiating salaries, a typical scenario has the opponent asking, "What do you consider to be the biggest weakness you'll bring to this job?" Naturally, a thorough and accurate answer would put you at a disadvantage. A positive, strategic answer might be, "Well, sometimes I get too caught up in my work and I'll stay until late at night. This really isn't fair to my family, so I have to learn to balance my time between family and work." This answer takes the advantage away from the opponent because it is difficult to fault a hard worker who is also a family person.

The real key to answering questions, then, is the ability to think on your feet. This task becomes easier with experience, but no substitute exists for rehearsing the possible questions and being prepared.

Channel

Face-to-face negotiation used to be considered the only viable channel, but this is no longer the case. Negotiators today must consider several communication channels when developing their negotiation strategy.

Whether the negotiation is conducted face-to-face, via the telephone, or electronically, written media often play a key role.[25] The most common in use is the *letter of intent,* which follows many negotiations. A person's memory is always much better five minutes after a conversation than five days later. The letter or memo of intent ensures that all the critical items are mutually agreed on.

The person who writes the memo or letter has the advantage, for this person interprets meanings and shapes words to reflect his understanding of the discussion. The question is not one of exploiting the party or catching the opponent in some trap. It is simply getting the area of agreement laid out in your own way, rather than leaving it to the opponent.

Of course, you do not write the letter in such a tone that it sounds as if the opponent cannot be trusted. You can achieve such tact easily. In one situation, a manager hosted several employees from an out-of-town office. She submitted an expense voucher for $400, but the next paycheck did not cover the expenses. A discussion with her supervisor followed, and after a long negotiation, he agreed to pay $300 of the $400. After the negotiation, the manager sent the following short e-mail:

DATE: March 11, 2015

TO: Chris Averson

FROM: Pat Harolds

SUBJECT: Expense Voucher

Thanks for taking the time to sit down with me and discuss the expenses incurred while hosting the engineers from St. Paul. I'll be looking forward to receiving the $300 with the next paycheck.

This quick e-mail not only confirms the result of the negotiation but also establishes goodwill.

Managers can also use written correspondence to de-emphasize an issue or soothe a highly emotional situation. Correspondence brings an issue back into perspective merely by tactfully showing that a matter is not of great importance. Often, the printed word can lend credibility that face-to-face communication lacks since some people are more apt to take seriously what they see than what they hear. Also, a carefully written memo tends to be less emotional than a face-to-face interaction.

Finally, managers can use written correspondence to present a position when a complex explanation is required. It is difficult to present a complex argument that includes cost figures and diagrams with only an oral presentation. A written statement or even a chart can be helpful when presenting such an argument. In addition, if the opponent has no such aids, counterarguments might be harder to formulate. Managers who believe that the only communication channel is face-to-face severely limit their options.

LAYER 4: CORE STRATEGIES

We have arrived at the core of our strategic managerial communication model (Figure 13–1). How a manager acts and looks, communicates the maximum supportable outcome, reacts to the adversary's style, uses time, establishes the environmental conditions, and asks and answers questions all contribute to the negotiation strategy. Managers combine these communication variables either by design or by accident to develop a core strategy for negotiating. Six general strategies reviewed in the following paragraphs can assist you in combining the different aspects of communication systematically. No particular approach is recommended over another; rather, these six approaches represent possibilities that may best fit a particular situation.[26]

Surprise

The surprise strategy involves unexpectedly introducing a goal or concession into a negotiation. For instance, a manager negotiating budget items with a vice president might suddenly request a new title. The total surprise may catch the other off guard so the additional request is approved, especially since it does not add additional expense.

A quick concession on a nonessential item is another form of surprise. Once again, this concession may be on an item unrelated to the main focus of the negotiation in hopes that the concession will foster a reciprocal concession by the opponent. Surprise may be particularly valuable with an opponent who is under time pressure, because it may stimulate some quick concessions.

Bluff

When playing poker, you may bluff by placing a large bet even though you do not have a strong hand to back it up. By bluffing, you hope to scare your opponent. This tactic is also occasionally appropriate in managerial negotiation. Bluffing, the act of creating illusions without the use of lies or outright misrepresentations, is fair play in negotiations because each side is attempting to maximize its own benefit. A difference exists between withholding information and presenting wrong data. For instance, when a person is negotiating to buy an office desk, it is not the same thing to say "I would like to pay no more than $900" as it is to say "I have only $900 to spend." A person may want to spend no more than $900 but has additional funds if they are needed.

Stacking

The stacking strategy is used when one idea is attached to another. For instance, a public relations manager might use this approach when negotiating a new strategy with her administrative vice president: "I was just reading in *Fortune* that ABC International has changed its approach for its stockholders' meeting. ABC used an approach similar to what I'm suggesting." This manager is stacking her approach on top of ABC's to build credibility.

Legislators also use a form of stacking when presenting bills. They will attach a controversial item as a "rider" onto something that has wide support. Managers use this tactic in negotiations when they stack an undesirable characteristic onto a desirable one. For instance, a person may be asked to take a transfer (undesirable) in combination with a promotion (desirable).

Fait Accompli

The *fait accompli* is a type of bluff that says, in effect, "Here it is, it is accomplished." You state the terms of an offer and act as if the terms are acceptable to the opposing party. The expectation is that when an issue is phrased as if it were a negotiated final settlement, the opponent will accept it with little or no protest. Assume an item has been discussed for some time, but no solid agreement has been reached. You may write a letter of intent regarding the negotiation and state the issue as settled. Using this approach, real estate agents will occasionally push stubborn buyers into action by jotting down the buyer's tentative terms onto a contract. Once the details are down, the buyer is asked to sign and often does.

Take It or Leave It

The take-it-or-leave-it position lets an opponent know this offer is your best one; it represents the maximum goal adjustments a person is willing to make. In making a take-it-or-leave-it offer (which is, in fact, an ultimatum), you take the risk that the offer will be rejected, so there may be no chance to improve it or even revive the negotiations. You could follow with a different offer if the initial take-it-or-leave-it proposal was rejected; however, credibility would be lost. You can use this strategy only once.

Screen

In negotiation, a screen is a third party used by the negotiator as part of the process. You act like a screen between the opponent and the final decision maker. For instance, assume you are negotiating with an outside contractor. You can say that certain conditions proposed by the contractor need to be approved by others in the company. When these conditions are not approved, the adversary may find it necessary to grant concessions to keep the deal going. The third party may actually be a phantom person in the background, but this procedure generates thinking time and may take away some of the opponent's offensive advantage. Instead of negotiating one on one, the opponent has two adversaries, and it is difficult to negotiate through a "barrier," or screen.

Negotiators often use the screen, but it has a serious drawback: It gives the impression that you have limited power. Use this procedure sparingly when negotiating salaries and budgets with your subordinates because it will soon appear that you have little decision-making authority; thus, both respect and influence are weakened.

If possible, do not let an adversary use the third-party technique. Instead, try to get directly to the decision maker. The screen filters out the communications, so much of the strategy used on the adversary is weakened.

These six strategies are only suggestions. Combinations of these or even other strategies are possible. Every strategy has potential drawbacks, strengths, and risks depending on the variables discussed in this chapter and summarized in the strategic communication model (Figure 13–1). Formulating the appropriate strategy is not an easy task. Good negotiation strategy requires analytical ability, an understanding of communication, a refined set of skills, and creativity. However, after you have studied this chapter, you should be able to enter a negotiation confidently.

SUMMARY

Negotiation is an appropriate tool for compromise in conflict resolution situations. Before negotiating, the manager should establish the maximum supportable outcome (MSO) and least acceptable outcome (LAO) to know the negotiation range. Both limits must be carefully thought out so managers can protect their best interests while negotiating in a credible manner. The MSO must be one the manager can support convincingly, and the LAO must be one the manager can live with. It is also wise to define BATNA, the best alternative to a negotiated agreement, to prevent a stalemate.

Negotiators need to consider when to negotiate, how long to continue, and when to make a counteroffer. Since negotiation is liable to be most fruitful when close to an opponent's deadlines, several suggestions about deadlines are appropriate: (1) do not reveal the true deadlines, if possible; (2) be patient; (3) use the clock. Strategic negotiators should also seek an optimum physical environment that benefits them without giving advantage to the opposition.

Another consideration is language used during the negotiation. Negotiators should use common, basic language, should strive for clarity, should be specific, and should not be apologetic. Questions asked during negotiations have five purposes: to create attention, to obtain information, to clarify, to stimulate thinking, and to conclude or summarize. In phrasing questions, strategy dictates whether to use open-ended, leading, or closed questions. In answering questions, the negotiator must protect his or her interests by taking time to think through the answer and respond only when the question is fully understood. The chapter suggests strategies for adapting answers to suit one's interests.

The channel chosen for negotiation is important. Which channel is chosen depends on the circumstances. The letter or memo of intent that follows many negotiations requires care in preparation and can work to the advantage of the person preparing it.

Six core strategies can be applied in negotiations—*surprise*, unexpectedly introducing a goal or a concession; *bluff*, creating an illusion without lying; *stacking*, linking one idea with another for argument's sake; *fait accompli*, acting as if terms are acceptable to the opposition before any agreement has occurred; *take it or leave it*, letting the opponent know that this offer is the last; and the *screen*, using a third party as part of the negotiation.

Cases for Small-Group Discussion

CASE 13–1

Negotiation and Technology

Jessie had just taken his second test drive in the new three-quarter-ton pickup truck he was considering purchasing. The salesman had become his "best" friend in the past three hours, pampering him with warm introductions with every "manager" in the dealership, free soft drink from the vending machine, curb service with two vehicles he had test-driven, and assurances that the salesman was "working for Jessie" and wanted to "earn Jessie's business." The salesman had barraged Jessie with a series of questions and baited him with "truck month" and "special deals" and "incentives for a short time only." He had informed Jessie of the "special financing, rebates, and dealer incentives" that would expire very soon and that Jessie would miss out if he didn't buy his truck today and that the dealership "seriously needed his trade-in and would offer top dollar." The salesman had figured out Jessie's payment for him, an amazingly low payment per month. Then Jessie did the smartest thing he had done in a long time. He said, "I have to be somewhere in twenty minutes, but I might come back tomorrow—when do you open in the morning?"

The next day, Jessie called one of his professors from college, followed up their conversation with phone research, and within twenty minutes, returned to the dealer with estimates of his trade-in value from three used car websites, a loan preapproval from his credit union, and a summary of the dealership's actual cost of the truck he was interested in from another website. He greeted the salesman and made an offer for the truck, below the invoice for the vehicle. "We just can't do that, Jess," said the salesman. "That's below what we have to pay for the truck."

"Well, first, you have added charged items that aren't even done yet, like the sprayed-in bed liner for $670 that I can have done for $230 from the same place you guys have it done. So I deducted that, and the special sealant extra charges that are included if a vehicle is painted, and all of them are (painted). . . . Here are some other items that are similar, and they come to $1,945. I deducted half of your destination charge, and then I deducted half of your holdback to arrive at this number." The shocked salesman took the information to his manager, who returned with another two managers to try to convince Jessie that his offer was not possible. The hard sell continued into a discussion of Jessie's trade-in, and finally, Jessie told them he just needed a deal and might find it at another dealer, or even with a different make of truck, and that if they were interested in trying to meet his offer, to call him. And then he left again, for the second time.

The next day, Jessie received a call. The manager had agreed to his offer. When Jessie arrived, the truck had been cleaned, had a large SOLD sign in the window, and was parked at the front door. Jessie walked into the wrestling ring. The manager had agreed to Jessie's offer on the new truck but had priced his trade-in at $8,000 less than the trade-in value Jessie had looked up. After another thirty minutes of hard-sell tactics, Jessie left the dealership for the third time. An hour later, Jessie got a call that the used car manager wanted to talk with him. After a visit with the used car manager, it was apparent that the call-back was for the purpose of talking Jessie down from his expected trade-in value. Again, Jessie left the dealership. That evening, the general manager called Jessie. He said that he could come within $450 of Jessie's offer and that if Jessie would come back to the dealership, the deal would be made. Jessie agreed and returned to the dealership the next day. The deal was indeed done, and written up, and the official "offer" reflected all of Jessie's requirements. And it was exactly $450 more than the deal Jessie had proposed. To a chorus of how much money the dealership was losing, he was hustled into the finance manager's office. Another barrage of deals flew Jessie's way. He was offered extremely overpriced credit, life insurance, gap insurance, extended warranties—and special deals on all four after he refused them all; he also refused the special deals on those items. The financial double-talk continued, but Jessie stood his ground, and the papers were finally finalized and signed.

That night, Jessie summed up the total additional costs the dealer tried to talk him into accepting. His truck would've ended up costing $42,360. The additional costs he could have incurred if he had given in to the hard sell totaled $19,763!

Jessie later acquired an extended warranty for 30 percent of the cost of the dealer warranty, and he had some custom touches added for a fraction of the cost the dealer had wanted to charge.

1. How important is it to be well informed about a negotiation before beginning the negotiation? Where would you go for guidance?

2. There was obviously a material cost of failing to negotiate effectively in this case. Can you think of other situations where costs of poor negotiation are high?

CASE 13–2

Purchasing and Accounts Payable

Saul and Latisha are both administrative managers in a machine tool company. Latisha is the director of purchasing and has four purchasing agents and a secretary reporting to her. Saul is the director of accounts payable and has two people reporting to him. The secretary for the accounts payable group also works for the accounts receivable group, so in effect, the accounts payable group has only a part-time secretary.

Saul and Latisha both have business degrees and graduated from college three and five years ago, respectively. They are both ambitious, and there is a high level of competition between them. The following discussion occurs in Latisha's office, which is down the hall from Saul's. Latisha is busy and has a lot of papers spread around on her desk. It is about forty-five minutes before the normal quitting time, but it looks as if Latisha may not be able to get away on time.

Everything has been rather hectic lately because it is nearing the end of the month. Both Latisha and Saul have numerous activities that need to be completed within the next few days.

QUESTIONS

1. Analyze the following conversation and indicate what could be done to improve the effectiveness of this interaction.

Saul: Latisha, could I use your secretary for a few hours tomorrow? We are really behind, and I've noticed that your secretary doesn't seem to be too busy.

Latisha: What do you mean "too busy"? We all have work backing up on us.

Saul: Well, you have one secretary, but we have to share time with accounts receivable.

Latisha: Well, I'm sorry, we're just too busy.

Saul:	How about asking her to work some overtime but charge it to our department? Does she like to work overtime?
Latisha:	She might want to do that. You can ask.
Saul:	Would you please ask? That might be better because you're her supervisor.
Latisha:	No, you go ahead and talk to her. Also, remember you will have to pay the time and a half for overtime.
Saul:	I really think you should talk to her.

As Saul says this, the telephone rings, and he walks out of the office.

2. Return to Figure 13–1. What are the major variables presented in the figure that influence the communication presented in this case?

CASE 13–3

Negotiating a Purchase

Reggie Blanchard's delivery van was recently totaled when someone ran a stop sign and struck the van. The other person's insurance company is going to pay Blanchard for the damages to his van, and for a week now, Blanchard has been looking at new vans while he temporarily leases one. The following scenario transpired when Blanchard talked to Kelly, a salesperson who tried to sell him a new van.

Kelly:	Yes, sir, may I be of service to you?
Blanchard:	I recently lost my delivery van in an accident. I am temporarily leasing a van, so I would like to get one as soon as possible.
Kelly:	What kind of van did you have?
Blanchard:	A 2005 one like this (pointing to a low-priced van). It had low mileage and was in great shape.
Kelly:	I know how you must feel. It is discomforting to lose a service van like that. And then you really don't get enough money from the insurance company to buy a van just like the one you had, do you?
Blanchard:	Yes, sir, that's exactly right.
Kelly:	How did the accident happen?

Blanchard then proceeds to explain how the other person ran the stop sign and demolished the passenger side of his van, and as he does this, Kelly nods his head in agreement with Blanchard's every word.

Kelly: That sorry old soul must have had mud in his eyes not to have seen you in that intersection.

Blanchard: Ha ha, I guess you're right.

Kelly: Well, now don't worry, because you've come to the right place at the right time. We're making good deals on all this year's models to be ready for the shipment of next year's vans due any week now.

Blanchard: That sounds good. Let me ask you, how much for this one?

Kelly: Well, these models are going like hotcakes. They're excellent vehicles and the prices are outstanding for the quality in the van. I can let you have this one for $37,000.

Blanchard: I hate to say it, but that seems a little high for this model.

Kelly: Oh, but this van has some great features, including our consumer protection package for $1,970 (smiling). This includes paint treatment, a sound shield underneath the van, and a three-year rust prevention guarantee. It also includes a membership in our motor club plan, which has some excellent benefits for businesspeople.

This last sentence was spoken while Kelly put his hand on Blanchard's shoulder.

Blanchard: Is that so?

Kelly: How much are you looking to spend?

Blanchard: I'm not exactly sure, but judging from what the book value of my old van is, and the amount of the notes I was paying on it, I'd like to spend not much more than $30,000.

Kelly: Well, like I say, I can give you this van for $37,000. We've already lowered the sticker price by $2,500. It normally sells for $39,500 (pause). If you can spend $30,000, then $7,000 more won't add that much to your payment. Besides, we're the only dealer in town that offers the consumer protection plan, and we feel that the benefits far out-weigh the cost. It's a steal, I tell you.

Blanchard: Oh well, in that case I guess $37,000 is fairly reasonable. Let me think about it, but it sounds good.

QUESTIONS

1. What negotiation style did Kelly use to move Blanchard toward this sale?

2. List some things Blanchard could do to improve his own position at the beginning of the negotiation.

3. Discuss some negotiation strategies that Blanchard should have used as the negotiation proceeded.

Exercise for Small Groups

Negotiating an Employment Agreement

Background: Managers seeking new positions may find there is far more to agree to than just pay, benefits, and job responsibilities. Today, companies want to protect their trade secrets, inventions, and clients. To do so, they ask new executives and managers to sign employment agreements that safeguard their interests.

Instructions: In pairs, students should negotiate the conditions for employment in the following scenario. One student is the candidate; the other is the hiring agent. The negotiators should determine the MSO, LAO, and BATNA for each topic to be negotiated.

Company: Bio-Analytics, Inc., a scientific software development company. The organization's chief clients are pharmaceutical companies, research and development laboratories, and universities. Products are software programs that support scientific research.

Position: Director of Marketing.

Responsibilities: Manage the Marketing Department, which is responsible for finding clients, selling Bio-Analytics products, and servicing the accounts.

Topics for Negotiation:

1. Noncompete clause—When the Director leaves, s/he cannot work for similar types of companies for a specified period of time or in a defined geographical area. S/he also cannot work for a competitor while employed in the current job.

2. Invention clause—The company, not the employee, owns whatever the employee developed or invented while working for the firm.

3. Nonsolicitation of clients—When the Director leaves, s/he cannot seek business from former clients for a specified time.

4. Nonsolicitation of employees—When the Director leaves, s/he cannot try to attract former colleagues to the new firm for a specified time.

5. Confidentiality agreement—When the Director leaves, s/he may not disclose to outsiders the company's private business and technical data, such as products in development, formulas, test results, and sales strategies.

Negotiation Tips for the Candidate:

- With noncompete clauses, try to limit the time in which you can't work for a competing company. As a bargaining chip point out that your useful knowledge about a company lasts only a limited time, such as a few months after you leave the company.

- With clients, ask to be allowed to identify which clients you can and can't contact after you leave the company.

- Focus the negotiation on conditions worth fighting for. For instance, the duration of noncompete and nonsolicitation provisions can limit your future ability to earn a living.

Student Study Site

Visit the Student Study Site at **study.sagepub.com/hynes6e** for web quizzes, video links, web resources, and cases studies.

Notes

1. D. G. Pruitt, *Negotiation Behavior* (New York: Academic Press, 1981).
2. Linda Babcock and Sara Laschever, *Women Don't Ask: Negotiation and the Gender Divide* (Princeton, NJ: Princeton University Press, 2003).
3. Tom White and Kimberly Gladman, "Female Chief Financial Officers and the Glass Ceiling," GMI Ratings, accessed January 23, 2014, www.gmiratings.com.
4. Barbara Safani, "Nuances of Negotiation," *Insider's Guide to Job Search,* accessed August 29, 2014, www.teglaloroupepeacefoundation.org.
5. Deborah M. Kolb and Blair H. Sheppard, "Do Managers Mediate, or Even Arbitrate?" *Negotiation Journal,* October 1985, pp. 379–388.
6. Roger Fisher, William Ury, and Bruce Patton, *Getting to Yes: Negotiating Agreement without Giving In,* 2nd ed. (Boston: Houghton Mifflin, 1992).
7. Stephen R. Covey, *The 7 Habits of Highly Effective People* (New York: Simon & Schuster, 1989).
8. John Ilich, *The Art and Skill of Successful Negotiation* (Englewood Cliffs, NJ: Prentice Hall, 1983), p. 33.
9. Michael Schalzki, *Negotiation: The Art of Getting What You Want* (New York: Signet, 1981), p. 33.
10. Fisher et al., *Getting to Yes.*
11. Peter J. D. Carnevale and Edward J. Lawler, "Time Pressure and the Development of Integrative Agreements in Bilateral Negotiations," *Journal of Conflict Resolution* 30, no. 4 (December 1986): pp. 636–659.
12. David D. Seltz and Alfred J. Modica, *Negotiate Your Way to Success* (New York: New American Library, 1980), p. 52.
13. Ilich, *The Art and Skill of Successful Negotiation,* p. 22.
14. Herb Cohen, *You Can Negotiate Anything* (New York: Bantam Books, 1980), p. 92.
15. Jeffrey Z. Rubin and Bert R. Brown, *The Social Psychology of Bargaining and Negotiation* (New York: Academic Press, 1975), p. 122.
16. Gerald I. Nierenberg, *Fundamentals of Negotiating* (New York: Hawthorn, 1973), p. 150.
17. R. Sommer, "Further Studies of Small Group Ecology," *Sociometry* 28, no. 2 (1965): pp. 337–338.
18. R. L. Birdwhistell, *Introduction to Kinesics* (Louisville, KY: University of Louisville Press, 1952).
19. P. A. Andersen and J. F. Andersen, "The Exchange of Nonverbal Intimacy: A Critical Review of Dyadic Models," *Journal of Nonverbal Behavior* 8, no. 12 (1984): pp. 327–349.
20. M. Cook, "Experiments on Orientations and Proxemics," *Human Relations* 23, no. 1 (1970): pp. 62–76.

21. R. V. Exline, J. Thibaut, C. Brannon, and P. Gumpert, "Visual Interaction in Relation to Machiavellianism and Unethical Acts," *American Psychologist* 16, no. 3 (1961): p. 396.
22. Dorothy Leads, *Smart Questions: A New Strategy for Successful Managers* (New York: McGraw-Hill, 1987).
23. Stuart Diamond, *Getting More: How to Negotiate to Achieve Your Goals in the Real World* (New York: Three Rivers Press, 2010).
24. Linda L. Putnam and M. Scott Poole, "Conflict and Negotiation," in *Handbook of Organizational Communication,* eds. F. Jablin, L. Putnam, K. Roberts, and L. Porter (Newbury Park, CA: Sage, 1987), pp. 549–599.
25. Joseph F. Byrnes, "Ten Guidelines for Effective Negotiation," *Business Horizons,* May–June 1987, pp. 7–12.
26. These strategies are partially drawn from Roy J. Lewicki and Joseph A. Littere, *Negotiation* (Homewood, IL: Richard D. Irwin, 1985).

CHAPTER 14

Conducting Interviews

Patience is the most necessary quality for business; many a man would rather you heard his story than grant his request.

—Lord Chesterfield (1694–1773), British statesman and author

A manager conducts many different kinds of interviews: performance appraisal, employment, persuasive, grievance, exit, problem solving, and informational. No matter what the situation, the process is an intensive communication transaction designed to obtain or share certain predetermined kinds of information. But successful managers must learn to avoid the special communication barriers that accompany the process. Accordingly, this chapter examines interviews from the perspective of the interviewer, suggests ways to overcome the special barriers, and offers guidelines for conducting the most common kinds of interviews.

BARRIERS TO EFFECTIVE INTERVIEWS

All the communication dynamics discussed in Chapter 2 are present in the interview, but six barriers are particularly relevant: (1) differing intentions of the people involved, (2) bias, (3) the fact-inference fallacy, (4) nonverbal communication, (5) effects of first impressions, and (6) organizational status.

Barrier 1: Differing Intentions

Managers cannot always assume all participants agree on the information that should be exchanged in an interview. In fact, rarely do both the interviewer and interviewee agree. One obvious instance is the employment interview. While the interviewer wants to know all the strengths and weaknesses of the applicant, the applicant (interviewee) wants to reveal only strengths to the interviewer.

Differences in intention operate at one of three levels. First, both parties consciously may intend to have a clear and accurate exchange of information. This type may be particularly relevant in a performance appraisal interview. This type is equally important during informational interviews at networking events. At the second level, one of the parties does not intend to disclose certain relevant information. This often occurs in exit interviews when the employee does not reveal the real reason for leaving. At the third level, both parties do not intend to disclose certain relevant information. This may happen when an employee interviewed for a promotion discusses the potential salary. The employee will probably not reveal the lowest acceptable salary, and the interviewer does not indicate the highest possible salary. Figure 14–1 depicts these three levels of intentions.

Skillful questioning, which is reviewed in the next section of this chapter, helps to overcome this barrier. Listening to the other person and understanding her point of view also help reduce this barrier. However, the key is to remember that the other person's goal may not always be the same as the manager's in the interview process.

Figure 14–1 Differing Intentions

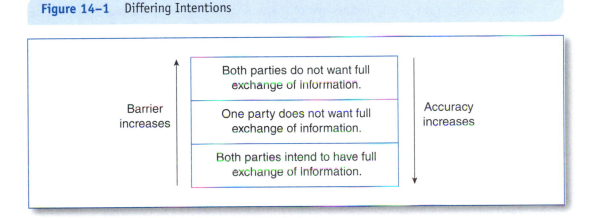

Barrier 2: Bias

Bias is a barrier because it slants people's perceptions, so they tend to see and hear only what they want to see and hear.[1] The most prevalent type of bias is the *halo effect,* which managers fall prey to when they allow the evaluation of one characteristic to be influenced by another characteristic or by a general impression.[2] One aspect of the job may affect the manager's impression of the employee in other areas. If an employee has a tendency to be late, for instance, the manager could let this shortcoming influence his impression of the employee on other, unrelated characteristics such as technical skills. The bias creates problems in performance evaluation interviews.[3]

Another type of bias is the *recency effect.* This occurs when the latest information disproportionately affects all the earlier information. Still other types of bias are *leniency* and *harshness.* In these instances, interviewers see everything as either positive or negative—they do not differentiate.[4]

Questions can also subtly bias an interview. For instance, one manager asked this loaded question: "Should the consumer group continue its generous support of the marketing research department when the research has proved to be of little value?" The question is obviously biased and would be difficult to answer in the affirmative. Appropriate ways to phrase questions will be discussed in the following section of this chapter.

Managers frequently become biased by coworkers' opinions. For instance, the following is the type of statement frequently heard: "You'll get nothing but trouble from Patrick, but you'll find Semkins easy to work with." Smart managers wait to form their own impressions of these subordinates.

Research has found that people who try hard can control their bias.[5] Thus, before entering the interview, the manager should try to review any bias that may interfere with his main goal and then make a special effort to remain objective.

Barrier 3: Confusing Facts With Inferences

Managers actually deal with very few facts in an interview. Rather, they must make inferences based on the words and actions of the interviewee. Sometimes, managers can be "almost certain" about their conclusions from an interview, but other times they are not too sure.[6] When they are not sure, however, problems can arise. Table 14–1 reveals some problems caused by discrepancies among words, facts, and inferences.

Managers need to be on the alert to determine when they are making plausible inferences and when they are jumping to unfounded conclusions. Many of the techniques discussed later in the chapter help to overcome this barrier. The simplest method for avoiding this confusion is to remember that a fact can be measured and proven, while an inference is an opinion or judgment and by definition subjective. Rereading the section in Chapter 2 about the assumption-observation error in communication may add to your understanding of this barrier.

Table 14–1 Facts and Inferences

Words	Facts	Possible Inference
"I like selling office equipment."	The record shows that the person has been selling for two years but before that was unemployed for six months.	This is the only work the person is able to get.
(When asked to fully describe college activities) "I did well in college and was involved in some extracurricular activities."	The person tends to avoid discussion on these activities and changes the subject when asked specifically about grades.	The person did not do well in academic work in college and had little involvement in extracurricular activities.
"I did not care for the atmosphere in that department." (by applicant for a job transfer)	The person received a poor performance review.	The applicant is a troublemaker.

Barrier 4: Nonverbal Communication

A quizzical look, a frown, a shrug, and a look of indifference are all important nonverbal messages, but those reading them must exercise caution before interpreting them. Nonverbal information can be a problem in an interview because interviews are generally short and intensive.[7] If a person slouches in a chair for a few minutes during a twenty-minute interview, this behavior is more noticeable than if he slouches for a few minutes during a four-hour meeting. Because of the compact time span, nonverbal signals have a greater impact.

Accurately reading nonverbal signals during a compact time span is complicated by the *primary effect*—one piece of information overpowering all others. In a short period, one nonverbal cue can more easily overpower the others.[8] This is especially the case when one has no baseline of nonverbal signs for judging the candidate. The careful interviewer is also aware that she can use nonverbal signs from the interviewee to judge the honesty of responses. Research has indicated that through training and practice, we can improve our ability to detect nonverbal deception.[9] This is further elaborated in the discussion of nonverbal leakage in Chapter 10.

Barrier 5: Effects of First Impressions

A manager may form a quick first impression that colors what he sees during the rest of the interview. If the interview is short, this strong first view may affect his overall impression since he does not have the time to find data to the contrary. Further, research indicates interviewers are influenced more by unfavorable than by favorable information, and the earlier in the interview the unfavorable information, the greater its negative effect.[10] In addition, it is more likely that the interviewer's impression will change from favorable to unfavorable than the opposite.[11]

STOP AND THINK
1. When you are forming a first impression of someone, how important are that person's nonverbal behaviors (eye contact, body language, appearance) compared to what they say?
2. Why do you think the nonverbals count more than the words?
3. What are the implications for your strategic processes?

This barrier may also be referred to as *hypothesis testing*, meaning the interviewer establishes a hypothesis early and then seeks information that supports it. The fear is that any information that does not support the hypothesis will be ignored.[12]

Since this barrier is so pervasive, managers must act to limit its impact. Part of the solution is simple: be cautious about making value judgments until evidence other than that available from first impressions has been considered. Then, too, be aware that short interviews encourage the manager to make a decision prematurely.

Barrier 6: Organizational Status

Perhaps the most pervasive communication barrier results from hierarchical rank.[13] In any interview situation, the parties involved know who holds the balance of power.[14] While a higher-ranking person may encourage candor, the lower-level person may fear the consequences of such openness. It is only human to worry about the reactions of people in powerful positions, so candor frequently suffers.

Several suggestions can prevent it. For one thing, managers should recognize that employees almost always want to make the best impression when communicating with the boss. An effective manager should try to create an open, supportive communication climate that minimizes power differences. And when a manager hears something unpleasant, harsh, or unwarranted from a subordinate, the manager should check her defensive reaction and try to remain open minded and fair.

QUESTIONS THAT LEAD TO EFFECTIVE INTERVIEWS

Thorough analysis and planning are required for effective interviews. We believe the numerous contingencies can best be managed by addressing the following seven questions.

Question 1: What Is the Interview Objective?

First, consider the interview objective. Are you trying to obtain general information, gather specific data, or persuade someone to accept an idea? The interview objective indicates the format. However, the objective is not always clear, or the interview may have more than one objective. Consider the employment interview in which a person is simultaneously trying to gather general information about the applicant and specific information about her skills in order to determine whether the applicant will fit in to the workplace. All the while, the manager is trying to sell the applicant on the benefits of joining the company. Because several goals may apply at one time, it is important to clarify the purpose of the interview and set priorities.

Question 2: Where Is the Best Place to Conduct the Interview?

Time and place have an impact on the success of an interview. Managers should select a time that is mutually convenient. Managers should also allow adequate time so neither party in the interview feels rushed. Finally, managers should be aware of the primacy-recency effect when scheduling a series of interviews. That is, people tend to recall most favorably the first and the last of a series of events. This psychological phenomenon can affect hiring decisions, in particular.

Privacy is also a primary concern. It ensures confidentiality and minimizes interferences. Many managers find they can best eliminate distractions by conducting the interview in a place other than their work area or office. Remember that a neutral setting also reduces the status barrier present in many interviews.

Question 3: What Is the Best Way to Begin the Interview?

This question and the next are closely related. The opening statements lay the foundation for the questioning to follow. The opening of an interview generally serves two purposes: (1) it establishes the communication climate, and (2) it explains the purpose of the interview.

The interview climate is established as soon as the manager meets the interviewee. At that point, nonverbal communication plays a crucial role. A friendly greeting, handshake, or smile will break the ice and help put the interviewee at ease. Friendly conversation about a neutral topic also puts everyone at ease. In her book *The Art of Civilized Conversation*, Margaret Shepherd suggests avoiding clichéd topics, such as the weather, and instead beginning by asking about the journey ("How was your trip?"), the situation ("What did you think of that speech?"), or the recent past ("How was your summer vacation?").[15] One to four minutes of small talk should be sufficient. No matter what the purpose of the interview, managers should always begin by establishing rapport. This makes the interviewee feel safe and ensures two-way communication.

Next, the manager should affirm the interview's purpose. Typical starters are

- summarizing the problem or task at hand,

- requesting advice or assistance,

- mentioning an incentive or reward for taking part in the interview,

- requesting a specific time commitment for the interview.

In addition to stating the purpose of the interview, the manager should check to be sure that the interviewee agrees. This encourages a participatory attitude and may stimulate the other person's involvement in the interview. Thus, the opening, which may take the least time of all the segments in the interview process, is a crucial part and sets the stage.

Question 4: What Is the Best Questioning Strategy?

Exact questions and their precise sequence cannot always be planned for an interview. However, developing a questioning strategy before the interview helps a manager reach the interview's goal (see Table 14-2). One strategy is the *structured interview,* in which the interviewer writes out preliminary questions in sequence. This may be effective for inexperienced interviewers or for situations where each question must be repeated exactly the same way and in the same sequence with each interviewee.[16]

Because a structured interview restricts the interviewer's flexibility and makes it difficult to adapt to unique situations, certain cases require an *unstructured interview.* Here, the interviewer has a clear objective but has prepared no specific questions in advance. With an unstructured format, the interviewer initiates the discussion, letting the initial responses lead into the next question. This type of interview is particularly valuable when it is important that the interviewee helps set the direction—as in some appraisal interviews or certain counseling sessions. Also, this type of interview facilitates the communication flow in informational interviews at networking activities.

A compromise between the structured and unstructured interview is the *semistructured interview.* In this format, the interviewer prepares a list of critical questions to make sure she covers all important points by the close of the interview. Meanwhile, she maintains flexibility because the sequence of the questioning is not completely planned. Many consider this the most appropriate format for most situations faced by experienced managers.

Table 14–2   Interview Questioning Strategies

Strategy	When to Use It
Structured	Inexperienced interviewer To compare interviewees' responses to the same questions
Semistructured	Experienced interviewer Flexibility of question sequence is appropriate
Unstructured	Interviewee should set the direction of the interview

Question 5: What Is the Best Sequence for the Questions?

For a semistructured interview, a funnel or inverted funnel question sequence is recommended. The funnel sequence opens with broad, open-ended questions and proceeds with increasingly restricted questions. The inverted funnel sequence begins with closed questions and gradually proceeds toward open-ended ones. Figure 14–2 shows these two sequences.

The appropriate strategy depends on the situation.[17] The funnel sequence works best when the interviewee is able and willing to talk freely, such as in a job selection interview. The inverted funnel works best when the interviewee is reluctant to participate or is hostile

Figure 14–2   Question Sequence

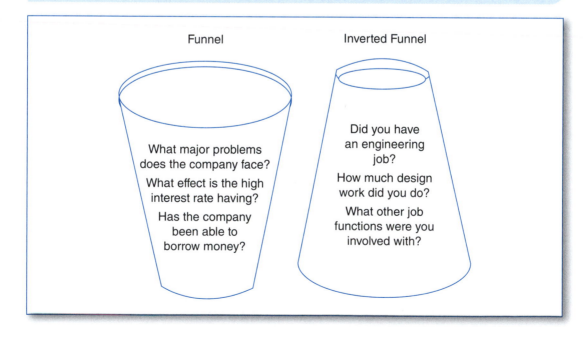

toward the manager. Thus, for example, during an exit interview, the manager might begin with specific, factual questions and move gradually toward general questions about changes the interviewee feels are needed in the workplace.

Question 6: What Are the Best Types of Questions?

The various types of questions have already been discussed in Chapter 9 and are reviewed next.

Interview questions fall into three wording categories: open–closed, primary–secondary, and neutral–directed. *Open* and *closed* questions are best explained using a continuum. An open-ended question has virtually no restriction on the type of response that is received. At the other extreme is the closed-ended question, which calls for specific, short responses. Look at the following examples of the two types of questions.

Open-Ended Questions	**Closed-Ended Questions**
1. How was your last job?	1. What part of your last job did you dislike?
2. Tell me more about the Niles project.	2. What percentage of the Niles project is completed?
3. How is everything in the Denver Division?	3. Did you complete the quarterly report for the Denver Division?
4. Tell me about yourself.	4. Have you ever been to Los Angeles?

Managers often use closed-ended questions when they should be asking open-ended questions. Managers need to ask themselves if they are looking for a general response or a specific answer. Are they trying to solicit information (open), trying to make the interviewee comfortable (open), or trying to get to a specific point or commitment as quickly as possible (closed)? The answers to these strategic questions help one decide when to use open or closed questions.

The second category of questions is *primary* and *secondary*. A primary question introduces a topic in an interview, while a secondary question follows up, probing further into the response to the primary question. A secondary question is most valuable when the primary question did not elicit all the desired information.

The following dialogue gives an example of the use of primary and secondary questions.

Interviewer: What was your most recent job? (primary)

Interviewee: I supervised the AR Department.

Interviewer: What is the AR Department? (secondary)

Interviewee: That's the accounts receivable group that does all the . . .

In this example, the secondary question elicited additional information for the interviewer.

A subtle form of secondary questions is a probe. Table 14–3 presents seven types of probes. Again, notice that in a relaxed interview, although these probes obtain additional information, they may not appear to be questions but rather part of the conversation. They are subtle but effective.

Table 14–3 Seven Probes

Probe	Definition of Probe	Illustration of Probe
1. Brief assertion of understanding	A indicates interest and understanding, thus encouraging B to continue.	"So, first I said to him, how'd you like a cup of coffee?" "You thought it would break the ice."
2. Neutral phrase	A elicits more information from B without affecting (biasing) the information.	"I don't know . . . kids today seem to be getting away with murder." "Huh."
3. Silence	A does not speak and looks attentively at B. The pause is under ten seconds.	"Wow . . . what a day I've had." Silence—two seconds. "I mean, I didn't have a minute to myself the way they kept me working."
4. Echo	A converts the last portion of what B says into a question . . . generally with almost the same words.	"I'm not sure that I can take any more. . . . I'm at the end of my rope." "At the end of your rope?"
5. Clarification	A tries to get a definition or further explanation from B that is not understood.	"I'll tell you, lowering the voting age isn't right." "Oh . . . how so?" "Well, for one thing, it's increased the likelihood of political conspiracies."
6. Elaboration	A requests new information that is directly related to something B already said.	"Bob, I'm really worried about the parade tomorrow." "Why are you worried?" "Well, I think we might be in for some trouble." "Oh . . . what makes you think that we might have trouble?"
7. Summary	A tries to pull together the main points B made during the past few minutes.	"And finally, Hank, we just don't get paid enough for the work we do." "Let me see if I have it straight, Ralph. First, you say the work is dirty, not carefully scheduled, and finally, you're underpaid, correct?"

Secondary questions help gain complete and accurate information, but they also establish a positive communication climate in the interview. The effective use of secondary questions and probes can help demonstrate that the manager is interested in listening. Initially, the interviewee may not know how much information is wanted or whether the manager is really interested in her comments; however, the use of secondary questions and probes helps establish a willing and open atmosphere.

Neutral and *directed* questions, the third category, may also be considered in terms of a continuum with neutral questions at one end and directed questions at the other. Since the correct answer is not implied in the question, a neutral question does not lead the interviewee to answer in one particular way. The directed question, at the other end of the continuum, leads the interviewee to give a particular answer. The classic example of a directed question is the courtroom ploy, "Isn't it true that . . . ?" In reality, this type of extreme directed question may be considered a plea for agreement rather than a true question even when an interrogative tone is used.[18]

Examples of neutral and directed questions are listed below to show the difference.

Neutral Questions	Directed Questions
1. What kind of car do you prefer?	1. Don't you think that foreign cars are superior to American cars?
2. What is your reaction to decentralization?	2. You are opposed to decentralization, aren't you?
3. What do you think of unionization?	3. Naturally, you are opposed to any kind of unions, right?
4. Do you feel we should hire more employees?	4. I don't think we should hire any more employees. Do you?

The skillful use of directed questions can be valuable since such questions can help keep the interview on track and be used effectively for persuasion. In persuasion, they point the interviewee in a particular direction and help him think about the benefit of some concept.

Question 7: What Is the Best Way to Close the Interview?

When it is time to close the interview, as with many other communications, it is important to summarize the main information and ensure understanding. The close also provides the opportunity to arrange for any follow-up activity and to express appreciation. Goodwill is always appropriate, whether the interviewee is a job applicant, a disgruntled customer, a networking associate, or a long-term, loyal subordinate. End with agreement, a statement of appreciation, and a handshake.

So far, we have given an overview of the barriers to interviews as well as the most frequent questions managers ask about the interview process. Next, we will focus on three specific interview situations that managers experience as well as the appropriate strategies for each: employment interviews, performance appraisal interviews, and networking.

EMPLOYMENT INTERVIEWS

Selecting the most qualified people available for a position is a major managerial responsibility. Many screening tools are used in employee selection, including application forms and aptitude and personality tests, but the most common is the interview.

While a member of the human resources department often screens applicants, the applicant's future manager generally makes the final decision. The ability to match competent applicants with the correct job leads to the success of an organization. Making good hiring decisions also reduces the cost of turnover, which can be significant. The US Department of Labor estimates that it costs a company one-third of a new hire's annual salary to replace an employee. More than 75 percent of turnover can be traced back to poor interviewing and hiring practices, according to a Harvard Business School study.[19] Managers have a responsibility to both the organization and the applicant to see that an applicant–job match exists.

As a manager, one way to create an edge for yourself is to rely on networking with peers and acquaintances for potential candidates. If a referred applicant is trusted and well qualified, this can save your company crucial overhead dollars and time by eliminating the search process. In fact, a 2006 study found that up to half of US jobs are found through families, friends, or acquaintances.[20] According to *BusinessWeek* contributor Stephen Baker, the increasing popularity of social and professional networking sites, such as LinkedIn and Facebook, is making networking easier than ever before. An online network of friends has turned into a turbocharged rolodex for both recruiters and job seekers inside and outside companies. In addition, every hand you shake or business card you exchange can lead to an online friendship invitation that can extend your professional network.[21]

Yet employment interviews are typically not used to their best advantage. While research shows that the interview is low in both reliability and validity,[22] no adequate replacement exists. It is the only technique that gives managers the chance to personally evaluate the candidate and to pursue questioning in a way that tests cannot.

STOP AND THINK

1. If a job applicant's résumé indicates she has the skill set required to do a certain job, why should you conduct a preemployment interview before making an offer?

2. What are some qualifications that can be determined only by an interview?

Planning

The employment interview, like all communication situations, requires planning, but in a more specific way.

Position Requirements

A manager's first step is to ensure a clear understanding of the job requirements. This effort helps to avoid putting too much weight on irrelevant information. An interviewer familiar with extensive details about the job to be filled (such as that provided by detailed job descriptions and job titles) enhances the reliability of employment selection decisions.[23] When no comprehensive job description is available, it may be necessary for the interviewer to complete a job analysis.

When reviewing the nature of the job, be careful not to compare the last *person* holding the job with present candidates. Doing so can inaccurately affect your impressions of a candidate. Also, many job incumbents change the nature of a position slightly to match their personal capabilities and interests. A good time to analyze the present and future qualifications required for performance on a job is when personnel changes are made.

Another consideration for interviewers who are preparing to conduct a job interview is the organization's culture, mission, and vision. C-level executives (CEO, CFO, chief information officer [CIO], chief operating officer [COO], etc.) in particular are likely to ask questions that will determine whether a candidate's values align with the organization's philosophy.[24] For instance, Barry Salzberg, CEO of Deloitte LLP, says that he looks for an applicant's speaking and writing skills, values, and "worldly experiences," including traveling and working for nonprofits. If he could ask only a few questions in an interview, they would be "What are the values that are most important to you? How have you demonstrated your commitment to those values in the last two years?"[25]

As a list of requirements develops, the interviewer should prepare questions that will determine whether an applicant can meet them. For example, if the job requires extensive teamwork, a poor question is "Are you a team player?" because it is closed-ended and because a yes response tells the interviewer nothing useful. A better question is "Describe the advantages and disadvantages of working on a team," because it is open-ended and will reveal the applicant's experiences, beliefs, and behaviors.

Time

Time and timing are also important parts of the planning process. The amount of time allocated for an interview varies. In general, it is better to allocate too much rather than too little time.

Timing is important in the employment interview due to the contrast effect, namely, the influence that earlier interviews may have on later interviews. The job candidate who is only average but follows a number of poor candidates will likely make a better impression than if she had followed other average candidates. One way to reduce this effect is to avoid interviewing a long series of candidates without a break.

In addition, allow enough time between interviews and arrange your schedule so fatigue does not become a factor. Applicants interviewed when the interviewer is tired may receive lower ratings than other applicants. These suggested strategies are valuable considerations when planning the interview.

Applicant Preview

Interviewers should review the application or the résumé before the interview to plan specific questions. Remember that the interview objective is to get information that written material cannot easily reveal, including motivation and personality characteristics. Clearly, time is wasted if the interview covers the same material that appears in the documents. But you can also use the interview to clarify inconsistencies or fill in gaps. In short, use the documents as a springboard for the interview topics.

Legal Concerns

By now, almost all managers are familiar with the Americans with Disabilities Act of 1990 and the Civil Rights Act of 1964, which was amended by the Equal Employment Opportunity (EEO) Act of 1972. Unfortunately, knowledge of the legal restrictions of employment interviewing is too often misapplied. Either managers may become too cautious in their questioning out of fear of the law and miss valuable information, or they may ignore the legal restrictions. Although the following paragraphs do not constitute a comprehensive discussion of the legal components of employment, several suggestions may help you in your employment interviews.

Probably the first thing that comes to managers' minds when discussing EEO is what is a legal or illegal question. To answer this, one needs to be aware of the concept of bona fide occupational qualification (BFOQ), which is *any characteristic that is a valid criterion of job performance*. Race, age, national origin, general health, religion, gender, ethnic background, number of children, and marital status are generally not bases on which people should be judged.

Firms with affirmative action programs are committed to ensuring that members of what are called protected groups (people over forty, people with disabilities, minorities, and females usually fall into this classification) will be actively sought for employment.[26] Equal employment opportunity and affirmative action are often confused because their goals have some similarities. However, EEO seeks a level playing field where all have an equal chance at gaining employment based on qualifications. A commitment to affirmative action is a commitment to make extra effort to identify and recruit individuals from protected classes.[27]

Generally, education, experience, abilities, and skills are the basic elements of BFOQs. Each job must be analyzed. In most situations, managers can follow guidelines that ensure no condition of the Equal Employment Opportunity Act is being ignored. The best advice is to ask only questions that are related to BFOQs or directly related to making an objective employment decision.

Keep in mind, too, that casual conversations with job applicants should respect the guidelines set out here. For example, suppose a job applicant is being treated to lunch. Do not confuse this with a truly social situation and make small talk about family, personal finances, or religion. These could be misconstrued by the candidates as irrelevant, non-BFOQ questions and represent grounds for later disputes should a job offer not materialize.

Table 14–4 presents guidelines regarding lawful and unlawful questions during the employment interview. These same considerations also apply to application forms. Discrimination

Table 14–4   Question Guidelines for Employment Interviews

Focus of Question	Nondiscriminatory	Possibly Discriminatory
Name	Have you ever used a different name in other jobs?	What was your name before you changed it?
Birthplace and residence	Which state do you presently live in? How long have you lived in Cedar Falls (or a given state)? Are you over 18 years of age?	Where were you born? In which country were your parents born? How old are you?
Physical characteristics including race	Do you have any distinguishing marks or scars?	Are you Asian?
National origin or ancestry	If hired, can you verify that you can legally work in the United States?	You're from Mexico, aren't you? Are you related to the Manuels from Hermosa?
Family status		How many children do you have? Are you married? Pregnant?
Religion	Here are the regular days, hours, or shifts to be worked:	Are you Jewish? Do you pray? What religious holidays will you be taking off if we hire you?
Citizenship	Are you legally able to work in the United States?	Are you a German?
Affiliations	Do you belong to any professional-related organizations?	Are you in the Daughters of the American Revolution (DAR)? Were you a member of the Catholic Students Club?
Arrest record and convictions		How often have you been arrested, and for what? (unless related to job performance)
Physical abilities or limitations	This job requires lifting and carrying; do you see any problems with that?	Are you handicapped? (similarly, avoid questions about the type and severity of the handicap)
Education	Have you received your CPM certification yet?	Do you have an MBA degree? (or similar questions when educational achievement has no relation to the skills needed for a given job)
Financial status		Have you ever had your wages garnisheed? What is your approximate net worth? How much is your house mortgage?

occurs when an individual who has an equal probability of being successful on a job does not have an equal probability of getting the job.[28] A manager is responsible for seeing that discrimination does not occur.

The Employment Interview Process

During the employment interview, the manager tries to find out as much as possible about a candidate that relates to potential job success. The best way to do this is to be aware of the various barriers and suggested strategies discussed previously. Also, to be fully effective, managers should be familiar with certain conditions specific to the selection interview. The following guidelines assist managers in their efforts to increase the reliability and validity of the employment interview.

Use Appropriate Questioning Strategy

Research indicates the form and sequence of questions profoundly influence the outcome of the interview.[29] Most interviews open positively with the manager attempting to put the interviewee at ease. The résumé can be a useful guide for selecting some strong point from the candidate's background to help make the interviewee comfortable in the beginning.[30] It is generally best to use a semistructured interview that not only ensures a definite direction is taken but also allows the opportunity to prepare additional questions as the interview proceeds. Table 14–5 shows possible questions that you might use as an interviewer.

When designing the questions for the interview, remember the difference between open and closed, primary and secondary, and neutral and directed questions. Know the benefits and shortcomings of each of these types of questions, so you can implement an effective questioning strategy. An employment interview generally uses open-ended questions, but it can also use closed and directed questions as probes.

A special type of question that is successfully used in employment interviews is the *behavioral question*. Based on the premise that past behavior predicts future behavior, these questions ask about specific instances of a particular action. Managers can use behavioral questions to probe for more information behind useless generalizations such as "I'm a people person" and "I'm flexible." Typically, behavioral questions begin with "tell me about a time when you . . ." and follow with situations or qualities relevant to the position, thus requiring evidence to "prove" the applicant's claims. Behaviors demonstrating leadership, conflict management, handling difficult customers, goal setting, teamwork, attention to detail, and the like can be effectively explored using behavioral questions. For example, if a manager of a diverse workforce is looking for someone who can interact with people with different values, cultures, or backgrounds, an appropriate behavioral question is "Describe a time when you adapted your behavior around another person's style," or "Describe something you did to optimize the benefits of diversity at work."

Another special type of question that is becoming popular in certain employment interviews is the *problem-solving question*. Its purpose is to seek out creative talent, a necessity for companies where competitive advantage is gained through its people. Microsoft, Boeing,

Table 14–5   Interviewer Question Options

Openers

Why would you like to join our company?

Why do you feel qualified for this job?

Tell me about your work experience.

Determining Motivation

Why do you want to change jobs?

What led you to enter this profession?

Where would you like to be in your career five years from now? Ten years?

What do you see as the perfect job for you?

Determining Experience

What did you do while you were in the military?

How would you go about improving our operations?

Who or what has influenced you the most? Why?

What aspects of your last job did you like best/least? Why?

What are your greatest strengths/weaknesses for this position?

What kinds of people do you like most/least as work associates?

What are your greatest achievements to date?

What equipment are you familiar with?

Why have you changed jobs so often?

What has been the biggest crisis in your career?

Why did you quit your previous employment?

May I see examples of your work?

Evaluating Educational Background

Describe your education for me.

Why did you choose your major field?

What extracurricular activities did you participate in that helped you prepare for your profession?

What honors did you earn?

To what extent do your grades reflect your full ability?

What courses did you like best/least and why?

What special training have you had for this job?

IBM, Southwest Airlines, and Weyerhauser are among the 20 to 30 percent of companies using situational or problem-solving questions, according to Professor Vandra Huber of the University of Washington.[31] The following are some sample problem-solving questions used during Microsoft interviews:

- Estimate the number of gas stations in the United States.

- If you could remove any of the fifty states, which would it be, and why?

- Design a bathroom for me.

- If you have a fishbowl with two hundred fish and 99 percent are guppies, how many guppies do you need to remove to get to the point where 98 percent of the remaining fish are guppies?[32]

Clearly, the answers to such questions are not as important as the process the candidate uses to (a) determine the problem and (b) develop solutions. A description of the steps in the rational problem-solving process can be found in Chapters 4 and 12.

Do Not Do Most of the Talking

In employment interviews, the manager is generally more talkative when reacting favorably to an applicant than when reacting unfavorably.[33] In other words, when an interviewer is impressed by the applicant, the interviewer is inclined to do less listening and more talking.

For whatever reason, extensive talking is efficient only when attempting to sell a candidate on a position; information relevant to hiring decisions is obtained through listening, not talking. Thus, be careful not to talk too much. A good rule of thumb is that the manager should talk only 30 percent of the time during an employment interview.

Keep Records

Given all the information revealed during an interview, it is unrealistic to expect that it can be remembered accurately for any length of time. One study showed that half the interviewers could not accurately recall the most critical information produced in a twenty-minute interview.[34] Thus, record notes or a summary of the interview immediately after its completion. One option is to use a rating system. This minimizes the possibility of erroneously making an early decision or letting one or two negative characteristics predominate. Another option is to have a routine form that reports on the same areas for each candidate interviewed or records answers to the same questions.

PERFORMANCE REVIEW INTERVIEWS

Periodically, managers are called on to conduct performance appraisal interviews. Over forty-five years ago, Maier cited several purposes for the performance review interview[35] and current objectives remain much the same.[36]

- Let employees know where they stand.

- Recognize good work.

- Communicate to subordinates directions in which they should improve.

- Develop employees in their present jobs.

- Develop and train employees for higher jobs.

- Assess the department or unit as a whole and where each person fits into the larger picture.

While the potential benefits of the performance review interview seem evident, its infrequent and ineffective use in organizations is widely recognized. Samuel Culbert, a professor of management at the University of California–Los Angeles and author of *Get Rid of the Performance Review!*, calls it "the most ridiculous practice in the world [because] it's . . . fraudulent, dishonest at its core, and reflects . . . cowardly management." Culbert sees performance reviews as a way to intimidate employees and concludes that they do more harm than good.[37]

This contradiction exists for several reasons, including that managers do not like to be put into the role of evaluator. Some managers may fear their working relationship with subordinates will be destroyed because of the discomfort created by a poorly conducted appraisal interview.[38] Another reason may be that managers often are not adequately trained in conducting these interviews.[39] Knowledge of the following information should encourage managers to conduct performance appraisal interviews that reach their intended purpose.

Purpose

The performance interview can meet two purposes: (1) it can focus on the worker's past performance in an effort to determine growth, or (2) it can focus on future activities and involve setting goals that will lead to increased employee performance. A critical question is relevant here: Does a manager discuss goals, performance improvement, and personal development in the same interview as salary increases? Extensive review of the available research on this question makes it clear that one should not combine specific developmental topics and salary discussions in one interview. The importance of the salary review typically dominates the interview so neither the manager nor the employee is in the proper frame of mind to discuss plans for improvement in a positive manner.[40] Instead, two separate interviews would be more appropriate. This requires more time but generally yields a more positive response from the employee.

Types

Three types of performance reviews are possible and vary according to the nature of the job and the employees.[41] *Developmental* appraisal interviews are used for high-performing, high-potential employees who have discretionary jobs giving them the opportunity to implement performance improvement.

The second type, the *maintenance* interview, is used for those who have performed at a steady, satisfactory level for some time and are not likely to improve due to constraints of ability, motivation, or the nature of their jobs. In this situation, the interviewee focuses on maintaining performance at the currently acceptable levels.

The third type of interview, the *remedial* appraisal, is used for low-performing or marginal subordinates in an attempt to raise performance to acceptable levels. This category involves two processes: evaluation and development. First, evaluate the present and past performances and then determine how they can be developed.

Each type of interview calls for a different degree of evaluation and development. More development is emphasized in the developmental and remedial interviews and more evaluation in the maintenance interview. A performance review interview does not always meet the same purpose; consequently, different communication strategies must be implemented to meet the established goals of either evaluation or development. In implementing the appropriate strategy, planning is required just as it is in other interview formats.

Planning

In terms of the strategic managerial communication model presented in Chapter 2, the three main factors to be analyzed in the planning process are the timing, the environment, and the message content—that is, when, where, and what—as shown in the third layer of the model.

Timing

Formal appraisals are most often conducted on an annual basis. Once a year seems to be a practical time frame; however, this should not preclude the feedback that should be provided to employees whenever needed. There should never be surprises during a formal review because it should be a summary of all the prior conversations between managers and their subordinates about positive feedback, corrective feedback, career path, and compensation.

Why perform a formal review once a year when more frequent feedback is provided? For one thing, an annual review helps to overcome the critical communication errors discussed in Chapter 2. A formal review also provides the opportunity to systematically review the possibility that different assumptions have developed between subordinates and managers. Periodic "course correction" makes sense for even very satisfactory subordinates. Also, certain situations such as the completion of a major project or unusually poor performance require formal feedback. Consider the entire situation when determining the best time for a performance interview.

Once the time is selected, inform the employee of the interview well in advance. The lead time required may vary from several hours to several weeks, depending on the employee and the type of job involved. In any event, avoid the "stop by my office as soon as you get a chance" type of preparation, which deprives the employee of the opportunity to prepare psychologically for the interview.

Environment

Once the necessary time and timing are determined, consider the best place for the interview. Managers tend to schedule the performance review interview in their own offices without realizing how potentially threatening this environment may be, especially when the subordinate is not accustomed to spending much time in the manager's office. Often, the best place for the interview is in a neutral, safe private location to maximize two-way interaction.

Message Content

Once the time and place of the interview are established, focus on the content of the session. Regardless of the specific interview purpose, review expectations and goals. To appreciate these fully, review the dimensions of the subordinate's job. In addition, review notes from the previous performance review and recent job performance items. You may even want to solicit information from customers or other managers who have observed the employee's performance. All these procedures allow a manager the opportunity to list specific items that must be discussed in the interview.

To give subordinates the opportunity to prepare for the interview, have them complete a self-evaluation form before the interview. Managers can use the standard performance evaluation form or a separate form similar to that shown in Table 14–6.

Table 14–6   Employee Self-Appraisal Checklist

The purpose of this form is to help you prepare for your performance review.
Be ready to discuss any of your specific accomplishments or problems that have occurred since the last performance review.
Set aside some time and review your job since the last review, so you can answer the following questions:
1. What are some unusually difficult problems you have solved?
2. What do you regard as your major strong points in knowledge, skills, or experience?
3. What do you regard as your challenge areas in knowledge, skills, or experience?
4. What are some working relationships you are pleased about?
5. What are some working relationships you feel need strengthening?
6. Did you carry out any special assignments with distinction or handle emergencies skillfully?
7. Determine one or two areas where you think you could improve something if you had the right support from your manager.

The more opportunity an employee has to participate in the process, the greater the possibility that open and valuable communication will result. Studies show that performance appraisal discussions based on a self-review of performance are more satisfying than are those based strictly on manager-prepared appraisals.[42] For the performance review to provide feedback to an employee and to establish goals, a trusting environment must be established.

The next section describes the process that will lead to a trusting environment.

Process

Although the parties involved already know each other and the purpose of the meeting is well established, it is still necessary to begin in a friendly, warm manner. It is a good practice to state the purpose of the session to ensure mutual agreement as well.

Once the climate is established, choose one of three approaches: tell and sell, tell and listen, and problem solving.[43] The *tell-and-sell* approach is used to tell an employee what is expected without any discussion and then to sell the employee on the idea. Those using this style assume employees desire to correct weaknesses if they know them. Unfortunately, employees' defenses may be raised as a result, and any independent judgment on the subordinate's part may be suppressed. This style is often appropriate for the subordinate who has little knowledge about the job (such as a relatively new employee). However, the possibilities for this style are limited because most employees generally have something to say.

The second style, *tell and listen,* includes the element of listening. As Chapter 9 emphasizes, listening is the key skill to learning. Tell the employees what you observed regarding their performance, emphasizing the positive behaviors you noticed, and listen to the reasons they give for their performance, whether it was satisfactory or unsatisfactory. The response probably indicates the cause behind the behavior, which you may then reinforce or redirect.

The third strategy, *problem solving,* expands on the second approach. The problem-solving approach is based on the premise that two-way communication leads to a mutually acceptable plan for performance improvement. This approach allows subordinates more freedom and responsibility than the other two; however, the climate must be right for subordinates to express themselves.

Supportive Environment

Table 14–7 draws on Gibb's classic works to differentiate the communication process that leads to a supportive rather than a defensive environment.[44]

Examples of communications from each of these categories assist in developing an effective communication strategy for the appraisal interview.

Evaluative Versus Descriptive

Communication that blames a subordinate naturally leads to a defensive climate. Avoid statements that make moral assessments of another or that question an individual's values and motives. Descriptive communication provides specific feedback and does not judge the receiver. The examples below show the difference that might occur during a performance review interview.

Notice that the evaluative examples typically are less specific and make inferences about the receiver's personality. These types of comments lead to defensiveness.

Control Versus Problem Orientation

Problem-oriented communication defines a mutual problem and seeks a solution. Controlling communication tries to do "something" to another person such as forcing a change in a behavior or an attitude. The problem orientation conveys respect for the employee's ability to work on a problem and to formulate meaningful answers to the problem. The following are some examples of control and problem-oriented communication.

Table 14–7   Supportive and Defensive Climates

Defensive Climate	Supportive Climate
Evaluative	Descriptive
Control	Problem orientation
Neutrality	Empathy
Superiority	Equality
Certainty	Provisionalism

Evaluative

You simply have to stop making so many silly mistakes.

Bob, you're tactless and rude.

The delay was definitely your fault because you didn't follow instructions.

Descriptive

We're still getting more than three errors per run with the new system.

Bob, some people say they are offended by your humor.

There seems to be some confusion about the instructions.

The problem-oriented comments develop more opportunities for two-way communication by using open-ended questions and indicating a concern for solving the problem in a cooperative manner. Listening is also a productive by-product of the problem-solving approach.

Control

Here is what you can do to reduce errors.

You definitely have a problem with that project.

Stop being so negative around here.

Problem Orientation

What do you think could be done to reduce errors?

We've got a problem with this project.

How do you think we could develop a more positive approach?

Neutrality Versus Empathy

Neutrality expresses a lack of concern for the well-being of the employee, whereas empathy shows that the manager identifies with the subordinate's problem, shares her feelings, and accepts the emotional values involved. Compare the following examples.

Neutrality	Empathy
That really isn't much of a problem.	Sounds like you're really concerned about it. Tell me more about the situation.
Everybody has to face that at one time or another.	That can be a tough situation. I'll tell you how I've seen it handled before, and then, you can give me your reaction.
Well, everyone is entitled to an opinion.	I think we disagree. Let's discuss this further and compare viewpoints.

Managers show empathy in the appraisal interview when they are willing to listen, when they inquire how employees feel about something, and when they attempt to understand and accept the employee's feelings. Empathy cannot be developed when a person is hastily cut off from communicating any further or the listener demonstrates lack of interest in the message.

Superiority Versus Equality

The less the psychological distance between the manager and the subordinate, the greater the probability of a productive assessment interview. Managers often inhibit subordinates by subtly indicating both verbally and nonverbally their superiority in position, wealth, power, intellectual ability, or even physical characteristics. The following are examples of verbal communication demonstrating superiority and equality.

Superiority	Equality
After working on this kind of problem for ten years, I know how to handle it.	This solution has worked before, so it should work here too.
I'm getting paid more than you, so it is my responsibility to make this kind of decision.	It's my ultimate responsibility to make the decision, but I sure want your recommendations.
The type of problems I face shouldn't be of interest to people at your level.	I want to share with you the type of situations I'm involved with.

Managers demonstrate superiority or equality by nonverbal as well as verbal communication patterns. Sitting behind a big desk, putting your feet on the desk, looking uninterested, and acting busy are all signs of superiority. Showing superiority can only add to defensiveness and reduce two-way communication.

Certainty Versus Provisionalism

Managers who emphasize certainty often phrase what they say as if the decision cannot be changed. This dogmatic approach makes the employee feel that offering new ideas or a different solution is futile. Provisionalism demonstrates that a manager is willing to be challenged to arrive at the best possible solution. Provisionalism promotes enthusiasm and provides a challenge to employees, as these examples demonstrate.

Certainty	Provisionalism
I know what the problem is, so there isn't much reason to talk about it.	I have some ideas, but it would be good to talk about it.
This is the way it's going to be done.	Let's try it this way for a while and see what happens.
I want it to be completed by June 1.	What needs to be done to ensure that it's completed by June 1?

These five elements of an effective communication strategy—description, problem orientation, empathy, equality, and provisionalism—are major factors in reducing defensiveness and developing trust. Once trust has been developed, managers must provide feedback to subordinates.

Providing Performance Feedback

Performance evaluation gives feedback on the employee's past performances. The performance appraisal interview allows managers to motivate their employees to higher levels of performance through positive feedback. Subordinates will see feedback as constructive criticism rather than as negative criticism if managers keep in mind the following principles.

1. *Identify concrete behavior.* Statements that identify specific, concrete behaviors are easier to accept than ambiguous, abstract statements. For instance, "You seem to have lost your self-confidence" is rather abstract. It is better to say, "You have not asked for any new projects since the hydraulic overhaul. I'd like to know why."

2. *Avoid inferences about motives, intents, and feelings unless you can cite specific behaviors to support these inferences.* A statement such as "You have lost interest in your job" is strictly an inference that does not lead to a constructive performance review.

3. *Focus feedback on a limited number of observable behaviors.* Employees can act on only a few feedback statements at a time. If one must deal with a large number of items, it is probably better to schedule several sessions.

4. *Time feedback to follow closely the behavior being discussed.* Immediate feedback almost always has more impact on the receiver than does delayed feedback. Accordingly, certain employees may require more than an annual review.

5. *Give feedback to help the employees rather than to make you feel better.* Avoid giving feedback when feelings are not under control.

Managers who experience difficult situations may ask, "What about the employee who receives extensive negative feedback? How can I continue to administer it in a positive environment?" Once again, the manner in which the feedback message is structured is important. Another factor to consider is that no matter how much negative feedback the situation calls for, positive comments can usually also be used; however, the old "sandwich" approach is not recommended.

In the sandwich approach, a manager places a negative statement between two positive comments. However, most employees quickly recognize the manager's attempt to manipulate the situation; consequently, the strategy usually falls short of its intended purpose. The current recommended procedure is to dispense supportive feedback almost exclusively at the beginning of the interview. This tactic helps to establish an initial positive climate, and once aware that the manager duly appreciates past success, the subordinate becomes more receptive to a thorough analysis of those areas where need for improvement exists.[45]

Goal setting is a valuable process when structuring feedback in a positive manner. The following discussion points out several implications that need to be considered when establishing goals that help to build a positive climate.

Establishing Goals

The performance review interview ought to be constructive. Instead of dwelling on past failures, focus on the actions an employee can take to improve and develop. Performance goals help keep the focus on the future. When these goals are clear, the performance appraisal is positively related to subordinate satisfaction with the interview process.[46]

Managers clearly state objectives when they include the elements of *time, quality, quantity,* and *priority.* Consider the following example:

During the next sixty days, you will set aside twenty minutes each day to meet with your crew and state what is expected in terms of their production and work schedules. You will counsel, on a daily basis, subordinates whose work schedules are not up to standard. If your turnover rate continues to be the same and you fail to counsel your employees, we will change your supervisory responsibilities.[47]

Notice that this activity is clearly stated: Quality is stated in terms of production and work schedules; quantity is established in terms of turnover and the frequency of the meetings. These are important priorities for the supervisor because, if the conditions are not met, the supervisor could be demoted.

To ensure that the objectives or action plans are clear, write down the agreed-on activity. This allows both parties to review the statements and ensure that all the meanings are mutually clear. Action plans guide employees' future activities to achieve established goals. Clearly stated expectations can reduce risk exposure from litigation if personnel or responsibilities change due to unmet objectives. The following section describes how to avoid potential legal issues that frequently arise from the performance review process.

Legal Concerns

According to the Bureau of Justice Statistics, the number of employment lawsuits filed in federal court from 1990 to 1998 more than tripled. When Congress declared that Title VII of the Civil Rights Act of 1991 granted employment law cases the right to request a jury trial, the number of cases filed in federal and state courts continued to increase as did the average award amount. Regardless of the outcome, businesses must allocate a significant amount of financial and human resources on the legal process.[48]

The number of lawsuits filed as a result of performance appraisals increased dramatically during the last two decades.[49] In response, firms have attempted to reduce risk by improving their performance review processes. Approaches involve two main components: (1) a legal performance appraisal system and (2) procedural consistency. Risk is further reduced when the forms, tools, and processes implemented for performance reviews are evaluated annually to validate expected outcomes. Legal, regulatory, and operational changes may require more frequent updates.

A legal performance appraisal system must pass a number of tests. First, employers must be able to show that their "selection" procedures do not disproportionately eliminate protected groups unless required for a *safe and efficient* performance. Second, the tool used for appraisals must be able to measure performance as it relates to the important aspects of the employee's responsibilities. (Recall the concept of BFOQ explained earlier in this chapter.) Third, to avoid bias by the manager, performance appraisals should be based on precise and objective criteria. Fourth, the appraisal should be performed by the employee's direct manager who observes the employee's performance daily. Finally, the manager should be adequately trained to perform appraisals appropriately.[50] Employers will find it difficult to prove nondiscriminatory practices during litigation if they fail any of these tests.

A biased and inaccurate appraisal is not illegal, but it becomes so if it results in adverse outcomes for protected groups. It has been estimated through studies that approximately 50 percent of merit raises and promotions result from discriminatory performance appraisals. Employers who provide due process and employee grievance channels can often resolve conflict before it results in litigation.[51] The key component in due process is to ensure consistency in the way employees' grievances are addressed.

Managers are responsible for overseeing the performance appraisal process. They are challenged with balancing the needs of the organization and the needs of their subordinates. Managers that approach performance review interviews fairly and free of bias can achieve their objectives and limit their organizations' risk exposure. Managers can acquire valuable information to improve their techniques for delivery of performance reviews and other duties through networking channels.

NETWORKING

Our discussion of managerial interviewing strategies warrants attention to a third application: networking. Social and professional networking provides excellent resources for intellectual and career management. Managers are very aware that knowledge is power and shared knowledge fosters beneficial relationships. Networking involves time and energy commitment to maximize managers' potential rewards. A clear understanding of purpose, mode, and potential outcomes enhance networking efforts.

Purpose

The main purpose of networking is to build relationships through informational interviews. As we saw in the previous chapter, networking skills can be useful during negotiations. But managers will fail at networking activities if their goals are merely to obtain something for themselves. Their motives may be transparent to others and hinder successful communication. Networking is a two-way street that succeeds when participants' intent is to share information in a mutually beneficial relationship.

Networking skills improve over time as participants are exposed to a variety of settings. Participants learn how to assist others and create long-lasting relationships. Participants provide assistance through their own expertise or by referring expert contacts. Activities as simple as sharing information on relevant events and articles with other participants are forms of assistance. By helping others, the participant demonstrates that she is a contact worth keeping and provides a reason to follow up with them again. These actions reinforce professional ties that may lead to reciprocity when the newcomer is in need of assistance.

Effective networking involves meaningful connections, relationships, and rapport developed through trust. According to a recent study by Pepperdine University's Graziadio School of Business and Management, successful professionals with annual incomes in excess of $200,000 cite networking as a critical factor in career advancement.[52] Networking activities allow participants to share experiences and develop best practices that continue to improve as they move through different networks. The number of contacts increase, and participants build a large pool of long-lasting relationships that are mutually beneficial.

How to Network

The number of networking associations and activities is endless. The most frequently used channels to exchange information for networking activities include electronic media, such as Facebook and LinkedIn, as well as face-to-face interactions. Networking occurs in formal and informal settings, and applying appropriate networking etiquette improves communication.

Managers can acquire valuable knowledge specific to their occupation, firm, and industry through a diverse group of professional contacts. Influential contacts within the company include mentors, colleagues, and other professionals. External network groups include professional associations as well as specialized groups for minorities, women, and executives. Internet searches reveal numerous sites to acquire specific activities for individual groups. Social networking through university alumni, former supervisors, previous colleagues, and casual gatherings increase one's pool of resources. Successful networking requires planning, setting goals, and tracking results.

Basic steps for successful networking include these actions:

- Identify networking groups that foster mutually beneficial interaction.

- Join professional associations and attend local and national meetings.

- Volunteer as a speaker, committee member, and/or officer.

- Know and promote your strengths, not your title.

- Display an attitude of enthusiasm, confidence, and sincerity.

- Listen carefully to identify opportunities to contribute to others.

- Mingle and meet several new contacts at every event.

- Ensure business cards are readily available.

- Follow up with former and new contacts.

Frequently, important relationships are created and maintained outside the work environment. It is important to recognize that every conversation and activity creates networking opportunities and career advancement.[53] First impressions are permanently embedded, so appearance is important. The rules of body language are as critical here as in other interview settings. Networking groups have a set of acceptable standards and expectations of group members.

Networking etiquette is founded on the golden rule that members are expected to reciprocate. It is equally important to recognize that the group's purpose is to share information. These are other networking etiquette guidelines:

- Never ask for a job.
- Return calls and e-mails promptly.
- Always respond as promised.
- Recognize participants' time constraints.
- Treat all participants as equals.
- Be knowledgeable on current events.
- Be helpful and grateful.
- Maintain participants' confidentiality.

These and other factors create an environment to develop mutually beneficial relationships that can lead to career advancement. Networking also requires the participants to be open minded, prepared, persistent, and patient. These characteristics combined with clear goals lead to successful outcomes.[54]

Outcomes

Many advantages for managers' career advancement occur as a natural turn of events with acquired knowledge. As time progresses, your credibility strengthens, and you gain a reputation as an expert in your field. You earn respect from your colleagues and upper management as you gain knowledge about your company or industry. You increase your pool of internal and external contacts through leveraged introductions. Opportunities arise to increase your potential customer base, and you may obtain consulting opportunities. You may connect with people who can assist, support, and accelerate your career advancement.

Promotion decisions are based on a number of factors: performance, image, style, and networks. Studies suggest that 60 percent of promotion decisions are based on networking activities within the organization.[55] This reinforces that visibility and communication within the company can accelerate career advancement. A manager's ability to generate new ideas and problem solve gain attention by upper management. According to Melanie Howard, a social trends forecaster and business advisor, "Professional networking has become central to the success of senior executives, and those who excel at it tend to rise to the top of their fields due to the added influence and problem-solving ability effective networking can confer."[56] Self-improvement is a continuous process that networking can make substantial contributions to. Managers who build strong relationships with key people are on the road to success. A critical element for building strong relationships is effective communication.

SUMMARY

This chapter presents general principles for conducting interviews and then applies them to special situations. The term *interview* includes many daily interactions that have a time limit and an identifiable purpose. It is an opportunity to gain and share information, but it is important to be aware of special communication barriers that make this difficult. First, the interviewer and interviewee might have different intentions. Second, personal bias results when people hear and see what they want to hear and see. The third barrier is the fact-inference problem. Nonverbal communication, the fourth barrier, presents problems because the interview is generally a short, intensive communication interaction where one nonverbal behavior may result in faulty conclusions. The last two barriers are the powerful effects of first impressions and organizational status.

To help overcome these barriers, seven questions should be asked by managers. A semistructured format is recommended for most interviews. This means some of the questions should be established before the interview, but others will depend on how the interview develops. Either the funnel or inverted funnel sequence of questions may be used. Three categories of questions are reviewed when discussing the phrasing of questions—open and closed, primary and secondary, and neutral and directed. Each may be appropriate at the correct time. Seven types of probes also are presented. Strategic analysis is required to use the appropriate questions in different situations.

Finally, consideration is given to ending the interview. Both the manager and the interviewee must be clear on the main points, future action, and goodwill close.

All managers conduct employment and performance appraisal interviews during their careers; consequently, they need to be aware of several aspects of each of these interviews. The employment interview requires planning to ensure the manager clearly understands the job opening. Legal concerns are unique during the employment interview, so it is necessary to be aware of the general guidelines for lawful questions.

An appropriate questioning strategy is important, and the manager can draw on a large number of potential questions to evaluate the applicants' motivation, education, experience, and fit. Each type of question has a specific purpose. The most common errors to avoid in the employment interview are talking too much rather than listening and keeping inadequate records.

Performance appraisal interviews are critical for a number of reasons; unfortunately, they are often not conducted or are ineffective. The effectiveness can be increased by scheduling the interview at the appropriate time, conducting it in the correct place, and discussing relevant topics. Legal issues can be avoided when performance appraisal interviews are fair, consistent, objective, and unbiased.

Strategic communication is essential when appraising performance; otherwise, defensive behavior may be aroused in the subordinate. Strategic communication allows the manager to develop a supportive, nondefensive environment that encourages a problem-solving approach. This communication should contain messages that are descriptive, problem-oriented, empathetic, equal, and provisional. These characteristics should also be present when giving feedback and setting goals.

Networking is founded on informational interviews. The main purpose of networking is to share information through mutually beneficial relationships developed through social and professional network channels. Following basic steps and etiquette for networking improves successful outcomes that can accelerate career advancement.

Cases for Small-Group Discussion

CASE 14–1

Conducting Interviews and Technology

Stacy Rollins was pensive as she waited for her interview with an investment banking firm. She felt well prepared because she had summarized all of her critical information into her résumé, which had been reviewed by her business communication professor prior to sending it to the recruiter. She felt well qualified for the position and wanted to make a good impression. She had been through three other interviews for different positions and had developed the ability to respond to questions that all of the recruiters seemed to have in common. Unlike the first three, however, this interview was going to be conducted as a teleconference. The recruiter placed the phone call, introduced herself, and added that she was placing Stacy on speakerphone, although she did not describe who else was in the room, listening in.

The recruiter began the interview by saying, "Stacy, we have the résumé you e-mailed yesterday. It looks good. You are familiar with the job requirements, I suppose. We are seeking a candidate with superb analytical skills, demonstrated ability to work in team settings, and the ability to communicate and to manage communication effectively."

"Oh, yes!" Stacy replied. "I think I am a good match for your criteria."

The recruiter was silent for a moment. "So . . ." she said finally. A prolonged pause ensued. The recruiter said nothing further, though the phone line was apparently still open. Stacy was perplexed. She had not experienced this in other interviews. She did not know what to do.

QUESTIONS

1. Place yourself in Stacy's shoes; knowing what you do about interviews, what would you do at this point?

2. What could the recruiter's objective be for posing the non-question and then saying nothing further?

3. What advantages and disadvantages of conducting interviews by teleconference does this case demonstrate?

CASE 14–2

Kern and the Quiet Nurse

Kay Kern is the director of the Corporate Safety Department for a large, multiplant manufacturing company in the Midwest. The company has six major manufacturing plants, and each has its own industrial nurses.

Twice a year, Kern has individual formal interviews with the nurses to find out if they have any major concerns or if Kern can help in any way. Since these nurses report to the personnel manager of each plant and not to Kern, this is not a performance review. Kern gets a lot of valuable information from the nurses through the interviews and seems to have developed a positive relationship with them. There is only one nurse, Joe James, who does not really open up to Kern and say much. On several occasions, Kern has tried to get information from James, but generally when Kern asks a question, all she gets is a one-word or superficial response. For instance, several months ago, all the plants instituted a new program for monitoring the number and types of visits to the nurses' offices. Kern asked James if everything was all right with the new program. James merely shrugged and said, "Yes."

This worries Kern because James is a young nurse with only two years of experience, and he probably has questions and could use some help. Kern has even asked some of the other employees in the plant if James was naturally quiet, but everyone said he was rather outgoing and easy to get to know. Kern is getting frustrated, because in her twenty-five years of experience, she has never had this much trouble getting someone to open up.

QUESTIONS

1. What are some possible incorrect interview strategies that Kern may be using?

2. What would you recommend to Kern?

CASE 14–3

Is It Harassment?

Jack Simpson, newly appointed human resources director for Geridan Contracting Corporation (GCC), had had an unusual morning. First on his agenda was an exit interview with Maria Johnson, the company president's executive secretary. Johnson had simply informed Simpson she was quitting, giving no reason. Judging from her performance reviews over the last few years, Simpson believed her to be a competent, enthusiastic, and dedicated employee. Even though Simpson had little knowledge of her workload, he could see no obvious reason for the resignation. He had set up this exit interview hoping to find out why she had quit.

Next on Simpson's agenda was an interview with Ryan Ross, the president of GCC, who wanted to talk to Simpson before Simpson began interviewing later in the day for the secretary's replacement. Simpson had never conducted an interview for a president's secretary before, but he had planned on getting a good idea of what to look for during his talk with Johnson. He believed Ross would also advise him on what he expected from the secretary's replacement.

However, when Simpson and the resigning executive secretary, Johnson, sat down in a quiet conference room at 8:30 a.m., the HR director's ears began to burn. Johnson explained that for the last six months she was being sexually harassed by Ross and that she was considering suing GCC (and Ross in particular).

Simpson needs to know more about this accusation in case it does develop into a more serious situation. Also, the more facts he has, the better prepared he will be to discuss the situation with the president. What interview strategy should Simpson use with the secretary?

QUESTIONS

1. What type of questions would you recommend? What sequence?

2. What do you think will be the major barriers in this interview? Why?

3. What can Simpson do to be sure he is getting the facts?

CASE 14-4

Motivation and the Performance Appraisal

Samuel Jones has worked diligently for his supervisor, Eric Donnell, during the past three years in the accounting department of a local bank. During that period, he has never been reprimanded for any of the work he has done. In fact, only recently, he received his first, supposedly annual, performance review. Although he received a raise in each of the two prior years, this was the first time he was formally evaluated. The first year, he received a memo from Donnell stating the amount of his raise. The next year, Donnell did not even inform him of a raise. Rather, Jones had to figure it out for himself from his paycheck stub.

After sitting through his first formal evaluation, Jones is stunned. Donnell informed him that his work effort is just average and that he does not always show enough motivation in the tasks he undertakes. This is the most Donnell has said to Jones concerning his work since Jones began working there over three years ago.

Donnell works on important matters alone in his office and shuts himself off from his employees' activities. Some of Jones's fellow workers see this as a sign the boss has faith in them to get the job done and to accept responsibilities on their own. But Jones believes Donnell is just avoiding responsibility and is not interested in involving himself with his employees. Jones believes his boss thinks, "I've got my own problems, so don't come to me with yours."

Jones has healthy working relationships with several other supervisors in the bank, and they all have told him more than once that his performance is above average. Because of this, Jones feels hurt that Donnell called him *average*. As far as motivation goes, Jones does not see what there is to be motivated about. He never receives rewards, verbal or otherwise, at those times when he does good work. Consequently, he is confused about what levels of effort and performance will lead to the recognition he feels he deserves.

QUESTIONS

1. What should Donnell do differently if he wants Jones to increase his work effort?

2. List some elements of job performance that Donnell must make sure are present to get better performance from his employee.

3. What can Donnell do to get the most out of his performance evaluations?

4. What, if anything, can Jones do to increase the flow of feedback from his supervisor?

Exercise for Small Groups

Create a list of behavioral questions you should ask when interviewing applicants for a faculty position at your university. The professor you hire would teach business communication.

Student Study Site

Visit the Student Study Site at **study.sagepub.com/hynes6e** for web quizzes, video links, web resources, and cases studies.

Notes

1. Susan T. Fiske and Steven L. Newberg, "A Continuum of Impression Formation, from Category-Based to Individuating Process: Influences of Information and Motivation on Attention and Interpretation," in *Advances in Experimental Social Psychology,* vol. 23, ed. Mark P. Zanna (New York: Academic Press, 1990), pp. 1–74.

2. Kevin R. Murphy and Douglas H. Reynolds, "Does True Halo Affect Observed Halo?" *Journal of Applied Psychology,* May 1988, pp. 235–238.

3. Elaine Pulakos, Neal Schmitt, and C. Ostroff, "A Warning about the Use of a Standard Deviation across Dimensions within Rates to Measure Halo," *Journal of Applied Psychology,* February 1986, pp. 29–32.

4. Terry L. Leap and Michael D. Crino, *Personnel/Human Resource Management* (New York: Macmillan, 1989), p. 332.

5. Fran F. Kanfer and P. Karoly, "Self-Control: A Behaviorist Excursion into the Lion's Den," *Behavior Therapy* 3, no. 2 (1972): pp. 298–300.

6. James P. Walsh, "Selectivity and Selective Perception: An Investigation of Managers' Belief Structures and Information Processing," *Academy of Management Journal,* December 1988, pp. 873–896.

7. S. L. Ragan, "A Conversational Analysis of Alignment Talk in Job Interviews," in *Communication Yearbook,* vol. 7, ed. R. M. Bostrom (Beverly Hills, CA: Sage, 1983), pp. 502–516.

8. R. L. Birdwhistell, *Kinesics and Context* (Philadelphia: University of Pennsylvania Press, 1970), p. 97.

9. J. K. Burgoon, D. B. Buller, and G. W. Woodall, *Nonverbal Communication: The Unspoken Dialogue* (New York: Harper & Row, 1989), p. 76.

10. Loren Falkenberg, "Improving the Accuracy of Stereotypes within the Workplace," *Journal of Management* 16, no. 1 (March 1990): pp. 107–118.

11. K. J. Williams, A. S. DeNisi, B. M. Meglino, and T. P. Cafferty, "Initial Decisions and Subsequent Performance Ratings," *Journal of Applied Psychology* 71, no. 2 (1986): pp. 189–195.

12. M. Snyder and B. H. Campbell, "Testing Hypothesis about Other People: The Role of the Hypothesis," *Personality and Social Psychology Bulletin,* 1980, pp. 421–426.

13. H. J. Bernardin and Richard W. Beatty, "Can Subordinate Appraisals Enhance Managerial Productivity?" *Sloan Management Review,* Summer 1987, p. 69.

14. R. I. Lazar and W. S. Wilkstrom, *Appraising Managerial Performance: Current Practices and Future Directions* (New York: Conference Board, 1977), p. 46.

15. Margaret Shepherd, *The Art of Civilized Conversation: A Guide to Expressing Yourself with Style and Grace* (New York: Broadway Books, 2007).

16. G. Johns, "Effects of Informational Order and Frequency of Applicant Evaluation upon Linear Information-Processing Competence of Interviewers," *Journal of Applied Psychology* 60, no. 3 (1975): pp. 427–433.

17. C. D. Tengler and F. M. Jablin, "Effects of Question Type, Orientation, and Sequencing in the Employment Screening Interview," *Communication Monographs* 50, no. 2 (1983): pp. 243–263.

18. Charles Stewart and W. B. Cash, *Interviewing: Principles and Practices,* 5th ed. (Dubuque, IA: Wm. C. Brown, 1988), p. 21.

19. Elizabeth Bradley, "Hiring the Best," *WIB, Magazine of the American Business Women's Association,* July–August 2003, pp. 12–15.

20. Linda D. Loury, "Some Contacts Are More Equal than Others: Informal Networks, Job Tenure, and Wages," *Journal of Labor Economics* 24, no. 2 (April 2006): pp. 299–318.

21. Stephen Baker, "What's a Friend Worth?" *BusinessWeek,* June 1, 2009, pp. 32–36.

22. Terry L. Leap and Michael D. Crino, *Personnel/Human Resource Management* (New York: Macmillan, 1989), p. 245.

23. Michael M. Harris, "Reconsidering the Employment Interview: A Review of Recent Literature and Suggestions for Future Research," *Personnel Psychology* 42, no. 4 (1989): pp. 691–726.

24. *CareerBuilder* survey of 2,775 hiring managers and 5,518 job seekers conducted in the United States and Canada, July 2013, www.careerbuilder.com.

25. Adam Bryant, "Corner Office: Barry Salzberg," *The New York Times,* May 22, 2011, p. 2.

26. Jeanne C. Poole and E. Theodore Katz, "An EEO–AA Program That Exceeds Quotas—It Targets Biases," *Personnel Journal,* January 1987, p. 103.

27. James R. Redeker, "The Supreme Court on Affirmative Action: Conflicting Opinions," *Personnel,* October 1986, p. 8.

28. "Employment Discrimination: A Recent Perspective from the 'Burger Court,'" *Industrial Management,* September–October 1986, p. 3.

29. Stewart and Cash Jr., *Interviewing: Principles and Practices,* p. 133.

30. Fredrick M. Jablin and Vernon D. Miller, "Interviewer and Applicant Questioning Behavior in Employment Interviews," *Management Communication Quarterly* 4, no. 1 (1990): pp. 51–86.

31. Wendy Kaufman, "Job Interviews Get Creative," *All Things Considered,* National Public Radio, August 22, 2003, http://www.npr.org/display_pages/features/feature_1405340.html.

32. William Poundstone, *How Would You Move Mount Fuji: Microsoft's Cult of the Puzzle* (New York: Little, Brown, 2003).

33. C. W. Anderson, "The Relation Between Speaking Times and Decision in the Employment Interview," *Journal of Applied Psychology* 44, no. 4 (1960): pp. 267–268.

34. R. E. Carlson, D. P. Schwab, and H. G. Henneman III, "Agreement among Selection Interview Styles," *Journal of Industrial Psychology* 5, no. 1 (1970): pp. 8–17.

35. R. F. Maier, *The Appraisal Interview: Objectives and Skills* (New York: Wiley & Sons, 1958), p. 3.

36. Robert D. Bretz Jr., George T. Milkovich, and Walter Read, "The Current State of Performance Appraisal Research and Practice: Concerns, Directions, and Implications," *Journal of Management* 18, no. 2 (June 1992): pp. 321–352.

37. Samuel A. Culbert, *Get Rid of the Performance Review! How Companies Can Stop Intimidating, Start Managing, and Focus on What Really Matters* (New York: Hachette Book Group, 2010).

38. R. M. Glen, "Performance Appraisal: An Unnerving Yet Useful Process," *Public Personnel Management* 19, no. 1 (1990): pp. 1–10.

39. B. Dugan, "Effects of Assessor Training on Information Use," *Journal of Applied Psychology* 73 (1988), pp. 743–748; and Timothy M. Downs, "Predictions of Communication Satisfaction during Performance Appraisal Interviews," *Management Communication Quarterly* 3, no. 13 (1990): pp. 334–354.

40. Michael E. Stano and N. L. Reinsch Jr., *Communication in Interviews* (Englewood Cliffs, NJ: Prentice Hall, 1982), p. 101.

41. L. L. Cummings and C. P. Schwab, "Designing Appraisal Systems for Information Yield," *California Management Review* 20, no. 1 (1978): pp. 18–25.

42. B. E. Becker and R. J. Klimoski, "A Field Study of the Relationship between the Organizational Feedback Environment and Performance," *Personnel Psychology* 42, no. 3 (1989): pp. 343–358.

43. Maier, *The Appraisal Interview,* p. 22.

44. Jack R. Gibb, "Defensive Communication," *Journal of Communication,* September 1961, pp. 141–148.

45. Douglas Cederblom, "The Performance Appraisal Interview: A Review, Implications, and Suggestions," in *Readings in Organizational Communication,* ed. Kevin L. Hutchinson (Dubuque, IA: Wm. C. Brown, 1992), pp. 310–321.

46. M. M. Greller, "Evaluation of Feedback Sources as a Function of Role and Organizational Level," *Journal of Applied Psychology* 65, no. 1 (1980): pp. 24–27.

47. Judith Hale, "Communication Skills in Performance Appraisal," *Industrial Management,* no. 22 (March–April 1980): p. 19.

48. Robert J. Grossman, "Law in the Slow Lane," *HR Magazine* 45, no. 7 (July 2000): pp. 62–70.

49. Peter A. Veglahn, "Key Issues in Performance Appraisal Challenges: Evidence for Court and Arbitration Decisions," *Labor Law Journal* 44, no. 10 (October 1993): pp. 595–606.

50. Giovanni B. Giglioni, Joyce B. Giglioni, and James Bryant, "Performance Appraisal: Here Comes the Judge," *California Management Review* 24, no. 2 (Winter 1981): pp. 14–23.

51. N. B. Winstanley, "Legal and Ethical Issues in Performance Appraisals," *Harvard Business Review* 58, no. 6 (November–December 1980): pp. 186–192.

52. Paula Ketter, "Social Net-What?" *T + D* 63, no. 2 (March 2009): p. 22.

53. Judy Estrin, "Networking: It's the Way to Grow," *T + D* 62, no. 10 (October 2008): pp. 100–101.

54. "Networking and Professional Etiquette," n.d., accessed June 1, 2009, www.career.caltech.edu/resources/handouts/Networking%20Handouts.pdf.

55. "Need to Know Networking," *Personnel Today*, March 24, 2009, p. 19.

56. Melanie Howard, "Social Networking: An Old Process in a New Form," *Market Leader*, no. 44 (Quarter 2, 2009), pp. 66–68.

Index

⊛SAGE research**methods**

The essential online tool for researchers from the world's leading methods publisher

Find exactly what you are looking for, from basic explanations to advanced discussion

More content and new features added this year!

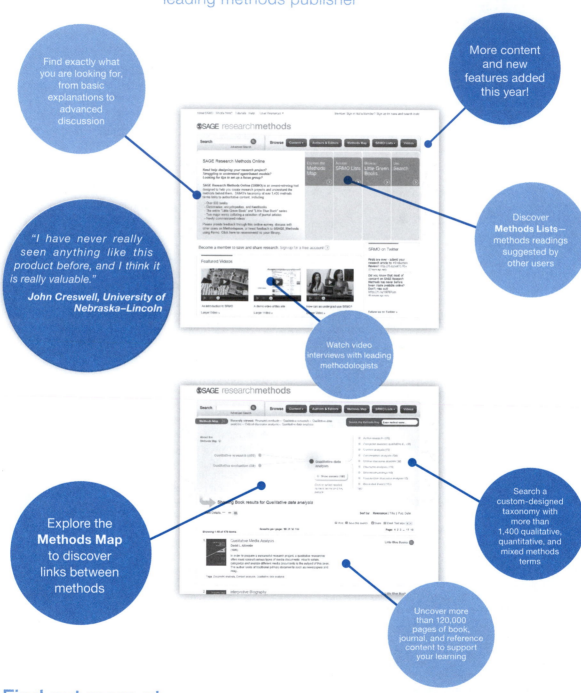

"I have never really seen anything like this product before, and I think it is really valuable."

John Creswell, University of Nebraska–Lincoln

Discover **Methods Lists**—methods readings suggested by other users

Watch video interviews with leading methodologists

Explore the **Methods Map** to discover links between methods

Search a custom-designed taxonomy with more than 1,400 qualitative, quantitative, and mixed methods terms

Uncover more than 120,000 pages of book, journal, and reference content to support your learning

Find out more at
www.sageresearchmethods.com